A FREEDOM BOUGHT WITH BLOOD

African American War Literature
from the Civil War to World War II
by Jennifer C. James

A FREEDOM BOUGHT WITH BLOOD

The
University of
North Carolina
Press
Chapel Hill

© 2007 The University of North Carolina Press

All rights reserved

Set in Quadraat, Franklin Gothic, and Boycott types

by Keystone Typesetting, Inc.

Manufactured in the United States of America

Library of Congress Cataloging-in-Publication Data

James, Jennifer C.

A freedom bought with blood : African American war literature
from the Civil War to World War II / by Jennifer C. James.

   p. cm.

Includes bibliographical references and index.

ISBN 978-0-8078-3116-8 (alk. paper)

ISBN 978-0-8078-5807-3 (pbk. : alk. paper)

1. American literature—African American authors—History and
criticism. 2. War in literature. 3. War and literature—United States.
4. African Americans—Race identity. 5. African Americans in
literature. 6. United States—History—Civil War, 1861–1865—
Literature and the war. 7. World War, 1914–1918—United States—
Literature and the war. 8. World War, 1939–1945—United States—
Literature and the war. I. Title.

PS153.N5J393 2007

820.9'358—dc22   2007008270

Gwendolyn Brooks's "Negro Hero" and "still do I keep my look,
my identity" are reprinted by consent of Brooks Permissions.

11 10 09 08 07 5 4 3 2 1

to my father, former sailor
to my brother, former soldier
to my mother, woman warrior;
and to my great-, great-, great-
grandfather,

    a former slave
    who fought for his freedom
    and for ours

CONTENTS

ILLUSTRATIONS

ACKNOWLEDGMENTS

This would not have been possible without the enormous love and unwavering support of my wonderful family: my parents, Aaron C. James and Maxine Allen James, who always knew I could do this even when I did not; my brother and sister-in-law, David Winston James and Leslie Daland-James; my niece and nephew, Reyna Maxine James and Donovan Aaron James; and finally, my cousins, Orien Reid Nix and Melvin J. Collier, who led me to my great-, great-, great-grandfather, Edward Bobo Danner, of the Fifty-ninth Colored Infantry.

I would also like to thank my terrific George Washington University colleagues and coworkers (past and present): my mentor, James A. Miller, whose intellectual insights, wit, and overall wisdom were indispensable; Robert McRuer, whose encouragement was constant; Randi Gray Kristensen, who kept me (relatively) sane; my fellow Americanists, Gayle Wald, Patty Chu, Antonio Lopez, Meta Jones, Gustavo Guerra, Melani McAlister, Kim Moreland, Ann Romines, and Ormond Seavey, who have made work a pleasure; my current chair, Jeffrey Cohen, and my former chairs, Faye Moskowitz and Christopher Sten, who have created a supportive department environment; and my former dean, William Frawley, who gave me time when I most needed it. And certainly not least, Constance Kibler and Karen Herbert, who both kept me laughing.

I am equally grateful to my former professors, who had faith in my work and provided me with models of excellence: Carla L. Peterson and Robert L. Levine, whose rigor was nearly intolerable but whose continued support is invaluable; and Sangeeta Ray, John W. Crowley, the late Thomas Yingling, and Joanne Braxton. I must especially thank the late Ronald Rogerson (who I hope is smiling wildly somewhere).

And, finally, I must acknowledge some of my dearest friends, who have helped me in ways both big and small, and whose love I cherish (listed in order of appearance): Andi Stepnick, Shellie Holubek, Lorin Brown, Seth Lavissiere, Levita Mondie, Rodrigo Lazo, Linda Cameron, Stephanie Batiste, LaVon Rice, and Jason Fults.

A
FREEDOM
BOUGHT
WITH
BLOOD

INTRODUCTION: SABLE HANDS AND NATIONAL ARMS

Theorizing the
African American
Literature of
War

In the face of death and danger,
  He met the foe, this soldier true,
Till, charging full upon them,
  Their bayonets had pierced him through.

He fell, and o'er the pavement
  A Negro's blood was flowing free
His sable hand was foremost
  To strike the blow for liberty.
—*Olivia Ward Bush-Banks, "Crispus Attucks," 1899*

In 1770, fugitive slave Crispus Attucks took two bullets in the chest during the Boston Massacre, the first of a series of volatile, often-bloody conflicts leading to the American Revolution. According to the early nineteenth-century historian Richard Botta, "a band of the populace, led by a mulatto named ATTUCKS . . . brandished their clubs and pelted [the British soldiers] with snowballs . . . the mulatto and twelve of his companions pressing forward, environed the soldiers. . . . The mulatto lifted his arm against Capt. Preston, and having turned one of the muskets, he seized the bayonet with his left hand. . . . Firing succeeds. Attucks is slain."[1] While Attucks's active resistance against the British prompted many white colonists to hail him as a hero—a "martyr" for independence—members of the increasingly conservative New England patriot movement were decidedly less enthusiastic about his contributions. In *Slavery, Propaganda and the American Revolution*, Patricia Bradley argues that the patriot press, led at that time by Samuel Adams's *Boston Gazette*, relied on the extant "body of attitudes toward black colonists" to keep from generating sympathetic feelings among white colonists that might upset the established social order.[2] The *Gazette* reported that Attucks simply "fell on a stick"; John Adams, the chief defense counsel during Captain Preston's trial, concurred, infamously characterizing the group led by Attucks as "a motley rabble of saucy boys, negroes and mulattoes, Irish teagues and outlandish jack tars."[3] Most blacks, not surprisingly, chose to believe the version offered by those who had praised Attucks; for them, Attucks's display of loyalty to the fledgling American republic stood as something more than a simple act of patriotism: it presented a definitive argument for black citizenship rights.

In *Strength for the Fight*, one of the most thorough histories of blacks in the American military, Bernard Nalty notes that blacks had fought alongside whites from the earliest of conflicts in the New World.[4] In 1652, blacks were required to stand as part of the Massachusetts militia; they also were recruited for numerous attacks against Native American tribes during that same century.[5] Joining the Spanish in 1736 to repress Natchez Indians in Mobile, Alabama, blacks served as officers within what is believed to be the first all-black military unit formed on American soil, comprising 19 percent of the total forces.[6] In the eighteenth century, blacks served with British forces in King George's War (1740–1748) and again with the Spanish in the French Indian Wars (1754–1763). Though a number of free black men joined in these struggles willingly, the enslaved had no choice in the matter; they either accompanied their masters as servants or were forced to serve while their masters received all or a portion of their pay.[7] Some of the enslaved population, however, did enlist of their own volition. For these men, military service was offered as a medium of exchange: they went to battle armed with promises of their manumission—a freedom that could only be earned, of course, if they returned from battle alive and if their masters did not betray them.

Attucks, however, was compelled to "fight" neither by a master nor on behalf of one. Nor was Attucks fighting for his own freedom; as a fugitive slave, he had already taken that matter into his own hands. Those blacks who had voluntarily taken up arms in exchange for liberty were doing so as mercenaries of sorts, fighting for whichever forces needed their services; during these earlier conflicts, there was no legally unified "nation" to fight for. But in 1770, when Attucks raised his arm against an officer of the British army, it had become increasingly clear that the colonies were poised to claim their sovereignty. It is true that those historians who have sifted through the many conflicting accounts of the massacre can only make conjectures about Attucks's motives; nonetheless, there is no evidence that the black man who led white residents of Massachusetts to attack their oppressors was doing anything more—or less—than agitating against an enemy of "the people." Therein lies Attucks's singular symbolic power. By aligning himself with the emerging nation-state and its nascent ideologies, and by willfully identifying himself with the "people"—white colonists—Attucks had done something extraordinary. He had imagined himself as a citizen.

As compelling as the argument for black citizenship raised by Attucks's death may have been, ultimately it would fail. Legal enfranchisement for blacks would continue to be deferred for nearly a century, although nearly 5,000 men of African descent followed in Attucks's footsteps, joining the ranks of the Continental army. Yet protracted debates over the wisdom of arming large numbers of blacks plagued their service, a trepidation arising from the numerous slave rebellions threatening the fictional stability of a society stratified by race.[8] Not surprisingly, the most fervent opposition to black military service came from those colonies whose economic machinery was driven ever more greatly by the extraction of free labor. In 1775, the Continental Congress bowed to pressure from southern leadership, voting "unanimously to reject all slaves, and by a great majority, to reject negroes altogether,"[9] creating the circumstances that prompted many black men to fight with the British. Indeed, Paul Revere's 1770 engraving of the Boston Massacre symbolized the long fight that lay ahead for African Americans. Although the caption accompanying Revere's rendition mentions Attucks specifically by name, the men who lay wounded and slain are depicted as "phenotypically" white. We cannot know with any certainty whether this racial erasure was an intentional political gesture. It may have reflected the technical challenges of the medium or the limitations of the artist himself.[10] It may have revealed his understanding of a "mulatto" body, or, in fact, represented Attucks accurately. Nevertheless, the visual effect of Revere's decision is the same, particularly for those unfamiliar with the rebel's identity and for those viewing versions reproduced without explanatory text. In eradicating any visible black presence, Revere presents the origins of the nation as white.

William Cooper Nell and the Origins of African American War Literature

Eighty-eight years after the appearance of Revere's engraving, the prominent black Boston abolitionist and historian William Cooper Nell sought to restore Attucks's central place in the mytho-historical narrative of the conflict. In 1858, Nell organized a festival in Boston's Faneuil Hall to simultaneously commemorate the Boston Massacre and to "Protest Against the Dred Scott 'Decision,' " as one advertisement declared. Held on the evening of March 5, the date of the Massacre, and extending into March 6, the date on which the Scott verdict had been issued a year earlier, the event marked both the "birth" of the nation and the premature "death" of black citizenship. Nell's festival—which promoted the

"The Bloody Massacre Perpetrated in King Street Boston on March 5th 1770 by a Party of the 29th Regt.," Paul Revere, 1770. Library of Congress, Prints and Photographs Division.

inclusion of "Humorous" acts and musical interludes[11]—proclaimed, in essence, that the allegedly decisive reports of black legal and social death had been greatly exaggerated, becoming less of a somber memorial than a carnivalesque celebration of black civic resurrection signified by the jubilant revitalization of Attucks's body. The handbills, pamphlets, and broadsides publicizing the festival prominently feature a wood-carved image of Attucks's slaying in which the slave is clearly black. His race thus inscribed, he is placed at the front of the white crowd, strategically positioned as its commanding presence. Attucks is shown falling backward into the assembly after being shot, his act against the British soldiers thereby incorporating the black fugitive into the body of citizens surrounding him. It is significant that in this artist's version, Attucks is depicted in medias res, his club still in the hand he has raised high in the air. The struggle, as Nell's event announced, is not yet over.

The festival at Faneuil Hall was not the first instance in which Nell endeavored to override images diminishing Attucks's presence at the Boston Massacre. Three years earlier, the frontispiece of Nell's pioneering book, Colored Patriots of the American Revolution (1855), the first full-length treatment of black participation in American warfare,[12] depicts a fallen Attucks encircled by "a cluster of concerned patriots."[13] A "combination of circumstances," he writes in his introduction, "has veiled from the public eye a narration of those military services which are generally conceded as passports to the honorable and lasting notice of Americans" (10). Nell's work, replete with acts of black valor and heroism equal to those of whites is yet another correction of Revere's engraving, though discursive: the historian "unveils" an altogether different version of the American Revolution for the "public eye," one decidedly inclusive of blacks. Nell's "veil" acts as a backslash dividing two narratives: one designed for the "public," and the other, it can be inferred, reserved for a "private" audience. Though Nell does not make clear who exactly comprises the public, nor does he elaborate on what "circumstances" have kept African American history from this public, he implies that the historical landscapes it is permitted to view are devoid of color—created by a state whose interest is to exclude blacks from the national political scene.

It would be easy, then, to place Colored Patriots into a simple narrative/counter-narrative formulation commonly used to characterize the insurgent praxis of "people's" histories. But Colored Patriots seeks to do more than be heard as an oppositional voice emerging from the "other" side of the backslash. Such binarism has too often led historical counternarrative to be conceptualized as parallelism: two wholly differing narrative lines, originating separately, that, while moving along a similar time/space continuum, never intersect. The gap between the narratives, therefore, appears both empty and unbridgeable. By filling that gap with a veil, which he then "lifts," Nell implies that the separation is a "man-made" construction; as such, it can also be "unmade." In much the same way, Nell's passport metaphor indicates a belief in the narration by the marginalized as rupture, opening the penetrable ideological boundaries a nation has drawn—or written, as it were—around itself. "The fact of the matter," as Benedict Anderson rightly observes in *Imagined Communities*, "is that nationalism thinks in terms of historical destinies, while racism dreams of eternal contaminations, trans-mitted from the origins of time through an endless sequence of loathsome copulations: outside history. Niggers are, thanks to the invisible tarbrush, forever niggers . . . no matter what passports they carry or what language they speak and read."[14] Nell in fact devotes several pages his work to the subject of passports, including a description of the former fugitive slave and abolitionist lecturer William Wells Brown's hard-won success in obtaining one before traveling to Europe on an antislavery speaking tour. Within the context of *Patriots*, the pass-port's language, offering its bearer the right "safely and freely to pass" outside of the nation's borders, is clearly meant to displace the slave pass's monitored movement with a state-authored black mobility originating from a stable domes-tic identity that can only be secured by citizenship.[15] But as a documentation of African American military history, *Colored Patriots* represents a passport of another kind: the proper "papers" allowing black Americans *entry* into a nation they have nonetheless occupied since its beginnings.

Nell thus recognizes that war was a means for blacks to demonstrate national loyalty, and that the narration of war was a means of writing blacks into the national "historical destiny." Too, however, he indicates that war may have yet another use for black Americans. In the conclusion to *Colored Patriots*, he writes: "The Revolution of 1776, and the subsequent struggles in our nation's history, aided, in honorable proportion, by colored Americans have (sad, but true, con-fession) yet left the necessity for a second revolution, no less sublime than that of regenerating public sentiment in favor of Universal Brotherhood. . . . Freedom's army" (380–81). In mobilizing the language of warfare to describe the forces he feels are needed to ensure change in the status of African Americans, which he labels a "battle for equality" (370), Nell also demonstrates an understanding that for Americans, the Enlightenment-based arguments validating the Revolution had forever altered the discourses of both war and liberation. That is, the "techni-cal" terms of war had become inextricably bound with those terms used to describe the "natural" rights of human beings: freedom and equality. He uses that shared national discourse to hail a white audience in hopes that it might recognize the call of its own democratic ideologies. This is the very strategy that had prompted the slave-writer Phillis Wheatley, the first black to publish a book

in the colonies, to embed these lines in a 1773 poem, "To the Right Honourable
WILLIAM, Earl of Dartmouth, His Majesty's Principal Secretary for North America, Etc":

> Should you, my lord, while you peruse my song,
> Wonder from whence my love of *Freedom* sprung,
> Whence flow these wishes for the common good,
> By feeling hearts alone best understood,
> I, young in life, by seeming cruel fate
> Was snatch'd from *Afric's* fancy'd happy seat:
> What pangs excruciating must molest,
> What sorrows labour in my parent's breast?
> Steel'd was that soul and by no misery mov'd
> That from a father seiz'd his babe belov'd:
> Such, such my case. And can I then but pray
> Others may never feel tyrannic sway?[16]

As a work of nonfiction history, *Colored Patriots* stands as one of thousands of
articles, books, and essays chronicling blacks' service in the armed forces. What
is not largely known, however, is that there also exists a substantial body of
imaginative literature by African Americans chronicling war: enough, I will argue, to be considered an identifiable and recognizable tradition within the larger
body of African American letters. One of the first original fictionalized treatments
of war by an African American, William Wells Brown's Civil War version of *Clotel,
or The President's Daughter*, was published in 1867 under the name *Clotelle, or the
Colored Heroine: A Tale of the Southern States*.[17] The antislavery activist, poet, and
fiction writer Frances W. Harper's novel *Minnie's Sacrifice*,[18] whose hero and heroine serve in the Civil War, was serialized in the *Christian Recorder* in 1869, just
fourteen years after Nell's publication. Harper would later publish her more well-
recognized novel describing blacks' role in the war effort, *Iola Leroy, or Shadows
Uplifted* in 1892.[19] These early examples have been followed by numerous other
novels as well as works of poetry and short fiction.

In spite of the wide range of historical and literary issues this writing raises,
however, African American war literature produced before the Vietnam War has
yet to be theorized as a whole. Nor have many individual works been considered
as a part of the broader tradition of American war literature. Wide-sweeping
studies of this genre, such as Wayne Charles Miller's *An Armed America—Its Face in
Fiction: A History of the American Military Novel*, Peter Aichinger's *The American Soldier
in Fiction, 1880–1963*, and Helen Cooper's anthology of essays on women's war
literature, *Arms and the Woman: War, Gender, and Literary Representation*, have, in the

main, omitted texts written by black Americans. And while critical attention has been paid to pre-Vietnam texts—Elizabeth Young's reading of *Iola Leroy*, Susan Schweick's and Ann Folwell Stanford's insightful analyses of Gwendolyn Brooks's war poetry, J. L. Greene's study of African American World War I fiction, and the numerous analyses of Chester Himes's brilliant home front novel *If He Hollers Let Him Go* (1945)[20]—several of the works I have chosen to consider have remained unexamined. Moreover, the war content in other works has often been overlooked in favor of other critical perspectives. Claude McKay's 1928 novel *Home to Harlem*,[21] for example, has been studied primarily as the urtext of the Harlem Renaissance, celebrated for the writer's unapologetic presentation of an unrefined black working class protagonist and his raw, uncompromised portrait of Harlem life. Undeniably, World War I is more of a spectral presence in the work; by the novel's seventh page, the Armistice has already been declared. To add dimensionality to standard readings of *Home's* subject matter, then, it is helpful to recall Aichinger's important redefinition of the war novel. Suggesting that the genre should include more than combat narratives, he argues that the war novel is simply "any long work of prose fiction in which the lives and actions of the characters are principally affected by warfare or the military establishment."[22] Although his rather expansive definition may seem too broad to be useful, it acknowledges something that many who have lived through war already know: that while war's epicenters might in fact be located on the battlefield or in the bombing area, the effects of war endlessly reverberate, traversing across both space and time. Interpreted in this way, *Home to Harlem*—a novel focusing on a black American army deserter's return stateside and his burgeoning friendship with a Haitian displaced by the military invasion of Haiti—can certainly be read as a "war" novel. However, while many critics have offered excellent interpretations of McKay's work, the centrality of World War I within it often goes unremarked, despite the war's effect on the status of McKay's main characters and despite McKay's extensive discussions of the war in other venues, including a short work of fiction about the violence confronting a black soldier upon his return to the South.

My book is therefore an effort to lay the foundation for a more comprehensive discussion on the subject of war and black American war literature than current scholarship has yet elicited. I will begin my study with an examination of Brown's *Clotelle* and will, from there, analyze histories, novels, poems, and first-person narratives by African Americans written about the major wars the United States fought before the official desegregation of the military in 1948. My study is structured chronologically by war, deviating only when subject matter demands, and is limited to those works published within approximately the same era of the wars they explore. In addition to *Clotelle, Minnie's Sacrifice,* and *Iola Leroy,* my book will offer discussions of two other works from the Civil War: Paul Laurence Dunbar's *The Fanatics* (1901),[23] and Susie King Taylor's memoirs, *Reminiscences of My Life in Camp* (1902).[24] I will then interpret histories and fiction about the Spanish-Cuban-American Wars and the U.S. wars in the Philippines: Herschel Cashin's and Charles Alexander's collection of historical essays, war poems, and military documents, *Under Fire with the U.S. Calvary* (1899),[25] T. G. Steward's military history, *The Colored Regulars in the United States Army* (1904),[26] and F. Grant Gilmore's *"The Problem": A Military Novel* (1915).[27] Next I will offer analyses of works using World War I as their subject: McKay's *Home to Harlem* (1928) and Victor Daly's *Not Only War: A Story of Two Great Conflicts* (1932).[28] Finally, I will end with World War II, examining four novels, William Gardner Smith's *Last of the Conquerors* (1948),[29] Chester Himes's *If He Hollers Let Him Go* (1945), Gwendolyn Brooks's *Maud Martha* (1953),[30] and John Oliver Killens's *And Then We Heard the Thunder* (1963).[31] I will also analyze Gwendolyn Brooks's war sonnets, "gay chaps at the bar," published in *A Street in Bronzeville* (1945).[32]

As I will show, many of these works are reminiscent of *Colored Patriots,* recalling and revising Nell's concerns. However, Nell's work, while providing a basic and useful framework for analyzing war writing by black Americans, does not wholly explain why blacks repeatedly assert their voices on the subject of war. In this study, I will isolate two main reasons. Given that the United States is a nation "made by war," a nation that has secured its position as a global superpower through numerous acts of aggression, domination, and conquest that have affected every ethnic group existing within its geographical boundaries (and most without), the literary history of any community within the United States must necessarily include war as text, subtext, or context. Moreover, just as Nell describes the contest for equal rights using the discourse of war, several black war writers use the nation's seemingly perpetual state of warfare to indict the United States as endemically violent, dividing their texts into two war narratives—the narrative of national warfare and the narrative of racial strife, a war within a war. Victor Daly makes this metaphorical relationship clear in the preface to his novel: "William Tecumseh Sherman branded War for all time when he called it Hell. There is yet another gaping, abysmal Hell into which some of us are born or unconsciously sucked. The Hell that Sherman knew was a physical one—of rapine, destruction and death. This other, is a purgatory for the mind, for the spirit, for the soul of men. Not only War is Hell" (7). Facing the second hell of racism, many of the writers examined here chose, as Harper writes in *Iola Leroy,* to take up the pen as a weapon and "wield it as a power" (212).

Another answer to the question is perhaps more complex: the destabilizing

effects of war—in which allegiances are made and broken, geographical boundaries crossed, countries renamed, and territories redistributed; in which women
become heads of households and neighbors become adversaries; in which the
oppressed may rise up against domination only to become oppressors—have the
power to disrupt even the most deeply ensconced notions of national, racial, and
gender identity. The use of war as a narrative context allows black writers to seize
these moments of historical rupture to assert newly formed notions of a black
"self"; the political and social aspirations these "selves" signify are translated
into representations of the body. My book will follow how physical representation and corporeal symbolism in African American war texts metamorphose as
the social conditions of blacks altered; as the circumstances under which blacks
participated in war changed (how and when blacks were allowed to serve); as the
goals and purposes of war shifted (for instance, the move from domestic to
imperial wars); and finally, as literary conventions continued to evolve.

The Military Creation Narrative: War, Manhood, and the Black Male Body

It hardly needs to be said that the falsely inclusive terms employed in the
language of the nation's documents—"men" and "the people"—have not always
meant all men or all people. Indeed, while Olivia Bush-Banks celebrates the
"sable hand" Attucks raised to signify his national allegiance,[33] that hand was of
course the very obstacle to his enfranchisement. Karen Sánchez-Eppler has famously argued that the idea of "men" and "the people" as nonspecific—what she
labels a "bodiless body politic"—was little more than a "fiction" designed to
mystify blacks and white women that they could be represented within these
terms by a white, male governing body: a political body comprised of human
bodies decidedly unlike those of many of the governed.[34] She substantiates her
assertion by claiming that the Fifteenth Amendment "unmasks" the very particular body represented in the Constitution all along. An amendment permitting any
man to vote, regardless "of race, color, or previous condition of servitude,"
clarifies the racial and sexual specificity of those who had already awarded themselves inclusion.[35]

As the recent outpouring of scholarship focusing on embodiment in early
African American literature has confirmed, the relationship between the corporeal representation of the body and the national body politic has concerned
black American writers from the very beginnings of African American literature.
Wheatley's most analyzed poem, "on Being Brought from Africa to America"
(1773), reveals the inherent instability in socially constructed notions of race:
"Remember, *Christians, Negroes* / Black as *Cain*," she writes, "May be refined / and

join the Angelic train."[36] As categories of "being" rather than bodily based actu-
alities, "whiteness" and "blackness" signified nominally ("*Christians*," "*Negroes*,"
"*Cain*") can thus be inhabited by any "body," irrespective of how that body is
inscribed biologically. More than an argument positing black Christians' preparedness for spiritual ascendancy, these lines of course imply that blacks can
and should be afforded other privileges of whiteness. Quite naturally, the problem of embodiment was central to the black abolitionist slave narrative. In order
to emphasize the barbarous cruelties of slavery, the writers of these narratives
were forced to present (although hesitantly, at times) tales populated with degraded bodies: bodies victimized by lynchings, whippings, rapes, murders, and
numerous other sadistic acts routinely implemented to beat the black body into
the objectified state that would retroactively "confirm" its proper status as a
commodifiable entity. At the same time, the slave narrators sought to reclaim the
black body by presenting an interior self that transcended the physical restrictions and violence to which their exterior body-selves were subjected. Internal
characteristics—intelligence, cleverness, spirituality, fortitude—provided the psychological emancipation from slavery that would lead to physical liberation. This
is not to say, as Katherine Fishburn also argues,[37] that the narrators wished to
escape their bodies; rather, the slave narrative, as a disembodied emanation from
the interior self, sought to rewrite the exterior self in such a way that the black
body signified something altogether different from the meanings it had accrued
within the institution of slavery and those discourses supporting it.

In a similar vein, nineteenth-century African American fiction writers used
literary representation to augment extratextual arguments for political representation. The light or white mulatta/o protagonists who crowded the pages of African
American literature before the turn of the century signified the material reality of
racial miscegenation and expressed, in part, the desire for racial miscegenation's
political equivalent,[38] dislocating whiteness from its containment in the white
body in a move that sought to redistribute the social and political rewards of
whiteness to the black national body. The "mulatto" heroine of William Wells
Brown's 1853 *Clotel*, for example, whom Brown imagines as the descendant of
Thomas Jefferson, served as a reminder that black Americans were already tied to
the nation by an irreversible blood-knot: it would be no more possible to extract
Clotel's "black" blood from her "white" than it would be to extract blacks from the
white national body. Brown's corporeal comingling is meant to render any exclusionary citizenship based in the construction of race meaningless.

Although Brown, Harper, and others chose to locate arguments for citizenship and liberation on the black female body, the dominant eighteenth- and
nineteenth-century black political discourse more often imagined the black citi-

zen's body as male. While the popularized shorthand for equal citizenship rights for blacks in the nineteenth century became "manhood rights," the myth of incorporeality this term implied was as suspect as white male leaders' use of the word "men" to assume the power to represent all bodies within the American body politic. That is, African American men relied upon a deracialized interpretation of the words "manhood," "men," and "people" to seek entry into the nation, not simply as citizens, but as de facto representatives of the black American body politic. Their biological proximity to their white male counterparts, they reasoned, extended them this right. As African American men pursued their efforts through formal organizations, particularly as the black convention movement gained momentum, black women, as Carla L. Peterson notes, "were officially excluded from those black national institutions . . . through which men of the elite came together to promote public civic debate on practical issues of racial uplift as well as those more theoretical considerations of black nationality."[39] The notion of an unsexed incorporeality nevertheless persisted. For instance, Paula Giddings describes a convention in 1855 during which one black male leader explained the need for equal rights: " 'As a people,' he declared, "we have been denied the ownership of our bodies, our wives, home, children and the products of our own labor."[40] While the speaker's generic language seems initially inclusive, corporealizing "people" by naming their specific political interests reveals an implicit male referent.[41]

However, before the Fifteenth Amendment was adopted in 1870, the black male's "proximity" to the white male body was not always recognized, legally or otherwise. Before black men could enact their "manhood"—their biologically inscribed position as the rightful leaders of the "nation within a nation," they had to demonstrate that they were men. War promised to be one ground upon which black manhood could be created.

In a prefatory note to *Colored Patriots*, abolitionist Wendell Phillips explains that the confirmation of black manhood was in fact the overriding importance in Nell's descriptions of black male military valor: "Some things set down here go to prove colored men patriotic—though denied a country:—and all show a wish, on their part, to prove themselves men, in a land whose laws refuse to recognize their manhood" (8). Barely a decade after the work was published, Frederick Douglass predicted that taking up arms during the Civil War would certainly secure "the black man's rights."[42] Historian Jim Cullen notes that during the same war, "in newspaper articles, government affidavits, and letters to officials, families and each other, manhood surfaces again and again as an aspiration, a concern, or a fact of life."[43] Abolitionist Thomas Wentworth Higginson, who commanded the First South Carolina Volunteers, the first African American regiment officially raised for the Civil War, issued this progress report on his black subordinates: they "were growing more like white men—less naïve and less grotesque."[44] Yet another white soldier commented: "Put a United States uniform on his back and the chattel is a man."[45] The remarks made by Higginson and the unnamed white soldier suggest that black men's first task in claiming manhood was to prove that they were not "grotesques" or "chattel"—that they were, in other words, human beings—a challenge recognized long before by blacks such as David Walker, who argued in his 1829 *Appeal* that blacks "are men, notwithstanding our improminent noses and woolly heads."[46]

Informed by the persistent veins of scientific racialism emergent in the eighteenth and nineteenth centuries, Higginson's "evolutionary" discourse reinforces a particular kind of racial hierarchy in which whites are naturally assumed to be an already-evolved species; blacks, therefore, must play "catch-up" or "get in synch" with the white race to be allowed entry into what Felipe Smith calls "white spaces," a concept derived from Benedict Anderson's enormously influential conceptualization of the nation as a temporal phenomenon.[47] According to Anderson, we envision ourselves as part of the modern nation through imagining acts of simultaneity, a collective imagining that becomes the unifying mechanism that creates a nation that conceives of itself as "a solid community moving down (or up) history."[48] For Western nations in particular, this movement is labeled "progress"—civilization marching ceaselessly forward. Those who are not thought to be on the same evolutionary trajectory thereby operate outside of nation-time and risk expulsion. Smith observes that in "denying simultaneity to nonwhite others, the politics of time" can be used as a means to refuse access to the nation-space where national identities are granted and "fraternité" assured. As such, time—and racism—become spatialized.[49]

The military, as both a white and a national space ("a white man's army," as it was frequently called), was especially ripe for exclusionary arguments based in evolutionary and physiological "difference." If, in the dominant culture's vocabulary, blackness signified subhumanity, it also came to signify congenital "disability," another, related, form of "difference" that further marked black bodies for expulsion. Historian Douglas Baynton clarifies this relationship between race and disability. "Disability," he claims, "has functioned historically to justify inequality for disabled people themselves, [however] the concept of disability has been used to justify discrimination against other groups by attributing disability to them. . . . Non-white races were routinely connected to people with disabilities, both of whom were depicted as evolutionary laggards or throwbacks."[50] The notion of the black body as congenitally disabled—inherently defective, afflicted with "deformity" and disease—was merely compounded by the dominant

COME AND JOIN US BROTHERS.

PUBLISHED BY THE SUPERVISORY COMMITTEE FOR RECRUITING COLORED REGIMENTS
1210 CHESTNUT ST. PHILADELPHIA.

"Come and Join Us Brothers," P. S. Duval & Son Lith., 1863. This recruiting poster for Camp William Penn, Pennsylvania, promises black soldiers fraternal inclusion. The Harry T. Peters "America on Stone" Lithograph Collection, National Museum of American History, Behring Center, Smithsonian Institution.

culture's attribution of another form of disability, but one that was acquired: the lingering "impairments" caused by the institution of slavery. In post–Civil War African American literature particularly, it was imperative that the black body and the black "mind" be portrayed as uninjured by the injuring institution of slavery in order to disprove one of the main antiblack arguments that surfaced after emancipation—that slavery had made blacks "unfit" for citizenship, "unfit" carrying a dual psychological and physical meaning.

Prior to emancipation, the "able-bodied" criterion used to eliminate "deficient" and disabled bodies from military service presented blacks with a more immediate and concrete reason to rebut these theories of black corporeal debility. Before black men were officially allowed to join the Union army, Frederick Douglass published an editorial that asserted that the powerful bodies of black men were needed to win the war: "Only a moderate share of sagacity was needed to see that the arm of the slave was the best defense against the arm of the slaveholder. Hence with every reverse to national arms, with every exulting shout of victory raised by the slave holding rebels, I have implored the imperiled nation to unchain against her foes, her powerful black hand."[51] Douglass's piece deploys black arms and hands as ready signifiers of ability, and, more importantly, of an ability that had been cultivated in slavery rather than compromised by it. During a manpower crisis during the Revolutionary War states such as Connecticut and Maryland allowed "able bodied" slaves to enlist with the permission of their masters, often, as I have mentioned, in exchange for their freedom. An "able body" could therefore directly translate into a liberated one. Just as often, however, the contention that the black body was an inherently disabled entity was used to prevent blacks from joining the military. Again, during the Revolution, the Continental Congress decided not to enlist "Negroes, Boys unable to bear Arms nor Old men unfit to endure the Fatigues of the Campaign,"[52] placing black male bodies somewhere along the continuum between the not completely formed bodies of children and the infirm bodies of the elderly. New Hampshire refused to accept "lunatics, idiots and Negroes,"[53] implying blackness was a similar mental deficiency.

The investment in the military as a site of rehabilitation was neither unique to the United States nor to African Americans seeking elevation. Michel Foucault has suggested that by the eighteenth century, the French army conceptualized the human body as a malleable form, an object that enters a "machinery of power that explores it, breaks it down and rearranges it."[54] The erect back, the head held high, and the chest thrown out are visible signs that the body has been "corrected," made pliant and docile; in short, they are signs that the body has been controlled, made something other, politically and physically, than it was upon entry. The "peasant," Foucault observes, becomes "the soldier."[55] And while it may be that the late nineteenth-century American military had yet to take on the structure and rigor that would be its hallmark in the twentieth century, the military was still thought to have the ability to transform its members; it was a space where boys were made men and men made more manly—where, as Higginson declares, blacks (or beasts, in other words) could be made men. Documents of African American military service abound with "before" and "after" photographs of black soldiers attesting to this radical reformation.[56] Serving as observable evidence of a rigorous and disciplined body, these photographs might suggest that the reason many African American men joined the army was not necessarily to be "transformed" (as many already considered themselves men) or "disciplined" (for many did not accept the nationalist ideologies that accompanied service), but rather to *display* a body that the nation would accept as "corrected," a body made "intelligible," in Foucault's terminology.[57] Very much like these photographs, the perfected body within African American war literature, particularly idealized representations of the black male soldier-citizen, became part of a larger set of cultural images designed to refute characterizations of deficiency and/or offer evidence of bodily rehabilitation, both tasks fueled by the necessity of imagining a black body poised to take up its position within the national body politic.

The Union army's willingness to believe in the military's ability to produce a rehabilitated black body fit to engage in national warfare was largely due to expedience; as the casualties mounted, the North made a concerted effort to corral all men available to serve. But the focus on rehabilitation further points to a somatic understanding of the state and to an attendant conceptualization of the military as an appendage of the "body politic." Richard Koenigsberg has theorized about how this corporeal "fantasy" of nation relates to the individual body of the soldier. Referring to the phrase used to exalt the sovereign upon his death, " 'The King is dead. Long live the King,' " he argues that the "body of the king is the dream of a body that lives on after the body of individuals die. . . . The concrete body of the King passes over into his immortal body. . . . The Second Body of the King is the foundational idea of nationalism: We die for the King (the leader) so that his name might live on."[58] If the military is both part of the sovereign's body and essential for ensuring his immortality—the well-being of the state—it would follow that the institution's enlistment of only the "able-bodied" was more than a matter of maximizing its efficiency but also a means of maintaining the "fantasy" of a healthy state when faced with circumstances threatening its ability to function or even signaling the possibility of its dissolution. Within this framework, Marcus Wood's reading of depictions of the escaped slave Gordon, one of the most reproduced images of a black body transformed by the military, offers another way of interpreting the North's faith in the army's capacity to rehabilitate African Americans. In the 1863 original from *Harper's Weekly*, a series of three engravings were printed illustrating Gordon's transformation. Published on July 4, the triptych details the route leading toward the subject's ostensible independence from slavery. He is first depicted as a "contraband," a barefoot slave in ragged clothing. In the next image, his scarred back is displayed with the caption "Gordon under Medical Inspection." In the final, he is standing, looking dapper in his uniform, a rifle by his side. Wood points out that the middle image, larger than the others, has the intended effect of positioning the subject as "a patient of the North."[59] Extending Wood's argument, I will suggest that the emphasis on the inspection is a way of assuring "quality control"; as a soldier whose possible death will absorb him into the body of the sovereign/body politic, he must be proved healthy, a noncontaminant.

While the northern forces may have needed to imagine themselves as selective, a popular 1864 war poem, "Sambo's Right to be Kilt,"[60] suggests that the ordinary white rank and file had less rigorous standards:

> I shouldn't object at all
> If Sambo's body should stop a ball
>   That was comin' for me direct;
> Though Sambo's black as the ace of spades,
>   His finger can a thrigger [sic] pull
> And his eyes runs straight on the barrel-sights
>   From under his thatch of wool[61]

The writer offers only a mocking acceptance of a black military presence. African American "inclusion" was predicated on the prospect of black death sparing white life; that is, "sameness" could only be accepted if the black male body were effectively removed from both national time and national space, allowing the white male body to retain its more deserving existence.

But if "all men" could be "buried equal," as historian Lerone Bennett Jr. has phrased it,[62] their equality while among the living was another matter. In fact, preoccupation with deevolutionizing the black male body during wartime—what Brooks calls the ascription of "congenital inequities" in one of her poems—only seemed to increase as the number of black men serving in the armed forces continued to steadily rise. Addie Hunton and Kathyrn M. Johnson, two African American women assigned to the American Expeditionary Forces during World War I, express dismay upon discovering that many French civilians believed rumors of blacks' savagery: "They had been systematically informed that their dark skinned allies . . . were brutal and vicious as to be absolutely dangerous.

|A TYPICAL NEGRO.|

We publish herewith three portraits, from photographs by M'Pherson and Oliver, of the negro GORDON, who escaped from his master in Mississippi, and came into our lines at Baton Rouge in March last. One of these portraits represents the man as he entered our lines, with clothes torn and covered with mud and dirt from his long race through the swamps and bayous, chased as he had been for days and nights by his master with several neighbors and a pack of blood-hounds; another shows him as he underwent the surgical examination previous to being mustered into the service —his back furrowed and scarred with the traces of a whipping administered on Christmas-day last; and the third represents him in United States uniform, bearing the musket and prepared for duty.

This negro displayed unusual intelligence and energy. In order to foil the scent of the bloodhounds who were chasing him he took from his plantation onions, which he carried in his pockets. After crossing each creek or swamp he rubbed his body freely with these onions, and thus, no doubt, frequently threw the dogs off the scent.

At one time in Louisiana he served our troops as guide, and on one expedition was unfortunately taken prisoner by the rebels, who, infuriated beyond measure, tied him up and beat him, leaving him for dead. He came to life, however, and once more made his escape to our lines.

By way of illustrating the degree of brutality which slavery has developed among the whites in the section of country from which this negro came, we append the following extract from a letter in the New York *Times*, recounting what was told by the refugees from Mrs. GILLESPIE's estate on the Black River:

The treatment of the slaves, they say, has been growing worse and worse for the last six or seven years.

Flogging with a leather strap on the naked body is common; also, paddling the body with a hand-saw until the skin is a mass of blisters, and then breaking the blisters with the teeth of the saw. They have "very often" seen slaves stretched out upon the ground with hands and feet held down by fellow-slaves, or lashed to stakes driven into the ground for "burning." Handfuls of dry corn-husks are then lighted, and the burning embers are whipped off with a stick so as to fall in showers of fire sparks upon the naked back. This is continued until the victim is covered with blisters. If in his writhings of torture the slave gets his hands free to brush off the fire, the burning brand is applied to them.

Another method of punishment, which is inflicted for the higher order of crimes, such as running away, or other refractory conduct, is to dig a hole in the ground large enough for the slave to squat or lie down in. The victim is then stripped naked and placed in the hole, and a covering or grating of green sticks is laid over the opening. Upon this a quick fire is built, and the live embers sifted through upon the naked flesh of the slave, until his body is blistered and swollen almost to bursting. With just enough of life to enable him to crawl, the slave is then allowed to recover from his wounds if he can, or to end his sufferings by death.

"Charley Slow" and "Overton," two hands, were both murdered by these cruel tortures. "Slow" was whipped to death, dying under the infliction, or soon after punishment. "Overton" was laid naked upon his face and burned as above described, so that the cords of his legs and the

GORDON AS HE ENTERED OUR LINES.

GORDON UNDER MEDICAL INSPECTION.

GORDON IN HIS UNIFORM AS A U. S. SOLDIER.

"Gordon under Medical Inspection," unidentified artist, 1863.
From *Harper's Weekly*, July 4, 1863.

They were even told that they belonged to a semi-human species who only a few years ago had been caught in the American forests."[63] As devastating as those rumors were to black morale, for most white men alarmed by the presence of blacks in the ranks of the military, simple demasculinization proved a far easier and a far more effective way to disempower colored interlopers. During wartime, the traditional paths leading to a recognizable militarized masculine subjectivity were routinely blocked. Black men were assigned low-level tasks and denied commissions, medals, and other accolades. After wartime, the demasculinization of black men often took narrative form. For instance, Amy Kaplan has read Theodore Roosevelt's conflicting accounts of the all-black Ninth and Tenth Calvary's performance during the famed Battle of San Juan Hill as an attempt to "restore domestic order" that required Roosevelt to reestablish the logic of a social and political hierarchy grounded in race. Shortly after the war, Roosevelt praised the troops' performance; later, he condemned the black men as "peculiarly dependent on their white officers."[64] Kaplan theorizes, in part, that a more balanced account of the battle—one that recognized the independence of the troops—would have "raised fear of armed insurrection and of national self-representation, which African American soldiers pursued in their printed rebuttals of Roosevelt's account."[65]

Black Americans' efforts to correct those portrayals of black men at war used to service a supremacist agenda gave rise to a genre of fictional war writing specific to African Americans: the black masculinist war novel. As I will later discuss, many of the African American writers in my study intentionally refer to traditions and themes from the dominant culture's nationalist war narratives, imprinting them with black social and political concerns. Harper and Dunbar revise those white postwar "reconciliation narratives" that depicted the nation as already "healed"; McKay suggests that the threat of lynching was a routine part of black veterans' "homecoming"; Brooks and Himes reveal that many blacks on the "home front" were anything but committed to the U.S. victory campaign. But the black masculinist novel has no ready counterpart in white American war writing. Its main concern, of course, is to present the black soldier-citizen as the epitome of manliness—honorable, ethical, powerful, and virile. In Killens's *And Then We Heard the Thunder*, the ambitious Solomon Saunders is cautioned not to "sacrifice" his "manhood" for any reason if he wishes retain his dignity in the white man's world (180). Very much like nineteenth-century African American male leaders' call for "manhood rights," the idea of manhood in these works is equally bound to the liberation, citizenship, and leadership of black men. Accordingly, many of these novels include depictions of the front that serve as a backdrop against which the black soldier-citizen can demonstrate his courage.

But this display of courage entails more than facing down the enemy "other" and his weapons. Invoking the dynamics of slavery to characterize relationships between black men and their white superiors, the novels invariably include a white antagonist, generally an officer who, through intense racial provocation, tests the soldier's commitment to military principles, and by extension his commitment to the nation he has sworn to protect. After black men became subject to formal draft policies during World War I and World War II—made to serve the country often against their wills—the analogy to slavery is amplified. Killens draws the parallel rather explicitly, creating a novel that might be thought of as a military neoslave narrative. A paternalist captain is labeled the "Great White Father" (284); his black company, "Rutherford's Plantation," and the men in it 'Rutherford's Slaves' " (284). In this vision of the military, the compliant black soldier quite clearly risks becoming another archetype from that era: the dreaded "house slave."

Of course, this will not be the case. Rather, the heroes of the masculinist war novel are descended from the new black males found in works such as race man Martin Delany's Black Nationalist novel *Blake, or The Huts of America* (1859–62),[66] or Douglass's *The Heroic Slave* (1853),[67] which locate the source of their protagonists' mental and physical fortitude in their undeniable blackness and willingness to rebel against the institution of slavery. Gilmore's soldier, the son of a "jet-black" slave father, is described as a "tall" and "active young colored man" whose "courage was never disputed" (13, 14). It is probably no coincidence that Gilmore's novel, one of the first black masculinist war novels (though certainly not the first to depict black male heroism) was set during the Spanish-Cuban-American Wars and the wars against the Philippines. Recalling Delany's and Douglass's efforts, the novel directly contradicts Roosevelt's misrepresentation of blacks as passive, disorderly soldiers in need of white leadership.

Thus, for men such as Douglass, who sent his sons to battle to fight for the manliness of the black race, actual warfare served as a proving ground for manhood; and for writers such as Gilmore and Killens, the narration of war permitted black men the opportunity to benefit socially and politically by creating idealized representations of black masculinity. Higginson's memoirs of his service with his black regiment attest to the power literary texts have in shaping national consciousness. He writes that while he was "expecting to find male Topsies"[68]— the unruly, minstrelesque orphan from Harriet Beecher Stowe's novel *Uncle Tom's Cabin*—he encountered men more courageous than in any "anti-slavery novel," perhaps referring here to the martyred titular character of Stowe's work.[69] Black male war writers, therefore, had some reason to hope their texts might effect change in the public's perception of black men. Many in fact describe black participation in the military as the *origins* of a new race. African roots and the experience of New World slavery are both historically displaced as war is declared the birthplace of the black American—a repeated gesture that I will refer to as the "military creation narrative." As a masculinist rhetorical strategy, women are omitted from this story, or assumed to be created from the black male warring body, little more than a race of black Eves. It is therefore critical to consider what opportunities for political and social gain African American women felt that war—and more importantly, black women's narration of warfare—offered them.

Fatal Feminization

As far back as the Civil War—and, as Nell claims, probably before—black women were active during times of war. Women such as Susie King Taylor, who wrote a memoir of her tenure with the Thirty-third U.S. Colored Troops, and activist Sojourner Truth served as nurses, teachers, cooks, and laundresses. The legendary conductor of the Underground Railroad, Harriet Tubman, served in the war as a spy and scout for the Union forces, leading an armed invasion into southern territories. As part of the Port Royal Experiment, Charlotte Forten Grimké taught newly freed slaves and acted as a nurse when the Fifty-fourth Massachusetts returned from its ill-fated attack on Battery Wagner, writing of her impressions in her posthumously published diaries.[70] Yet another African American woman, Elizabeth Keckley, who lost her son during the Civil War and who also helped found the Contraband Relief Association, offers her thoughts on the conflict in an autobiography that focuses on the years she served as Mary Todd Lincoln's modiste in the White House.[71] Frances Harper, an active abolitionist before the Civil War, also played a central role in uplift education after emancipation. Harriet Jacobs founded a Freeman's school in Alexandria, Virginia. During the Spanish-Cuban-American War, Nanahokye Sockum Curtis recruited a small number of black nurses for duty in Cuba. Hunton and Johnson spent fifteen months abroad as spiritual counselors and soldier-teachers for black soldiers, detailing that experience during the First World War in their memoirs of that period, *Two Colored Women with the American Expeditionary Forces*.[72] In World War II, more than four thousand black women were part of the Women's Army Auxiliary Corps. Hundreds of these women were sent overseas.[73] Five served in the Coast Guard, and others joined in the U.S. Army Nurse Corps, although quotas limited the numbers of black women allowed to participate.[74] Black women currently comprise a plurality of the 15 percent of women in the military; many have enlisted for the same socioeconomic reasons that have historically led minority men to turn to the military as the most viable peacetime employment option, a choice made even more likely by recruitment practices that strategically target poorer communities for potential recruits. But before women's military assignments were legally expanded after the Second World War, many black women who actively participated in war or organized in its aftermath did so in caretaking capacities—a "logical" extension of their prescribed "civil" duties. Nevertheless, their gender did not protect them from segregationist policies, from witnessing firsthand the ravages of war on the minds and bodies of black men, or from falling victim to the brutalities of war themselves. While the works by African American women vary widely in scope and purpose, all offer invaluable insight into how they viewed themselves as women in relation to the nation, war, and African American men.

Indeed, the construction of war as a solely masculine domain is as misleading as the debunked division of public and private spheres. Feminist theorists have aptly demonstrated that the public "male" sphere (under which war would logically fall) and the private "female" sphere are symbiotically linked, so much so that one can image the "female" domestic space as a "house without walls" into which the "male" ideologies of government and the marketplace may enter with little interference. In the same way, though women are often viewed as ancillary to the project of war, they are essential for its continuation. Hunton and Johnson acknowledge what is often viewed as the most troubling role women play in war, writing that their work is "dedicated to the women of our race, who gave so trustingly and courageously the strongest of their young manhood to suffer and die for the cause of freedom.[75] In *Woman and the New Race*, published not long after World War I, birth control activist Margaret Sanger indeed holds women responsible for creating " 'fodder for cannon.' " Listing other, attendant "horrors of war," Sanger claims that "it is out of her womb that those things proceed."[76] If war, she reasons, is created by the struggle for the world's limited resources, population control could effectively put an end to it by decreasing the number of human beings in need of those resources. Sanger chastises women for the same reason Hunton and Johnson praise them; all, however, assume that women's primary weapon in relation to war is the womb: the incubator for warriors. In this conceptualization, the womb loses its private function and becomes, in essence, a public property to be used either for evil, in Sanger's conceptualization, or, as Hunton and Johnson imply, for good. In spite of the obvious biological relationship women have to war, however, the womb is neither the beginning nor the end of women's involvement in war. Just as the public/private dichotomy proves fragile at best, feminist war critics have also noted that essentialist extrapolations corresponding to the idea of separate spheres—men are "pro-war aggressors," women are "anti-war pacifists"—are equally weak.

The female speaker in Alice Dunbar-Nelson's well-known World War I poem, "I Sit and Sew," appears burdened by her "useless" domestic task in the face of war:

I sit and sew—my heart aches with desire—
That pageant terrible, that fiercely pouring fire
On wasted fields, and writhing grotesque things
Once men. My soul in pity flings
Appealing cries, yearning only to go
There in that holocaust of hell, those fields of woe—
    But—I must sit and sew.[77]

If men have indeed wandered into the private sphere to plunder the womb for bodies, women, in the very act of writing about war, have invaded a "public," "male" territory—a narrative manifestation of the longing expressed by the speaker of the poem to unloose her hands from the ties binding her to a needle. The final question asked in the poem—"Why must I sit and sew?"—invites an interrogation of a patriarchal political order in which women are not able to choose freely how they will participate in national affairs. The hands, engaged in "women's work," the body, confined to a chair, become a metaphor for political confinement located in bodily based understandings of citizenship roles.

During the period my study covers, essentialism remained at the core of policies preventing women from being fully integrated into the armed forces in more than supportive capacities. The primary rationale is perhaps best summarized by an assertion made more recently. In *Women in the Military: Flirting With Disaster*, Brian Mitchell claims that "[Women's] expanding presence is destroying the military's body and soul,"[78] a manner of prophesying that Kim Field and John Nagl have critiqued as the "fatal feminization" theory of women's military service.[79] Corporeal metaphors predicting the military's "death" draw their power through a familiar recourse to biological dichotomies, the ostensible distinctiveness of men's and women's bodies. Men are big, hard, strong, phallic, made to penetrate. Women are small, soft, round, weak, made to procreate. Accordingly, men and women house different interiors; women's minds, like their reproducing, menstruating, expulsive bodies, are governed by emotional "excess." Too flighty, chatty, and malleable, they are too undisciplined to be regulated. Too loving and caring, they recoil at inflicting injury. When confronted with the injury, pain, and death of those around them, they dissolve into fits of hysteria. Outside of the theater of war women are the embodiments of life; when their bodies are brought within its realm, they are transformed into bodies of death, hastening the military's demise by weakening its constitution. The belief that women are life-givers also undergirds "protectionist" arguments currently restricting women from formal assignments as combat personnel (though they can be part of combat units and are as a matter of course trained in weaponry): the idea that their bodies are too valuable to be harmed or annihilated in warfare.

Too, those who lobbied against integration argued that the introduction of women in the military would necessarily mean the introduction of heterosexual sex, characterized as a radically destabilizing force (in denial of the presence of homosexual sex that has always been part of a military that has isolated men, encouraged homoerotic rituals, and included gay members, even if they are forced to be closeted). Hunton and Johnson, who were able to spend much of their time at the front, write of becoming keenly aware of their female bodies while in an all-male environment; although they claim to have kept their virtue intact, they take care to note ongoing flirtations that tested their "Christian ideals." Hunton's and Johnson's temptation to abandon a morally "acceptable" female identity operates as a metaphor for other women writing about war: how (and whether) to maintain their "female" identities in a "male" territory (both actual and literary) in which traditional gender norms are prone to transgression.[80] For example, not only does Hunton and Johnson's preface disseminate the ideologies used by men to justify war (war is "freedom"), they apply the terms typically reserved for warring men ("courage") to describe black women's sacrifice, in effect inscribing masculinity onto the female body. Susie King Taylor uses her autobiographical narrative to reenvision herself as a soldier rather than a laundress, her assigned duty. In Minnie's Sacrifice, the character who makes the ultimate sacrifice men at war make for their countries—death—is a woman. To write about the Second World War, Gwendolyn Brooks "cross dresses" as a male soldier, as Susan Schweick has noted. All but one of her war sonnets are written in the persona of a man.[81] In general, in writing about war with "womanly comprehension," in Hunton and Johnson's words, black women war writers often (but not always) liberate themselves from traditional gender roles—sometimes overtly, more often covertly—confusing and complicating notions of the "feminine" and "masculine," prompting a critical analysis of what ideas of a "womanly comprehension" of war truly denote and what a woman's place in war ought to be.

Representing War: The Enemy Within

The already wide array of problems accompanying representations of the black body in African American war writing is further broadened by the difficulties of representing war itself. Much of the conventional wisdom about war literature comes to a single conclusion: that war is nearly impossible to describe. Of course, this particular consensus is more often than not grounded in cultural and psychological analyses of "trauma." Stated briefly, a great number of these theories argue that when the already faulty cognitive processes of perception and memory are confronted with a traumatizing event, these processes become even less reliable, prone to disruptions both physiological and psychological in origin. Theories focusing on the linguistic translation of those perceptions and memories, however corrupted, have suggested that any articulation of the traumatic event is necessarily compromised by the structural limits of an abstract system of referents already removed from material "reality." Forms of posttraumatic syndrome resulting from the indelible and exact impression of horrific scenes on the survivor's mind—the inability to forget rather than remember—has lead some to speculate that trauma lies not in the failures of memory itself, but in the failures of language, in the survivors' struggles to translate these experiences in a manner others will comprehend. While we may never know with certainty how accurate such theories are, the belief that war is "unnarratable" does have sources that can be separated from the study of trauma, at least to some degree. In Just What War Is, a study of the Civil War writers Ambrose Bierce and John W. DeForest, Michael Schaefer has pointed out that those arguably most interior to warfare—combat soldiers—are often the least capable of rendering it in its totality.[82] This inability is not completely reducible to whether or not they were actually traumatized; alternatively, it may be attributed to something far simpler—what they did or not witness. Certainly, visual capacity is often diminished in the "fog of war," but the limitation of the visual field is also a matter of purposeful strategy. Drawing from soldiers' descriptions of Civil War battles, he observes that large-scale combat often necessitated that the soldier narrow his sight lines to what is in front of him and little more; soldiers' lives and the lives of their comrades depended on the ability to tunnel their vision through an onslaught of sensory information, zeroing in on whatever targets lay ahead and then quickly advancing. Although this might be partly a consequence of older, more formalized troop formations, a soldier recently demobilized from the war in Iraq has described his experience of battle quite similarly: "Being artillery you're firing upwards of 15 miles away. You don't get to see your target. You normally don't get to see the results . . . every time we would see these kind of things, like, you know, dead bodies on the road, burnt and destroyed vehicles, we'd just keep going, because, you know, mission accomplishment. We have a position to get to."[83] To further guard against succumbing to the chaos and devastation surrounding them, soldiers learn to develop an intense and focused relationship with their weaponry, loading and reloading guns, correctly activating and lobbing grenades, filling mortars: repetitive, controlled acts that also provide emotional insulation from the combatants' own thoughts and fears.[84] The irony is therefore clear. What we commonly understand as "true" images of war lie in the stimuli an "effective" soldier must attempt to filter out—the smoke emerging from weapons and burning buildings, the relentless noise of artillery, the groans and cries of the wounded and dying, the smell of flesh and fire. Schaefer notes that even those writers who had been in the midst of battle, as combatants or medical personnel, were later forced to turn to other sources to fill in what they did not know, see, feel, or remember, relying instead on photographs (sometimes staged, as with Mathew Brady's images of the Civil War),[85] strategic manuals, journalistic accounts, and paintings.[86] Thus battle, war's "violent essence,"[87] is subject to infinite refraction and deferral; the very bodily and psychic locus of its "truth" becoming, perhaps, the most unreliable conveyer of its larger reality.

Efforts to define war, as opposed to describe its manifestations, further complicate a precise apprehension of "what war is." In *On War* (1832), the famous nineteenth-century military strategist Karl von Clausewitz endeavored to do just this, using his sprawling tome to discuss war's origins, functions, and operations. It was there that he issued his oft-cited maxim: "War is . . . a continuation of policy by other means. It is not merely a political act but a real political instrument, a continuation of political intercourse."[88] He goes on to suggest that this political element, part of a "trinity" of warfare, is quickly subsumed to the other two elements. War is, he explains, "composed of the violence of its essence, the hate and enmity which are to be regarded as blind, natural impulse; of the play of probability and chance . . . [and] of the subordinate character of a political instrument."[89] The part of Clausewitz's theory positing the primacy and recession of politics has proved essential to answering a quite broad and quite impossible question I crafted when beginning this study; that is, whether a collective African American vision of war can be ascertained from black American war narratives, particularly given war's ability to elude description and definition. What I have discovered might be characterized as a reversal of Clausewitz's claim of subordination—that black American war writers' presentation of war often downplays the other elements of war to focus on its political instrumentality. Yet this emphasis on instrumentality manages to avert an examination of the fundamental machination of war—a government's use of unlimited and absolute "force" to "compel" its "adversary . . . to do [its] will," as Clausewitz suggests.[90] Rather, many, though not all, black war writers appear more invested in assessing black participation in U.S. warfare as another political instrument, one wielded in the struggle for civic inclusion and equity, as my prior description of the literature suggests. This is not to argue that African American populations in general were disengaged from discussions of war on its own terms: its just or unjust nature, its effectiveness or ineffectiveness, its inevitability or aberrancy. The literature simply tells a different story, reflecting concerns more immediately related to blacks' national and racial well-being. If, as it has been said, "all politics are local," in these works, all wars are domestic (with a few notable exceptions).

The tendency to ensconce war within domestic conflicts is, I believe, a latent effect of the Civil War, the war that "freed the slaves" in deed if not intent, an event still sacred in black collective memory. Judging from the descriptions of that war in the literature, it appears that the outcome of that conflict gave rise to an initial reluctance to offer unsettling depictions of war and its damage, lest these images be construed as antiwar statements that might retroactively call into question the very means that facilitated black emancipation. Therefore, in many instances war exists in what I consider rather abstract terms, a subject apparently too hot to touch, even as it must be handled nonetheless. My interpretations of the works in this book will expand from those overlapping and interrelated strategies that coalesce into this "domestication" of warfare:

1. War as a field of oppositions. In describing war's most basic structure, Clausewitz claims that war "is nothing but a duel on a larger scale."[91] In other words, war is a contest between two people, the "self" and the "other," enlarged into a battle between multiple selves (the same as you) and multiple others (different from you but indistinct from one another). Conceptualizing war as a space determined by such binaries has become a kind of cognitive reflex—what Paul Fussell calls the "imaginative habit" of "gross dichotomizing."[92] In war, there are "winners" and "losers," "allies" and "adversaries," "imperialists" and "subjects," an "us" and a "them." War insists upon an identification with one side or the other of two opposing forces; " 'We' are all here on this side," Fussell writes, " 'the enemy' is over there."[93] African Americans, however, as a people both racially and culturally hybrid and as a people who at once identify with and are excluded by national democratic ideologies, have traditionally existed between oppositional terms. "Hitlerism at home," for instance, became a popular phrase for American racism circulated among blacks during World War II, collapsing the ideological distinction between "the enemy" and "us" and further dissecting the "us" (Americans) into two distinct warring camps: blacks and whites.

Capitalizing on these divisions, American adversaries frequently propagandized themselves as the allies of African Americans. During World War I, the Germans dropped leaflets designed to make African Americans question their allegiance to the United States:

Hello boys, what are you doing over here? Fighting the Germans? Why? Have they ever done you any harm? . . . Do you enjoy the same rights white people do in America, the land of freedom and Democracy, or are you not rather treated over there as second class citizens? . . . Can you get into a restaurant where white people dine? . . . To carry a gun in this service is not an honor but a shame. Throw it away and come to the German lines. You will find friends who will help you.[94]

During the wars against the Philippines, similar tactics were used by Filipino insurgents, and by the Viet Cong during the Vietnam War. How, then, do African Americans negotiate their positions within a discourse characterized by oppositions, particularly in narratives that waver between subverting American "egalitarian" ideologies and heralding their validity? And how do they choose to align themselves racially as they participate in imperialist wars waged against other people of color?

2. War as a national space. During World War II, the army general staff issued this bulletin:

Every effort should be made by the War Department to maintain the social and racial conditions which exist in civil life in order that the normal customs of white and colored personnel now in the Army may not be suddenly disrupted. The Army can, under no circumstances, adopt a policy which is contrary to the dictates of a majority of the people.[95]

Until Truman mandated the end of legal segregation across the armed forces, most branches of the military enacted the discriminatory practices at work in the nation at large. In practice, the exigencies of war made total segregation difficult. During World War II, white and minority military troops were frequently thrown together on the battlefield; minority soldiers serving in the army were in many instances sent to fill in all-white regiments depleted by death and injury. In the navy, complete separation proved structurally unworkable because of the close quarters in which sailors were made to work. Despite this spatial problematic, however, some semblance of division was maintained through restricting blacks' official assignments (for instance, they could be radio men, boatswainers, and machinists). More commonly, black sailors were given menial duties, as they were in the other branches, serving as galley workers or janitorial personnel. While segregated black units often excelled in military terms, the Tuskegee Airmen as one familiar example, the practice of separation nevertheless proved demoralizing. The champion boxer Joe Louis, exulted as an unlikely embodiment of nation after winning the world heavyweight title from the German Max Schmeling in 1938, was drafted into the army four years later. President Franklin Roosevelt, who had written him a letter of commendation after his celebrated bout, deemed it a welcomed opportunity to boost morale among black servicemen. Hardly uplifted by his own experience of military life, Louis tells of being shocked at the extent to which segregation organized every aspect of army life in a 1948 piece published in *Life Magazine*: "One time down in Camp Silbert in Alabama I went into a bus station to telephone for a cab and I was sitting on a front bench and an MP said I would have to sit in the back—the Jim Crow part. . . . I wouldn't go. Ray Robinson, the Negro welterweight was with me, . . . they took Ray and me to the stockade."[96] Within black American war narratives, the black soldier-citizen who triumphs over racist practices within these spaces is an embodied index of African Americans' postwar expectations, signaling his preparedness to compel the nation to reorganize racially upon his return. What, however, are the implications of using the military and war as sites from which a viable black subjectivity emerges?

3. War as a site of sexual struggle. Aside from black women's determination to transform war from a traditionally masculinist space to one where they can participate in the making of nation, war acts a site for another form of sexual struggle within the African American war narrative. Even in the twenty-first century, nations are still imagined as sexed entities, referred routinely to by the feminizing pronouns "she" or "her." In the case of the United States, that "she," of course, has been racialized as white: Blind Justice holding her scales, Liberty holding her torch. The flag of one black Civil War unit was emblazoned with a black soldier and a white, gowned woman jointly holding an American flag. If blacks felt the Civil War was waged for their freedom, this emblem serves to remind them that all U.S. wars are, in effect, wars fought to preserve the bodies of white women.[97] After that war, as we know, these same bodies would be marshaled as essential weapons in the domestic war against a population of newly freed black men. The somatic symbolism was evident; if the white woman represented nation metaphorically, by no means would black men be permitted to penetrate her boundaries. Accordingly, as the United States engaged in wars abroad in European nations, "foreign" white women's bodies were transformed into American territorial possessions and made subject to the same restrictions. Pressured by the United States, in 1918 the French Military Mission issued a directive intended to solve the problem: because "[white] Americans become greatly incensed at any public expression of intimacy between white women with black men," the French population was advised not to "indulge" any black soldiers socially. A similar directive issued by an American commander forbade his black male troops from fraternizing with white women, whether the women

"solicited" the attention or not.[98] Whether informal or formal, these regulations reemerged during the Second World War, sparking a number of violent racial clashes abroad. As a means of further exposing racial injustices in the armed forces, many of the black masculinist novels choose to center their narratives on the restricted access to the white female body, particularly as the sexual domestic war followed them overseas. This focus has the effect of positioning this prohibition as the most virulent form of regulatory violence these men experience. What is the intention of emphasizing this aspect of racial relations within the context of national warfare?

4. War as a zone of violence. War is an act of violence—or, as it were, a zone of multiple acts of violence. And while violence in war tends to be spoken of as "a means to an ends," Elaine Scarry has suggested that violence is not the means, but the ends.[99] The purpose of war is to wound, maim, or kill, and to risk being wounded, maimed, or killed, until the most injured forces cede defeat. Winning is a by-product of intentional injuring; injuring is not, Scarry argues, the unfortunate by-product of winning. This uncomfortable reality—the necessity of wounding human beings in war—is lost, she claims, when the human element goes unmentioned; dead and wounded bodies are missing from terms such as "casualties" and "collateral damage." Writing of the Iraqi conflict in *Parameters*, the organ of the U.S. Army War College, Ralph Peters argues against such subterfuge, asserting that "we don't need discourses. We need . . . the will to close with the enemy and kill him. And to keep on killing him until it is unmistakably clear to the entire world who won."[100] Peters realizes his frank advocacy of waging a "war of attrition" will prove disconcerting to many; looked at from a rhetorical standpoint, one reason his words carry a disruptive potential lies in his use of the pronoun "him"—his willingness to repersonify an enemy who is often depersonified as a standard diversionary tactic. During the Persian Gulf War, General Colin Powell laid forth the strategy of the American forces during one of many televised briefs: to cut off the Iraqi army and "kill it." More recently, an army general declared it "fun to shoot some people," justifying his exuberance by arguing that Afghani men "who slap women around . . . because they didn't wear a veil . . . ain't got no manhood left anyway. So it's a hell of a lot of fun to shoot them."[101] The dehumanization of the enemy other in these statements serves the same purposes as the deanimatization of black bodies within American white supremacist ideology; it permits acts of violence and subjugation against that entity to be committed with impunity. As such, using violence against the "enemy/ other" to "make" a black American national identity—the tool that the dominant culture has wielded to "unmake" that same identity—might be expected to pose a problem for African American war writers.

Indeed, as a representative of the black body politic, the soldier-citizen's physical body tends to be extraordinary, as I have noted. One reviewer of Killens's novel in fact denounced the portrayal of the hero as "too handsome and too irresistible to women."[102] These magnificent male bodies are partly meant as somatic signifiers pointing to an inviolate ethical and moral black interior. Analyzing what happens, or what does not happen, to these spectacular bodies within zones of violence—and what acts they do or do not commit—is therefore essential to understanding how invested these writers had become in portraying a physical body that projected their political longings. Yet there are curious and notable silences surrounding the subject of violence. While one might expect any socially conscious literature about war to include realistic depictions of wounded and altered bodies as a matter of course, graphic "damage imagery" in relation to the black male body is rare within these texts, or described only tentatively.[103] Also missing from many of these works are portrayals of the black male body acting offensively: killing or wounding the adversary. If the very meaning of masculinity in the U.S. cultural lexicon is to "embody force,"[104] the omission of moments describing offensive violation might comprise the claim to manhood these writers wanted to secure. What, therefore, are the purposes (and the consequences) of exempting the black body from the violence of war?

4. War as an immaterial/rhetorical creation. It scarcely needs to be said that the forgetting of the main goal of war—to injure—is encouraged by the obscuring languages of the state. It is standard practice for governments and their militaries to place the violent reality of war into relief by purposefully emphasizing its ideological aspects. The United States fights wars "to save democracy" or for "the American way"; it fights wars "against fascism" or "against terror." "His truth is marching on," not the Union forces. "Freedom is on the march," not U.S. troops with heavy artillery. Lifting war into the lofty realm of the abstract quite naturally rids it of its dirty, physical, earthly nature; denying war its human agency brings it closer to an act of God than to a work of man. African Americans were hardly exempt from participating in these obfuscations. As an interesting instance, one of the many World War II propaganda posters targeting black communities features an image of Joe Louis, muscular and uniformed, leaping forth with a bayonet, his body nearly breaking through the single dimension of the flat plane. This image, although valorizing aggression, is coupled with a soothing message: "We're going to do our part . . . and we'll win because we're on God's side." Many of the blacks in African American war narratives espouse similar rhetoric, inviting an investigation of the relationship between the black speaking subject and what is spoken. Looking at the Louis poster and knowing that it is propaganda, one cannot help but wonder if those are, in fact, *his* words

"Private Joe Louis Says—," unidentified artist, 1942.
National Portrait Gallery, Smithsonian Institution.

stamped across his form (especially in light of his disillusionment with the military). They are. But encounters with such language within black war texts, so very reminiscent of state-generated sloganeering, raise a significant question. *Who*, one asks, is speaking? Are the writers pointing to an enunciatory gap, contrasting the very real oppression of black bodies with the abstract notions of freedom and democracy they voice? Or do "patriotic" and religious narratives of war provide a subterfuge, becoming another means of averting the "real" nature of warfare?

5. War as something other than war. African American literature produced after emancipation necessarily grapples with the legacy of slavery, not simply its lasting effect on matters racial, social, and political, but also the imprints slavery left on a tradition of black writing that had been largely abolitionist in its purposes and which sought, accordingly, to contest images of black Americans in proslavery literature. Both bodies of work, anti- and proslavery, depended on mobilizing a host of "stock" figures: the "heroic" slave, the "tragic mulatto/a," the amoral overseer, the northerner/abolitionist, the "darky," the "benevolent" plantation patriarch. As I earlier noted, these figures reemerge in varied and derivative incarnations, populating the postemancipation war literature produced by black (and white) Americans. However, in terms of African American war literature specifically, this gives rise to another query. What happens when the racial dynamics of slavery are grafted onto the racial dynamics of the military and warfare? How useful is the "heroic slave," for instance, when placed on the battlefield?

The multitude of questions raised by these representative strategies, what I have labeled the domestication of warfare, inevitably lead to a final, overarching question asked by most of the writers in my study: *what*, exactly, are *we* fighting for? The response most texts supply—citizenship rights—seems simple enough. Given, however, that these rights would continue to be deferred in the aftermath of war upon war, there is nothing at all simple about that answer.

1 CIVIL WAR WOUNDS

William Wells Brown, Violence, and the Domestic Narrative

In 1867, William Wells Brown, the first published black American novelist, wrote a fictionalized account of the Civil War, becoming, it appears, the first black American war novelist in the process. However, *Clotelle; or, The Colored Heroine, a Tale of the Southern States* was not a war novel in its origins.[1] Brown, who manifested an unparalleled talent for repetition throughout his career, took one of his several revisions of the 1853 *Clotel; or, The President's Daughter* and added four chapters dealing with the Civil War.[2] Brown admits in his preface that all but these chapters were completed "before the breaking out of the recent rebellion" (4). Approximately six months before the publication of *Clotelle*, Brown had also become the first black American to publish a book-length historical account of the Civil War, *The Negro in the American Rebellion: His Heroism and His Fidelity* (1867).[3]

The 1867 version of Brown's revisions of *Clotel* brings the fugitive slaves Clotelle (daughter of the original Clotel and named Mary in the first novel) and her black husband Jerome home from their refuge in France to participate in the Civil War. Joining the Louisiana "Native Guards," one of the first black regiments raised to fight in the war, Jerome is killed off four paragraphs into the Civil War section of the narrative when a white general asks that his black subordinates charge into an onslaught of bullets and shells to retrieve the body of another (assumedly white) officer. Four by four, they are fed into the fire until, on the fourth try, the body is rescued. Very nearly out of danger, Jerome is decapitated by a shell. What Brown labels "human sacrifice" (106), was of course, "black sacrifice"; black men willingly— and here, forcibly—laying down their bodies at the altars of freedom and citizenship. Jerome does not die in sacrificial glory, as Frances Harper's slave-martyr Tom will in *Iola Leroy*, saving black and white men alike; Jerome's death is senseless and the scene absurd. Moreover, Jerome's commanding officer is not the concerned abolitionist/

commander both Harper and memoirist Susie King Taylor will both put to use in their works, but "a sorry tribute to white humanity" (106).

This episode is a fictionalized representation of an event in the war that apparently had made a deep impression on Brown. In *The Negro in the American Rebellion*, the writer allots the incident an entire chapter, rendering it in explicit, uncomfortable detail. In historical actuality, a noncommissioned black officer, Captain Andre Cailloux, whom Brown describes in the most elevated terms of black masculinity—"the blackest man in the Crescent City. . . . Finely educated, polished in his manners . . . bold, athletic and daring"—was killed in a poorly planned attack on the rebel works at Port Hudson, Louisiana (169). Although it was evident that the works could not be taken without extraordinary loss of life, a General Dwight ordered that the mission continue. His subordinate, Colonel Nelson, made seven charges of the Confederate batteries, each unsuccessful, and each bringing more deaths and casualties. "Humanity," Brown writes, "will never forgive Gen. Dwight . . . for he certainly saw he was throwing away the lives of his men. But what were his men? 'Only Niggers' " (170). Brown asks the relevant question: "But had they accomplished anything more than the loss of many of their brave men?" Unwilling to let the query hang too long, he answers it quickly and affirmatively. "Yes: they had," he writes, explaining that the bravery of the black troops "created a new chapter in American history for the colored man" (172). His assurance seems more than a bit disingenuous. Brown indeed is trying to have it both ways: these black lives were both carelessly disposed of in battle *and* honorably preserved by historical record—not just his, but the dominant culture's, who, Brown writes, "paid . . . tribute" to these men (172). When read within the context of his preface—he writes that he is "feeling anxious to preserve for future reference an account of the part which the Negro took" in the recently ended war—Brown's insistence that the blood of black lives lost, even those lost in this most obscene manner, had *already* written this "chapter in American history" appears to be more hopeful than truthful.

Brown's attempt to have it both ways underscores the difficulty he faced in creating a usable African American history of the Civil War: writing a realistic portrayal of black military life that exposes the psychological and physical assaults blacks endured at the hands of both the Union and Confederacy (the aspects Harper will later choose to forgo) while at the same time idealizing the dignity and bravery of the troops. The Civil War was nothing if not a conflict rife with conflicts: a war that was and was not about slavery, that freed some slaves but not others, where blacks were used as both Union and Confederate soldiers, and where those blacks who did don Union uniforms were paid no more than fugitive slave laborers. It was a war whose end seemed to promise total liberation, but that brought about a freedom so limited that many blacks were left to wonder whether emancipation had taken place at all. Looking at Brown as Civil War writer, what intrigues me are his troubled endeavors to produce and manage a black body that can negotiate this contradictory historical terrain. As I will explain, Brown used his early nonfiction and literature to create male and female heroic bodies that could take their proper places within an evolutionary, linear narrative of black historical progress, a narrative designed to combat the devolutionary temporal narratives that would preclude blacks from inhabiting national space. In a work published during the Civil War, The Black Man: His Antecedents, His Genius and His Achievements (1863), Brown argues that blacks, who "belong to the great family of man," are not debilitated by a "natural inferiority" that would prevent them from achieving equality "on this continent with the white man."[4] The argument that belonging to the same evolutionary time should secure blacks' right to live with whites in the nation, rather than be expatriated or expelled to a more "backward" elsewhere, is a variation of the claim he used to demand the abolition of slavery. Throughout his lectures and speeches Brown maintains that blacks, if indeed in a degraded condition, were made that way from the intellectual and physical deprivations of bondage; given time, they would emerge as enlightened, capable beings.

For Brown, that linear narrative of black progress almost always crosses the threshold of the domestic, the allegorical space where he enacts his fantasies of national inclusion. The manner in which Brown constantly moves his hero and heroine across geography and circumstance—from the United States to Europe and back to the United States, from slavery to freedom—demonstrates that Brown's particular notion of a politically useful domesticity relies less on the creation of a perfected material space than on an idealized heterosexual union whose hallmark is its very mobility: black men and women forming a political alliance that is impervious to time, space, and history. For African Americans, whose historical experience has been defined by geographical movement, displacement, and loss, the notion of a movable "homespace" defends against the "lack" implied by an inability to construct a stable physical domesticity. This holds particularly true for Brown, who was a fugitive slave. His sketch of Madison Washington, the instigator of the revolt on the slave ship Creole, included in The Black Man shows the extent to which Brown articulates black progress within the trope of a mobilized matrimony. While Frederick Douglass's fictionalized version, The Heroic Slave, has Washington's wife dying before the insurgency takes place, Brown places Washington's beautiful mulatta companion (with "marbled" skin, "mild blue eyes," a "finely chiseled mouth")[5] within the group of slaves freed by her husband. As Richard Yarborough observes, Brown's realization of liberation results in "a restoration of the integrity of the domestic circle," revising Douglass's idealization of a solitary male heroic figure.[6] Brown was intent on creating a decidedly black and decidedly heroic male protagonist who could access public male power and perform domesticity at once.[7]

However, as the 1867 *Clotelle* demonstrates, a marked shift takes place in the narrative Brown produced after the war. In abandoning the heterosexual domestic imaginary, and with it, the powerful set of meanings it had accrued within his work—as I will suggest he does—Brown raises the question of whether the cultural vocabulary dominating nineteenth-century American culture can remain functional within black postbellum protest fiction. He raises a similar question in abandoning the black corporeal fantasy embodied by the hero and heroine he sculpted so meticulously within the *Clotel* novels: can highly stylized, aestheticized representations of blackness still perform the political work necessary for African Americans in the post–Civil War United States? Jerome's magnificent body, as we have seen, is very certainly "transformed," but the equally magnificent mulatta Clotelle is also altered, nullified, as it were, through Brown's linguistic neglect. In these chapters, he refuses to enshroud her in the idealizing terms standard for the literary figure whose very comeliness had come to represent the political and social promise of the black nation. Focusing on the alterations made to these bodies and the alterations to the *Clotel* narratives, I will argue that Brown's unwillingness to provide Jerome and Clotelle with either a protective domestic narrative or a protective corporeal language in the Civil War section of the 1867 revision reflects the writer's disillusionment in the years following the conflict, a disillusionment that led him to create a depiction of the "Rebellion" that rejects the laws that govern sentimentality for the laws that govern the frankly unsentimental project of war.

It almost seems unnecessary to explain the degree of optimism that the war gave black Americans, and therefore the corresponding degree of disappointment African Americans experienced when their hopes for prosperous lives as freed people were dashed repeatedly. Long before the abolition of slavery was declared an official war aim, and well before the Emancipation Proclamation, most blacks understood that any war between the northern and southern states would turn on the issue of slavery. Brown, a tireless antislavery activist, had ample reason to believe that everything he had worked for his entire adult life would come to fruition. In 1865, the Congress both ratified the Thirteenth Amendment abolishing slavery and enacted legislation establishing the Freedmen's Bureau. However, the opportunities the bureau provided were all too often negated by the "Black Laws" that many states had rushed to enact in the wake of the Emancipation Proclamation, hoping to keep contraband from securing employment. Most of these laws appeared after the war, when free blacks were seen as even more of a threat to white labor. Called "Black Codes" in the South, they imposed restrictions in nearly all aspects of African American life, giving whites the opportunity reign over blacks with impunity. Blacks in South Carolina, for instance, one of the states most devastated by the war, could not marry if "paupers"; orphaned black children were forced into indentured apprenticeships.[8]

Brown transcribes some of these laws in his Civil War history, commenting acerbically on what he views as their absolute hypocrisy: "And yet Connecticut, with her proscription of the negro, and receiving their aid in fighting her battles, retains her negro 'black laws' upon her statutebook by a vote of more than six thousand" (143). The war within a war that Martin Delany, Frederick Douglass, and other black activists had waged to force the Union to accept black soldiers had already given blacks an inkling of the obstacles they would face as freed-people. Indeed, Brown, who had been vocal in this movement and who later recruited blacks to join Union forces after Lincoln agreed to raise African American troops in 1862, abandoned his recruiting efforts in 1864, angered by the Union's refusal to grant black soldiers adequate wages.

I return, then, to the dilemma *The Negro in the American Rebellion* presented to Brown in 1867 as he sought to write a "nonfiction" history that balanced the real and the ideal, and as he strived to present a black male body capable of transforming physical and psychic humiliation into a transcendent state of heroism. He tries to solve this problem by reimagining the conflict as a race war taking place almost exclusively between black men and their oppressors, attempting to construct a black male body in which two modes of violence are reconciled: a body that is both injured and injuring.

Calling the war the "Slaveholders' Rebellion" in his preface, he begins his chronology with Crispus Attucks, the fugitive slave who was the first to fall in the Boston Massacre. Writing of Attucks's escape in one sentence and the massacre in the next, Brown presents Attucks's flight from slavery and involvement in the war as one fluid movement, from fugitive to American revolutionary, collapsing the distinction between slave and patriot. He devotes the next three chapters to Nat Turner, Denmark Vesey, and Madison Washington, all leaders or planners of slave revolts. He follows these installations with "The Growth of Slave Power," a chapter characterizing the expanding proportions of slavery as an overfed "monster" (40). The next describes John Brown's raid on Harpers Ferry, emphasizing the role played by John Copeland and Shields Green, the only two blacks captured alive. Quoting an article from the *Baltimore Sun* that marvels at Copeland's "unwavering fortitude" in the moments before his execution, Brown adds that Shields "behaved with equal heroism" (49). He concludes: "Shields Green . . .

died as he had lived, a brave man, and expressing to the last his eternal hatred to human bondage, prophesying that slavery would soon come to a bloody end" (49).

In Brown's book, the Civil War begins thereafter, with black men heeding (albeit unsuccessfully) Lincoln's call for seventy-five thousand Union volunteers. By positioning black soldiers within a continuum of American slave revolutionaries, Brown transforms the Civil War into the greatest in a series of slave revolts, placing the black male in direct, armed confrontation with his master/monster: "an opportunity of settling with the 'ole boss' for a long score of cruelty" (157). Far from being something as removed from African American life as a conflict over "state's rights," the war instead becomes slavery's bloody finale, the inevitable conclusion to an inhumane institution prophesied by a black man with his dying breath. Indeed, in his 1854 meditation on the slave revolution in Santo Domingo and its leader Toussaint L'Ouverture, Brown predicted that if slaves rose up, "the God of Justice would be on their side," envisioning uprising as the completion of the "revolution that was commenced in 1776" and defining revolt as a morally righteous materialization of Republican ideology and divine retribution.[9] In the 1853 Clotel, Brown had already fused the philosophies of black slave "revolt" and white American "revolution." Protagonist George Green (who will become Jerome in the 1867 version), on trial for insurgency, makes this provocative speech: "Did not American revolutionists violate the laws when they struck for liberty? They were revolters, but their success made them patriots—we were revolters, and our failure makes us rebels" (226).

Thus, while the history of slave revolts left a slew of "failed" bodies—wounded, wrecked, or even obliterated by violence—it was nevertheless a heroic violence of their own making, in which they chose to use force to assert selves that centuries of enslavement had attempted to decreate. These bodies, then, represented willing and necessary forfeitures in the making of a manly race, and as Brown sees it, in the making of a black American.

But the powerful association Brown makes between the war and slave revolution has the effect of obscuring a simple fact: the Civil War was not a slave revolt, and at Port Hudson, these men did not have the choice of volunteering for the charges—a crucial fact that Brown alters within his novel when he writes that the black soldiers were *asked*, not commanded, to put themselves in harm's way. The fictionalized account in Clotelle therefore becomes puzzling. Within the space of the imaginary, Brown could have chosen to portray many events in the war less bloody and less tragic. He could have chosen events that showed an emerging fraternity among white officers and their black subordinates. In other words, he could have taken this as an opportunity to create an uncompromised heroic black manhood—the decision Douglass made when he chose to write *The Heroic Slave*—a depiction of a black man who waged a successful revolt, rather than a fictionalized version of, say, Nat Turner, whose body ended up dangling from a noose. Instead, Brown is distressed enough by the white male's willingness to wound black male subjectivity (on many terrains) that he finds it necessary to reviolate the black male body himself: "His head entirely torn off by a shell," Jerome is simply and unceremoniously snuffed out (106). "Imagery of slaying," as Kenneth Burke observes in an analysis of Milton, is an act of transformation; "the killing of something is the changing of it."[10] Brown willfully presents a grotesque in the place where once stood a whole black man.

Certainly, then, this seems an odd fate for a character the writer had carefully chiseled across the span of four versions of his novel. Indeed, Brown did not initially imagine his hero as a man physically black enough to be Andre Cailloux's double. Named George in the first *Clotel*, he more resembles the white aristocrats in the first text, Henry Morton and Antoine Devenant—who marry mulatta characters—than he resembles most of the other prominent black males in the narrative. In part, George's whiteness serves one of the same fundamental purposes as the mulatta's: it renders him a reasonable facsimile of the chivalric heroes of white sentimental literature generally, and, within *Clotel* specifically, it allows him to supplant the white male figures who form ultimately unsuccessful relationships with Brown's mulatta heroines. Influenced perhaps by the symbolic blackness of what Delany called his "New negro" black male hero in his *Blake; or, The Huts of America*, Brown concluded that George was too white to signify black manhood, physically and ideologically. More than a bulked-up, colorized version of George, Jerome consolidates the two distinct manifestations of black heroic masculinity in the novel: the ultralight black romantic hero who marries the mulatta heroine and is allowed access to the domestic sentimentalized narrative, and the ultrablack slave-revolutionary, whose acts place him within a differing narrative, one that distinctly disallows for domestic stability.

In fact, in *Clotel*, it appears that physical proximity to the darker African ancestors to a large measure determines revolutionary potential; thus, as a light-skinned rebellious hero, George is an odd man out, standing apart from the other black men in the texts who also engage in overt acts of resistance against the system of slavery, particularly the figures of Nat Turner and Picquilo (whose messianic blackness is coded in opposition to the minstrel blackness of the comic folk in Brown's work). Showing no hint of "African blood," George possesses hair "straight, soft, fine and light"; but William, the slave who ushers Clotel to freedom and flees to Canada, is "tall, full bodied" (224, 171). George had a "prominent" nose and "thin" lips; Turner is "full-blooded" (224, 213).

Brown reserves his most detailed description of a black man for the catlike, stealthy Picquilo—a "large, tall, full-blooded Negro with a stern and savage countenance . . . his step oblique, his look sanguinary" (213, 214). For Brown, the tribal marks on this African's skin were signs of inner power made visible, as if they were carved from the "bold spirit" of his interior (214). It is no wonder, then, that after George takes part in a slave insurrection at the end of the original *Clotel*, he arrives in the next version physically inscribed by revolution: "This slave, whose name was Jerome, was of pure African origin, perfectly black."[11] Brown enacts another change; the defiance that lands George in jail is downgraded from insurgency to insolence[12]—from participation in a slave revolt to a refusal to be whipped by his master. While these modifications might seem minor when compared to his wholesale purging of the extratextual documents woven into the first narrative, they nonetheless represent a profound change in the way in which Brown wished to present his primary representative of heroic black masculinity. An act of will replaces insurgency but elicits the same consequences; revolution, Brown appears to say, can take place on a small scale.

The writer is nevertheless playing it safe. In replacing insurgency with insolence, Jerome does not commit a revolutionary act so implicitly violent that it would risk placing him permanently outside of civil law and evolutionary discourse, and therefore outside the permissible boundaries of domestic sentimentality. A fugitive slave who has run from his master's cruelty can be reintegrated into civil society; a fugitive slave who has murdered whites would be a fugitive for life, even if no longer a slave. Moreover, while Brown and other abolitionists celebrated the Santo Domingo uprising, whites terrified by the prospect of rebellion in North America pointed to the bloodshed as a sign of black savagery. Ever cognizant of the way the dominant culture perceived African Americans, Brown might very well have been reluctant to corroborate theories of the beast lurking within the black. These two significant alterations to the narrative, merging the two manifestations of masculinity—the sentimental hero and the black revolutionary—and reducing the gravity of Jerome's rebellion, allow the black heroic figure to fulfill two narrative functions. Jerome can participate in the creation of the idealized social imaginary that republican domesticity signifies in the sentimental text and still be fiercely black, with the implicit threat that a messianic blackness carries.

The transformation of Jerome is just one of many changes the writer made in revising *Clotel*. It is indeed ironic that Brown, a man of so many "firsts," appeared to delight in seconds and thirds, repeating characters, plots, and passages verbatim from one novel to another. And not only did the writer borrow from his own historical publications for the 1867 *Clotelle*; as a basis for a subplot for the

1853 version, he used a panel from the guide to the panorama he had staged while a fugitive in Britain, *A Description of William Wells Brown's Original Panoramic Views of the Scenes in the Life of An American Slave, from his Birth in Slavery to His Death or His Escape to His First Home of Freedom on British Soil* (1850).[13]

That Brown mined his own historical material for his novels is interesting but certainly not improper. Historical fiction is inherently a return to prior representation. Rather, more important to understanding Brown's writing is the nature and frequency of his returns. We must ask what that echoing might signify within the body of the writer's work, a body filled with echoes. And although it remains true Brown often repeats without revision, I will assume the theoretical position that Brown's instances of repetition can be thought of as similar but never as the same. For example, in *Clotel*, Brown includes part of Andrew Jackson's 1814 address recommending commendations for blacks who participated in the War of 1812. He embeds the document within a discussion between Mrs. Carlton and her husband, who are debating plans to manumit their slaves from their plantation. During the course of this discussion, Mrs. Carlton remarks upon the ineffectiveness of Jackson's declaration. "And what did these noble men receive in return for their courage, their heroism?" she asks. "Chains and slavery" (164). Recontextualized and reprinted in 1867 as part of *The Negro in the American Rebellion*, the address becomes something else altogether: evidence Brown offers to make the case that white Americans have always understood and valued the contributions blacks have made to the military.[14] What is revealed here is, of course, the inherently unstable condition of any text; re-placed, the text itself accrues altered meanings. In light of the now-familiar poststructuralist argument that history is only text, a discursive recreation of "the thing itself," Brown's act—taking a document produced from a historically messy moment and attempting to impose a tidy evolutionary reading on it, beating back prior interpretations with his newer one—shows us how Brown might have approached the writing of America's slave past, not only in *The Negro* but in his imaginative works as well (especially since Brown insisted on blurring any distinctions between the two).

I am suggesting that Brown recognized the instability of both text and interpretation—that Jackson's letter, and thus the fruits of black military labor, could be read differently in 1853 than in 1867. It follows then, that in the case of the *Clotel* novels, the writer's compulsion to repeat and revise is, in part, an attempt to retroactively ascribe meaning to previous incarnations of the work. Throughout the versions written before 1867, he faithfully adheres to the most significant aspects of the plot of the first *Clotel*, adding more elements, such as the reunion of Clotelle with her slaveholding father, that show Brown anticipating positive historical developments, and in my speculation, anticipating the possibility that he at last might be able to ground Jerome and Clotelle in a stable, integrated home on domestic soil. Each subsequent novel appears as an evolution made along a linear narrative of progress that was moving, if slowly, toward liberation. From the position he wrote these earlier versions, as an antislavery polemicist, Brown's mission as fiction writer had been indisputably clear: to use the medium as an abolitionist tool. In the tumultuous, contradictory state the nation found itself during the years immediately following the war, his mission became less certain, and his outlook grew increasingly bleak. The final *Clotelle* registers these changes, and powerfully so: as the rending of Jerome's head from his torso suggests, the four chapters completing the 1867 publication represent a break from the other narratives that is so drastic that it can only be described as complete.

If the killing of Jerome is one marker of the writer's shifting perspective, so, then, are the alterations he makes to his heroine. After the hero's death, the black protagonist who remains in the narrative is the widowed Clotelle, dubbed "the Angel of Mercy" for her ministrations to the suffering. But Brown will not have her take center stage in the narrative. Grief-stricken, Clotelle "withdrew from the gaze of mankind" (106). More than a self-imposed act of mourning within the story, her withdrawal serves as Brown's cloaking of the mulatta body. Brown takes the "impassioned and voluptuous" form he described in detail on the first page of the novel, the woman who stood upon an auction block with a crowd "gazing and feasting" upon her, the creature locked in a cell as onlookers "gazed at her," and hides her from the audience/spectator (5, 43, 74). Instead, he has her "pass" for white, as a "rebel lady" in Georgia, then again in Alabama (107, 112). With Clotelle hidden, the gaze is reversed as she becomes a spectator to the kind of "repulsive" scene the reader witnessed in the episode with Jerome. In the Georgia hospitals, she sees "emaciated Union prisoners, worn down to skin and bone with disease and starvation, with their sunken eyes and wild looks . . . hideous in the extreme" (107); in Alabama, she is taken in by a black woman whose husband lopped his hand off rather than serve in the Confederate army. As is true with Brown's other disjointed, episodic, and strange incarnations of this narrative, it is difficult to determine just what Brown is up to. One possible interpretation is that removing from the reader's view the highly charged mulatta body, a body already overly determined by the multiple sexual and racial ideologies ascribed to it, allows him to redirect that gaze to the disfigured bodies (and nation) produced by war.

While that very well might stand as one interpretive possibility, Brown himself complicates it in *The Negro in the American Rebellion*. It would seem that his historical account of the Civil War, though a patchwork of newspaper articles, first-hand narratives, rumor, and information from other historians, would be no place to insert the tale of (yet another) beautiful mulatta who is part of (yet another) idealized "domestic" union. That, however, is exactly what "The Colored Historian" does. In Chapter 31, Brown addresses the massacre at Fort Pillow, which, because of its scope and calculated execution, came to symbolize Confederate atrocities in the war. On April 12, 1864, a group of soldiers led by Nathan Bedford Forrest (who would later found the Klan) entered the Tennessee fort with the intention of slaughter. Although the fort had been captured already, blacks did not have the option to surrender and were summarily shot; some were "burned alive."[15] Although whites were also killed, at least one hundred African Americans, among them women and children, were murdered. A black New Yorker wrote the secretary of war, suggesting that black soldiers be allowed to kill an equal number of Confederate prisoners of war.[16] The Union government made the requisite noise about punishing the Confederates but did nothing. Brown, after including the lengthy and detailed report of the Committee on the Conduct of War on the Fort Pillow Massacre, tags on a story, which I will reproduce in a slightly abbreviated version:

> When the murderers returned, the day after the capture, to renew their fiendish work upon the wounded and dying, they found a young and beautiful mulatto woman searching among the dead for the body of her husband. She was the daughter of a wealthy and influential rebel residing at Columbus. With her husband, this woman was living near the fort when our forces occupied it, and joined the Union men to assist in holding the place. Going from body to body with all the earnestness with which love could inspire an affectionate heart, she at last found the object of her search. He was not dead; but both legs were broken. The wife had succeeded in getting him out from among the piles of dead, and was bathing his face. . . . At the moment she was seen by this murderous band; and the cry was at once raised, "Kill the wench. . . !" The next moment the sharp crack of a musket was heard, and the angel of mercy fell a corpse on the body of her husband, who was soon after knocked in the head by the butt-end of the same weapon. (247)

As contrived as Brown's version appears, whether the story of the mulatta is true or not becomes secondary to a greater consideration: why the writer would insist upon inserting this overdetermined body into what many historians agree remains the most tragic single incident of the war, particularly since he announces in the preface that faced with the overwhelming amount of information about the Civil War, he "did not feel bound to introduce an account of every little skirmish in which colored men were engaged" (vi). The mulatta, however, makes it through the rigor of Brown's selection process and winds up as the finishing touch to a factual chronicle of carnage. Brown's decision transforms a field of blood into a page straight from a sentimental novel: his own. Like the heroines in the *Clotel* novels, this young woman is a product of a white man in high places (though less than a president or a senator). And as in the 1867 novel, he labels this unnamed heroine "the angel of mercy." Given these similarities, it seems appropriate to read this anecdote in relationship to those narratives.

In the era Brown was writing his works about the Civil War, the white female body, Columbia, was the corporeal symbol of the Republic.[17] Not so for Brown, who, as I have mentioned, sees the nation embodied in the mulatta, "the representation of two races,"[18] standing for a Republic ancestrally linked—a symbolism that will become even more important in Civil War fiction as Harper makes use of this figure in *Iola Leroy*. The dual ancestry of the mulatta does not mean he presents her as unified ideal; as a figure both black and white in a country divided by race, this biracial female will not live an unembattled condition until both of her identities can coexist within the boundaries of her nation/body. Thus, despite the manner in which the varied endings of the novels taken together produce an evolutionary narrative—each revision a cautious step toward freedom—each of the *Clotel* novels also repeatedly defers closure, ending tentatively, with the heroine's ultimate fate undetermined.

At the end of the first *Clotel*, written three years after the Fugitive Slave Law was passed, Mary is trapped in Europe with George, unable to come home lest she fall prey to slave catchers. In 1861, when a version of *Clotel* was serialized in the *Weekly Anglo African* under the name *Miralda; or, The Beautiful Quadroon: A Romance of American Slavery, Founded on Fact*, it had become evident that the nation would divide over the issue of slavery. Brown closes his novel with a statement voicing his optimism that "in the world to come," equality would reign.[19] The nation was still warring when *Clotelle: A Tale of the Southern States* was published in 1864; consequently, Brown leaves his heroine safely in Europe, reconciled with her father, who is making plans to free his slaves and to "end his days in the society of his beloved daughter."[20] Still recovering from the war in 1867, the new nation is under construction, and we find Clotelle correspondingly performing the work of reconstruction as a schoolteacher in New Orleans.

As idyllic as this scenario might appear, the route that has taken Clotelle back home belies any genuine sense of narrative stability or closure. After Clotelle is accused of helping a female Union sympathizer in Alabama, she defiantly announces her allegiance to the North. Clotelle learns from a slave woman that she will be jailed for her offense; the heroine, still passing as white, is whisked away in the dead of night by a black servant and taken to a cabin, the home of Jim and

Dinah, an embattled black couple, where she hides for a week.[21] Brown draws a rather unflattering picture of the U/union that has replaced Clotel and Jerome's in the narrative. Describing the hero and heroine's state of matrimonial bliss, he writes that "few unions had been more productive of harmonious feelings" (106). In contrast, the uneducated, unrefined Jim and Dinah bicker incessantly; their fights ending when Jim, who has purchased his wife as a slave, threatens to sell her back into enslavement. It is in this "place of concealment," a psychically violent space where the folk are unmercifully taunted by slavery—and not, as in the other narratives, on a boat sailing safely away from her former position as chattel (114)—that Clotel reemerges as black. Reinhabiting her black subjectivity thusly, in the slave cabin, she later purchases the land where she herself once lived in bondage, "where at this writing,—now June, 1867,—resides the 'Angel of Mercy' " (114). Far from being the end of anything, or even being a moment that points toward a definitive conclusion, the novel's ending leaves Clotelle still suspended, still in the present tense, and still on the geographic terrain of slavery.

The differences between the close of this final *Clotelle* and the closure of the story Brown attaches to the Fort Pillow massacre report further reveal his struggle with interpreting the war in terms of its ability to secure a future for black Americans. In the Fort Pillow narrative, Brown feels compelled to turn his reader's attention to his mulatta's physicality by calling her expressly "a young beautiful mulatto," the very corporeality he subsequently attempts to conceal in the Civil War chapters of *Clotelle*. In addition, while Clotelle, the other "angel of mercy," who, in her capacity as nurse, is positioned as a *spectator* to the "hideous" bodies of Union men, the Fort Pillow "angel" plows through piles of mangled dead and dying bodies, and dies herself intermingled with them. I will later suggest that it is exactly this—the gruesome situation this woman (and Brown) encounters—that necessitates her specific embodiment as a "young beautiful mulatto," a corporeal code that signifies a spiritual and physical fecundity that stands in frank opposition to death.

Five years before *Clotelle* and *The Negro in the American Rebellion* were published, Brown remained sanguine about the changes the Civil War might bring about in African American civil life. In 1862, in a speech given before the New York Branch of the Anti-Slavery Society, Brown assures his audience that the freed slaves will prosper—on their own—if permitted "the opportunity to exercise their own physical and mental abilities."[22] Using himself as an example, Brown boasts that he "did not ask society to take me up. . . . All I asked of the white people was, to get out of the way."[23] As Ronald Takaki notes, on the first anniversary of the Emancipation Proclamation, a still forward-looking Brown characterized the war as an opportunity for racial union: "This rebellion will extinguish slavery in our land,

and the Negro is henceforth and forever to be a part of the nation. His blood is to mingle with that of his former oppressor, and the two races blended in one will make a more peaceful, hardy, powerful and intellectual race than America has ever seen before."[24] Brown's psyche, shaped by his own mulatto body and its tortured origins,[25] insists upon a corporeal understanding of nation, so much so that even the unsettling image of black blood spilling into a common stream with that of his oppressors proved comforting to the writer. The excess of the mulatta's "impassioned and voluptuous" form stands as a less painful version of this liberational paradigm. As a material manifestation of Brown's unwavering faith that "God hath made one blood of all nations for men to dwell on the face of the earth," the bountiful, ripe figure who in Brown's mind has always been able to bring forth a "hardy," "blended" race without the violence of war symbolizes a nation ready to deliver peacefully the promise of both God and the Republic. Therefore, giving the "angel of mercy" the (re)productive corporeality he later disposes of in the 1867 Clotelle enables Brown to present that body as a reminder of that promise. Showing the mulatta dead atop a heap of wounded black masculinity offers Brown an opportunity to depict the purposeful and violent slaughter of the promise her body represents. In the same way, showing a black wife dead atop her prostrate husband offers Brown's readers insight into what will become of his matrimonial ideal.

Indeed, at the point that Brown returns to the mulatta body in Clotelle, the tears in his veil of optimism had become visible. It is not the body he had circulated within the first and second versions of Clotel, or even in the chapters leading up to the Civil War in the third. Throughout Brown's fiction, the mulatta's beauty is both an attribute and a detriment; if it causes her to be objectified and coveted by white men, it also rescues her from the auction block and wins her the lifelong devotion of the narrative's black hero. Her beauty is also transcendent. Even when Mrs. Miller, her jealous mistress, chops off the mulatta's hair to diminish her allure, she still radiates; disguised as a male to escape slavery, her fine "Spanish" looks attract a group of female admirers. Most certainly, her ability to mesmerize was Brown's manner of making her inferior to no white woman; but, as a representative of nation, her comely face parallels the promises of her corporeal excess.

However, in the 1867 Clotelle, her beauty is not simply hidden temporarily as she masquerades as a white woman, it is permanently extinguished. Brown, who hardly lets a passage about Clotelle pass without remarking on some aspect of her attractiveness, fails to make a single mention of it in the Civil War section of the 1867 narrative. The only comment made about Clotelle's physical appearance is the remark Dinah makes as Clotelle emerges from the storm, likening her to a "drownd [sic] rat" (112). Brown does not expressly say that this old woman is the same grinning Dinah who conspires with Mrs. Miller in the violent haircutting scene—" "Gins look like a nigger, now" (40)—but he does bring attention to her name as he introduces her in the novel's concluding chapter: "Dinah," he writes, "for such was her name" (113). I believe that Brown is asking the reader to make the link in order to highlight the difference in his heroine's "before" and "after" appearance: before and after the Civil War had altered Brown's authorial disposition. In the span of four short chapters, Jerome, the "very fine looking" defiant hero of the antebellum portion of the novel, is transformed into a decapitated torso; Clotelle, the " 'beautiful quadroon,' " into a rodent.

In eradicating mentions of her beauty and cloaking her form, Brown dislocates the mulatta from her body; in killing Clotelle's second husband and leaving both her son and her long-lost father abandoned in Europe, he wipes out her family. The noncommittal yet definitely sentimentalized endings of the other *Clotel* works give way to an ending that undercuts domestic sentimentality by refusing the heroine the safety of heterosexual union and family. Attached to no man romantically and bereft of blood kin, her primary ties to the domestic narrative have been severed. Brown provides his heroine with an alternative to her previous life of domesticity: a life dedicated to work. The romanticized antidote Brown provides in the part of the novel written before the war stands in stark contrast to the more sober, practical remedy offered in the section written thereafter. This change is explained by the fact that Brown actually has written two very different novels posing as one. The first belongs to the school of sentimental abolitionism, relying on the moral, social, and civil pedagogical instructions of domesticity to convey its message; the second is a war narrative, questioning a pedagogy that posits overly simplified answers to problems that only grew increasingly complex in postbellum America. It is as though Brown realized that neither fictive depictions of black heroism on the battlefield nor idealized representations of black matrimony would bring about the drastic changes necessary for black equality to be realized in real, not imagined, worlds.

For that reason, I will argue that his four short chapters on the Civil War stand as an important contribution to African American war literature—and an aberration within that tradition—precisely because of what the writer has refused to do. Within war writing in general, the wound serves as an essential metaphor, linking physical trauma to the body to the psychological trauma suffered by all whom war has affected, directly and indirectly. The nature of the wound (its location, its severity, its effects on the body's many functions) can be interpreted as an index of the nature of psychic trauma inflicted to other bodies elsewhere, inside and outside of the text: those bodies that are represented by the particular fleshly incarnation the writer chooses to depict as assaulted. In this understanding, Jerome's wound, and therefore, the wound to the black body politic, becomes even more severe, for the damage done to his body is not simply terrible but irreversible.

Moreover, before the destructive capabilities of the modern weapons used in the Civil War had made such an injury far too common, having a head blown from a body was a relatively unfamiliar form of wounding. This unfamiliarity adds to its symbolic potency: Jerome's decapitation renders antiblack violence appropriately shocking and strange precisely because it is offered to the reader in less recognizable form than, say, the lynching of the unnamed black man he details in the 1853 novel. Adding to the strangeness of the decapitation is its very legal appropriateness, which distinguishes it from the lynching: it is a "civil" war wound, inflicted within the bounds of "civil" law, sanctioned and authorized by a representative of the state. Though Brown sees the general's order as an undeniably deadly racist calculus in which sixteen live black bodies were "sacrificed" for a single dead white one—described by Brown as an inhumane choice—the act hides within the bounds of civil law, becoming, in the rules of war, something other altogether.

Although Brown invests his characters with little interior motivation, we can assume that Jerome's decision to fight for the Union parallels that of the thousands of black men who did the same. As I have noted, throughout the history of warfare on the American continent, African Americans had offered their lives to gain recognition: to be recognized as human beings who in turn deserved to be recognized as citizens. This method of "recognition" is, of course, ironic: not simply because of its seeming futility, but because of what the body may become when met with violent death—unrecognizable in relation to what it was before. Scarry observes that a civilization embeds itself in the body; a handshake, a gait, a wave are signs of that civilization carried within an individual human form. As such, she claims, the inherent contradiction in the concept of "dying for one's country" lies within the radical deconstruction of the body slain on a battlefield. When the "chest is shattered," the nation is emptied from the body; "the civilization as it resides" in the body is unmade.[26] Any notion of the Republic inside of Jerome's form exited through his headless neck.

Even if we reject Scarry's theory, the idea that African American war literature might repeat Brown's narrative, resulting in works full of black bodies dying for their country, is nevertheless disconcerting. Fundamentally, the desire to be recognized as a citizen is an expression of a desire for self-representation—to be considered a "speaking subject" rather than an object "spoken for." Drawing energy from Benedict Anderson's reading of the rise of French nationalism,

Sharon Holland makes a simple but significant observation: "The ability of the emerging nation to speak hinges on its correct use of the 'dead' in the service of its creation."[27] A dead body very quickly surrenders its agency (hence, for example, the note attached to a suicidal body in an effort to ensure the "meaning" of its death). Anderson's analysis itself examines how one of the more influential French historians of the eighteenth century, Jules Michelet, reads the bodies of those who died in the violence of the French Revolution (also decapitated, it should be noted). Speaking *for* them, as Anderson notes, on their behalf, Michelet pronounces them sacrifices in making the French nation "*even when these sacrifices were not understood as such by the victims*" (Anderson's emphasis).[28] In a similar manner, Brown attempts to speak for Jerome's dead form, but not as a mouthpiece for the state. When Brown labels him both a "hero" and a "sacrifice" to the general's inhumanity, he supplements and disrupts the postwar official language that tended to speak of dead black Union bodies as only "heroic" (in the same leveling way nations honor *all* of their soldiers as "heroic"), a language that failed to acknowledge the specificity of what it meant for a black body to fight and die in the war: a language that did not, in effect, endeavor to ascertain what a black body might say from the grave.

While Brown's decision to allow Jerome to be injured and killed raises many intriguing questions—possibly more interesting than those raised if this character had lived—after Brown, graphic, specific depictions of the wounded black male body and representations of the grotesque virtually disappear until the literature of the Second World War. In part, the reluctance to depict violence to the black male body in the black American war novel, a public text, can be explained as response to a historical legacy in which the routinized torture and mutilation of the black body was made public in events that allowed whites the opportunity to witness the transformational power of violence, the black body diminishing before their very eyes, forced into an object status. The rituals accompanying lynching, as many historians have documented, included displaying body parts collected as trophies; photographs of lynchings were routinely mailed and traded as postcards (a practice finding its contemporary parallel in the disturbing images of Arab and Muslim prisoners in Abu Ghraib). Too, as we know, antislavery activists depended on exhibiting and photographing the scarred and deformed black body as material evidence of the barbarity of slavery; antislavery literature offered its literary equivalent. Even if the use of the wounded body in antislavery efforts asked onlookers and readers to gaze not too long upon the body itself but instead to turn that gaze upon the spectral image refracted by the body—in other words, the slaveholder—the wounded black form was intended to linger in audiences' minds, that ocular lingering necessary for arousing a desire for change. The risk of specularity is apparent: the body risks being imagined in a permanent state of damage or injury. The absence of the wound in the literature following Brown's effort can be interpreted therefore as an attempt to shield the violated black male body from the gaze of the spectator-audience.

In terms of the specific concerns of African American war writers, the dearth of references to black corporeal damage can be interpreted as a literary version of bodily rehabilitation, mimicking the purposes of the rehabilitative technologies used to reconstruct bodies disabled and altered by the violence of war. Although the purposes of those technologies might seem self-evident—to help the injured body regain its corporeal functions—disability scholarship has shown us that the goals of ontological restoration are all too frequently bound to ideological objectives that have little to do with any needs the disabled individual may have (including the very real possibility that he or she might not deem bodily intervention as necessary). Indeed, in *A History of Disability* French cultural critic Henri-Jacques Stiker concludes that Western societies' rush to "fix" bodies labeled "disabled" stems from a growing unwillingness to acknowledge circumstances—poverty, for example, or unsafe industries—that continue to create socially produced (i.e., nonaccidental, noncongenital) forms of disability.[29]

Locating the emergence of this "new" rehabilitative imperative within post–World War I France, Stiker claims that the unprecedented numbers of soldiers returning with permanent injuries prompted a shift in attitude regarding the proper treatment of disabled veterans. Any genuine sense of moral and ethical responsibility toward the injured individual—whose wounds were viewed as lingering memorials to the epic disaster of the war—was complicated by a competing desire to limit the impact of the conflict on French society and to reduce, even deny, human culpability in its making. According to Stiker, what would prove an ultimately dangerous consensus began to take shape: the decision to view the injuries soldiers suffered as inevitable, "natural" occurrences rather than the results of an avoidable social calamity. Naturalizing disability in this manner required, he writes, behaving as one would in the face of an earthly catastrophe, such as a flood, an event for which no one can be held responsible and from which complete recovery can be imagined: "We can and must repair . . . in other words, efface, expiate."[30] Thus, very much like a bridge torn apart during an earthquake, the injured body was transformed into an "object of repair," something that could be returned to a "prior, normal" state.[31] To be most effective, this return also needed to be wholesale. Consequently, in 1916, the National Office of the War Maimed enacted a policy authorizing "the general use of prostheses" for all veterans who could presumably benefit from them.[32] The compulsion to physically "repair" the disabled body, to reverse corporeal "damage," was henceforth intertwined with the impulse to "redeem" society. Modern technology became indispensable to this project; the advanced prosthetic, unlike its cruder and more apparent predecessors, "the crutch and wooden leg," could eradicate the physical signifiers of disaster, facilitating the forgetting of a war that France wanted to purge from its collective memory.[33]

But it is the intermediate step that Stiker describes, the step between fixing and forgetting, that renders his analysis critical to understanding how rehabilitation operates in African American texts. Successful rehabilitation was believed to facilitate the "formerly" disabled body's reintegration into the nation's significant social structures, such as work and the family. Made "ordinary" again, "identical" to "normal" citizens, the disabled would "disappear" within these institutions.[34] The intentions of those African American war writers who resist representing injury might be characterized quite similarly. A slippery slope of conflations—blackness and "disability," disability and "deficiency" (both physical and psychic), injury and disability—made the presentation of an always-already able-bodied masculinity unmarred by slavery, antiblack violence, and warfare crucial to "rehabilitating" the perception of black men as an argument for national and structural (re)integration. In other words, these writers wished that African men be considered "normal" rather than "aberrant" or damaged, *identical* to the racially, physically, and mentally "able" spectator. In that way, the black body could elude what Foucault has called the "medical gaze."[35] More than looking at the "other," the medical gaze is at once visual *and* discursive, a knowing look whose conclusions have already been determined in the languages of science. Seeing "specimen" rather than "spectacle," it allows the viewer, with a simple "glance," to assess corporeal signs as symptoms, to bore into the body's interior and then diagnose, finding the presence of "pathologies" without need of further investigation. Although Foucault argues this way of seeing was born in "the clinic," he also suggests it has influenced visual apprehension well beyond that institution and its origins: the nineteenth-century freak show, for instance, is merely the hospital's commercial cousin. It seems apparent that African American war writers understood the dangers in displaying "damage." If hidden, obscured by an image of sameness, the rationale for categorization and exclusion no longer exists, and integration becomes a possibility.

In comparing the issue of injury in African American war literature to antislavery literature (or antilynching literature, for that matter), the very source of the infliction further complicates the meaning of the wound for these writers, as Brown's work aptly demonstrates. If violence to the enslaved or lynched body can readily be read as "unjust" and "nonconsensual," the injury stemming from battle resists similar cultural interpretation, particularly as many of the wounded men who *are* depicted in African American war literature volunteer to place themselves in a position where their bodies might be readily deformed or destroyed. The involuntary wound, in other words, was readily mobilized in a "useful" capacity. The symbolic potential of the voluntarily, "consensually" disfigured or disabled black body produced by war has less accusative power in a tradition of war literature that is very much accusatory, operating in the same vein as antislavery literature: as evidence of the dominant culture's unwillingness to extend African Americans civil and human rights. Thus the brilliance of Brown's decapitation of Jerome—his "civil" war wounding—lies in the writer's successful elision of the differences between nonconsensual and consensual injury, between slavery and war, allowing the wound to exist somewhere between the voluntary sacrifice of battle and the involuntary injury inflicted by the oppressor.

The second element Brown rejects in his war narrative—protective domesticity —will return when Harper, who borrows as freely from Brown as Brown does from himself, reconstructs the ending from Brown's 1867 *Clotelle* for her 1892 novel *Iola Leroy*. While Brown's Iola, like Clotelle, chooses a public life of work, Harper will rebuild for her the domestic structure Brown has dismantled, constructing correct black marriages as political unions stronger than the reunited nation itself. The idea of black matrimony as the basis of civilization and a politically committed union as "the consummation" of the couple's "desire" to be racially rather than sexually engaged will dominate the African American literature of that period.[36] Harper will follow those literary edicts, even as she strives to write about war.

2. FIGHTING FIRE WITH FIRE

Frances Harper,
Paul Laurence Dunbar,
and the Post–Civil War
Reconciliation Narrative

When William Wells Brown allowed his black hero to die in a frankly unsentimental fashion in the 1867 *Clotelle*, he placed himself in the company of a distinctly small group of writers who introduced elements of realpolitik into fictional interpretations of the Civil War. Most of these writers, such as Ambrose Bierce and Stephen Crane, would not appear until late into the nineteenth century when "realism" had begun to shape the American literary consciousness. Although critics still debate what, exactly, the increasingly capacious term denotes, theories making the war central to the rise in the number of writers experimenting with mimetic strategies speculate that the effects of the war itself contributed to the beginnings of a more representational, "honest" mode of fiction. The secession had effectively shattered fantasies of nationhood; the war's scale, length, and destruction had tainted the illusory glory of warfare. Accordingly, fictional literature began to register a general and growing distrust of the rhapsodizing sentimental languages the nation had used to lull its members into thinking it was a family devoted to—and dying for—a common cause. A related argument claims that the decades-long period of avoiding "authentic" depictions of the Civil War, fought, John Limon claims, within a historical literary milieu incompatible with it, necessitated a belated documentary response to other damaging aspects of American modernity, such as the human fallout of industrial capitalism.[1] What remains clear, however, is that most of the hundreds of Civil War novels of the nineteenth and early twentieth century were decidedly unconcerned with realistic presentations of modern war. Writing for popular audiences who had not yet lost their taste for sensation and sentimentality, most of these writers simply grafted the chivalric, romanticized exaltations of preindustrial warfare onto a U.S. landscape that improved technologies of killing and the politics of internecine war had nevertheless permanently altered.

Two of the most substantial African American novels of the Civil War published after Brown's, Frances Harper's Iola Leroy (1892)[2] and Paul Laurence Dunbar's The Fanatics (1901),[3] were written well after the advent of American literary realism. Dunbar, in fact, published a Civil War novel fully divested of sentimental content after Crane wrote The Red Badge of Courage in 1895. Moreover, during the nine years between the 1892 publication of Iola Leroy and the 1901 publication of The Fanatics, Charles Chesnutt had begun to work outside the black American sentimental tradition when blasting plantation mythology in The Conjure Woman (1899) and writing a startlingly forceful fictional version of North Carolina's Wilmington Race Riot of 1898 in The Marrow of Tradition (1901). Yet Dunbar and Harper forgo the possibility of using newer models of fiction to engage the Civil War, choosing to develop projects making full use of sentimentality as a discursive strategy. Frances Smith Foster explains that a decision to produce a sentimental novel hardly seems remarkable for Harper, who was writing during "The Black Women's Era," a period in which African American women almost uniformly used the sentimental ethos to, among other things, express a politics of racial uplift within a narrative frame already familiar to their reading public, adopting an aesthetic that those readers could readily assimilate.[4] Foster understands Iola Leroy in part as an instance of an author "fight[ing] fire with fire"— writing and encouraging a black literature with the power to correct the demeaning images of blacks found within the fiction of the Plantation School of the New South.[5] The fact that Harper's novel was possibly the best-selling novel by an African American in the nineteenth century is ample evidence that her aesthetic choice allowed her politics a means of dissemination they might not have had otherwise. Dunbar's novel hardly fared as well, gaining scant attention in literary circles and going relatively unnoticed by the reading public.

In this chapter, I take Foster's observation about the urgency of Harper's interventionist poetics a step further, suggesting that a deeper understanding of her and Dunbar's novels as sentimental texts can be generated by examining them as works that intentionally place themselves in conversation with a particular genre of American sentimentalist war fiction that flooded the marketplace in the decades following the war: the reconciliationist/reunion narrative. Virtually bereft of any of the markers of realism, these narratives acted as powerful cultural counterparts to a national movement toward postwar reconciliation, promoting themes of sectional reunion and purposefully downplaying the differences that drove the South to secede from the Union and that subsequently drove the nation to war. This was particularly true of those matters pertaining to race. As responses to this genre, Iola Leroy and The Fanatics should be read as novels arising from the writers' awareness that the forgetting necessary for intersectional fence mending hinged on an unspoken but definite understanding that black political progress would be hindered in the process. Inverting the analysis I made about Brown's moment of realism in the previous chapter—that sentimentalism collapsed structurally and ideologically after Jerome's decapitation—I will argue that for Harper and Dunbar, the self-conscious use of an excessive sentimentalism becomes a vehicle for asserting a black cultural realism that engages dominant white narratives of the Civil War and its legacy.

I use the term "cultural realism" to refer to the nineteenth-century black literary production that, while not expressly mimetic, refers to the dominant culture's literary conventions and themes as metaphorical vehicles whose tenors are those "truths" of black existence obscured and distorted in mainstream interpretations of U.S. racial relations. As an example, Pauline Hopkins's proto-science fiction novel *Of One Blood* (1902–3), in which a black doctor travels back and forth from the United States to the imaginary African civilization of Telasaar, can be considered a spatial allegory for black liminality, pointing to American blacks' psychic suspension as their originary displacement and continued expulsion from U.S. social structures forces them to exist between two cultures. Too, as critics have pointed out, the passing narrative implicitly suggests that the "science" upholding "fictions" of race is in fact science fiction.[6]

Harper's and Dunbar's formulations of "realism" will also entail a revisionist historicism of the Civil War, rescuing African Americans from rhetorical and political erasure. As I noted in the last chapter, in spite of the insistence of many northerners that the Civil War had been about "preserving the Union" and, for southerners, that it was the culmination of an escalating political tug-of-war over "state's rights," the issues driving a wedge between the North and South—slavery, the Civil War, Reconstruction—of course had at their roots the citizenship status of black people. However, the compromise between Republicans and Democrats that ensured that Rutherford B. Hayes would be elected president in 1876 also ensured that former slaves would no longer have the economic and political support systems vital to their successful integration into the nation as freed people. The premature end of Radical Reconstruction the following year sent a clear signal to African Americans that their needs and interests had been forfeited readily for the "greater" interests of the nation. These greater interests were in part commercial: southerners wanted subsidies for infrastructural development; regional stability would help the South seem less risky to northern capital. In fact, by the time the Hayes decision would be reached, the federal government had begun to structure reunion politically, and the nation had started, if tentatively, to embrace reconciliationist sentiment on other fronts.[7] In 1872, as David Blight notes in *Race and Reunion: The Civil War in American Memory*,[8]

Congress passed the General Amnesty Act, allowing most men who had served in the Confederacy to hold national office. The first of a succession of Blue-Gray reunions would begin only two years later, inaugurating a form of racially exclusionary white fraternalism that only quickened the erosion of any former differences.[9] In general, African Americans, recognized as inconvenient and deemed expendable, were pushed to the background of the national political scene so that intersectional political reconciliation could be acted out without distraction.

Blight further explains that black spokespersons such as Douglass and Benjamin Tanner, the editor of the *Christian Recorder*, understood very well that a rush to reunion placed the "emancipatory legacy" of the Civil War in a perilous position.[10] Placed in an equally perilous position was all that this emancipatory legacy meant in terms of forcing the nation to heed what Douglass held as the "moral" lessons stemming from the massive enslavement of blacks and the massive, devastating warfare that resulted from it.[11] Both Harper and Dunbar made statements during their careers indicating the difficulty of sustaining such a vision in a political climate disinclined to remember that blacks had participated in their own liberation and had fought for the cause of Unionism. Speaking out against lynching and disenfranchisement in "A Duty to Dependent Races," a speech given before the National Council of Women in the United States just prior to the publication of *Iola Leroy*, Harper argued that "the negro" had a right to be a "member of the body politic," presenting his "patriotism," most recently demonstrated in the Civil War, as proof.[12] In 1898, Dunbar penned "Recession Never," a fiery essay in reaction to the Wilmington Riots, expressing outrage over the violent tactics used to expel blacks from the political process. He argued that the problem was not limited to the South: "The race spirit in the United States is not local but general. . . . The new attitude may be interpreted as saying 'Negroes, you may fight for us, but you may not vote for us. . . . You may be heroes in war, but you must be cravens in peace.' "[13] For African Americans, as Blight notes, a real "reconciliation" meant "equality."[14]

While many critics have offered extensive discussions of the literature of reconciliation and reunion,[15] I wish to describe the literature here in some detail in order to provide an adequate framework for the discussion of Harper and Dunbar that will follow. Although the specific variation the writers draw from would not reach the pinnacle of its popularity until late in the century, the theme of reconciliation began to make its way into northern and southern popular literature published shortly after the war. This body of work quite clearly performed a critical emotional and ideological function for a country still stunned by the scope of the war's destruction. Reminders were everywhere: cities burned to the earth, amputated veterans begging in the streets, families mourning the deaths of fathers, sons, and husbands. Frances Miles Finch's famous poem, "The Blue and the Gray," appeared in an 1867 issue of the *Atlantic Monthly*, exalting themes of mutual loss and forgiveness ("Love and tears for the Blue, / Tears and love for the Gray").[16] Such sentiment as that found in Finch's poem or the feelings intended to be generated by the many fictionalized scenes of comradery between Yankee and Confederate soldiers allowed the nation to forget the "mutual slaughter" of the war, as Amy Kaplan has suggested, and to rewrite it instead as "shared sacrifice for reunion."[17] In the 1880s the reunion genre—in poetry, fiction, and autobiographical reminiscences—emerged in full force (almost coincidentally, it should be noted, with American literary "realism"). Blight argues that of the many magazines publishing this work during this period, *Century* played the most influential role in promoting reconciliationist writing. Its wildly popular war series explicitly solicited pieces, as the magazine phrased it, with "a non-political point of view,"[18] prompting writers from both sides to forgo partisanship in favor of financial remuneration. *Century* also sought to forget "slaughter," publishing only tidy pieces for its readership, ones that did not touch upon the unwieldy and terrifying physical and psychological consequences of warfare.

The absolute centrality of blacks to the causes of the Civil War, and the indisputably violent nature of war in general, get lost in *Century*'s case to monetary motives. But it and other periodicals publishing reconciliationist literature also should be read as a cultural symptom indicating what W. E. B. Du Bois, writing some seventy years after the Civil War in *Black Reconstruction*, calls the propensity of Americans to substitute "pleasant reading" for accurate historicism.[19] The pleasure of embracing narratives of reconciliation, stories of healing, enables an endless deferral of a more painful engagement of history, one that necessarily would grapple with two defining, persistent facts of U.S. existence: its tactical reliance on violence for the development of the state and on the willful subjugation of African Americans for its economic benefit. Du Bois elaborates on the motives behind the revision of the war in the field of American history:

> War and especially civil strife leave terrible wounds. It is the duty of humanity to heal them. It was therefore soon conceived as neither wise nor patriotic to speak of all the causes of strife and the terrible results to which sectional differences led. And so, first of all, we minimized the slavery controversy which convulsed the nation from the Missouri Compromise down to the Civil War. On top of that, we passed by Reconstruction with a phrase of regret of disgust. But are these reasons . . . sufficient for denying Truth?[20]

According to Du Bois, "Truth," or by another name, "realism"—be it historical, political, psychological, or other—had little place in a white American consciousness grappling with the most damaging war it would ever know; a fratricidal war in which white men killed one another over the fate of blacks (a fact that was nevertheless tellingly remembered in the very compulsion to forget).

What Du Bois labeled the "truer deeper facts of Reconstruction" would be obscured even further as northern magazines such as *McClure's* began "court[ing] Southern writers and stories of the Old South" in the 1880s and 1890s,[21] allowing a distinctly southern brand of reunion literature steeped in Lost Cause ideology to reach an ever-widening bisectional readership. A politically ingenious mixture of plantation school nostalgia, sentimental war literature, and reconciliation narratives, the white nationalist fantasies imagined by southern nationalists such as Thomas Nelson Page and Thomas Dixon aimed to deny the deep fissures created by the war by diminishing the racial and sectional strife engendered by the slave system, reconceiving slavery as a natural hierarchy in which blacks knew and understood their proper places. At the same time, these whitewashed imaginaries portray the South as a lost, grand civilization that ultimately will be returned to its former state of glory.

More than a longing for a past that never was, the revision of slavery and the Civil War in these fantasies projects both a need to stabilize contemporary racial relations in the tumult of post-Reconstruction America and a desire to alter the destiny of future race relations. Informing these works is a lateral notion of black history in which slavery, the Civil War, and Reconstruction are understood as a continuum. Blacks, finding themselves in the New World friendless and backward, were nurtured in the benign civilizing paternity of slavery. Helpless and immature, they could not have fought with any intent or "manliness" on their own behalf against the South. In the final, tragic phase, the civilizing process was abruptly halted, leaving them absolutely unfit to hold the franchise in freedom. Any reading of the war as a site that changed the course of history, an unexpected moment of rupture producing citizen from slave, is quite inconceivable in these works. African American men in military uniform, the iconic symbol of a black future, simply signify two alternatives of regressive black masculinity: slaves who had followed their masters to war or illegitimate soldiers masquerading as the masters of whites during the military rule of Radical Reconstruction— characterized as a topsy-turvy, nightmarish period of "nigger domination." The former image of black men was meant to evoke nostalgia, the latter, terror; a terror that was destined to become increasingly sexualized as the genre reached its end.

Both northern and southern reconciliationist culture conceptualized its desire for reunion within a familiar sentimental lexicon of domesticity, family, and the body: the need to rebuild the national home, mend fractured relationships, and heal open wounds. Not surprisingly, the courtship plot is ubiquitous, the split between North and South, depicted in much of the fiction as the rupture of a previous mythical state of domestic bliss—"a house divided"—is shown as remedied with the marriage of lovers representing the opposing sides of the war: the projection of a democratic imaginary in which the nation's differences are easily mended. For defenders of the South, the body became a particularly potent metaphor in evoking the sympathetic response that sentimentalism demanded. Defenders of the South were quick to imagine the region as a fallen soldier— quite logically—but also as a "cripple," a widow, or, in the most resonant and ideologically productive corporeal metaphor, the "prostrate" victim of rape.[22]

The corporeal implications of the marriage/courtship trope thus supplied a perfect vehicle for white nationalist reunion fantasies. In their most overdetermined form, the North-South romantic pairing was amplified into a double love story: a "southern brother/sister pair marrying a northern brother/sister pair."[23] The northerners, of course, concede to the politics of the South, a transformation completed when the northerners choose to abandon their homes for permanent residence in the South. At the time Dixon introduced the most notorious of these novelistic doublings in his best-selling novel *The Clansman: A Historical Romance of the Ku Klux Klan* (1905),[24] the matter of whether the nation would be geographically unified had long been settled. Still unsettled, however, was the question of what to do with a growing free black population increasingly intent on securing full citizenship rights—a question, in Dixon's mind, causing the North and South to remain as essentially separate as they were when the issue of slavery had ripped the nation apart. Blacks were, therefore, the real and only threat to white national reunion: the reestablishment of undivided, white national domestic space.

In *The Clansman*, the white national domestic space is symbolized by a "fallen slaveholder's mansion" (185), destabilized by the dissolution of the institution that built it, both literally and metaphorically. Already reduced to a state of fragility, the white national home, Dixon warns his audiences, is further threatened by the black man who will—if allowed enough power—seize control of government and legislate himself into the white man's bedroom. This threat is confirmed through the character of Silas Lynch, the black governor elected in the first election of Reconstruction. Depicted as a duplicitous political opportunist and a dangerous sexual grotesque, he proclaims his intent to "take . . . [the white man's] daughter in marriage"—specifically, the northern heroine Elsie (275). "Marriage," in Dixon's vocabulary, becomes a code for "rape." Dixon's hysterical vision attempts to demonstrate that opening the "doors" of sacred white institutions to blacks—the doors of government or those of the home—has devastating consequences. Dixon effectively renders any legitimate claim blacks have to political and social parity null and void, and, significantly, lends moral justification to the expulsion of blacks from national spaces. The racially pure, politically harmonious, and vaguely incestuous neoplantation household created by Dixon's double love story—an impenetrable fortress against black invasion, a quarantine, really—is made possible only by the elimination of Lynch. Naturally, blacks will be permitted to enter this hermetically sealed household, but only conditionally: in a subservient position, economically, politically, and sexually disabled.

Returning to Foster's claim that Harper and other writers of her generation needed to "fight fire with fire," it is difficult indeed to conceive of black writers fashioning effective fictionalized responses to such preposterous racial scenarios out of the authentic stuff of war—death, carnage, disability, disease. Rather, in avoiding the explicitly documentary and mimetic modes of realism, and in deploying the tropes of sentiment, Harper and Dunbar are able to create works that engage the nationalists on their own metaphorical turf: the purified white domestic space, the space from which the nationalists seek to derail black evolutionary history by altering the meaning of the Civil War and staving off the implications of its aftermath. If the nationalists' aim is to reinterpret the war retroactively (an emancipatory reading of the war must be a misinterpretation because black suffrage and representation, its outcome, is quite obviously a grave and frightening error), Harper and Dunbar also attempt to review the war's success in light of blacks' sociopolitical circumstances in the postwar period, both engaging the white nationalist understanding of black historical "progress" as lateral rather than evolutionary.

Similarities aside, what makes Iola Leroy and The Fanatics most interesting to consider together is, in fact, the radically different meaning each ascribes to the outcome of black military participation. In the first half of the chapter, I will read Harper's novel in a manner to suggest the writer finds it necessary to disrupt the nationalist continuum by re-presenting the notion that the future for African Americans was transformed by the Civil War, particularly by what Harper presents as blacks' uniformly noble and heroic efforts. The Civil War becomes a site of racial rebirth, eradicating the memory of slavery; it becomes a site of national rebirth, cleansing the sins of the nation. While her submersion of the war within redemptive biblical narratives and an overabundant sentimentalism hardly constitutes what we accept as the "real," she calls on the structures and scenes from the reconciliation narrative only to alter their meanings. First and foremost, Harper argues that the reconciliation most necessary to African Americans is not the reuniting of the North and South, but the reconciliation and reestablishment of a strong, viable black community, a force against the escalating political and racial terrorism targeting black Americans during the 1890s. Her revision of the dominant culture's reconciliation narratives also asks that her audiences see the nation as still fundamentally fractured, a corrective that emerges as a quite accurate and "real" apprehension of the contemporary political scene.

If Harper's insistence on the war's success in transforming blacks into viable citizens nevertheless betrays a lingering doubt regarding the actual possibilities of an irrevocable, uncontested integration, Dunbar makes that doubt explicit, wholly resisting the notion of black transformation in *The Fanatics*, a deeply bitter novel that presents the Civil War as having done little for black citizen rights. In effect, Dunbar agrees with the race nationalists' interpretation of the conflict, rejecting the idea that the war was fought between the "good" North and "evil" South over slavery. Instead he replicates important aspects of the reconciliation narrative, depicting the war as mere misunderstanding between northern and southern racists, or more accurately, between those whites sympathizing with the Union and those aligning with Confederates. Dunbar implies that when the war ended and passions cooled, these "misunderstandings" were very quickly "forgotten" so that the nation could get on with the real national business: finding ways to keep blacks in a permanently subjugated position. In illustrating his point, Dunbar, like Harper, engages in generic excesses, but his are the excesses of parody, in the Bakhtinian sense of the term,[25] "quoting" the narratives' conventions, themes, and content. These repetitions will service Dunbar's self-conscious assertion of the black cultural real. Within this reconceptualization of realism, Dunbar's use of sentimentalism and minstrel characterization are made to operate allegorically. For instance, sentimentalism's romanticized endings, in which "fractured bonds" are quickly healed at the expense of more complex resolutions, are typically discussed as creating literary "imaginaries" that attempt to "correct" the social and political deficiencies of the "real" world. However, Dunbar's repetition of these endings in *The Fanatics* suggests that he views these tidied, hurried literary closures as paralleling a quite "real" and devastating political impulse in the postwar nation. Similarly, Dunbar's rather disconcerting decision to configure his representative of black masculinity as a minstrel represents the very real way black men's place in the white (national) home is secured by a performative dissembling: the ability to rescind any self-determining manhood earned in the military, which requires, in Dunbar's mind, the willingness to reproduce the sentimentalized, whitewashed versions of the war the dominant culture wished to hear.

Iola Leroy

Frances Harper's Iola Leroy tells the story of a woman raised as white by a white father, Eugene Leroy, and a mulatto mother, Marie. Sent away from the South to be educated in an elite boarding school, Iola remains unaware of her racial heritage until the eve of the Civil War, when her father dies, his marriage to Marie is invalidated, and Iola and her mother are remanded to slavery. Iola's brother, Harry, initially stunned by the revelation, stays north, eventually joining a black regiment in the Union army. Rescued from slavery by the northern forces, Iola serves as a nurse in the Civil War where she meets her uncle, Robert Johnson, who has enlisted with the Union troops. They vow to search for their mothers after the war. The family is happily reunited after the war ends. Both Iola and Harry marry members of the activist elite; Iola marries the accomplished mulatto Doctor Latimer and Harry marries Lucille Delany, a well-educated "pure" black. The entire extended family moves south to commit themselves to the work of racial uplift. Harry, Lucille, and Iola become educators; Latimer becomes a community physician; and Robert Johnson embarks upon a project of communal farming among the poor. "Blessed themselves," Harper ends her narrative, "their lives are a blessing to others" (281).

To properly understand Iola Leroy as a revision of race nationalists' representations of the Civil War and Reconstruction, it is first essential to note the writer's preoccupation with the issue of memory as it relates to what was, in 1892, a quite recent experience of slavery. Harper chooses to open her work as the moment of the Emancipation Proclamation draws near, when the possibility of freedom for blacks is approaching, an opportunity for the writer to create a narrative break from the slave past and imagine a historical trajectory moving toward a "future . . . rose tinted and rain-bow hued," as Robert muses when he initially recognizes the Union army is within distance (35). "All the ties" that "bound" him to slavery, she writes, fall away like "ropes of sand," the mere presence of the army making the psychological shackles of slavery dissolve into minute, insubstantial fragments (35). Harper herself expressed similar sentiments upon receiving news of the Proclamation: "The President reached out his hand through the darkness to break the chains on which the rust of centuries had gathered. . . . Once the slave was a despised and trampled on pariah; now he has become a useful ally to the American government."[26] The chains have been broken, the past is gone, the move upward "for the slave" to a "higher destiny" swift and definitive.[27]

In Robert's case, the quick dissolution of the memory of slavery is merely metaphorical, but other slave characters in Harper's novel are depicted as actually unable or unwilling to psychically process a preemancipatory life, finding it simply too troubling to contemplate. Harry, upon learning he was a slave born of an illegitimate marriage, experiences a kind of amnesia: "it seemed as if the past were suddenly blotted out of his memory" (123). Falling ill for several months, he emerges from his sickbed believing the story of his upbringing a "dreadful dream" (123). Iola, speaking to her mother after the war, also characterizes her past as a "dream" and declares it "useless . . . to brood over the past" (195). The characters' repeated response to the trauma of slavery—repression—is, as I have suggested, also Harper's. This is not to imply that this suppression is altogether pathological, following the logic of popularized interpretations of the Freudian psyche: that trauma must be revisited, made "conscious" through the powers of narrative lest it return in a monstrous, destructive form. Her move to repress reflects the attitude shared by many African Americans at that time that dwelling on the wrongs of slavery was not only painful but ultimately paralyzing, drawing vital energy away from the struggles of the present. Toward the end of the work, Mrs. Leroy remarks that "Slavery . . . is dead, but the spirit which animated it still lives" (217). Slavery is a corpse, never to be resurrected. What is necessary, then, is to locate the "spirit's" latest incarnation and to fight it in its most recent embodiment—"lawless white men who murder, lynch, and burn their fellow citizens" (217).

Much of Iola Leroy indeed reads as a primer for African Americans on memory, emphasizing which events of a collective black historical experience are to remain safely dead and buried and which can be summoned forth (safely) to do work in the present. Examinations of Iola Leroy often point out that William Still, Harper's dear friend who wrote the introduction for the work, had wondered whether or not it was wise to return to slavery as a subject for a novel in 1892. But Still's hesitation is indicative of what I see as continuing misreading of this work: Iola Leroy is a novel that is not as much about slavery and its legacy as it is about the Civil War and its legacy. If in Harper's thinking slavery needed to be pushed to the realm of distant memory because it was an unrecoverable void in a narrative of black progress (as many blacks believed), the war can and should be recalled on the basis of its instrumentality—both as a costly lesson to the nation and, even more significantly, as the origin of a newly formed black race. The language Harper wields to describe the war gives us insight into her belief in its utility. She intimates in "A Duty to Dependent Races" that before blacks were allowed to join the Union forces, the slaughter white men had engaged themselves in was merely a wasteful expenditure of life: "men," she said, "poured out their blood like water."[28] After the northern army "walked abreast" with black men "to victory" Harper's blood-water metaphor will take on a different tenor,[29] signaling forms of bodily making much more than corporeal undoing. In *Iola Leroy*, the blood spilled on the battlefield is transformed into holy water in a rite of black baptism: "The lost cause went down in blood and tears, and on the brows of a ransomed people God poured the chrism of a new era, and they stood a race newly anointed with freedom" (138). Her meditation on Lincoln's death once again associates blood with water in a cycle of renewal and rebirth: "the white flower of freedom" had sprung from "the crimson sods of war."[30] To be sure, Harper's redemptive rendering of the war is also facilitated by a long tradition in which African Americans have sought to interpret the history of U.S. blacks in an allegorical relationship to Biblical narratives. The Civil War is a holy war, the Union army "deliverers" of the black people (*Iola*, 14), and Abraham Lincoln, a martyr. Harper's Christian vision led her to see "divine retribution" in the war's "desolation and carnage."[31]

Quite differently from Brown, Harper conceives of the war as a moment that operated bidirectionally in the production of a black subjectivity, wiping out the body of the slave and bringing forth "men," an essential part of constructing a black American creation narrative from the Civil War. This requires romanticizing and sentimentalizing black participation in the conflict—finding glory in patriotic death, finding honor in injury, and, in general, finding a means to avert war's more horrific aspects. Two years after the war ended, Douglass referred to African American history as a traumatized body; borrowing language from the Irish nationalist Daniel O'Connell, he declared that it could "be traced like that of a wounded man through a crowd, by the blood."[32] In an important sense, then, Harper seeks to alter this conceptualization by erasing the traces, mopping up the messy scene, suturing the opened flesh shut.

In the first part of my discussion, I will connect Harper's dis-remembering of slavery, her "cleaning up" of the Civil War and idealization of black Reconstruction in *Iola Leroy*, to the writer's increasing anxiety about the preservation and restoration of the black body (in its fully metonymic relationship with the black body politic) as this body attempted to withstand the innumerable assaults, physical and political, leveled against blacks during the period that has come to be known as the "nadir." Indeed, in spite of the novel's promising ending, some twenty years before its publication, Harper had already begun to anticipate the failure of the racial uplift ideology whose virtues she extols in *Iola Leroy*. From 1864 to 1871, Harper traveled extensively in the South as a lecturer and teacher, often recording her observations in letters to Still, who collected them, publishing them in his book *The Underground Railroad* (1872).[33] In one letter dated from the year *Underground* was published, she agonizes over what she perceives as her race's declining commitment to the cause she had made her life's work, expressing once again a need to be distanced from slavery's memory: "Oh," she writes, "if I could only see our young men and women aiming to build a future for themselves which would grandly contrast with the past—with its pain, ignorance and low condition."[34] Harper had ample reason for concern. Despite the numerous social and political inroads blacks had made since the end of the Civil War, in 1870, approximately 80 percent of southern blacks were still illiterate. A decade later, black voter participation in the South had declined markedly—in some states, the number of voting blacks had dropped by half. Correspondingly, the number of black members in Congress plummeted from a high of seven in 1873 to zero in 1887.[35] Social Darwinism, polygenesis, phrenology, and other pseudoscientific forms of racialism were still culturally influential, redeployed after the war to justify social, political, and sexual segregation in a miscegenated nation. White terrorism, spearheaded by the founding of the Ku Klux Klan in 1865, had only grown after the end of Reconstruction, an issue Harper would engage in her serialized novel, *Minnie's Sacrifice* (1869),[36] whose heroine dies at the hands of the "Invisible Empire."

When Harper began to write *Iola Leroy*, her anxiety over postwar racial relations had escalated, manifesting itself around a set of concerns arising from the effects of reconciliationist politics and sentiment on black American social and political elevation. A letter to Still from Athens, Georgia, in 1870 registers her belief that a rapid reunion would be detrimental to black progress. Noting the gradual pace at which former slaves were elevating themselves, Harper writes that "keep[ing] Georgia out of the Union about a year or two longer" would allow "the colored people [to] continue to live as they have been doing."[37] In another letter she asserts that "basing national reconstruction on the votes of returned rebels, and rejecting loyal black men" was "fallacy."[38] Harper was not only troubled by the laxity in the formal policies dictating reunion but by the North's apparent unwillingness to put energy into reforming their own racist political structures, which helped create an informal sympathy between the two regions. In *Minnie's Sacrifice*, Harper describes an unintended complicity between the North and South in relation to black voting rights, implying that the "illegal" political terrorism of the Klan was validated by the "legal" political disfranchisement of blacks in the North:

> The times were evil, and the days were very gloomy. . . . State after State in the North had voted against enfranchising the colored man in their midst. The spirit of the lost cause revived, murders multiplied. The Ku Klux Klan spread terror and death around. Every item of Northern meanness to the colored people in their midst was a message of hope to the rebel element of the South,

which had only changed. Ballot and bullet had failed, but another resort was found in secret assassination. Men advocating equal rights did so at the peril of their lives (85).

Given the wariness Harper expressed about northern/southern collusion, whether she interprets it as purposeful collusion or not, the flourishing culture of reunion of the 1890s, with its will to "forget" the strides blacks had made since emancipation, was still a matter with which Harper felt she needed to contend—particularly as this forgetting became intertwined with the ideology of white supremacy in race nationalist reconciliation literature.

Thus in Iola Leroy, Harper rethinks the meaning of reconciliation for African Americans at the same time she rejects what reunion has come to mean in white American civic and social life. As the close of Iola Leroy suggests, Harper's plan for an alternative notion of reconciliation begins (and ends) with regathering the scattered black family into a prosperous community: "the reunion of severed hearts" (216). The continued success of that process depends upon reconsolidating the community racially—an argument that implicitly undermines the importance granted black-white reconciliation moments appearing not only in white reconciliation literature but also in some African American postwar literature of the period.[39] But as we will see, in Harper's novel, black reconciliation demands the expulsion of whites from black American private life, particularly the domestic space. It is white, not black, men whose desire crosses the color line; it is the white body, not the black, that becomes the source of disease and physical degeneration. In that way, Harper attempts to turn the sexual politics of the race nationalist narratives inside out. Harper's novel does lobby for civic inclusion, however. Evoking the language of Horace Greeley's famous admonition that the North and South must "clasp hands across the bloody chasm" to avoid deepening sectional divisiveness,[40] Harper suggests that true national reconciliation, based in a "cohesion of justice," will not be achieved until the nation "clasp[s] hand with the negro" (24) as it did during wartime. Yet these interesting and important revisions are nonetheless accompanied by a problematic body politics. More specifically, the success of both forms of postwar reconciliation that Harper deemed critical for black survival, the communal and the national, or put differently, the intraracial and the interracial, are predicated upon a conservative racial ideology in which "worthy" blacks must be separated from those deemed less so. In so doing, Harper crafts a eugenicized social and corporeal fantasy (what Houston Baker calls a "mulatto utopia")[41] that in the end invokes the racialist logic it seeks to overturn. The Civil War, so important to Harper's racial genealogy, is the moment where these bodily matters can begin to sort themselves out.

Reconciliation and Black Expulsion

In "A Duty to Dependent Races," Harper extensively quotes Henry Grady, who, as the managing editor of the *Atlanta Constitution*, became one of the most vocal advocates of the New South's commercialism and continued movement toward reconciliation:[42]

> Mr. Grady said, I believe, "We do not directly fear the political domination of blacks, but that they are ignorant and easily deluded, impulsive and therefore easily led, strong of race instinct and therefore clannish, without information and therefore without political convictions, passionate and therefore easily excited, poor, irresponsible, and with no idea of the integrity of suffrage, and therefore easily bought. The fear is that this vast swarm, ignorant, purchasable, will be impacted and controlled by desperate and unscrupulous white men and made to hold the balance of power when white men are divided."[43]

In her novel, Harper places parts of Grady's speech in the mouth of Doctor Latrobe, a character designed to represent the racialist sector of the white medical profession. Latrobe is then quickly corrected by Robert. Harper's desire to combat such claims of black inferiority fueled the insistent, rectifying sentimentality in her work that resembles, however ironically, the agitated tone of southern nationalists desperately trying to confront the uncomfortable fact that millions of black bodies had been freed to live among them. "Black hordes of former slaves," frets a character in Dixon's novel, "with the intelligence of children and the instincts of savages, armed with modern rifles parade daily in front of their unarmed masters" (289). Grady's and Dixon's exaggerated expression of fear is of course the dominant's standard response to social disorder—a disorder that can only be assuaged by justifying the implementation of controls over the disruptive body. In America, that body is most often black, especially that body that is visibly racially inscribed.

Harper's offsetting depiction of the black community as ordered and contained, in all ways so apparently opposite of Grady's and Dixon's, can be interpreted nevertheless as a response to the "masses," "hordes," and "swarms" of blacks whom, Harper writes in a concluding note to *Iola Leroy*, "the fortunes of war threw, homeless, ignorant and poor, upon the threshold of a new era" (282), and whom Harper felt it was her duty to "help . . . forward."[44] Describing her impressions of Alabama, she offers this assessment: "I should think this has been one of the lowest down States in the South, as far as civilization is concerned. . . . Men talk about missionary work among the heathen, but if any lover of Christ wants a field for civilizing work, here is a field."[45] Certainly, the late nineteenth-century rhetoric of racial uplift lapsed far too easily into a language evocative of the imperialist ethos emerging in a nation increasingly devoted to global expansion. Just as it became necessary for the United States to dismiss other nations and peoples as "uncivilized" to justify its emerging dominion in the Western hemisphere—a subject I will treat in Chapter Four—in order for educated black elites to assume an instructive position in relation to the blacks of lower classes, it was necessary that they presume intellectual and moral superiority. This is not to say that Harper believed in biological "infusionism," the theory that the black elite, who were often mixed race, were inherently more advanced than the common folk, their white blood elevating them genetically. Rather, her writings suggest that she adhered, at least in part, to the notion of civilizationism. Harper thought blacks of the lower strata to be "behind," very much in the same way her work also suggests that African culture, once progressive and glorious, was simply outpaced by Anglo-Saxon development. "Uplifting the race" therefore meant rushing to put disadvantaged African Americans on the evolutionary trajectory—morally, spiritually, and economically. And who better to perform that task than educated members of their own race?

Accordingly, everywhere in Iola Leroy—as in The Clansman—the notion of "civilization" is juxtaposed with the behavior of the common black, who, in the words of one character, should be taught how to "eliminate paganism of caste from our holy religion and the lawlessness of savagery" from civil society (260). During a conversazione held after the war, Lucille Delany, one of the few elites whose skin is clearly black, repeats with great alarm a newspaper article claiming that black women had become "unfit to be servants for white people" (199). Rather than issuing a more radical interpretation—reading black women's behavior as an act of passive resistance to servile conditions—she concludes that black women who were not disciplined enough to serve whites would never make proper homemakers and vows to open a school to "train future wives and mothers" (199). At another gathering of black elites, one participant explains his fears about the criminal element within the black race: "I am concerned about the lack of home training" (259).

While the novel repeatedly reminds the reader that white oppression, particularly violent intimidation, largely contributes to blacks' inability to rise above their current status—"The Anglo-Saxon race," Dr. Gresham asserts in Iola, ". . . has more capacity for dragging down a weaker race than uplifting it"—blacks are nevertheless held responsible for introducing the savagery that influenced the white civilization in the first place (116). In denouncing the rise of lynching, Gresham makes a circuitous argument that initially seems to lay the blame for white lawlessness squarely in the laps of whites, but winds up, in a strange twist of logic, returning to the black as the origin of white "barbarity":

Both races have reacted on each other—men fettered the slave, and cramped their own souls; denied him knowledge and darkened their spiritual insight; subdued him to the pliancy of submission, and in their turn became the thralls of public opinion. The negro came here from the heathenism of Africa; but the young colonies could not take into their early civilization a stream of barbaric blood without being affected by its influence, and the negro, poor and despised as he is, has laid his hands on our Southern civilization and helped mold its character (217).

After Gresham finishes his speech, Iola's mother simply agrees: "Yes" (217). No dissenting opinions are registered. I point out these moments in *Iola* to show that within a novel largely devoted to reasserting the promise of the black race, Harper nevertheless demonstrates a nagging preoccupation with what to do with the common black body—often referred to as undisciplined and undisciplining, and often constructed as a racial "other."

For the most extreme race nationalists such as Dixon, disciplining the disorderly black body provided a perfect occasion for national reunion. The emergence of white nationalist reunion narratives coincided with a solidifying belief that the United States, increasingly divided since the Civil War, could be brought together over the domination of dark bodies abroad.[46] This does not hold true for Dixon who, as Walter Benn Michaels argues, belonged to the class of supremacists who believed that imperialist efforts overseas drained energy away from the immediate task at hand: keeping blacks under control domestically.[47] Extending the United States' domain would only further destabilize the already unstable "Nation" by bringing an untold number of unruly bodies within its boundaries. In *The Clansman*, the Ku Klux Klan is heralded as an organizational model for the country. Whites of differing regions, classes, and political allegiances push their antagonisms aside for the greater good: to discipline the offending body. That body is either chased to the outskirts of town or relegated to a subjugated, pre–Civil War condition of servitude. For instance, Aleck, a former slave, is made sheriff under "negro rule," but after a threatening visit by the Klan, renounces his position and returns to calling white men "master" (348). In the most expedient disciplinary strategy, the most disorderly body, the rapist, is simply killed. In this instance, the "misdirected" violence of the Civil War—fratricide—becomes rechanneled into an appropriate manifestation of that impulse, onto the black beast.[48]

As I have claimed, for Harper, the division to be healed is not between two sections of a previously warring nation, but between two nations emerging as separate and unequal: the white nation and the black. Like many of her era, Harper believed that white Americans were more likely to accept blacks who demon-strated characteristics of elevation. A white journalist who had heard Harper lecture made this remark about her poise and appearance: "Many more like Harper are greatly needed, especially in the South, to remove the bad odor from the name 'negro.' " To demonstrate the worthiness of her race, Harper bathes her blacks, as it were, filling the pages of her novel with exemplars—bodies which are already rehabilitated or ready to undergo the rehabilitation process necessary to enable them to "add their quota of good citizenship to the best welfare of the nation" (282). Harper is especially careful to write only of those of the "folk" classes who can further the novel's purpose. Thus some folk can be narrated: Uncle Ben, who is elected a congressman; John Salters, who fought in the war; Tom, who courageously sacrifices his life in battle; and Aunt Linda, who takes a temperance pledge. Most of these characters live on a settlement located on a former plantation, an oasis of black ownership and thrift where "the school-house had taken the place of the slave-pen and auction block" (152). Yet, in an 1870 letter to Still, Harper admits that she cannot "pretend" that all [former slaves] are saving money and getting homes," and in another laments that too many "are living in the old cabins of slavery."[49]

But pretend she does. The truly undisciplined black body—the spendthrift, the criminal, the drunkard—never disrupts or disturbs Harper's narrative by making an appearance in her text. They are, however, spoken of throughout. The most startling analysis of this class comes from Aunt Linda: "But dere's some triflin' niggers down yere who'll sell der votes for almost nuffin'. Does you 'member Jake Williams an' Gundover's Tom? Well, dem two niggers is de las' ob pea time. Dey's mighty small pertaters an' few in a hill (176)." Robert issues a brief objec-tion to Aunt Linda's use of the word "nigger": " 'Oh Aunt Linda,' said Robert, 'don't call them niggers. They are our own people' " (176). Aunt Linda responds by explaining her reasoning: "Dey ain't my kind of people. I jes call em niggers and niggers I mean; an' the bigges' kine ob niggers" (176). In the discourse of Harper's novel, blacks are blacks—whether educated or not, whether mulatto or full-blooded—but, in this passage, "niggers" are something else altogether, con-signed to a category outside of black humanity entirely. Like Gresham's speech naming black barbarism as the source of white lawlessness, Aunt Linda's point of view about "niggers" remains unreconstructed in the text; the content of her speech reflecting Harper's eventual disavowal of universal suffrage and belief that "educational and moral tests" should be administered to all seeking the franchise.[50] "Well after all," she writes Still, "perhaps the colored man is gener-ally not really developed enough to value his vote and equality with other races."[51] Given Harper's tendency in Iola Leroy to allow enlightened characters such as

Robert the privilege of lengthy, meticulously detailed monologues refuting incorrect positions on matters of race and equality (some monologues are constructed from Harper's own speeches), Robert's (and Harper's) relative silence becomes troubling.

Harper's reunion fantasy is thus one disconcertingly similar to the race nationalists—a world where the "other" can be rehabilitated into behaving according to the social codes of the dominant order, and those bodies that cannot are narratively and rhetorically banished from that world altogether.

The Mulatto Body as a Site of Reconciliation

For many Civil War writers, using war as a narrative frame became a means of heightening the importance of other domestic politics by associating them with those issues dire enough to cause national rupture. For the writers of race nationalist narratives, the Civil War becomes a literary springboard for a longer, more complex political war: the battle over what bodies would be considered "American." As Kaplan has noted, Dixon's first novel, The Leopard's Spots (1902),[52] "is punctuated by a repeated anxious refrain: 'Shall the future American be an Anglo Saxon or a Mulatto.' "[53] Dixon was repeating a phrase drawn from Charles Chesnutt's inflammatory essay, "The Future American";[54] in this piece, Chesnutt asserts that the United States is destined to become a nation of mixed-race people, theorizing that the inability to distinguish bodies racially might be the sole way equality will ever be achieved. He even suggests that this could be achieved "mechanically" under a "sufficiently autocratic" government.[55] One can almost discern a refrain similar to Dixon's echoing throughout Iola as Dr. Gresham expresses a desire to take Iola as a wife and hide her blackness and as army officers suggest that both Harry and Robert bury theirs by joining all-white regiments. All resist. In Harper's work, the "future American," it seems, will not be white (nor black, for that matter) but will be a mulatto.

Well before the war, Harper lamented white America's steadfast refusal to recognize black and white biological kinship: "we are treated worse than aliens among a people . . . whose blood flows and mingles in our veins."[56] In Iola Leroy, the repetition of the mulatto body—male and female, spanning several generations—repeatedly forces the nation to confront an image of itself, to see in the mulatto body the circumstance that brought together two groups of people in the making of a new republic. Harper has Dr. Latrobe give voice to a reading of this body antithetical to hers. White negroes," as he calls blacks, are of "illegitimate origin" and therefore social undesirables (228).

It is not the illegitimacy of the mulatto's origins that Harper disputes necessarily, given her belief in the virtues of lawful, Christian matrimony; rather, she contests the notion that the "origins" delegitimize any claim to social equality. Her ideas parallel Nathaniel Hawthorne's description of the birth of the black American in "Chiefly about War Matters," published in the *Atlantic Monthly* just a year into the Civil War. After describing an encounter with contrabands in Virginia that caused him to consider where these "Africans" belonged—North, South, Africa, or the New World—he decides that blacks and whites have sprung "from an identical source": "They are our brethren, as being lineal descendants from the Mayflower, the fated womb of which, in her first voyage, sent forth a brood of Pilgrims on Plymouth Rock, and, in a subsequent one, spawned slaves upon the Southern soil,—a monstrous birth, but with which we have an instinctive sense of kindred, and are so stirred by an irresistible impulse to attempt their rescue, even at the cost of blood and ruin."[57] Hawthorne and Harper both characterize the Civil War as the nation's reluctant acceptance of a familial relationship (though Hawthorne sees it as a matter of historical rather than biological coincidence).

But more important, the heroine of Harper's novel, who in one life is a wealthy defender of slavery living in the North and in the next, a poor black southern slave, disturbs all notions of national identity emerging from facile antonymic relationships. She is neither slave nor free, black nor white, northern nor southern. Her body refuses any particular inscription or permanent identity because it is already a location of multiple, contradictory inscriptions and identifications. National reconciliation takes place on Iola's body: an amalgamation of race and class, unmarked by geography.

Reconciliation and White Expulsion

Crucial to Harper's project of stabilizing and reproducing this "future American" is the manner of household that emerges in *Iola* after the war. Indeed, if the mission of the white reunion narrative is to reconcile the white national family in one household that has successfully withstood varied forms of black attack— political, social, and sexual—Harper's goal is to create domestic spaces immune to the same forces of whiteness. In the years following the official death of Reconstruction in 1877, whites in both the North and the South were intent upon resegregating the nation. Jim Crow separated blacks from whites socially, disenfranchisement practices separated them politically, and both antimiscegenation and lynch laws attempted to separate blacks from whites sexually. Denying the real rationale for these divisions—white economic hegemony, as the antilynching activist Ida B. Wells argued—whites once again turned to claims that blacks, as beastly, "other," and so forth, were outside the social order, or at least at the bottom of a racial hierarchy. Blacks also were rumored to be rife with syphilis and gonorrhea; interracial sex, besides being simply taboo, could carry the severe penalties of madness or death. Such antimiscegenationist postwar discourses fingered the black body as a site of degeneration, death, and disease, combining "the wish for black extinction with the fear of white race extinction."[58]

Whites were not the only racial group distrustful of the mulatto body. Robert Reid-Pharr has argued that antebellum black literature, consumed with the project of drafting, defining, and stabilizing a recognizably black subjectivity, demonstrates a similar phobic reaction to the body of the mulatto. Borrowing the trope of a well-ordered household from white domestic literature—a symbol of a stable nation, a site where republican identities could be produced and reproduced—early black novelists such as William Wells Brown, Frank J. Webb, and Harriet Wilson essentially kicked the inherently "messy" body of the mulatto out of the black national home. Reid-Pharr theorizes that "proper black bodies can only be produced within proper black households, households that must be cleaned literally and figuratively of the unsettling stench of white intrusion. In the process mulatto bodies are either killed off or reinterpellated as black."[59]

Harper melds the tropes of marriage and the home to the metaphors of death and disease to underscore the importance of such disinfected households: clean of the contaminating presence of whiteness. Reversing the purpose of the "house-cleaning" so central to white nationalist literature, Harper turns the insidious racialist discourse that characterized the black body as "contaminant" onto itself, transforming the discourse into an idiom that accommodates her concerns with "preserving" the black race. In Harper's novel, the mulatto body, rather than being a threat to whiteness, is threatened by it—threatened by further hybridization, threatened, therefore, by the prospect of further interracial marriage. If Dr. Latrobe believes that Dr. Gresham's solution to social inequality, "the absorption of the negro" into the white race, would "be a death blow to [white] American civilization," there is evidence that Harper is equally unwilling to level that death blow to black American civilization (228). In order to resist utter dissolution in a pool of white blood, the mulatto in Iola Leroy must marry mulatto, or marry a body visibly black. Thus, in juxtaposing Iola's mother Marie's marriage to her white master with Iola's rejection of Gresham, who is white, for Dr. Latimer, who is mulatto, Harper is positing the Iola's decision as an assurance of black generativity. To underscore her point, Harper consciously parallels the collapse of Iola's mother's marital union to a man whose life is marked by sickness to the collapse of the national Union, implying that a nation unified must be rid of the "virus" of slavery that had been allowed to fester in her mother's home.

Iola's mother's acceptance of marriage was also an acceptance of the "privatization" narrative of standard tragic mulatta stories, found within novels such as Brown's earliest version of *Clotel*, which Harper sets out to destroy, as Carla L. Peterson has recognized.[60] Characterized as a man with only a fleeting grasp of racial politics, Leroy decides to send his slave Marie north to be educated and to free her and take her as his wife, a decision prompted by the tenderness she displayed while nursing him during a period of illness. Her establishment as the mistress of Leroy's southern plantation—certainly that irony is not lost on Harper—is the beginning of her total isolation from any social contact with anyone other than her family and her slaves. The couple is only visited by Leroy's friends, who stare upon Marie as an exotic curiosity; Marie, it is implied, has no friends of her own. As Peterson further observes, Marie's promising public oratory—the rousing antislavery speech she delivered at her graduation had the power to move "strong men" to tears—is silenced upon marriage, her opinions on racial matters reduced to protests that make her husband "uncomfortable" (75, 78). "If it annoys you," Marie says, "I will stop talking" (78). Their insular existence renders them oblivious to political and social developments outside of their "joyous dream" (76). Unaware, then, of the regional fissure deepening between the North and South, Leroy dismisses warnings of national conflict: "There are some prophets of evil that tell us the Union is going to dissolve. But I know it would puzzle their brains to tell where the crack would begin. I reckon we'll continue to jog along as usual" (78). When war actually erupts, both are taken aback, but Marie is more surprised than her husband: "A civil war about what?" she asks, with a surprise that will be duplicated when Marie learns that her "marriage certificate is not worth the paper it is written on" (87, 95). Shortly after learning of the war, the couple heads north for Iola's graduation but are stopped short by an outbreak of yellow fever. The disease overcomes Leroy, "creeping slowly but insidiously into his life, dulling his brain, fevering his blood, and prostrating his strength" (92). He dies. His contaminated body cannot be brought home. After returning to the plantation, Marie discovers Leroy's cousin Alfred Lorraine has convinced a judge to declare a flaw in her manumission. Her family's disintegration begins.

I detail the events of Marie's marriage to Leroy to demonstrate that Harper purposefully forges links between "private" and "public" households, slavery and disease, to lay the basis for one of the novel's most fundamental arguments: any union tolerant of slavery—marital or national—is doomed to failure. Leroy's claim to be committed to the principle of Unionism is based in his belief that the North had always let the South be when it came to deciding matters concerning slavery. Both kinds of slave-based unions, private and public, marital and national, are also described in the novel as infected. Toward the end of Harper's narrative, Iola has a conversation with Dr. Gresham in which she likens slavery to "a fearful cancer eating into the nation's heart, sapping its vitality, and undermining its life" (216). Gresham agrees with Iola, adding that war "was the dreadful surgery by which the disease was eradicated. The cancer has been removed, but for years to come I fear we will have to deal with the effects of the disease" (216). In other writings, Harper refers to slavery as a "virus" and a "deadly gangrene."[61] If slavery is disease, it is then no coincidence that Eugene Leroy, a slaveholder, and Gresham, whose views on race are often shown to be retrograde and paternalistic, are associated with contagion, illness, and decay. Before Gresham proposes to Iola, he confides that he is "recovering from malaria and nervous prostration" (213). "Time and failing health," Harper writes, "had left their traces" on the aging man (214).

In Harper's work, whiteness is shown to be an illness both deadly and contagious, physically, morally, and politically. As a diseased man, Leroy transmits whiteness to his children by insisting their blackness be hidden from them, a decision Marie calls "oppressive" and a move that will prove lethal to their blackness (82). He also transmits, by example, a tolerance of slavery. Although the consequences of his death are dire, his death is necessary to "clean" Iola's household of "white intrusion," just as war became necessary to cleanse the nation of slavery. In rejecting Gresham (who also reappears as an amputee, his arm cut off in a gesture of symbolic castration) and subsequently choosing Latimer, Iola is proceeding in a manner her mother did not: rejecting privatization for public service, alienation for community, white for black, silence for speech, vitality for decay.

Reconciliation and Gender: Black Men, Black Women, and War

Harper's decision to spare her Iola the predestined fate of the "tragic mulatta" —ostracism or death—centers the novel by clearly drawing a line between a pre– and post–Civil War social order and by reconfiguring white nationalist hysteria about black male predatory behavior by redirecting miscegenationist desire to white men. The reversal also speaks to Harper's desire to create a viable, generative black female subjectivity. Accordingly, *Iola* ends quite differently from Harper's earlier work, *Minnie's Sacrifice*. In the conclusion of *Minnie's Sacrifice*, Harper makes two interesting statements: "While some of the authors of the present day have been weaving their stories about men marrying beautiful quadroon girls, who in doing so were lost to us socially, I conceived of one of that same class to whom I gave a higher, holier destiny" (91). Two paragraphs earlier,

Harper assesses the desire of the black race: "The greatest want, if I understand our wants aright, is not simply wealth, nor genius, nor mere intelligence but live men and earnest, lovely women" (my emphasis, 91). Harper's growing advocacy for black women in the years following *Minnie* (detailed in speeches such as "Coloured Women in America" [1878] and "Enlightened Motherhood" [1892]) reflects her increased understanding that not only must she give black women a higher fictive destiny than marriage to white men, but that they also, like black men, must live. While Minnie, Harper's earlier representative of black female subjectivity in her Civil War fiction, is "sacrificed" at the hands of the Klan, Iola will be spared any such fate.

In spite of Harper's undeniable commitment to doing literary justice to African American women, it would be an error to assume that Harper's work, particularly because it is what it is—a work of sentimental fiction by a black woman with a black female heroine—is largely unconcerned with the status of black men in the new nation. Tate notes that "seldom is there a story of the struggle for public male power in the female domestic fictions,"[62] which is certainly true for those domestic fictions in which the majority of narrative action takes place in homes or homesites such as schools. While Harper does use the household—the "women's sphere"—as a location of black generativity, nearly one-third of *Iola Leroy* takes place while the nation is at war, a site exterior to the home.

One reading of Harper's representation of a "public" and "masculine" site in a domestic fiction could suggest that writing about war allows Harper to complicate the public/private dichotomy by reinserting black women into the narrative of war, a goal that Susie King Taylor makes explicit in her autobiography, *Reminiscences of My Life in Camp* (1902). In her study of women Civil War writers, Elizabeth Young suggests that in spite of the numerous representations of black male heroism during wartime in *Iola Leroy*, the novel is essentially a female text; war becomes a feminized, domestic space because of Iola's presence near or on the battlefield. Young augments her reading of the novel's feminine center with an extended analysis of Harper's novel as an effort to find a "black maternal legacy" lost within the institution of slavery, restored only when Iola, her brother, and her uncle are reunited with their mothers after the war.[63]

While I do not entirely disagree with Young's argument, placing *Iola Leroy* within the context of the nineteenth-century sentimental war literature once again helps facilitate a more expansive reading of a novel whose gender politics are as complex as its racial politics. First of all, as Young also notes, the nineteenth-century war narrative was hardly the sole preserve of male writers. Augusta Jane Evan Wilson, a southerner and one of the most popular women writers of the midcentury, began publishing war novels before the conflict had ended. Robert Lively, the author of a study of over five hundred Civil War novels, credits women, particularly southern women writers such as Wilson and her contemporary Sarah J. C. Whittlesey, with governing the "earliest general conventions" of the Civil War novel, imprinting it with the sentimental discourse defining women's writing of that era.[64] By the time Harper wrote Iola Leroy, rendering the war in so called "feminine" terms was nothing new and certainly nothing radical. Moreover, in nineteenth-century sentimental war literature by women, war is a performance where those men and women who reflect the standard of citizenry valorized in that era are designated "heroes" or "heroines" and granted lives after war befitting of their show of courage and patriotism.

As in those works, in Iola Leroy the Civil War acts a national stage upon which blacks, female and male alike, "audition" for citizenship in the re-forming nation. I will argue, then, that while Harper does make room for women at the front, making the war "feminine" or an alternative domestic space is not her primary purpose. The insertion of war as a public site of the creation of black subjectivities outside the home permits Harper to provide a space where black men can achieve what Tate has called "public male power"; this power is earned and implemented in the same public arena occupied by whites, where "the world," as Harper writes in Minnie's Sacrifice, can "see the grandeur of . . . [black men's] courage and daring of their prowess" (66).

Furthermore, at war, where black men and black women worked together, this empowered black male subjectivity is conjoined with an empowered black female subjectivity. For Harper, who expresses worry in her writings about how the white nation viewed African American men, depicting black men as good, productive citizens—as good and productive as black women—was necessary to help form a conciliatory link to the larger white nation. In an 1871 poem, "An Appeal to the American People," Harper, speaking on the behalf of black men, asks for their inclusion based on their performance during the Civil War: "To your manhood we appeal."[65] In addressing a masculinized American populace, Harper asks the nation to consider blacks on the basis of the amount of "manliness" they have already offered the nation: "With your soldiers, side by side, / Helped we turn the battle's tide."[66]

In Iola Leroy, four black male characters help "turn the tide" of the Civil War. Aunt Linda's husband, the aging John Salters, reveals late in the novel that he had enlisted. Tom, though of "herculean strength," is not made a soldier because of his unnamed "physical defects," but he becomes a "helper," setting up camps, scouting, and tending to the wounded (40). Harry and Robert emerge as well-respected members of their troops. These men comprise Harper's fictive representation of the 186,000 black men who served as soldiers for the North. More than latecomers to the war, black soldiers played an integral part in conquering the South: they were the first to take possession of the key city of Charleston and among the first to seize control of Richmond.[67] Captain Sibyl, Robert's white commander, is moved enough by the overall performance of black troops to make this statement: "I hope . . . that the time will come when some faithful historian will chronicle all the deeds of daring and service these [black] people have performed during this struggle, and give them credit" (130).

As a chronicler of the Civil War, Harper certainly does much to reposition the black male—both common and elite—as essential to the success of the Union army. If all of Harper's warring men are courageous for their participation in war, it is Iola's family members, in particular Harry and Robert, who exemplify the citizen-soldier. They stand out not simply for their bravery but, just as important, for their intelligence, an essential combination in Harper's vision of a generative black masculinity.

In the chapter that most greatly elaborates on Harper's ideal of a black masculinity based in brain and brawn, "Robert and his Company," Harper uses a camp setting in which Robert engages in lengthy exchanges with his white superior officers, intermingling fraternally. This black-white fraternalism deeply contrasts with the white exclusionary fraternalism of reconciliation culture and underscores an irony Harper emphasizes in the novel and in her speeches: that while white southerners were bent on seceding from the Union and forsaking their countrymen, "black men rall[ied] around the Stars and Stripes" (36), more devoted to the Union and to their fellow Americans than the "secesh." Robert is depicted as his superiors' comrade and their equal, making astute commentary on northern strategy in the war, sharing information about early American history he gained reading as an autodidact, and, importantly, narrating an anecdote about Uncle Jack, a slave, which allows Harper to position Robert as an adept cultural interpreter of "the folk."[68] He can, therefore, do all that the white man can, and more: provide the crucial form of mediation that will be necessary as poor and uneducated blacks rely on the "uplifters" to negotiate their place in a racially reconciled postemancipation nation.

While visiting the homestead after the war, Robert states a need for "young folks to keep their brains clear, and their right arms strong, to fight the battles of life manfully" (170). This comment demonstrates that Harper is not merely interested in how black men appear on the national public stage during the war but is also concerned with the fate of black men in postbellum America. As a member of the clergy in Iola Leroy claims, black men are "growing away from the influence of the church and drifting into prisons" (259). Before Iola delivers her paper on the "Education of Mothers," Lucille Delany insists upon the need for "enlightened fathers" to further the progress of the black race. Another woman adds, "We can[not] begin too early to teach our boys to be manly" (253). When Dr. Latimer asks Iola to be his wife, she expresses a wish that he "prove a good soldier . . . when there is no battle to fight" (269). Harper's new black masculinity is predicated on a manhood cast in language of wartime bravery; in her postwar vision, soldiering, literally and figuratively, becomes a fundamental component of a rehabilitated black manhood.

While tales of black sacrifice and valor during the Civil War are certainly not all mythical, Harper's picture of black service is missing critical components. Preserving the lore surrounding the enlistment of black men—that all who could fight did, and that only those who were not able to fight did not—enables Harper to construct black men as heroic defenders of their own people and, more essentially, as unhesitant patriots prepared to give themselves to the greater good of the nation, the portrait of the black soldier that would eventually become an archetype in African American war literature. At the beginning of the Civil War, many men did rush to serve, but others held back, waiting for an end to slavery to be declared the primary purpose of the war. The Colored A.M.E Church asked that blacks not serve a nation that had systemically denied them liberty.[69] As the war became increasingly a war of attrition, black soldiers were often drafted from groups of contraband, frequently forced to leave their families behind. There was at least one grievance filed against the Grand Army of the Republic for pressing African American men into service:

> We were pressed into Service by force of numbers without any Law civil or militry to Sanction it[.] Many of us were knocked down and beaten Like dogs[,] others were dragged from our homes in the dead hour . . . and forced into a Prison without Law or Justice. Others were tied and thrown into the river and held there untill forced to subscribe to the Oath. Some of us were tied up by the thumbs all night[,] we were starved[,] beaten . . . and but one alternative to join the service or nearly suffer death.[70]

Harper also does little in the way of honestly depicting the numerous indignities suffered by black men who enlisted, willingly or not. Brown's refusal to continue recruiting black soldiers because of discrepancies between the pay of white and black men was more than justified. Black "soldiers" toiled as laborers, digging trenches and building fortifications—doing the work refused by white soldiers—all the while routinely subjected to insults from Yankees who simply felt it was unfitting to serve with blacks (something Harper does mention to help dispel the myth of the North as the bigotry-free promised land). The discrepancy in work detail and pay were often compounded by the differences in camp conditions. Because black troops were more stationary than whites, they fell victim to diseases at twice the rate of white northern soldiers; one out of eleven of the thirty-six thousand blacks who died in service died from illness. They also received less medical care and of a poorer quality.[71] Made into a nurse in the South Georgia Islands, where she was aiding the Union forces, Harriet Tubman in fact remarked that wounded white men were routinely sent to nearby hospitals, while black men were often sent back to camp where volunteers like Tubman herself attended to them. A former slave who had enlisted in the army wrote President Lincoln with his concerns:

> I have a wife and 3 Children . . . and my wife is sick. . . . And she has sent to me for money And i have No way of getting Eny money to send to her Because I cant Get my Pay. . . . We are not treated Like we are soldiers in coleague Atall we are Deprived of the most importances things we Need in health and sickness Both That surficinct Food And quality As for the sick it is A shocking thing to Look into thire conditions Death must be thire Doom when once they have to go to the Hospital Never Return Again such is the medical Assistance of the 20th Rig n.y.[72]

Returning to the notion I raised in the introduction of this chapter, I would like to argue that Harper's decision to present a tidied, romanticized version of black male participation in the Civil War serves as an attempt to exercise control over the "reading" of one racially traumatic moment from the vantage point of another. Kali Tal, a cultural critic who has studied psychorhetorical responses to trauma engendered by war and sexual violence, posits "mythologization" as one form of "cultural coping."[73] The result is something larger than an individual interpretation of a traumatic event: "Mythologization works by reducing a traumatic event to a set of standardized narratives (twice- and thrice-told tales that come to represent 'the story' of the trauma) turning it from a frightening and uncontrollable event into a contained and predictable narrative."[74] The "story" becomes codified through repetition, the repetition leaving no space for the emergence of competing narratives. What I have labeled Harper's romantic "creation narrative" varies little from the way in which her contemporary, George Washington Williams, characterized black military participation in the Civil War in the introduction to his influential work *A History of Negro Troops in the Rebellion: 1861–1865* (1888),[75] which may have very well shaped Harper's own descriptions: "The part enacted by the Negro soldier in the war of the Rebellion is the romance of North American history . . . from clanking chains to clashing arms; from passive submission to the cruel curse of slavery to the brilliant aggressiveness of a free soldier; from a chattel to a person; from the shame of degradation to the glory of military exaltation; and from deep obscurity to fame and martial immortality."[76] The horror of the Civil War—a horror made only worse if a participant were black—is somehow assuaged as Harper re-presents the story of heroism and "birth" over other less comforting versions of events.

Black rehabilitative narratives of war must of course carefully control what happens to black bodies during warfare. As with Brown's work, analyzing the way Harper deploys the wound is therefore critical to understanding what I earlier called Harper's "instrumental" interpretation of the Civil War. In thinking about the meaning of the novel's ending, it is crucial to note that Iola's family is presented intact and ready, by means of matrimony, to become regenerative. Harper's reconstitution of family is a gesture that quite obviously stands in opposition to Brown's, who, as we recall, leaves Clotelle as a war widow and a black single mother whose child has been obliterated from the novel by its end. The fatal injury of Brown's hero is, I argued, an attempt to introduce African American historical trauma into his novel by disabling the black male body and disabling, therefore, the black family's future generativity. Harper's familial reassembly, made possible only by safeguarding the heroic black male body, can be viewed therefore as another means of avoiding the invocation of trauma by remembering a black collective body that had been dismembered by slavery and that remained, despite the promise of the war, "wounded," to repeat Douglass's characterization.

Interestingly enough, Harper's tendency to romanticize black male service does not lead her to protect her male characters wholly from experiencing violence to the body. Harry is "severely wounded" and even "forced to leave his ranks for a bed in the hospital" (191). But his wound is sentimentalized, his "sickness and suffering" largely alleviated when he finds his mother "tenderly bent over" his bed. Still, while he "rapidly recovered," Harper writes that he was "too disabled to re-enter the army" (191–92). What is telling here is that despite the "severity" of his wound and the subsequent damaging effect it had on his body, Harper does not even attempt to describe it. Robert, too, suffers a "flesh wound" (169), yet again, no description is offered, no location on the body named. The wounds remain dislocated, unanchored, abstract, and therefore materially separate from the black body they should "realistically" mark.

The only death comes to the already physically "defective" Tom, who is described as "black as black can be," is likened to a "Pagan," and who believes that the Yankees have horns until Robert corrects him (44, 40). With his damaged form, dark body, and childlike ignorance, he cannot possibly represent the evolved black masculinity Harper presents as counterargument to accusations of racial backwardness and demonstrates the extent to which Harper understood disability—"defect"—as a primary ordering concept in racially hierarchical processes. As we know, in racialist thinking, bodily "regularity" was a characteristic of whiteness: a symmetry of form and figure, a "refinement" of features. Harper consistently uses this vocabulary to describe her "white" blacks, her heroine, Iola Leroy, in particular. The "irregularity" of Tom's body therefore marks him immediately as different, as "othered" within a group already designated "other," signifying his distance physically and intellectually from the mulatto characters. This irregularity also makes him expendable. Becoming instead Harper's "martyr," Tom dies saving his superiors, his body easily disposed of with little political or narrative complication. Like Aunt Linda's loathsome "niggers," he does not survive to disrupt either Harper's eugenicized notions of blackness or her idealized presentation of masculinity, both embodied by the heroic mulattos Robert and Harry. Avoiding a realistic or detailed description of Harry's and Robert's injuries is therefore essential for her project: their wounded bodies could be too easily conflated with Tom's physically defective one, evoking the meanings that a damaged black body like his had come to signify. Tom's death remains therefore Harper's small sacrificial offering to the "real" consequences of war.

Noting the absence of "action" taking place on the battlefield in Iola Leroy, Don Dingledine suggests that Harper might have felt it unnecessary to portray masculinist heroics because black men had already been put through the ultimate "test" of their masculinity during slavery.[77] While Dingledine's analysis fails to specify what is meant by "action," I doubt Harper's unwillingness to depict action comes from her feeling satisfied that her reading public understood black men as already properly masculine. I do suspect, however, that the reason Harper carefully averts depictions of violent action on the part of black men—in other words, killing and injuring—stems in part from her steadfast belief that fiction should aid in the uplift of African Americans, which requires they conform to the standards of "civility," a concern Young also notes. If the wound allows civilization to spill from the body, killing, even if socially sanctioned, risks placing the offending body outside of civilization, a point I raised earlier in endeavoring to explain why the "threat" carried within Jerome's messianic blackness remains merely a threat, a sign of the slave-revolutionary's violent power, but a power that his hero never uses.

Antiwar critics often argue that moments of state-authorized violence must be recuperated if a belief in the benevolence in the nation-state is to be maintained. The nation and its populace are to regard wars as anomalies, or as the necessary unleashing of force in defense of national principles, boundaries, ways of being. The white nationalist narratives implement this strategy, turning the most vile acts against blacks into stories of white rescue, manifestations of white love. In essence, these acts become sentimental. If we think of Harper's romantic presentation of the Civil War as an effort to rescue a "wounded" black American history, we might then say that to deflect offensive violence away from African American men as they fought for the future of their race is also to sentimentalize killing by default, even as it is not actually represented, in absentia, as it were. What we are left with in terms of "real" violence in *Iola Leroy* is the impression that white men were made to slaughter one another in a divine plan to end slavery; and in the war's wake, ruthless racists unleashed violence against African Americans in an effort to prevent interracial reconciliation. While this impression does perpetuate a notion that all violence stems from the "white Other," a subject I will later explore more deeply in analyzing World War I and World War II narratives by black American men, it also corrects white nationalist interpretations of the Civil War and Reconstruction, and in so doing, posits an alternative black historical and political realism squarely within a sentimental landscape. At the same time, Harper employs "cultural realism." Through appropriating the tropes and scenarios the nationalist fiction writers used to make interregional white reconciliation seem imperative—such as the fear of black sexual contamination and politically divided households—she endeavors to arouse anxieties that similar fates could befall black communities separated by racial castes and an affinity for whites. "As did most survivors of the Civil War," Foster has written, "African American writers saw themselves as architects for the rebuilding of the nation, who would salvage the best of its past, make the most of its present, and integrate its future."[78] For Harper, the Civil War and the promising new beginning Radical Reconstruction seemed to offer stood as twinned symbols of the fruits of interracial cooperation and fraternity. Together, they were the best of the black past and an antidote to the terrifying present, and, even more significantly, they gave her the necessary hope that she might live to see the integrated future for which she had worked ceaselessly.

The Fanatics

At the turn of the century, Paul Laurence Dunbar, widely acclaimed at that time as an accomplished and prolific poet, published two novels, *The Uncalled* (1898) and *The Love of Landry* (1900).[79] Though quite different in subject matter, both novels center on white protagonists, and both were published to generally unfavorable reviews. Undeterred, in 1901 he published yet another. Set in the town of Dorbury, Ohio, a fictionalized representation of Dayton, Dunbar's hometown, *The Fanatics* follows three white families ripped apart over political differences raised by the Civil War, taking the theme of a house divided and rendering it in dizzying triplicate. Stephen Van Doren, a staunch Democrat, rejects his son Robert for refusing to align himself with either the northern or the southern cause. Bradford Waters, an equally ardent Republican, lauds his son Tom's choice to join the Union army, but disowns his daughter Mary for her unwillingness to break off her romance with Robert, a son of the "enemy." Waters does, however, approve of a relationship between his son Tom and Nannie Woods, a young woman devoted to the Union. Colonel Alexander Stewart, a displaced southerner, denounces his Unionist son Walter as a traitor to his heritage and moves back to Virginia to support the Confederacy. Waters loses his son; Van Doren's returns with an arm missing after having joined the war to assuage his father. The one black who can be considered a character in the novel, the town crier "Nigger Ed," is ridiculed as a degenerate until he joins the war, nursing the dying and wounded of Dorbury. Ed is then "welcomed" into the community. At the close of the conflict, all families reconcile, recognizing the unnecessary price all paid for their "fanaticism."

From this synopsis alone it may appear that Dunbar has abandoned his novel to the narrative pleasures of an unrestrained sentimentality. Certainly, Dunbar's novelistic landscape, strewn with broken homes and fractured relationships, seems a bit crowded, even by the genre's standards. Many of the more recent assessments of the novel, written a good decade before the critical recuperation of sentimental literature in the 1980s, struggle with the text, viewing it as a "primitive" or inartistic work of fiction, recognizing in The Fanatics a political message, but one buried too far beneath the formulaic surface to be uncovered. These critics, however, have missed an important point. In Dunbar's Civil War novel, the medium is the message. Nearly immediately, in fact, the writer calls attention to the use of melodrama, a defining convention of sentimentalism. Of one discussion taking place among the white characters, the narrator offers this wry comment: "It was a strange talk and a strange scene for these self-contained people who thought so little of their emotions; but their fervor gave a melodramatic touch to all they did that at another time must have appeared ridiculous" (27).

Edmund Wilson contends that war is particularly vulnerable to political myth making simply because bloodshed demands explanation.[80] The Civil War, longer and more brutal than either the North or the South had anticipated, required that each side couch its purposes in a rhetoric that roused support to a fevered pitch. For the Union, Wilson continues, slavery "supplied the militant Union North with the rabble-rousing moral issue which is necessary in every modern war to make the conflict appear as melodrama"[81]—the "good" North vying for dominion over the "bad" South. The threat of the demise of slavery provided the Confederacy with circumstances that could be characterized in equally agitated language. The Civil War, then, as political "melodrama" became easily translated into literary melodrama, precisely because depicting the Civil War in that manner was as overly reductive and romantic as the formulaic plots that sentimental literature, in its least imaginative form, had offered the early American and nineteenth-century reading public.

In noting the "fervor" that gives a "melodramatic touch" to what the people of Dorbury "did"—what they did, of course, is lend emotional fuel to the war— Dunbar thus makes a sharp statement that antedates Wilson's observation. By prompting the reader to consider how this heightened state of emotion would have appeared "at another time" and by denaturalizing the effusions of "these people . . . who thought so little of their emotions" normally, the writer reveals an artifice in the sentiment that prompted the characters to take sides in the conflict, a revelation that threatens to undo the artifice of Dunbar's novel itself and, ultimately, the artifice of the entire Civil War.

After all, the logic of literary melodrama demands a polarization that is often missing in its "referent": the "real" world. Melodrama finds it purpose in positing a morally instructive universe in which good triumphs over evil; this triumph is necessarily predicated on a conviction that binaries—right and wrong, good and bad, heroes and villains—do exist and are, most importantly, *actual* forces in the world.[82] The hyperbolic emotional reactions that mark a work as melodramatic are exaggerations of natural responses to the manifestations of good and evil within the text. One must overcome the other; no synthesis emerges from the tension created by the two. The "middle," as Peter Brooks explains it, remains expressly "excluded."[83] In this understanding of melodrama, sentimental reconciliation narratives, which rely on constructing the "middle," inherently transgress the very melodramatic logic they invoke. This is not to say that there are no heroes and villains in these war narratives and that emotion does not permeate their pages. However, the major assertion these novels make—that the war was more of an interregional "miscommunication" than a profound political conflict—belies the authenticity of the emotions that pulled the regions apart. A subplot in Dunbar's novel exemplifies this point.

Walter Stewart, the young Unionist, has to defy his father in fighting for the Yankees. Certain that he must stand by his principles, he anguishes as he watches his family leave Ohio for Virginia. However, when his father becomes ill, Walter immediately abandons the army to go south but is captured by the Confederates. When he declares his relationship to the well-positioned Stewart family, the Confederates take him home. There, the family is reconciled, and when his father dies, content to see his son come home, Walter becomes the head of his father's plantation. "A unionist on parole" and a man who will eventually oversee his father's black workers, he realizes he was neither "with" the southern people "nor against them"; Dunbar writes that Walter feels "a sense of peace, even joy at the reconciliation" with his family (154, 150). The transition from rupture to reconciliation, from Union soldier to southern planter, happens far too easily for the rupture to have stemmed from any deep-seated convictions about the war. Walter's heightened emotional state about the Union was confused with genuine political concern, and when his emotions subside, so go his politics. Here and elsewhere in the novel, Dunbar shows that melodramatic sentiment—fanaticism—is not a pedagogical tool pointing to right and wrong within a morally instructive universe; it merely appears to operate that way within a universe that is morally inert. There is neither "good" nor "bad," no Union vs. Confederate, no abolitionist vs. slaveholder. There is only and always the "middle," which proves a dangerous space for black Americans.

Dunbar takes that dangerous middle space and places it at the center of his novel. And while I cannot claim that Dunbar's brief but telling announcement of sentimentalism's operations at the onset of the work signal overt satire, what I have labeled Dunbar's parodic, allegorical use of sentimentalism in The Fanatics—his "cultural realism"—is evidenced in a subtle yet persistent ironic distance placed between the writer and both the subject matter and the literary framework he uses to narrate it. Brooks claims that the emotional hyperbole in melodrama is the human condition made legible. I will assert that the emotional excess in The Fanatics is sentimentalism writ large, so large that it becomes distorted. This distortion calls the reader's attention to one trope most specifically: the divided house metaphor, and even more specifically, the divided house metaphor in the southern nationalist postwar narratives, with its emphasis on the "excluded" and exclusive middle.

Divided Houses and Homosocial Fraternity

I again return to The Clansman to provide a framework for my argument. The Civil War, in Dixon's mind, was a lesson, a course at "the University of Hell," where the "great North" and "equally wise" South enrolled for the express purpose of learning an essential lesson of domesticity: how to get along under the same roof (4). Unsurprisingly, both sides discovered that they could fare much better without troublesome blacks in the way. Thomas Dixon casts Lincoln in the role of teacher, a "Friend of the South" whose dream of a purely white nation died prematurely with his assassination. "I have urged the colonization of the negroes," he tells Congressman Stoneman (a representative of Thaddeus Stevens), "and I shall continue until it is accomplished. . . . There is no room . . . for two distinct races of blacks and whites" (46). Lincoln continues his justification for his scheme to expel blacks from the United States: "God never meant that the Negro should leave his habitat or the white man invade his home. Our violation of this law is written in two centuries of shame and blood. And the tragedy will not be closed until the black man is returned to his home" (47). Dixon's Lincoln—far from the Great Emancipator—is the man who in historical actuality congregated with black leaders shortly before the Emancipation Proclamation to lay forth his plans to send blacks to Central America. The language Dixon's Lincoln wields in speaking of slavery, the war, and the war's aftermath— "room," "home," "habitat"—reinforces the domestic rhetoric linguistically structuring sentimental literature. The path this Lincoln says the South should take to render the nation whole again—"come back home" (49)—is the same avenue used to solve the myriad of problems, both "private" and "public," explored in sentimental texts.

With the recent emphasis on uncovering the political subtexts submerged beneath the melodramatic storylines of sentimental fiction, it has become easy to forget that the genre succeeded in securing audiences precisely because it was "sentimental," unapologetically tugging on the heartstrings of the American public. Accordingly, the effectiveness of the divided household trope used in postwar reconciliation narratives relies on constructing the Civil War as a transgression of emotional, not political, "law," violating what Joanne Dobson claims is the "principle theme of the sentimental text . . . the desire for bonding":[84] "Violation, actual or threatened, of the affectional bond generates the primary tension in the sentimental text . . . in the sentimental vision, the greatest threat is the tragedy of separation, of severed human ties: the death of a child, lost love, failed or disrupted family connections, distorted or unsympathetic community or the loss of hope of reunion and/or reconciliation in the hereafter."[85]

To foreshorten the lingering "tragedy of separation" caused by the Civil War, the broken bonds of affection that must be mended under the roof of the national home are bonds between statesmen, fraternal bonds, bonds between men. When tempered by the language of domesticity, the political, professional, and social alliances among white men—so necessary to exercising hegemonic dominance over the black body—seem distinctly more benign than if these alliances were constructed in the mercenary language of the marketplace, the calculated language of government, or even the frankly racist language of the lynch mob. Ostensibly, these men, so worried about the "domestic," want neither money nor power, but merely a nation they can all call "home." More mask than metaphor, the reunited household turns out to be a place where white men hide the "baser" aspects of the desire they have for one another. These men are not performing some self-domesticating ritual by carving out a national homesite for themselves;

instead, they are creating a closeted male space within the white national home in which they can decide how to (re)domesticate blacks, or, in the words of a Dixon character, how to "manage the Negro" (163). In an even more obfuscating maneuver, this desire for masculine bonding is easily and safely rerouted to the heterosexual courtship plot. The subsequent establishment of the real material heterosexual home in the works is not, therefore, the primary vehicle for national reunion in the nationalist texts; however, it does become a potent symbol of its rewards: a romance between men and women spawned by the male unions created in the larger national home. The true love, as A Romance of the Ku Klux Klan, the subtitle of Dixon's novel indicates, is homosocial.

In his study Fiction Fights the Civil War, Lively writes of The Fanatics, asserting its "literary superiority" but concluding, nevertheless, that the book is "distinguished in no way . . . from stories by white novelists on the same theme."[86] In one sense, Lively is absolutely correct. Like Dixon, Dunbar takes great pains in his novel to show just how essential fraternal bonding is to white national generativity, the continuing project of creating and keeping homes and households that reproduce the exclusionary whiteness essential for consolidating white power. The first fractured relation in the text occurs when two long-standing patriarchs in the town, Bradford Waters, "a typical Yankee pioneer," and Stephen Van Doren, "a gentlemanly old man" from "the old South," heatedly debate the South's decision to secede from the nation (4). The argument becomes emotionally explosive, and the two men are forcibly restrained from one another. Waters' daughter Mary and Van Doren's son Bob watch on in disbelief, hand in hand: the two will later be forbidden to court because of their fathers' political differences.

Dunbar cleverly entitles this opening chapter "Love and Politics," emphasizing the sentimental novel's penchant for interweaving the two. What is important here is that Dunbar grants narrative primacy to the rupture of the affectional bond that occurs between the male friends, both widowed, and allots the young couple a secondary role. Most of the relationships that will come undone in The Fanatics are male—Waters and Van Doren, Van Doren and his son, Walter Stewart and his son. The Civil War, then, is an event in which men who should be engaging in harmonious relationships are instead distracted by fighting over who will control the fate of the black body. The interregional and interpolitical heterosexual love affairs thus become ancillary to the problem of homosocial national reconciliation. An afterthought, they are, in fact, made possible only when and if men of opposing viewpoints work out their differences. The affair between Van Doren's son and Waters' daughter is validated when the end of the war brings their fathers' quarreling to a halt, and Stewart's son meets and weds the southerner Dolly when he returns home to be by his father's side. Significantly, Dunbar attempts to lessen the sociopolitical significance of these heterosexual relationships by making them impervious to the political disunity that left the male relationships in ruins.

In examining the use of two collusive elements in Dunbar's novel—the trope of a house divided and the figure of the black body—I will argue that Dunbar's reproduction of the excluded and excluding middle maintained by homosocial national reconciliation, the mending of political bonds between white men, northern and southern, "abolitionists" and "slaveholders," in nationalist texts unravels the seams in a war-to-postwar transition that the writer strives to present as seamless. In Dunbar's Civil War "middle," slavery is not positioned as the cause of the conflict; the causes are ambiguous, at best. Accordingly, the North and South, despite their differing identities as "free" and "slave," respectively, are not shown to be greatly divergent politically at the onset of the war; after the war, Dunbar implies that the two regions have good reason to form an ideological merger: neither ever intended to enfranchise blacks fully and equally into the "new" nation.

As much as this might coincide with race nationalist narratives on its surface, Dunbar's understanding diverges at a significant juncture, pointing to an important contradiction in the plan to bar blacks from an inclusive citizenship. The Fanatics seeks to demonstrate that while neither North nor South purported to want African Americans in their new national home, a reunited national household exclusive of blacks will never be realized for a single, significant reason: the fantasy of a political reunion predicated on expulsion denies the very necessity of the black body to both regions' economic, political, and ideological enterprises. Dunbar characterizes the North and South as too wedded to prewar political identities to give them up easily—the North needs to continue to see itself as "savior" to take the upper hand in the reconstruction of the South and industrial expansionism; the South needs to see itself as "master" to perpetuate the domination of blacks. The Civil War, in Dunbar's mind, will continue long past Lee's surrender, the North and the South incessantly fighting over the position of the black body that provides the basis for this distinction, however imaginary the distinction itself might be.

Urban Darky

The name Dunbar gives the representative of this contested black body, "Nigger Ed," recalls the self-conscious act of naming in Our Nig, Harriet Wilson's 1859 novel.[87] "Nig," as she is called by the whites in the novel, is the name the author gives herself: *Our Nig* by " 'Our Nig.' " In the work's very construction—a semiautobiographical novel told in the third person—the author points directly to her own objectified status, going so far as to create a character who exhibits minstrel-like behaviors. Similarly, "Nigger Ed," called so by the townspeople and the author, is less human than object, less a character than a caricature. The "town drunkard," "the bell-ringer," Ed skirts around the narrative edges of the novel, appearing only periodically, and then as a generally disruptive figure, unintentionally creating confusion, consternation—or laughter—wherever he appears. He is, then, a stock plantation darky, but "free," urban, and living in the North, in a plight much like the one Wilson crafts for her heroine, made clear by the full title of her work—*Our Nig; or Sketches from the Life of a Free Black, In a Two-Story White House, North. Showing That Slavery's Shadows Fall Even There.* Dunbar offers a description of Ed early in the novel: "The servant is always curious; the negro servant particularly so, and to the negro the very atmosphere of this silent house, the constrained attitude of the family were pregnant with mystery. . . . Ed had a picturesque knack for lying, and the tale that resulted from his speculations was a fabric worthy of his weaver" (38–39).

Picturesque, blundering, gossipy: for writers of plantation fiction, the comic darky was a useful creation. Primarily a product of the southern nationalist imagination, the darky reflected the amalgam of anxiety and desires of whites who needed, Leonard Cassuto reminds us, "a contented participant in a pastoral fantasy."[88] Part domesticated "animal," part "culturally stunted" African, part child, part entertainer, the minstrelesque black posed no threat physically, sexually, politically, or intellectually.[89] Thus an angered Walter Stewart can say that he would rather his daughter marry "Nigger Ed, the town crier, than cross my blood with that Van Doren breed" (10), because of its very impossibility. Ed, as a darky, stands as an already castrated figure; exclusion from the world of white homosocial relations corresponds to an exclusion from white heterosexual circuitry. This manner of literary containment in prewar plantation fiction offered much-needed relief from the incriminations and implications of miscegenation, of course; but of equal importance, containment also reduced anxiety stemming from the real threat of a discontented slave population that mounted hundreds of rebellions, many bloody, against the whites who repressed them. It is no surprise, then, that during the war, popular southern fiction attempted to diminish the threat of black service by making African American soldiers into "Sambos." As Alice Fahs notes in *The Imagined Civil War*, southern writers "imagin[ed] black men refusing to fight, kidnapped by Yankees, and always eager to 'belong to somebody.' "[90] In postwar reconciliation literature, as I have mentioned, the comic darky was used to paint a picture of freemen as hapless and lazy watermelon eaters, unfit for the franchise. Absent a clear referent in the "real world," the darky became ideologically overdetermined in southern nationalist literature, readily mobilized in whatever capacity political circumstances necessitated.

It is significant then, that Dunbar takes this figure—the one Harper needed to kill off—and makes him the sole representative of black military service in the novel. However, Dunbar does not have "Nigger Ed" enlist as a soldier but has him enter into the army as an officer's servant. After Ed has joined league with his townspeople in the Union forces, he stumbles upon a debate:

> Another speaker, half-hearted and little trusted rose to address the assembly. He was a fiery demagogue and depended for his influence upon his power to work upon the passions of the lower element. His audience knew this. He knew it, and for an instant, paused embarrassment. Just at that moment, "Nigger Ed" strolled up and joined the crowd. The eye of the orator took him in and lighted with sudden inspiration. Here was all the text he needed. Raising his tall, spare from, he pointed in silence until every face was turned upon the negro. Then he said, "Gentleman, it is for such as that and worse that you are shedding your brothers' blood." Without another word he sat down. It was the most convincing speech he had ever made. The negro had put a power into the words of a man who otherwise would have been impotent. (180)

Dunbar's narrator makes the clear analysis himself. The black body becomes text, "putting power into the words" of whites.

Paul H. Buck's 1937 assessment of the emergence of southern reconciliation narratives in The Road to Reunion: 1865–1900 demonstrates just how necessary the black body was in "putting power in the words" of whites, giving white southern literature a raison d'être. Buck describes the South as "an unproductive literary section before 1860," then positions plantation writer Irwin Russell as the "postwar discoverer of the Negro character in [southern] literature": "'Christmas Night in the Quarters' (1878) stands on the threshold of greatness. Certainly Russell's Negro is the type familiar to Harris and Page—the superstitious, mercurial fellow . . . possessed of shrewd bits of homely wisdom, fond of the banjo and the 'possum, happy irresponsible, and good natured."[91]

The greater part of Buck's examination of post-1860 work assesses southern literary output in the same way he treats Russell's book: almost exclusively on the basis of how well southern writers used black stereotypes in their fiction.[92] While Buck never directly attributes the development of New Southern literature to the "discovery" of "negro" character, this is precisely the argument he makes by placing blacks at the center of his analysis. If the economic success of southern

agrarian society depended on African Americans as laborers, southern nationalist fiction depended on them as characters; the pen simply replaces the whip as a
tool to force submissive behavior. Buck's interpretation of southern literary development exposes another facet of the nationalist writer's extratextual dependence on slavery: the forced slave performance. Assuring his readers that the
scene he renders is "true," Martin Delany presents a disturbing rendition of this
phenomenon in Blake. Promising to show his company a "sight," a slave owner
brings out a young boy: "With a peculiar swing of the whip, bringing the lash
down upon a certain spot on the exposed skin . . . the boy commenced to whistle
almost like a thrush; another cut changed it to a song, another to a hymn, then a
pitiful prayer . . . to oaths which would make a Christian shudder; after which he
laughed outright; then from the fullness of his soul he cried: 'O, maussa, I's sick!
Please stop little!' casting up gobs of hemorrhage."[93]

Cassuto analyzes forced slave performance within the Hegelian master/slave
dialectic: masters needed to delude themselves into believing that slaves coerced
into displays wanted, indeed begged, for recognition and had therefore asked the
master to assume the superior position of the approving or disapproving spectator. The master's identity as master was bound to the slave's self-identification as
slave; eliciting recognition in a "voluntary" show for the master was one means
masters could believe this self-identification had taken place. In this conceptualization, slavery itself—not just dancing, singing, and clowning at the request of
the slaveholder—was a "forced performance," a subject Saidiya Hartman has
also treated.[94] Masking their feelings about the institution and modifying their
behaviors accordingly, slaves played, as Cassuto writes, "the part of [willing]
industrious worker."[95] For the master to remain master, to retain his subject
position, and therefore his or her identity, the slave's performance was integral.
Thus divested of the title of "master" after the war, southern nationalist writers
coerce blacks who have retired from the stage into giving a final performance: the
perpetuation of the nationalists' identity rested on it.

Dunbar understands that his black character is not only caught in a master/
slave configuration perpetuated by southern nationalist literature, he is also
trapped within a complex system of sociolinguistic subterfuge that simultaneously seeks to refuse the presence of the black body while using it, nevertheless. Throughout the novel, the monologues and arguments white characters
make about the reasons for war are stumbling and weak; characters repeatedly
refer to their "principles," but these principles are unconvincingly articulated.
When a friend asks Mary whether the war is for "those people," she replies, "Oh,
no, not at all. . . . It's for the Union, and against states' rights, and—and—
everything like that" (24). Denying the black body has rendered her virtually

speechless; her words are hesitant and faltering. Conversely, the crisp, succinct statement made by the "fiery demagogue" invoking the black body facilitates an oratorical command previously unknown him. The speech creates a fury, with Republicans, Democrats, and Copperheads fighting one another, all claiming that no issue involving blacks would ever turn countrymen against each other: "One side was furious that blood should be spilled for such as the negro bell-ringer, while the other was equally incensed at being accused of championing his cause" (180). This is Dunbar's Civil War reenactment. At this gathering, as in the larger nation this gathering represents, the black body has been allowed to create chaos, with those involved all the while steadfastly denying that the black body has anything to do with the conflict at all.

Through the dissonant sounds of the debate that ensues, a unified message manages to emerge: "Both sides hated" blacks (181). Even Harper, looking through her "rose-hued" glasses, recognized that the "good" North/"bad" South binary did not hold. Dunbar imagines Ed as a "shuttlecock" that is not to land on either side of the geographical or political net (181). To make his point clear, Dunbar includes two narrative digressions that illumine northern antagonism toward blacks. The first, a chapter entitled "The Contrabands," undoes myths of white northern saintliness but also tackles a taboo subject in the era of racial uplift: the deep-rooted class antagonism between the free northern "negro aristocracy" and newly freed slaves (167). The term "freed" is only accurate in the most technical sense. Before the Emancipation Proclamation had been issued, General David Butler declared that southern slaves be treated as any other property seized during the state of war. As Robert Johnson quite aptly explains in *Iola Leroy*, "It means that if two armies are fighting and the horses of one run away, the other has a right to take them. And it is just the same if a slave runs away from the Secesh to the Union lines. He is called a contraband, just the same as if he were an ox or a horse" (16).

Just as Harper makes it clear that the "chattel" slave owned by the southern slave owner becomes no more than an "ox" possessed by the northern soldier, Dunbar draws an equally unromantic image of the "contraband" who have sought haven in the mythical land of freedom. The contraband are described by the narrator as "negroes of all ages and conditions . . . worrying and embarrassing the soldiers . . . conducting themselves like the great, helpless, irresponsible children that they were . . . wandering in the darkness of their ignorance" (155–56). The narrator continues: "the word 'Contraband' became a menace to the whites and a reproach to the blacks" (160). Rejected by the black church despite their plea—" 'We's all colo'ed togethah' "—the "black horde" is victimized by the mob violence growing more prevalent in the northern states (163, 167). The leader of the mob asks the contrabands: "why don't you people stay where you belong?" (169) In the second narrative digression elucidating racism in the North, Dunbar uses an aside to insert an embittered but accurate account of Ohio's reluctance to raise black regiments until late in the recruiting process. As a result of the state's hesitation, many blacks enlisted in Massachusetts: "When the chief executive of Ohio was consulted, he was so far from objecting to the use of his negroes by another state, he expressed himself to the effect that he would be glad if they would take 'every damned nigger out of the state' " (186). The flow of contraband into the "free states" and the decision to arm blacks unleashed prejudices that northern whites had heretofore kept relatively quiet. Moreover, Lincoln's position that blacks could not be let into the nation on an equal footing with whites resonated among whites, even some abolitionists who believed that, while bondage was wrong, blacks were nonetheless their inferiors.

In an ironic twist that blurs the distinctions between the regions even further, Dunbar has Stephen Van Doren, the embodiment of the manners, mores, and convictions of the South, act as rescuer of the contrabands. His paternal instincts, well honed from years of living below the Mason-Dixon Line, make it natural, in the character's mind, to take charge: "he understood these people, who have for two centuries been the particular wards of the South . . . and believed all these blacks must eventually go back into slavery whence they had come, yet he reasoned that they were there, and such being the case, all that was possible, ought to be done for them" (164). Dunbar continues: "The negroes were quick to recognize a friend" (164). The indictment of the "not in my backyard" vein of northern abolitionism and black elitism here is unmistakable. The literal and metaphorical "homeless" condition the contraband have been reduced to has left them little choice other than to hope for benevolence in Van Doren's deeply racist paternity. Dunbar's rendering of the homelessness of the contraband can also be interpreted as a backward projection of contemporary political problems facing Dunbar and other blacks in the late nineteenth and early twentieth century. Dunbar's novel was created at a time when blacks found themselves suspended between two political parties unresponsive to their needs. In historian Lerone Bennet's description of the period, the Republican Party, the "party of Lincoln," had become the party of big business, capitulating to labor practices that were "objectively anti-black"; that is, practices that favored white workers. Furthermore, industrial expansionist policy required making bedfellows of the most viciously racist southern business profiteers.[96] The Democratic Party had not evolved from the thinly veiled supremacist organization it was during the Civil War. Southern political opportunists seized this dilemma to renew neoproslavery arguments resting on the premise that the North and the Republican Party were both turning their backs on African Americans. In 1889, Reverend A. D. Mayo, a northern clergyman who had made a career ministering in the South, made this claim:

> If the Negro, as so many Southern people believe, is only a perpetual child, capable of a great deal that is useful and interesting, but destitute of the capacity for "the one thing needful" that lifts the subject of paternal[ism] up to the citizen of a republican government, then the thing to do is leave him to the care of the superiors of the South, who certainly know this side of him far better than the people of the North. . . . The outward opportunities for full association with the white population in the North, are after all, of little value in comparison with the substantial opportunity for becoming the great laboring class and of capturing the field of mechanical labor. It will be his own fault if he permits the insolent naturalized foreign element that now dominates out northern industrial centers to elbow him off into a peasantry or menial subordinate laboring population.[97]

The "choice" that Mayo sees for blacks is a decidedly unfortunate one—industrial peasantry or agricultural slavery—a choice as problematic as the choice between Republicans and Democrats. The "incapable" black body is expelled from politics, made absent as national reunion called for the North and South to put aside their differences; yet, as this passage demonstrates, the black body persisted as a contested space, made present as political necessity dictated.

Though Dunbar and Harper see white supremacy as a bond holding the North and South together, white nationalist reconciliation narratives manufactured an artificial sense of a more general harmony between the regions. However, Reverend Mayo's distinctly nonfictional discussion of which region could provide African Americans with better "opportunities"—a common national debate—serves as evidence to contradict any notion of a genuine truce: beneath the literary and political accord, the tension between the North and South surrounding the management of the black body persisted.

As late as 1900, a former colonel in the Confederate army and ex-slaveholder made similar arguments in the European edition of *Harper's Magazine*, warning the North that "as the negro advanced so well under our tutelage . . . it may be well for the people of the North to realize that in the nature of things we are better qualified to make a correct diagnosis of the negro's case."[98] He then confesses a motive less "humanitarian" and more economic: "We need him." Dunbar understood that the black body remained a site of contestation, particularly as a source of labor. In an episode at the end of *The Fanatics*, Ed receives a telegram from Walter Stewart, urging Ed to come to the Virginia plantation to work, promising him he will not be "teased . . . it will be much better than going about ringing an old bell" (310). The young lawyer whom Ed solicits to answer the letter is outraged because, in his words, " 'You *belong* to Dorbury' " (my emphasis, 311). He suggests that Ed send a succinct statement to the young plantation owner: " 'You be damned' " (311). Instead, the letter, written in officious prose, states that "Nigger Ed" preferred to "retain his official position, in view of the fact that the emoluments thereof had been materially increased" (311). The paper-pushing Yankee lawyer and the hands-on southern planter, stock representations of regional values in postwar sectionalist literature, create the tug-of-war that pulls the black body simultaneously north and south.

Homeless, Ignorant, Poor

In light of the social and cultural environment that produced The Fanatics, in which there seemed to be no obviously viable political alternatives for African Americans, the question the lynch mob asks the contrabands, "Why don't you go back where you belong?" rings throughout the text at a piercing pitch: in a postslavery, post–Civil War world, where do blacks belong, politically and geographically? In other words, where is home?

My examination of Dunbar's understanding of "home" has focused on the particular use of the divided house trope in southern nationalist fiction. I have argued that the forging of the middle essential to the divided house trope within this subgenre stands in violation of melodrama's most pronounced concern: the maintenance of poles necessary for the contest of good and evil. I have also claimed that within nationalist works, the national home, the metaphorical household of homosocial reunion, can only stand if free of black inclusion: political and economic segregation. The white heterosexual household bringing interregional lovers together is a byproduct of homosocial reunion, a racially pure house that refutes miscegenation: sexual segregation. The black can be affiliated with these homes, but only in a subjugated status, as servant, literally or metaphorically. While the domestic tropes signifying sociopolitical disorder—the divided house/broken home/unstable household/unclean quarters—have accrued distinct meanings in this southern nationalist fiction, they are of course conventions appearing in the sentimentalist genre as a whole. Dunbar's invocation of the divided house trope therefore goes beyond the bounds of southern nationalist fiction, putting him in conversation with Page and Dixon, yes, but also Stowe and Child, as well as Dunbar's black contemporaries, writers such as Griggs, Harper, and Hopkins. Moreover, using sentimentalism meant that Dunbar invoked the work of his antebellum African American predecessors: Wilson, Webb, and Brown. As such, Dunbar's deployment of the household trope, the primary signifier of domesticity, becomes that much more complex. Dunbar is writing within a black tradition of sentimentalism that was from its antebellum beginnings, as Reid-Pharr notes, quite "hostile" to some modes of sentimentality.[99]

The alluring promises of republican citizenship purportedly to be fulfilled by the conventions wielded in white bourgeois sentimentalism, most apparently the marriage trope, are frequently marked by those promises' "deferral" in black American literature, undermined by reminders of their tentative nature.[100] Reid-Pharr points out that homes are led by single mothers, set on fire, plagued by disease, wrecked by slavery; they are places of violence and concubinage, and, in the case of Hopkins's *Contending Forces*, "tainted" by an undercurrent of lesbian desire. Even if the final, triumphant household emerging at the closure of many nineteenth-century black narratives is "proper" in terms of race, gender, and class stratification and in terms of being a close facsimile of the white household (like Harper's), the "dysfunctional," inappropriate black household always remains in the psychic neighborhood, reinforcing the idea that social disaster lurks just around the corner. I therefore would like to emphasize that the most important characteristic of this "proper" household to black writers is not that it is "authentically" black or socially secure. Rather, its most important characteristic is that it is discrete, a physical and metaphorical refusal on the part of black American writers to have blacks sleeping in the slave and servants' quarters, attached to the big "white house" from which they have escaped.

Undoubtedly, Dunbar knew this and would blatantly satirize this black domestic ideal in *The Sport of the Gods* (1902).[101] The "little cottage . . . somewhat in the manner of the old cabin in the quarters" to which Berry Hamilton and his wife return at the close of the novel is a remand to metaphorical enslavement; the house is close enough to Berry's former employer's home that they can hear the crazed man "shrieking in the background from across the yard."[102] Somewhat differently, Dunbar has disallowed for any notion of a discrete black home altogether in *The Fanatics*. During the course of the novel, "Nigger Ed" is associated with no black household, divided, dysfunctional, or otherwise. A "free" black, he is loose in the novel, unmoored, having neither a house nor a black kinship community. In one way of thinking, he is then in a position much like the wandering contrabands who mistakenly see in Van Doren a friend, a position both vulnerable and dangerous. In another way of thinking, Dunbar's "free" black can only remain liberated if he does not get that which he should want according to the prevailing logic of domestic sentimentality: a place to call home. By the end of the novel, Dunbar will reconceive narratives of "domestic desire" by using the change in Ed's homeless status to warn us that the deferral of the

promises made by having a "home" might not be as dangerous as their fulfill-
ment. For as he later clarified in Sport of the Gods, there is only one home available:
an extension of the neoplantation household.

When Dunbar writes that "a new cap and a soldier's belt had had their effect
on . . . [Nigger Ed] and he marched upon his deriders, very stern, dignified
erect" (53), Dunbar presents Ed's body as ostensibly successfully "rearranged"
by the military's altering, rehabilitative machinery. Nevertheless, a gathering
crowd "laughed" (53). The town still refuses to recognize the "manhood" that
rearrangement has promised: "the people greeted him in more serious tones, as
if his association with their soldiers, light though it had been, had brought
him nearer to the manhood which they still refused to recognize in him" (122).
Superficially, they treat him as though he were a man, though they are not convinced. In this passage, Dunbar exposes the profound ambivalence many northerners had about the meaning of black military participation. Fahs notes that
while much of northern literature published after blacks formally conscripted
often celebrated service as the arrival of "black manhood" and interracial fraternity, much of it also attempted to avert "the implications" by killing off black
heroes, "imagin[ing] white control of black actions," and also by "ridicule"
(180). The town laughs in part because the culture has instructed it to do so.

The narrator of The Fanatics echoes the town's ambivalence about Ed's status:
"What he felt is hardly worth recording. He was so near the animal in the
estimation of his fellows (perhaps too near in reality) that he could be assumed to
have really few mental impressions. He was frightened, yes. He was hurt, too. But
no one would have given him credit for that much of human feeling. They had
kicked a dog and the dog had gone away. That was all. Yet Ed was not all the
dog. His feeling was that of a child who has tried to be good and been misunder-
stood" (182).

Dunbar allows the text's authoritative "objective" voice an opportunity to
move beyond a mere description of Ed's buffoonish behavior and to assess him
both psychologically and biologically. In so doing, Dunbar demonstrates how the
dominant culture's narratives silence black voice and ignore black "feeling" in
order to read and transcribe the black body as it sees fit. Ed's "manhood"—
established through service then rescinded as he is demoted to animal and
infant—will not grant him equal status in the reforming nation. In "Recession
Never" Dunbar writes of this shift in status: "Thirty years ago the American
people told the Negro that he was a man with a man's full powers. They deemed
it that important that they did what they have done few times in the history of the
country—they wrote it down in their constitution. And now they come with the
shotgun in the South and sophistry in the North to prove to him that it was all

wrong."[103] The article argues that the postwar black is a "different man" whose entry into the nation will not be denied. He sees the forces gathering against black enfranchisement as hypocrisy:

> We are presented with the spectacle of people gushing, through glowing headlines, over the bravery of its black heroes. In an incredibly short space of time—almost too brief, it would seem for the mental transition of the individual, much less the nation—we found mouth pieces of this same people chronicling the armed resistance to the Negroes in the exercise of those powers and privileges for which the colored men fought. The drama of this sudden change of heart is incongruous to the point of ghastly humor.[104]

This piece illustrates Dunbar's doubt as to whether black participation in the Civil War had truly brought blacks into national esteem; what he calls the "recent and sudden change" in feeling happened far too quickly for the "gushing" to have been genuine. This stands as yet another statement Dunbar makes about the transitory nature of melodramatic sentiment and the artifice of politics shaped by that sentiment. Considered too strong for *McClure's*, which had originally commissioned the article, the attitude Dunbar takes toward this national about-face is documented in several of his other works about the Civil War. Two years after "Recession Never," Dunbar published a sonnet eulogizing Colonel Robert Gould Shaw, the white officer who commanded the Fifty-fourth Massachusetts, the first black regiment formed in the North. In 1863, six short weeks after his regiment was formed, Gould was shot dead in an attack on Battery Wagner that claimed half his troops in casualties. He was then tossed in a mass pit, buried undistinguished from his men in an act the Confederates believed fit for a white who dared to lead black soldiers. "Robert Gould Shaw" laments more than the death of the colonel and the decimation of his regiment; it laments the failure of military participation to secure enfranchisement: ". . . thou and those who with thee died for right / Have died, the Present teaches, but in Vain!"[105] "Shaw" expresses more intensely feelings articulated in an even earlier poem, "The Colored Soldiers" (1896), in which the speaker insists that the virtuous "traits that made them worthy" of becoming "citizens and soldiers" are "not dead."[106]

By the time Dunbar published *The Fanatics*, any residual doubt he harbored about the utter failure of black military participation to secure "manhood rights" had become solidified. The trick the town of Dorbury needs to pull off—indeed, the trick the nation needs to pull off—is to keep Ed the "man" in the demasculinized position Ed the "nigger" occupied before the war. However, Ed's "new" body no longer fits the older, prewar proslavery narratives that could "sentimentalize" the black body in its safely bound state. This trick, then, will be a discursive one, finding an alternative discourse that will accommodate Ed's transition into postwar narratives without actually elevating his degraded status.

Home at Last

In this "new" discourse, master/slave hence becomes, as we have seen, colonel/servant; John Pendleton Kennedy's Swallow Barn becomes Page's In Ole Virginia. As Orlando Patterson reminds us, slavery was repetition:[107] the institution required the constant influx of new bodies to fill the position of slave, thereby reproducing the position of master. And as Homi Bhaba has theorized, the force of a stereotype is repetition: the devalued body must be constantly reinscribed with its status, and the "stories" devaluing it "must be told (compulsively) again and afresh" to give the construction "fixity" in "the face and space of disruption and threat."[108] Southern postwar nationalist narratives did it all. In repeating the discourse of prewar proslavery fiction, the narratives repeat slavery metaphorically, and repeat the stereotypes necessary to maintain this slavery in "the face" of freed blacks demanding civic equality and in the "space" of a politically altered landscape. In using the structure of national reconciliation narratives, itself a reiteration, Dunbar shows how this process of repetition operates within southern nationalist fiction and within the postwar nation. Ed's shift from bell-ringer in the largely white town of Dorbury to militia servant and nurse within a white regiment was horizontal movement only, a repetition of position—from one occupation that serviced whites to another.

The course Ed's future in the new nation will take is exemplified in one of the "occupations" that has helped him increase his material fortunes: storyteller. "There were," Dunbar writes, "women who begged him to come in and talk about their sons who had been left on some Southern field, wives who wanted to hear over and over again the last words of their loved ones" (312). This job has been filled before: for instance, by Sam, the narrator of Marse Chan's Confederate glory and by Uncle Remus in Harris's "A Story of the War." Southern nationalist fiction did more than allow the nationalist writers to narrate blacks as they wanted, but in a greater exercise of power, they could force blacks to tell the same stories they did. In The Clansman, Ben, the southerner, first falls for the northerner Elsie when she picks up a banjo and sings in black dialect. It is not so much Elsie that mesmerizes him but her channeling of the southern plantation black: "No Yankee girl could play or sing these songs . . . !" (12). The "darky" voice, called "soft" by Dixon (12), is indeed music to the ear when the grating sounds of black political protest are muffled beneath the soothing tones of white nostalgia. Dunbar's 1903 poem "The Unsung Heroes" calls for a "seer" to sing "a song" of Civil

War soldiers that would make "hate / of race grow obsolete and / cold."[109] Within this poem, Dunbar recognizes that a different voice was needed for this role. This "seer" would replace the "minstrels . . . of old."

Ed will not be that voice. No longer considered the "town buffoon" at the end of the narrative, he becomes the town mascot, "petted and spoiled" very much like the "dog" the narrator labeled him earlier (312). In the first movement on the horizontal plane in the novel he is made a servant and nurse from a bell ringer. A second movement on the horizontal plane has taken him from servant and nurse to minstrel. This lateral shift has also taken him from the streets of Dorbury to the battlefield to a "home." He has been properly domesticated, but he has not created a domestic space of his own. When invited into the Stewart household early in the text, he was snoop and sneak, spreading rumors and creating chaos. Invited into homes at the end of the text, in his newer capacity, he brings solace and security; as a result, the townspeople "gave him a place for life" (312). But that position comes at a cost. "Nigger Ed" has lost his ability to trouble the white household, and that, Dunbar implies, is a dear sacrifice indeed.

In replacing the iconic black soldier-hero with a "darky" servant following whites to war, Dunbar attempts to reveal how the Union "really" envisioned black service and, of course, the black "manhood" it had argued that African Americans had earned by blood. The value of Dunbar's bleak version of the outcome of black military participation is clarified when set against Harper's valorizing portrayal. Writing of the psychic aftermath of the Holocaust, Jack Kuglemass suggests that refusing the more troubling aspects of the past "robs history of its critical power to disturb."[110] Dunbar wanted to disturb. As a man whose father served in the Civil War with little tangible reward, it would be unlikely that he would desire anything less.

3 NOT MEN ALONE

Susie King Taylor's
*Reminiscences of My Life
in Camp* and Masculine
Self-Fashioning

Susie King Taylor's 1902 autobiographical narrative, *Reminiscences of My Life in Camp with the 33rd United States Colored Troops Late 1st S.C. Volunteers*,[1] the only known extant memoir by an African American woman who directly participated in the Civil War, provides a factual account of what life might have been like for the warring women in Harper's and Brown's fictionalized worlds. Born a slave in Savannah, Georgia, King gained her freedom in the second year of the war after her uncle took his family and Taylor to St. Catherine's Island off of the coast of Georgia, where they were then transferred to St. Simon's Island as contraband of war under the protective custody of the Union army. Though Taylor was only fourteen years old at the time, her ability to read and write prompted a commander in the Union forces to ask Taylor to enlist her services as a laundress and soldier-teacher in the Thirty-third U.S. Colored Troops, one of the first all-black regiments trained to fight for the North after Congress eased restrictions on the use of black personnel in the military. Taylor remained with the Thirty-third from 1862 until the war ended in 1865, eventually taking on the role of company nurse as the number of wounded and diseased began to overwhelm those trained to care for the afflicted. The book Taylor produced detailing her experiences is rather slim—only eighty-eight pages in its original form. She opens her work with two chapters conventional to autobiographical writing: the first, a brief outline of her genealogy; the second, an abbreviated selection of reminiscences from her childhood. The bulk of her volume—eight chapters—describes her memories of life working with the regiment. The remaining four chapters focus on Taylor's life after the Civil War, concluding with a chapter detailing a visit to Louisiana that allows Taylor to comment on the state of race relations in the South.

The rare status of Taylor's memoirs seems remarkable in consideration of the great numbers of African American women who gave their services to the Union forces. While agitation for black inclusion in the Union army had heightened the call for "manhood" rights, black women inherently understood that the war was also about them. As historians Darlene Clark Hine and Kathleen Thompson point out, "black women took an active, aggressive role in the Civil War even when it meant tremendous sacrifice."[2] Like Taylor, many served in roles that were an extension of women's prescribed civil duties: as cooks, nurses, laundresses, or teachers. Some, however, offered their services in less conventional occupations. They were employed as Union messengers, recruiters, and spies; others performed reconnaissance missions. "They worked for the army in part because they had nowhere else to go," Hine and Thompson continue, "and in part because they wanted to be involved in the struggle for freedom."[3] Black women often had "nowhere to go" because the Civil War was largely fought in the South, where the majority of black Americans lived. The war was brought "home," quite literally. Black women also carried "home" to the war. The "contraband" freed from plantations often lived on the edges of army units as families; black women also followed male family members, "reconstruct[ing] their domestic life" near or on the outskirts of camps.[4] The proximity of women to the front helped blur the distinction between "feminine" and "masculine" spaces, undoubtedly making it easier for some black women such as Taylor to proffer their services to the military.

If the extension of the war into the South brought the war home literally, the fact that the Civil War became "a struggle over freedom" brought the war home in metaphorical terms. In "Civil Wars and Sexual Territories," Margaret R. Higonnet rightly claims that nationalist wars—wars fought against an external "other"—require the suppression of a nation's internal political differences in order to unite citizens against an exterior threat.[5] Indeed, nationalist wars are often waged for the precise purpose of maintaining a nation's way of life—an effort to preserve rather than disrupt the status quo. Civil wars, on the other hand, are sparked by internal friction: an internal friction so great that a nation can no longer ignore the extent of divisions within its geographical boundaries. As such, civil wars have the power to transform women's understanding of their gender roles and identities precisely because they anticipate a change in government, allowing women to conceive of broadened political choices for themselves.[6] This holds especially true for many black women during the American Civil War, who not only understood that a war over slavery meant the larger white nation was poised for political transformation, but also that the possibility of emancipation could bring about even more dramatic changes within the black "nation within a nation" that had heretofore been regulated by its own specific set of gender and social norms particular to a largely enslaved community. Slave women, of course, were often women without men: husbands and lovers were frequently "leased out" to other plantations and work sites or sold away from their families. In many instances, slaveholders actively prohibited marriage. Free black women in the North and South were also affected by slavery; in both regions, free black women tended to outnumber the available population of free black men.[7]

In writing about the Civil War, then, Taylor also was writing about a time in which black women were about to experience a major upheaval in their lives. As freedpeople, black women who had been enslaved would have the task of reunderstanding, reinterpreting, and renegotiating their positions in relation to black men. The strata of already free black women faced the self-ascribed responsibility of "uplifting" their sisters from their downtrodden condition. The politically efficacious strategy of prioritizing black men's enfranchisement over black women's would be more vocally challenged than it had been before the war, undergirded by a growing women's movement inside and outside of the black community. It is especially significant that Taylor wrote *Reminiscences* well after the Civil War was over, thus after the political changes black women had been long desiring for themselves had begun to be realized. Indeed, in 1902, Taylor—as a founder of a school, a teacher, an organizing member of the Women's Relief Corps, and finally, a writer—was one of an emerging group of black women who had consciously carved out activist lives for themselves. As Carla L. Peterson notes in *Doers of the Word*, many black women speakers and writers in the antebellum North—Sojourner Truth, Harriet Jacobs, and Charlotte Forten as examples—never married, married late in life, or were widowed early. Some remained childless.[8] Other racial spokeswomen and black cultural workers who rose to prominence after the war, such as Ana Julia Cooper, led similar lives. Peterson argues that such women, while not rare, were nonetheless considered " 'anomalous,' " particularly from the viewpoint of the dominant culture.[9]

The original published introduction to Taylor's narrative, written by Thomas Wentworth Higginson, the white colonel who had commanded the Thirty-third while it was still a volunteer regiment, reinforces Taylor's "anomalous" status:

Actual military life is rarely described by a woman, and this is especially true of a woman whose place was in the ranks, as the wife of a soldier. . . . No such description has ever been given, I am sure, by one thus connected with a colored regiment; so that the nearly 200,000 black soldiers (178,975) of our Civil War have never been delineated from the woman's point of view. All of this gives peculiar interest to this little volume, relating wholly to the career of the very earliest of these regiments,—the one described in my volume "Army Life in a Black Regiment." (xi)

He later adds that Taylor was "very exceptional among the colored laundresses in that she could read and write" (xi). Although Higginson's description of the singularity of Taylor and her text is fundamentally correct, his choice of language also signals that his assessment of the worth of both is guided by an implicit logic of masculinity. This logic does not seek to interpret Taylor as a black woman per se, but as a black woman "connected to" the black men who fought for the Union—in her proper "place . . . as a wife," no less—and as such, as a woman who could offer "peculiar" insight into their experiences. Yet, in Taylor's own preface, positioned before Higginson's, Taylor writes that she "presents these reminiscences" to show that there were " 'loyal women,' as well as men, in those days, who did not fear shell or shot . . . women who camped and fared as the boys did" (vi). Nowhere in her remarks does Taylor state that she wishes to detail the circumstances of those "200,000 black soldiers . . . from the woman's point of view." In imposing that reading on Taylor's book, Higginson altogether misses the significance of Taylor's autobiographical act: to grant narrative primacy to her female body and the other female bodies it represents. She offers herself neither as an "exceptional" woman nor as an anomaly, but as one of many other women whose service, in Taylor's estimation, has largely remained undocumented. In most instances, this service also went financially uncompensated, something that held true for Taylor herself. Even Harriet Tubman, who worked for the Union as a laundress, cook, nurse, spy, and scout in the South Georgia Islands where Taylor served (though whether they met is not known) was initially unsuccessful in securing a pension despite the letters written on her behalf by several well-respected army officers, including Generals David Hunter and Rufus Saxton, confirming the critical role Tubman played in the Union military.[10] In what would prove her most valuable contribution, Tubman designed, implemented, and commanded the famed Combahee River mission, a wildly successful stealth attack on South Carolina coastal planters and the Confederate works securing the region. The expedition was, in words that have been attributed to Saxton, "the only military command in American history wherein a woman, black or white, led the raid and under whose inspiration it was originated and conducted." Before the incursion was executed, Tubman had carefully laid the groundwork, secretly moving in and out of the targeted area, gathering critical information from slaves and from unsuspecting white planters. The Boston Commonwealth reported that the gunboats of "Col. Montgomery and his gallant band of 300 black soldiers, *under the guidance of a black woman*" (original italics),[11] averted river mines planted by the Confederacy—explosives Tubman herself had located.[12] Tubman also went ashore with Union soldiers to raid plantations and Confederate stockpiles and helped rescue the nearly eight hundred slaves who had made the decision to flee their masters. In spite of this remarkable military achievement, she drew money from the government only after her husband, a former soldier, died and Tubman was allowed to claim widow's benefits. This was not until 1892, some four years after his death. Finally, in 1899, Tubman would be allotted an increase in her widow's pension in recognition of her own service; though at twenty dollars, it was five dollars less than the pension given "official" Union soldiers.[13]

Just as the work Tubman performed for the Union confirms that gender boundaries during wartime were crossed, Taylor's narrative demands that Higginson's claim that his "point of view" stands "wholly different" from hers be questioned on this very basis. Certainly, his matter-of-fact declaration would be readily accepted by a turn-of-the-century reading public. He was, after all, a free white male and Taylor an enslaved black woman; their social statuses hardly could be less comparable. Too, their "oppositely" sexed bodies would make natural the assumption that their reflections on war, a "masculine" enterprise, would be as substantially different as the essential "natures" signified by their distinctly gendered corporealities. However, Taylor's assertion that some women at the front "camped and fared as the boys did" clearly indicates that she desires that her audience understand that the space and conditions of war required that these women behave in ways exceeding circumscribed notions of the "feminine."

In fact, those women who "fared as the boys did" had to overcome "material" gender restrictions, quite literally. In a letter Tubman dictated for publication in an 1863 issue of the *Boston Commonwealth*, she describes a particular complication she encountered during the Combahee raid: "In our late expedition up the river, in coming on board the boat, I was carrying *two pigs* for a poor sick woman, who had a child to carry, and the order "double quick" was given, and I started to run, stepped on my dress, it being rather long, and fell and tore it almost off, so that when I got on board the boat there was hardly anything left of it but shreds."[14] Aware of the irony, she explains that she "made up my mind then that I would never wear a long dress on another expedition of the kind."[15] Though Tubman goes on to make a public request "to the ladies" for "a *bloomer*" rather than trousers, many women did choose to don male attire during the Civil War, cross-dressing as men in order to serve in the military in capacities other than those typically reserved for women. It was also commonplace for African American women during the antebellum era to masquerade as male during escapes from slavery (Harriet Jacobs and Ellen Craft are prominent examples).[16] While we can be reasonably sure that Jacobs and Craft were cross-dressing for expeditious reasons, it is difficult to know how many others who cross-dressed "temporarily" were in fact exteriorizing an interior "masculine" gender identity. As a case in point, Sara Emma Edmonds, a white woman who served in the Union army as a man, had been passing as male well before she enlisted, selling bibles in the North under the name Franklin Thompson; Edmonds had adopted this identity after fleeing an unwanted engagement being forced upon her by her father.[17] And yet, as transgressive (and correcting) as such instances of cross-dressing might be, this mode of masculine self-fashioning also raises the possibility of relief—that "natural" gender roles can be restored by a simple unmasking of the sexual impostor (William Craft's giddy description of his wife's "return" in *Running a Thousand Miles for Freedom* certainly attests to that). Thus while Taylor's narrative crossing-dressing might not seem as radical or provocative as that of women who actually performed masculinity in full drag, the possibility of restoration is precisely why Taylor's writing of her body-self in masculine terms, if "only" rhetorically, can be viewed as equally transgressive. Unlike Craft's or Edmonds's narratives, there will be no retrieval of the "feminine" body from the sexual tumult cross-dressing creates, no neat reversal to gender "normalcy." Taylor's masculinization is presented, instead, as a "permanent" gender corrective, an "authentic" representation of self that transcends the space of the military and the exigencies of war; a bodily and psychic state that, in Taylor's understanding, should allow her to access those prerogatives labeled "masculine" well beyond both circumstances.

As she intimates in her preface, Taylor's representation of self is tied to larger issues pertaining to black women's social, political, and historical representation. In *Female Masculinity*, Judith Halberstam argues that the cultural meanings ascribed masculinity are made most legible outside of the male body proper; that is, that if we wish to understand what masculinity means in a particular society, we must look at how those bodies gendered as "other" assume and perform those behaviors and attitudes considered "masculine" within a sexed corporeal lexicon.[18] In Taylor's case, the very act of writing her female body onto the scene of the Civil War becomes a flesh-based argument asserting black women's right to be "public" beings: to do the public/male work of war, to challenge the public/male history of war writing, and to be included within the public/male domain of black "manhood rights." By identifying herself with the duties, the postures, and the bodies of the men who surround her—and by openly documenting her transgressions—Taylor therefore makes a dual gesture intended to negate arguments of essential sexual difference that relegated "proper" women to the private domestic sphere and constricted them to similarly "proper" and "feminine" discursive acts. If this dual gesture is improper, even more improper, then, is the manner in which Taylor handles the black men in her text. Rather than heralding their fabled transformations from "slaves to citizens," she silences them, and in some instances, physically displaces them; her voice and body speaking and acting in their stead.

Thus it is interesting that much that has been written about Taylor's short narrative tends toward a discussion of the absence of Taylor from her own autobiography. In her introduction to an abridged edition of Taylor's work, Willie Rose comments that Taylor, rather than writing about herself, submerges herself within descriptions of the soldiers of the Thirty-third. "One wishes," she writes, "that Taylor had written as much about herself as she wrote about 'our boys.'"[19] Joycelyn K. Moody places *Memoirs* into a larger tradition of "self-effacement" in nineteenth-century black women's autobiography. Noting that many black women purposefully "withdraw" from their narratives, Moody argues that this consciously engineered rhetorical strategy allowed black women, whether free or enslaved, whether writing before or after the Civil War, to "adopt deliberately subversive means of rendering self-inscribed black American female lives acceptable to 19th century readers."[20] "Acceptable" meant, of course, creating identities that would compare favorably to those of their white female counterparts. As many critics have noted, writers of slave narratives were faced with the task of executing a series of difficult negotiations. On one hand, they attempted to project a "chaste" self, while on the other, they recognized that a full apprehension of slavery necessitated focusing on the innumerable indignities inflicted upon their bodies, rendering the image of "purity" virtually impossible. Lest they be accused of embellishment or fictionalization, these writers desired credibility yet also understood that "naming" might be considered "indelicate." And finally, as black women who dared to write autobiography, they knew that the very decision to commit their lives to paper meant they were breaking gender norms. "Self-effacement"—apologizing for descriptions of bodily violations, concealing unpleasant "facts," adopting pseudonyms, and claiming a hesitancy to write at all—permitted these writers both to tell their stories and to distance themselves from them. In this way, self-effacement does not constitute actual withdrawal, then; more accurately, it merely constructs the appearance thereof. Such a strategy, Moody astutely points out, permits Harriet Jacobs to employ "eleven self-referent pronouns" in one short passage from the preface to *Incidents in the Life of a Slave Girl* (1861) and, in the same passage, claim that "it would have been more pleasant for me to have been silent about my own history."[21]

Like Jacobs, whose authorial "I" pervades her narrative, I argue that Taylor is also very much present in her work. On virtually every page of *Memoirs*, Taylor asserts the "I" repeatedly; indeed, her readers have no opportunity to forget through whom the events of the Civil War are being filtered. Nevertheless, despite Taylor's rightful insistence in occupying the narrative space of her own making, Taylor's "I" is frequently disembodied—present psychologically, but not physically. This stands in stark contrast to the fully corporeal "I" in Jacobs, who understands that her project necessitates frank descriptions of the sexual and physical ordeals her body endured. Given the horrendous conditions of camp life during the Civil War, particularly for blacks, one might expect Taylor to write more extensively about the physical toll laboring with an army regiment must have taken on her young body. In addition to the constant threat of gunfire, raids, and shelling, epidemics of small-pox and influenza ravaged encampments. Tent life provided scant shelter against cold, snow, rain, and heat. The humid climate and dense vegetation of the South Georgia Islands created a haven for mosquitoes and other insects. Although Taylor insists that she "shall never forget that terrible war until my eyes close in death," recalling nights where "I would stand at my tent door and try to see what was going on, because nights were the times the rebels would try to get into our lines and capture our boys" (50–51), Taylor often writes, to use her own words, from the "tent door": as a witness to the many atrocities of war, rather than as a potential victim of the conditions she painstakingly details. While Taylor allots both depth and breadth to the many dangerous situations endured by the troops, Moody observes that accounts of threats to her own body "frequently end *in medias res*. . . . The fact of her narrative is apparently . . . survival."[22]

The notion of survival may extend beyond the threats of enemy fire, sickness, disease, or mental and physical exhaustion. Though Taylor never dwells on the fact, she was, after all, a young woman—one of only a handful—in a company of men. Women living within or near army encampments were particularly vulnerable to sexual exploitation. In a letter written to the commander of the Department of Missouri, three black soldiers complain that the wives of some of the contraband "have been molested by soldiers to gratify their licentious lust, and their husbands murdered in endeavoring to defend them.[23] One can only speculate whether Taylor's quick marriage to a soldier in the Thirty-third was a means of deflecting the inevitable sexual overtures—or threats—made by the "boys" she had enlisted to serve. In the same year she joined the regiment, Taylor married Edward King, an officer in the unit. She omits, however, any details of their meeting or courtship, burying the fact of her marriage within a passage explaining the death of two Union soldiers, John Brown and Charles O' Neal, during a confrontation with the "rebs." "Charles O'Neal," Taylor writes, "was an Uncle of Edward King, who later was my husband and a sergeant in Co. E., U.S.I." (13). Her husband, to whom she subsequently refers to in only the most formal manner—"Sergeant King"—died in 1866; Taylor neglects to mention how. In the same sentence, Taylor adds that King's death left her "to welcome a little stranger alone" (54). One paragraph later, Taylor explains that she left her baby—given neither gender nor name—with her mother in 1868 to "enter into employ with a family" after the school she had opened four years earlier failed (55). One learns, once again in passing, that after King's death, Taylor married her second husband, Russell Taylor, at age thirty-one. Her child resurfaces in the final chapter of Taylor's work, thirty-two years after his birth, when Taylor is called to Shreveport to be at his bedside as he lies dying from an unspecified illness. Aside from his sex, Taylor says little else about him or their relationship.

The most startling omissions in *Memoirs* are configured around these circum-stances: Taylor's narrative is conspicuously devoid of any personal detail that might call attention to her body as a sexual or sexualized entity. While Moody rightly suggests that her "self-imposed silence" might have stemmed from a sense of decorum and modesty,[24] that assessment may not entirely explain why Taylor also keeps quiet on subjects decidedly less provocative: the duties of child rearing and domestic responsibility. Not only does it appear that Taylor is unwill-ing to position herself as a de facto sexualized subject within the hypermascu-linized space of an army camp, she is equally unwilling to position herself as wife, mother, or homemaker: the precise roles that would make her, returning to Moody's argument, "acceptable" to a white readership. The sentence in which Taylor mentions her marriage is merely an aside within a longer passage describ-ing a skirmish between the Union and Confederate soldiers. King's death and the birth of her child—the former, allotted all of three sentences, the latter, given a mere six words—are wedged between accounts of Taylor's employment as a teacher in two of the many schools that were established for black children after the Civil War.

If one version of Taylor is missing from her narrative, it is a version whose body-self simultaneously denies being contained by female sexuality and refuses to be inscribed with the typical signifiers of nineteenth-century ideals of woman-hood. Taylor was not the only nineteenth-century black woman whose text resists such details. For example, Jarena Lee and Julia Foote, who produced autobiogra-phies that largely served to justify black women's right to interpret the Word and preach the gospel, leave textual lacunae around similar issues.[25] The frequency of these omissions across black women's autobiographies (Truth's is another) is worthy of noting, but not altogether inexplicable. If none wanted their occupa-tional endeavors to be confined by ideologies of gender, neither did they want their narratives—their emancipatory acts—to work against them by inviting the kind of judgment that might be inspired if their readership were too frequently reminded of what these black women "ought" to be doing. It seems, then, that Taylor is neither self-effacing in the *exact* manner Moody suggests, nor, as Rose claims, does she hide beneath accounts of the Thirty-third. Rather, in excluding explicitly gender-related subjects from her texts, Taylor replaces what would be a recognizably female identity with a defeminized body-self prepared to work. It is not, however, the "private" work of a wife and mother, but public work: the work of war and the American nation, and the work of building yet another nation—a black nation of newly freed, newly enfranchised citizens. Her narrative thus departs significantly from the "confessional mode" of women's autobiography in which deeply interior, private revelations become a lens through which these writers view the exterior, public world. Freed from the conventional narrative expectations of personal disclosure and "female" confidences, Taylor throws herself and *Reminiscences* into the public domain of history. "Many people," she writes, "do not know what some of the colored women did during the war . . . These things should be kept in history before the people" (68).

From the very first chapter of Taylor's memoirs, "A Brief Sketch of My Ancestors," a solely matrilineal narrative of her roots, Taylor seeks to align herself with the long tradition of self-reliant women Peterson describes. In the simple, declarative sentence that initiates her autobiography—"My great-great grandmother was 120 years old when she died"—Taylor establishes herself as a descendant of a long line of vital, robust women: her great-grandmother, Taylor also writes, lived to be 100. While the longevity of Taylor's foremothers might be viewed as a simple statement of fact, read differently, it can be linked to Taylor's construction of her body as especially resilient later in the narrative—a body fit to withstand the perils of war. Taylor also foreshadows the minimal narrative space she will allot her own husbands. As with the description of her own life, Taylor places the men her grandmothers and her mother married under a form of erasure; their names are offered as merely one bit of information within other details of her female family members' lives. In fact, Taylor does not associate the first woman of her genealogy, her great-great-grandmother, with any male figure; whether Taylor knew of her great-great-grandfather or not is thus left to speculation.

Taylor provides yet another clue as to the manner of self she will construct in *Memoirs*. The chapter is dominated by memories of her grandmother, who, Taylor writes in her second chapter, raised her and facilitated her literacy. Praising her grandmother as a "hard laborer" and a "practical" woman, Taylor notes that she "made a good living" for herself: "My grandmother went every three months to see my mother. She would hire a wagon to carry bacon, tobacco, flour, molasses and sugar. These she would trade for eggs, chickens, or cash. . . . These, in turn, she carried back to the city market, where she had a customer who sold them for her" (2–3). Taylor's detailed account of her grandmother's business acumen foregrounds the priority she will give her own work in her autobiography. Taylor's grandmother, as the mother of only one living child, was loosed from the familial responsibilities of Taylor's great-great-grandmother, who bore seven children; her great-grandmother, who bore twenty-four (but was nevertheless "a noted midwife"); and her mother, who bore nine. As a result, Taylor's grandmother was free both to travel and to do the kind of "public" work Taylor would eventually pursue herself.

Suggesting that the first two chapters of *Reminiscences* "frame the text in such a way that when war does appear in Taylor's narrative, it is against the background of a black matrilineal legacy and a female tradition of literacy," Elizabeth Young links Taylor's work as a nurse, soldier-teacher, and laundress to her grandmother's insistence on Taylor's literacy and her grandmother's work cleaning "bachelors' rooms."[26] Young also interprets Taylor's work in the Civil War as an extension of the "mothering" Taylor's grandmother bestowed upon her. She notes one particular passage in which Taylor writes of the gratitude her soldiers expressed for what Young conceptualizes as her "maternal" interest in them. "It is as though the war itself," Young argues, "were one event on the continuum of mothering."[27] As interesting as this reading may be, when placed alongside Taylor's unwillingness to "mother" her biological child within the pages of her memoir, the desire to mother Young ascribes to Taylor is thoroughly confounded. Though Young does use the word "work" to describe her grandmother's *work* as a cleaning woman and Taylor's own *work* in the war, because these tasks are performed by women, it seems, Young insists that these acts be read as "mothering." During the war, nursing, one of Taylor's primary tasks, was not in fact a "female" occupation. Approximately 80 percent of field nurses were men.[28] For Taylor, "mothering" is a mere biological fact rather than a consumptive social destiny that would define a woman's choice of labor. Her description of mothering in these early chapters is purely genealogical, limited to the enumeration of the children each of her foremothers bore. If a continuum exists in Taylor's narrative, it is a continuum of work.

That Taylor wishes to assert herself as part of a legacy that has prepared her to occupy not only the public sphere but specifically the sphere of war is further evidenced in the first chapter of her narrative. Just after Taylor writes that her great-great-grandmother died at age 120, she notes that five of the woman's sons served in the Revolutionary War. In doing so, Taylor effectively claims participation in war as her birthright, associating herself with the warring men within her familial lineage. Characteristically, Taylor does not mention these men by name— though they were, indisputably, an important part of African American history. Taylor's pattern of diminishing black male presence in her text serves another purpose here. This act of unnaming is merely the first of many times Taylor silences black male soldiers in her work, forging a narrative "hole" into which she then inserts herself. For instance, although Taylor notes that she "had a number of relatives in this regiment,—several uncles, some cousins . . . and a number of cousins in other companies," she offers no other information about the male members in her family with whom she served (16). Unnaming allows Taylor to exercise narrative power over these men, de-creating the black male soldier and re-creating herself in his place. On a textual level at least, Taylor succeeds in subjugating their existence to her own. Taylor deploys yet another tactic to ensure their subjugation: they and the majority of other black men in her work are denied the privilege of language. Virtually all speech uttered by any black man in Taylor's narrative is paraphrased, translated through Taylor's own authorial voice. What little is actually heard from the soldiers with whom Taylor has contact is narrated as a collective utterance. Taylor re-creates one conversation in which soldiers from outside of her unit ask her why she so kindly administers to their needs: "I replied, 'Well, you know, all the boys in other companies are the same to me as though in my Company E; you are all doing the same duty, and I will do just the same for you.' 'Yes,' they would say, 'we know that, because you were the first woman we saw when we came into camp, and you took an interest in us boys ever since we have been here, and we are very grateful for all you do for us'" (29–30). Taylor's use of collective speech reinforces the de-creative effect of unnaming, leveling all soldiers into a "sameness" that permits Taylor to forgo the task of creating any individual, viable black male subjectivity. Here, Taylor's "I" is heard as the words of the emerged, differentiated subject among the undifferentiated "they." Taylor is the speaking subject; the soldiers are the spoken. In speaking *for* them, Taylor eliminates the chance that any black male voice will compete with hers within the boundaries of her text; in speaking *of* them, she exercises rhetorical control over their bodies. The use of collective speech here has an additional benefit: the synchronous, affirming words "spoken" by the soldiers refract the dutiful, active image of self Taylor strives to maintain in her narrative. In essence, Taylor manipulates these soldiers in an act of textual ventriloquism; their mouths may move, but it is her voice that is heard.

Having effectively muted the black male soldier in her narrative, Taylor further attempts to usurp his position by reimplementing the strategy she uses when claiming herself as heir to Revolutionary soldiers: identification. Even in his diminished form, the black male soldier—both his body and his duties—becomes a measure against which Taylor can favorably compare her own body and her capabilities. If Taylor's meticulously orchestrated disassociation of her body from female sexuality and "womanly" obligations allows her to determine a self unfettered by the prescriptions of femininity, her persistent associations with the male body and the "manly" responsibilities of war have the inverse effect. In one instance, Taylor lauds her own soldiering skills by writing of her adeptness with a rifle, acting not as a traditional woman would, but presumably, "as the boys did": "I learned to handle a musket very well while in the regiment, and could shoot straight and often hit the target. I assisted in cleaning the guns and used to fire them off, to see if the cartridges were dry, before cleaning and reloading, each day. I thought this great fun. I was also able to take a gun all apart, and put it together again" (26). Cleaning guns, shooting them, taking them apart: Taylor presents a passage ripe with phallic content. Not only does she handle guns—and very well for that matter—she enjoys it. If, however, Taylor was not intending to offer her reader a sexualized metaphor, a veiled allusion to the pleasures of the phallus, she quite certainly succeeds in prying it from the hands of "the boys." Halberstam has claimed that such props are necessary for constructing a powerful cultural vision of masculinity; iconic figures (she refers to James Bond specifically) are made virile, even complete, through their access to and possession of prosthetics such as weapons, cars, high-tech instruments.[29] By describing how she takes control of the musket, Taylor shows that masculinity is not the sole property of the male body "naturally"; and that it can therefore be appropriated, and with it, the power masculinity carries.

Elsewhere, she places her female body beside the men in her unit, measuring her resilience against theirs, and declaring hers superior. In the third chapter of *Reminiscences*, for example, Taylor writes that an outbreak of variloid, a strain of smallpox, had "caused some anxiety" in camp (17). After describing how, in spite of her care, a member of the regiment "succumbed to the disease" she immediately adds that she "was not in the least afraid of small pox. I was vaccinated and drank sassafras tea constantly, which kept my blood purged" (17). Moreover, the "masculinization" of Taylor's body is further accompanied by a masculinization of consciousness: "Outside the fort there were many skulls lying about; I have often moved them one side out of the path. The comrades and I would have quite a debate as to which side the men fought on. . . . They were a gruesome sight, those fleshless heads and grinning jaws, but by this time I had become accustomed to worse things and did not feel as I might have earlier in my camp life" (31).

The men here are not "boys" but "comrades"; in their company, Taylor engages in the kinds of games men at war play—blackly humorous, designed to alleviate the "gruesome" nature of war. Taylor's tenure at war has transformed her into a woman who can and does write about "limbs blown off . . . without a shudder" (31), and importantly, without loading her prose with the sympathetic sentimentality one might expect from a woman writing about this subject at the turn of the century. While it is true that nineteenth-century antislavery women writers such as Harriet Beecher Stowe and Harriet Jacobs had long before depicted all manners of bodies wounded and deformed by violent slaveholders, these bodies were meant to arouse feelings of compassion in their audiences; in Taylor's passage, these bodies are also meant to support her claim that her constitution was toughened by an assumption of masculinity made necessary by war.

Compare, for instance, Taylor's authorial disposition to that of Charlotte Forten Grimké, who served as a contraband teacher in the South Georgia Islands (as with Tubman, it has not been ascertained that they knew one another). Unlike Taylor, who makes no claims to literary aspirations, Grimké harbored a profound desire to be an artist, publishing highly sentimentalized poetry and essays in antebellum abolitionist publications such as the *Liberator* and attempting to publish short stories in literary magazines.[30] Peterson uses the term "seeking the 'writable,'" derived from a phrase used in Grimké's diary, to theorize her near obsession with rendering the world in terms of the picturesque. The writer seems to harbor an especial need to discover the "picturesque" in the black body, to which she developed a problematic relationship, complicated in part by her association with white abolitionists and her dependence on conventional white sentimental imagery, romantic racialism in particular.[31] My inquiry into Grimké as a chronicler of the Civil War leads me to a conclusion quite similar to Peterson's. Grimké can write about the Civil War only inasmuch as she can render it in sentimentalized, romantic terms. She adorns her account of her tenure with the Port Royal Experiment with images of beautiful black children, detailed descriptions of gallant white soldiers, and long passages devoted to the scenery of the South Georgia Islands. So overdetermined is Grimké's mind and imagination by her search for scenes and people that she can absorb into romantic prose that upon learning of the fate of the Fifty-fourth Massachusetts, she is at a loss for words: "It is too terrible, too terrible to write. We can only hope it may not all be true. That our noble, beautiful young Colonel [Shaw] is killed and the regt. Cut to pieces! I cannot, cannot believe it. . . . I can scarcely write."[32] Although Grimké undoubtedly created vivid images of the event in her imagination, she abruptly aborts any effort to give those images language or to portray the depth of her feelings: "But I can write no more to-night."[33] Over the next week, she manages a few more passages attempting to describe the wounded soldiers, but she undercuts the horrific reality by returning to depictions of beauty whenever possible, noting, for example, a soldier's handsome face or the spectacular grounds of the officer's hospital. Positioned as makeshift nurse to mangled male forms, Grimké could not resist suturing the wounds with threads of sentimental discourse. Conversely, Taylor leaves them wide open.

It is possible that Taylor rejected assuming a posture perceived as feminine because she imagined her memoirs, an attempt to rescue black women who served in the Civil War from historical obscurity, as wedged between two manifestations of public historical writing: the accounts of African American history, such as Nell's *Colored Patriots* and Brown's *The Negro in the American Rebellion*, produced primarily by African American men, and of course, "general" American history, produced primarily by white American men. Taylor is thus attempting to negotiate a space within two dominant historical discourses. Historical texts written by those in positions of domination have come to be understood as sites in which narrative strategizing—selection, forgetting, diminishment—allow the writer of history to interpret social relations in such a way that the marginalized remain marginal and the powerful remain powerful. Taylor's translation of those methods in her autobiography—unnaming, silencing, and displacement—enables her to give precedence to her experiences as a woman within two male spheres: that of war, and that of war writing. Exploring the tactics women autobiographers wield to conceptualize an emancipated narrative "I" resistant to the western, male, imperial "I" of "traditional autobiographical practice," Sidonie Smith suggests that women, like men, willfully and purposefully use suppressive narrative strategies. Women, she argues, "mime the textual politics of 'man.'. . . Speaking from this location proffers authority, legitimacy, readability. It proffers membership in the community of the fully human."[34] Taylor's maneuvers of occlusion may therefore reveal a desire to create authority and legitimacy for herself both inside and outside of her text.

Indeed, in *Martin Delany, Frederick Douglass, and the Politics of Representative Identity*, Robert Levine argues that autobiographical, fictional, and political writing, all arguably forms of the historical, served as an important means through which these two black leaders each attempted to claim status as the representative of the black race. In particular, Levine notes that Douglass "remained virtually silent, in his autobiographical narratives, about his interactions with his black contemporaries. In fact, he did not mention Delany by name in any of his autobiographies."[35] Though Taylor hardly shares Douglass's stature, his omission of Delany and his submersion of other black political leaders can be compared to Taylor's repression of black male soldiers in her work (and, it should be added, her failure to mention many other black women). That is, not only does Taylor position herself as a representative African American woman, standing in for other women who participated in the Civil War, but in clearing the narrative field of black male subjectivity in *Memoirs*, she leaves herself standing as the representative black historical subject of the war, representing the black race generally, men and women alike.

If Taylor's narrative is in fact a contestation of black male historical writing and of the black male's exclusive claim to representational status, the relationship of her narrative to white male historical writing (and white male power) comes across as decidedly less rivalrous. To begin, Taylor does not dedicate her work to the women who labored beside her, nor to the "boys" with whom she served. Instead, *Reminiscences* is dedicated to Higginson, who, as I have mentioned, wrote one of the introductions for her volume. A second introduction, a letter, was written by Colonel C. T. Trowbridge, who succeeded Higginson when the latter left the Thirty-third because of disability. These prefatory materials serve unquestionably as legitimizing mechanisms, recalling, of course, the prefaces attached to the eighteenth- and nineteenth-century slave narratives. Given the purposes of the prefaces of slave narratives—to validate the truthfulness of the narratives and deem the voice that follows them as worthy of speech, and given Taylor's persistent attempts to loose herself from black male authority—it seems odd that she would immediately enter into a relationship with Higginson and Trowbridge that signifies a form of racial hierarchy reminiscent of an ancien régime. While Taylor positions her introductory remarks before theirs, Higginson ensures that her narrative is read as ancillary to his, describing her work as a "little volume" of "peculiar interest" while noting that his version of events had been "long since translated into the French by the Comtesse de Gasparin under the title 'Vie Militaire dans un Régiment Noir' " (xi): a remark so pompous and unnecessary that it can only be construed as a self-serving attempt to establish the grandeur of his work, particularly when compared to Taylor's.

In dedicating the work to Higginson, Taylor appears to agree with his assessment of his own significance. Additionally, his and Trowbridge's names—along with the names of numerous other white male officers—are consistently invoked within the pages of her work, an altogether differing treatment from that afforded black men within the same narrative space (and a very different treatment than black men are given in Harper's novel). Both Higginson and Trowbridge are each given a single page on which their portraits appear; only one black man's image graces the pages of *Reminiscences*, that of Henry Blanchot, a steward of John and Abigail Adams. His picture appears not singly, but amidst portraits of white officers on the same page; his affiliation with the Adamses is mentioned in a line beneath his portrait. Because no blacks other than Taylor appear in portraiture, it can be assumed that his connection with a prominent white family was the sole reason he merited inclusion. Although it is quite likely that Taylor had little to do with illustrative decisions, her narrative choices reinforce the story told by the selection of images. Just as pictures of unnamed black males are placed beside pictures of fully identified white men, Taylor silences black men within her work while she liberally quotes their white male counterparts. She includes, for instance, the entire speech Trowbridge made when the regiment was officially disbanded at the end of the war. And while Taylor may seek to become "one of the boys," an equalizing gesture, her identification with white officers in her text takes on the same coloration of the relationship of her narrative to Higginson's and Trowbridge's prefaces: one of validation. Taylor repeatedly refers to their praise of her work and to her esteem in their eyes. In one instance, Taylor writes of Trowbridge: "I shall never forget his friendship and kindness toward me, from the first time I met him to the end of the war. There was never anyone from the North who came into our camp but he would bring them to see me" (45).

Why Taylor would so freely give the authority she wrests from black men to their white commanders certainly might be puzzling from a political point of view, but from an economic perspective, it makes sense. The letter printed in Taylor's book from Trowbridge expresses regret that she is not eligible to receive a pension because she was not technically an army nurse: "among all the number of heroic women whom the government is now rewarding I know of no one more deserving than yourself" (xii). Although little is known about Taylor's life other than what is contained in her book, it is not unlikely that Taylor, like many other black women before her, was moved to write for financial reasons. (Similarly, the profits from Sarah Bradford's 1886 biography of Tubman were intended partly to make up for the pension she had yet to procure and to make an argument for it.[36]) Taylor self-published her work in Boston, where Higginson and Trowbridge were both renowned figures (like Higginson, Trowbridge was also a published author); with no publisher to market or distribute her book, their stature might have lent interest enough to increase sales. Within her memoirs, Taylor comments that she "gave" her "services willingly for four years and three months without receiving a dollar," yet claims to feel her services were appreciated, if not financially rewarded (21). Whatever her reason, offering these white men the authoritative space she denies black men seems especially odd given her claim to want the old black soldiers to be remembered (a claim already undermined by the narrative that has preceded it): "I look around now and see the comforts that our younger generation enjoy, and think of the blood that was shed to make these comforts possible, and see how little some of them appreciate the old soldiers. My heart burns within me, at this want of appreciation. There are only a few of them left now, so let us all, as the ranks close, take a deeper interest also, and remember that it was through the efforts of these veterans that they and we older ones enjoy our liberty today" (52). It is important to remember that while black

Civil War writing is preoccupied with the project of writing the black body in such a way that it illustrates the writers' perceptions of postwar political and social relations, this project must necessarily position the black body against the white, especially the white male body. The white male body carries no fixed meaning across the literature; however, most consistently, it is marked by its power and desire to consume blackness. In *Iola Leroy*, Dr. Gresham wishes to marry Iola and place the mulatta's race under erasure; the heroine's refusal of his hand essentially reinscribes the heroine as black. Harper perceives Gresham's desire to absorb Iola into his whiteness as so potent that she found it necessary to cut his arm off—a wound sustained in war—in an obvious gesture of symbolic castration. In the same novel, the bodies of Harry and Robert, who are asked by white men why they would not choose to pass undetected into a white manhood, are also defined as black by the rejection of that proposal. In the 1867 *Clotelle*, a white general feeds black body after black body into the killing field until the dead body of a white officer is recovered. In Dunbar's *The Fanatics*, Nigger Ed's black body is pulled back into the domestic "white hole" of homosocial race nationalist narratives. In *Behind the Scenes*, Elizabeth Keckley largely expresses the worth of her black body by its proximity to the "greatest" white man of the era, Abraham Lincoln, detailing his accomplishments until her own life is diminished in relation to his: "I am not writing," she admits, "altogether the history of myself."[37] Over and over again, white masculinity takes on the characteristics of a devouring machine, a characteristic rooted in the slave system, and one that undoubtedly intensified as the nation continued to swallow darker geographical regions. Whether these writers' renderings of the relationship of the black body to the white male's are rooted in anxiety, like Brown's, or apparent admiration, like Keckley's, they speak—loudly—to the recognition of white male power. Accordingly, the issue each of these works addresses, consciously or unconsciously, is how that power should be confronted in a postslavery, postwar world.

This struggle is made nowhere more apparent than in the way black Civil War writers and commentators treat Keckley's white man, Lincoln, a treatment that will provide a context for elucidating Susie King Taylor's discursive relationship to Higginson and Trowbridge.

As I mentioned in the last chapter, despite Lincoln's own reservations about the roles blacks could possibly play in a society comprised completely of liberated people, the Emancipation Proclamation succeeded in transforming a deft politician into a hero within black communities. Whether the black population as a whole knew of the president's reticence about an integrated society became irrelevant; the fact remained that Lincoln had set African Americans free. The assassination of the president only assured his martyrdom, as the following passage from Mattie J. Jackson's 1866 "as told to" narrative attests: "On the Saturday after the assassination of the President there was a meeting held in the common, and a vote taken to have the President's body brought through Indianapolis, for the people to see his dear, dead face . . . a thousand black hands were extended in the air, seemingly higher and more visible than all the rest. Nor were their hands alone raised, for in their deep sorrow and gloom they raised their hearts to God, for well they knew that He, through martyred blood, had made them free."[38]

As in Harper's holy vision of war, Dr. L. S. Thompson, the black female physician who wrote Jackson's narrative, here transforms Lincoln into a mythical figure akin to Christ; Lincoln, like Christ, was unjustly murdered for attempting to realize God's will on Earth. Her passage retroactively reconfigures the Civil War as a religious crusade: a vision that Lincoln himself forwarded during his lifetime. In his Second Inaugural Address, the president, "searching for the meaning of emancipation," Blight writes, ". . . declared that the 'Almighty had his own purposes' and gave the country 'this terrible war, as the woe due to those by whom the offence came.' "[39] Jackson was not alone in her view of Lincoln. Brown, Harper, Douglass, Du Bois, and Keckley are just a few of the many black writers who eulogized Lincoln as a martyr. Even the cynical Dunbar fell in step in his poem "Lincoln" from Lyrics of Love and Laughter (1903). Not every literary and political response from African Americans about Lincoln consented to his coronation, however. In "Lincoln and Douglass," Alice Dunbar-Nelson took the occasion of Lincoln's birthday to make a radical statement about blacks' deification of the fallen leader. "Every school boy in the nation" knows the story of the fallen leader, she proclaims, "His life with its romance of poverty and toil, its tragic sorrow and its tragic end."[40] She argues that blacks should reserve some of their adulation of Lincoln for Frederick Douglass, imploring African Americans to "pour out at his altar the incense he deserves"—a call for the nation within a nation to seek out its own national narratives with its own national icons.[41]

This is not to say that none of the other black writers I mentioned were discontented with Lincoln's uneven, equivocating leadership. "Faults he had," Brown writes in The Negro in the American Rebellion, "but we forget them in his death."[42] In the same vein, the famous 1876 speech Douglass delivered before a mixed audience honoring the first Memorial Day and the eleventh anniversary of Lincoln's assassination hardly extols the president's virtues unhesitatingly. Douglass used the oration to recite a long list of Lincoln's failures in racial policy; he tempered it, however, with another list of Lincoln's accomplishments, equally lengthy. His oration, double-voiced though it is, depicts Lincoln more favorably than not. During the course of the speech, Douglass labels Lincoln a "martyr" and "glorious friend" to African Americans.[43] More significantly, in calling blacks Lincoln's "best step-children," Douglass figures the president as a father, though perhaps a reluctant one; blacks, his lineal descendants through "adoption."[44] To be sure, the exigency of the speech and an audience filled with white statesman—including President Grant—required that Douglass be kinder than he might have preferred. Praising the sculpture of Lincoln unveiled that day, he later criticized the depiction of the slave, shackles broken, kneeling before Lincoln as counterproductive to images of black progress and manliness.[45] Overall, however, Douglass's attitude toward "the Great Emancipator" was insistently forgiving; his writings about Lincoln reveal that he preferred to think of Lincoln as the man he was becoming rather than the man he actually became. He was, to Frederick Douglass, a man both "great and good."[46]

Blight has argued that Douglass's thinking was informed by a religious "cosmic dualism"—the struggle between good and evil—that permeated his work. As I noted previously, this cosmic dualism also formed the basis for the melodramatic underpinnings of the sentimentality that characterized many of the discourses of the Republic, political and literary. This mind-set also reveals itself in Douglass's stubborn adherence to the Republican Party. In 1870, he warned blacks how to vote: "One is the party loyal to liberty, justice, and good order, and the other is the party in sympathy with the defeated rebellion."[47] Again, in 1883, at a Memorial Day gathering in Rochester, he reiterated his stance, announcing, "I shall never forget the difference between those who fought for liberty and fought for slavery; between those who fought to save the Republic and those who fought to destroy it."[48] Douglass spoke for the majority of black Americans, who could forget (if they knew) that Lincoln had blamed blacks for the war and wished for their expatriation, but who would not forget that the Yankees were their friends and the Confederates their enemies. Despite the good work Dunbar, Harper, and other black writers such as Hopkins did to emphasize the falsity in the antonymic binaries, North and South, it was simply too tempting and far too easy for blacks in the postwar nation to seek to divide white men into two categories that fell along those lines, those who were "for us" and those who were "against us," labels emerging from the division between the two white male figures who loomed large in pre–Civil War black life and imagination: abolitionist and slaveholder.

I suggest, then, that Taylor's scripting of Higginson and Trowbridge as her "friends" and her deference to their authority flows from a logic shaped by three factors: the cosmic dualism of Republican discourse, the desire to ascribe the North with a postwar "abolitionist" sentiment that reinscribes North/South binaries, and the need to perpetuate iconographic representations of white "saviors." Toward the end of her autobiography, Taylor writes of how she "does not condemn all the Caucasian race because the negro is badly treated by a few of the race" (66). "No!" she continues, "for had it not been for the true whites, assisted by God and the prayers of our forefathers, I should not be here to-day" (66). Shortly thereafter, she admits that living in the country of the "negro-hating white man" and remembering the atrocities of the Confederacy confuses her ability to repeat the mantra "no North, no South" (59, 68). She wrestles with eliding the South and the negro-haters out of hand, yet feels a need to distinguish "true whites"—the friends of blacks—as those who assisted the Union in the war. Those people are, in the main, northerners. Taylor's scripting of the kind white male northern Union officer in *Reminiscences* places him squarely and safely in the category of the "true white."

The widespread iconography of Lincoln as martyr and Taylor's insistence that "true whites" such as Higginson and Trowbridge exist seems a containment strategy, much like the creation of the plantation darky. If every black has the potential to rise up in slavery to demand freedom or rise up in freedom to demand the vote, that potential for disorder is quelled in the creation of the contented figure guaranteed not to challenge the status quo. If every white man, even he who issued the Emancipation Proclamation, can be a potential (or undercover) racist, transforming him into a martyr deadens that potential by permanently silencing his troubling politics. The Higginson Taylor praises, though a lifelong abolitionist, was also the man who claimed the military had made black men less "grotesque." *Army Life in a Black Regiment*, the work he demands be taken more seriously than Taylor's, is full of the musings of the romantic racialist. Blacks are "picturesque" objects to be written about, not subjects, like Taylor, fit to write themselves—"Sambos," with "simple natures" like those of a "child."[49] In one particularly long passage, he takes a cue from scientific racialists, detailing the black soldiers' "splendid muscular" bodies, which are "smoother and more free from hair" than whites. He announces: "I always like to observe them when bathing."[50] Higginson also implies that he expected less of them initially because he spied only one or two mulattos in the bunch and elsewhere struggles to divorce them from the fictional images of blacks he encountered in Stowe's novel. Whether infantilizing, dissecting, eroticizing, or romanticizing the black male body, Higginson's objectification is a sure sign that he does not place them on a plane equal to whites.

Taylor, literate and rhetorically astute, must have grasped the implications of her colonel's depictions of the black soldiers (and it is interesting that both writers use the narrative control they exercise over these black men as a means of consolidating visions of their own bodily identities.) Given that awareness, her subsequent diminishment of the black soldiers' bodies and her valorization of the white officers illuminate the utter urgency of the two overriding needs that guide her narrative: to put her body before the black male's historically, and to believe, at all costs, in the presence of "true whites" in a country that made that belief difficult. In a moment of exasperation in one of her closing chapters, she asks the underlying question posed by all of the Civil War writers in my study: " 'Was the war in vain' " (61)?

It must be noted that Taylor voices her insecurity about the war's success in 1902, after the Spanish-Cuban-American War, and that this insecurity appears to be tied to concerns about the United States' imperial designs in the Caribbean. Although Taylor organized on behalf of black troops returning from that conflict, she nevertheless expresses fear that oppressive American racial structures would be instituted abroad if the United States were to gain complete control of Cuba. In "Thoughts on Present Conditions," the same chapter in which she attempts to make sense of the political circumstances facing blacks after the Civil War, Taylor remarks on the role the United States had assumed as a Cuban temporary "protectorate" upon its defeat of Spain. Characterizing Cuba as a nation previously immune to color stratification, she suggests that it has suddenly—if explicably—become racially corrupted: "With the close of the Spanish war, and on the entrance of the Americans into Cuba, the same conditions confront us as the war of 1861 left. The Cubans are free, but it is a limited freedom, for prejudice, deep rooted, has been brought to them and a separation made between the white and black Cubans, a thing that had never existed between them before; but to-day there is the same intense hatred toward the Negro in Cuba that there is some parts of this country" (63). Taylor was not alone in her assessment. As the next chapter demonstrates, African American debates over the role of the United States as a rising empire at the turn of the century would heighten blacks' awareness of the relationship between those "domestic" policies involving their own constitutional rights and "foreign" policies involving people of color abroad.[51] "We have before us," Taylor writes, "still another problem to solve" (63).

4 IMAGINING MOBILITY

Turn-of-the-Century
Empire, Technology,
and Black Imperial
Citizenship

As early as the 1840s and 1850s, black intellectuals had denounced white politicians who envisioned Mexican conquest and the possibility of Cuban annexation as ways to extend the United States' slaveholding territories. During the Ten Years' War that Cuban revolutionaries waged against the Spanish preceding U.S. involvement in that conflict, blacks nearly unanimously supported the insurgents, awed by the leadership of Antonio Maceo, "the Bronze Titan," whom some African Americans viewed as a fellow black. Reminiscent of Toussaint L'Ouverture's revolutionary liberation of Haiti, Antonio Maceo's command led radicalized black Americans to anticipate what President Cleveland's administration later said it feared: "an establishment of a . . . black republic" in the Western hemisphere.[1] When the United States formally declared war against Spain in 1898, African Americans voiced concern that the possibility of a Cuba under American rule would mean that more people of color would become victims of the blatant discrimination and racism that American blacks had endured for centuries. While some wholeheartedly endorsed the United States' declared goal—the liberation of Cubans from Spanish domination—a prolonged occupation or permanent annexation was another matter. Forced to live with the daily and ceaseless indignities of Jim Crow, many blacks were unwilling to become integral to a process in which African Americans might be "used to subject non-white colonials to that same system."[2]

By the time of the Philippine-American War (1899–1902), when it had become clear that Filipino revolutionaries led by Emilio Aguinaldo would not accept American sovereignty, prowar military and political officials—aided by the yellow press—escalated a brutally racist rhetorical campaign against their former allies, dismissing them as a "stunted" and "inferior" race. Black anti-imperialist sentiment became more fervent as reports of white soldiers calling the insurgents "niggers" surfaced, and the popular press printed cartoons in which Aguinaldo, a refined brown-skinned man who had studied law in Manila, appeared as a pitch-black "primitive" or a pickaninny. For many African Americans, these caricatures merely confirmed the sinister character of the racism influencing imperial policy and military practice. The impunity with which McKinley had refused autonomy for the Philippines was perceived as colonial and supremacist; his concession to the Sultan of Sulu, which allowed the sultan to retain slavery within his Philippine territory, was met with disbelief and outrage.[3] The treatment of black soldiers who fought Spain in Cuba helped solidify antiwar sentiment. Though the performance of black regulars in the famed battle of San Juan Hill prompted the white and black press alike to praise them as heroes, they were initially denied commissions upon their return. Narratives of bravery were quickly overshadowed by rumors of incompetence. In fact, the War Department alleged that its hesitance to send black volunteers to the Philippines was based on the units' poor showing in the earlier conflict. Two volunteer formations were eventually sent to join the black regulars, but African Americans widely believed that the decision was reversed only so that black men could be used as fodder in a war that was proving bloody, long, and costly.[4]

It is of little wonder, then, that black anti-imperialist efforts had become more organized than during the prior war. African Americans formed a colored auxiliary of the New England Anti-Imperialist League in 1899; similar groups emerged that same year. The most vocally opposed to McKinley's policies included recognizable and weighty figures such as lawyer Archibald Grimké, antilynching activist Ida B. Wells,[5] educator Anna Julia Cooper, and the president of the Afro-American Council, Bishop Alexander Walters. Even Booker T. Washington, while not expressly anti-imperialist, articulated serious doubts about the wisdom of supporting actions in the Philippines that would divert resources from the critical work of racial uplift within the United States.[6] While it is not my purpose in this chapter to tease out all the various strands of thought within the black anti-imperialist movement, the commonality, as I have intimated, was African Americans' refusal to believe that the United States should govern people of color abroad, having failed to do so justly on its own soil. Thus, while black men clamored to join in the war against the Filipinos, as they had done in every war before, black anti-imperialists asked African American men already in the military to refuse service and others not to volunteer. The rationale was plain: blacks should not aid and abet the United States in its plans to deny other "dark-hued races" their natural right to freedom and their political right to self-determination.

Although proimperialist blacks would dismiss these concerns as thoroughly unmodern—just so much old-fashioned black paranoia—the fear that domestic racial practices would be carried abroad was not without historical basis. Anne McClintock has famously argued that English colonial endeavors during the Victorian era were often articulated as a desire to transform foreign spaces into domestic ones, the colonizer believing that the civilizing "rituals of domesticity" would tame the wild savages now housed within the walls of the national home.[7] Amy Kaplan has extended this concept to antebellum white women writers in the United States, suggesting that these women alleviated anxieties about westward expansionism by imagining contact with the other as a similarly domesticating enterprise.[8] As American continental expansionism traveled overseas, the idea of setting up household abroad might have therefore assuaged misgivings about overseas imperialism for some white Americans, who could envision slipping into the familiar role of domesticators to barbarous "others." However, as evidenced by the increase in black anti-imperialism as Philippine occupation became imminent, the extension of disciplining "rituals" of American domesticity overseas in the guise of a protective governmental practice was not nearly as comforting for African Americans.

Even in its rhetorical capacity, as a trope that diverted attention away from the ramifications of a range of violently oppressive national practices, domesticity had been critiqued steadily by black American writers. As I have shown, a good number of African American Civil War writers were reluctant to invest in a domestic sentimental fantasy that embraced Republican civil ideals as a solution for racial relations. Presenting contrived images of black "domestic tranquility" as a form of racial protest was, in essence, a violent act of self-domestication, forcing oneself to be civil when civility was not in order. Brown's disillusionment with postwar racial politics, recall, drove him to disavow a bourgeois matrimonial imaginary, leaving readers with portraits of two politically imperfect households: the quarreling Jim and Dinah's "slave" cabin and a widow's house, built on the land where she was raised in bondage. Dunbar's equal bitterness prompted an ironic attack on blacks' debased position within the neoplantation household. King refused the sexist repression of the white private/female domestic sphere to take up a liberatory black female public subject position. Nevertheless, even if these writers were bringing the domestic under question, a civil war fought on domestic soil begged that they discuss the black body in relation to the home and the household.

I return to these writers' endeavors to distance themselves from domestic tropology, an issue raised in prior chapters, to point out that the desire for domestic inclusion, finding a way "in," was often simultaneously articulated as the need to escape forms of domestic repression—finding a way "out." This "out" might be metaphorical (through dismantling or complicating the rhetoric, for instance), literal (the flight to Canada, emigration, exile, African "repatria-tion"), or ideological (a repudiation of the dominant culture's politics). Protest-ing U.S. imperialism was most certainly a way out ideologically, a means of both dissociating blacks from the manner in which the nation chose to conduct itself abroad and of furthering an identification with people of color outside of the boundaries of the United States, particularly those who had been suffering under European colonialism. A.M.E. clergyman H. T. J. Johnson was eager to claim Filipinos as "foreign members of his own [black Americans'] racial household" in an effort to galvanize blacks against American imperial enterprises.[9] Yet such broadly encompassing pan-Africanist or pan-Afro-Asian modes of thought—based primarily in a perceived similarity of "race" and circumstance—tended to generalize an understanding of the global oppression of darker races from do-mestic racial sensibilities, creating a model of "global" racism that could not be divorced from the American context that generated it. The "foreign" Filipinos belong to African Americans' "racial household" rather than belonging to their *own*. Whether the ethnocentrism inherent in this kind of analysis suggests an inability to transcend a racial consciousness bound by domestic politics or an impulse to co-opt the struggles of American people of color elsewhere for do-mestic use, the gesture outward, away from the national, often returned black American anti-imperialists squarely inward.

In this chapter, I will examine two African American works supportive of the Spanish-Cuban-American War and the American wars in the Philippines to sug-gest that embracing imperialism, rather than rejecting it, offered some blacks an alternative way "out." The first, the celebrated military history *The Colored Regulars in the United States Army*, was written by the influential Colored A.M.E. minister and army chaplain T. G. Steward, a well-regarded member of the free-born elite, and only the third black clergyman to secure a commission within that branch of the armed forces. Completed in 1899 and published in 1904,[10] *Colored Regulars* was written largely to refute claims of black military ineptitude. The second, a little-known work entitled *"The Problem": A Military Novel*, published in 1915 by Prince Hall Mason F. Grant Gilmore,[11] details the exploits of a noble, gifted black soldier who fights valiantly during both wars and is duly rewarded by the white military establishment for his efforts. I will use these works to argue that the transformation of U.S. imperialism from a continental phenomenon to a practice exercised abroad—away from "home"—prompted some African Americans to perceive in that movement a route away from domesticity in all of its manifesta-tions: domestic repression, domestic tropology, and domestic models of race and racial relations, especially those models elevating the black domestic sphere as the principal structure for the creation and enactment of a black bourgeois subjectivity. Indeed, the significance of Steward's and Gilmore's works lies in the ways both narrate black military participation to do more than align themselves with new U.S. imperatives as a means of demonstrating national allegiance, or to hail black service in a bid for a fully recognized national citizenship. Those aspects are certainly forcefully present, but they would hardly differentiate these writers from Nell, Williams, Harper, and other black "patriots" writing about the wars that preceded the U.S. military's overseas interventions. Steward and Gilmore instead take those elements distinguishing the Revolution and the Civil War from the turn-of-the-century imperial warfare—its civilizing rationale, its location "elsewhere," and its association with the nation's technological and geopolitical future—to construct a black imperial masculinity that displaces versions of the black male body limited by domestic interpretative frameworks.

Many of these interpretations, such as the archetype of black social and physical immobility (the agricultural, land-based slave tied to the plantation), or Harper's new national males (former slaves building homesteads in the South), suggest various modes of boundedness, a condition that empire explicitly refuses. It is a condition that the writers also refuse, rejecting what Houston Baker has very helpfully labeled "domestic immobilization" for "public sphere mobility," the ultimate sign of black modernity.[12] Thus, while Steward's and Gilmore's black military male signals a desire to recover the liberating movement that had characterized the icon of black heroic masculinity during the era of slavery—the fugitive slave—there are critical points of departure arising from the context of a postemancipation American imperialism. Perhaps most important, the compulsory movement of escape and exile (in which the subject looks nervously over his shoulder or longingly at what he might have left behind) is transformed into a movement that permits the subject to look in one direction only: toward the future. Differentiating it even more from the movement of escape and exile, a movement which is often perpetual and infinitely displacing, black imperial mobility inherently (and perhaps paradoxically) signifies rootedness. It does so precisely because it is imperial, following empire's geographical duality. That is, just as empire simultaneously exists here and there, grounded in the nation-state yet traveling outside itself, the black military imperial male is deeply connected to the nation but able to move beyond it as a legal "citizen"—without, therefore, forsaking citizenship and without implying a lack of citizenship status. Baker in fact argues that black public sphere mobility depends on the safety of U.S. "documentation":[13] the "passport" that Nell fetishizes in Colored Patriots.[14] Ostensibly, then, as a passport-carrying member of a postemancipation U.S. empire, the African American military male can propel himself into modernity, unafraid of finding himself in a state of permanent dispossession.

Additionally, I will read the production of the black imperial body within historian James A. Field Jr.'s paradigm-altering contention that "technological feasibility" was a critical factor determining when and if the United States would become an overseas empire.[15] Field made this claim in the 1970s as an intervention: most historical accounts of this period, he argues, erroneously elevate racial and ideological rationales for turn-of-the-century imperialist warfare, missing the essential role industrial innovation played in opening vistas, creating the means to seize territories, and inspiring confidence in the military's efficiency. Empire, he writes, is "in one sense the product of the new technological developments."[16] His fundamental assertion characterizes the impetus for the wars in Cuba and the Philippines as startlingly banal—the United States went to war abroad because it could. Only retroactively, then, did proimperialists, and later, historians, frame the motivation for empire within imperatives more ideological in nature. Yet Field studiously avoids moralizing about the ethical implications of allowing technology to govern decisions about warfare. But a moral critique had been made many times before, most aggressively by Marxists, who had analyzed empire in terms similar to Field's if for altogether differing ends. For example, the Marxist cultural critic Walter Benjamin, a victim of the rise of European fascism, explicitly blamed the misuse of technology in industrialized nations as transforming states into deadly, desiring machines:

> If the natural utilization of productive forces is impeded by the property system, the increase in technical devices, in speed, and in the sources of energy, will press for an unnatural utilization, and this is found in war. . . . The horrible features of imperialistic warfare are attributable to the discrepancy between the tremendous means of production and their inadequate utilization in the process of production—in other words, to unemployment and lack of markets. . . . Instead of draining rivers, society directs a human stream into a bed of trenches; instead of dropping seeds from airplanes, it drops incendiary bombs over cities."[17]

Of course, the direction of the determinism presented in Field's and Benjamin's assessments has been rigorously debated.[18] Others have in fact argued that the transformation of the United States into a military power, a nation perpetually at war, created a need to discover means of increasing industrial productivity and spurred technological innovations that could be implemented in the armed forces,[19] the beginnings of a military-industrial state. In either case, what is important here is that Steward's and Gilmore's modernization of black liberatory movement—the "upgrade" into imperial mobility—registers industrialism's powerful impact on the course of U.S. geopolitics. That is, both endeavor to construct a technologically "determined" and "technologically feasible" black male body by associating it with the advances in military technology that made Caribbean and Pacific empire possible and by presenting that body as perfected by the military's organizational and disciplinary "sciences." In so doing, they create a black male subjectivity that is "expansionist": entering the temporal space possessed by "civilized" races while distancing themselves from the "primitive" cultures with whom black pan-Afro and pan-Asianists sought proximity. As Field suggests, in imperial reasoning the technological capacity for movement into the territory of the "other" often cooperated with "biological" rationales, particularly those justifications of empire supported by faulty analogies drawn from Darwin's influential 1859 study of the natural world and his later work, *The Descent of Man*, published in 1871. Put reductively, in this manner of conceptualizing empire, some dominant nations (like hardy, aggressive species and organisms) would naturally propagate and expand, eventually needing to overtake others in a global "race" for land and resources. The ability to implement technology in whatever capacity to accomplish that, such as worthier ships, advanced weapons systems, and so forth—the material production of an industrialized nation with a organized state—served as evidence of cultural superiority, a display of a creative and intellectual inventiveness that supplemented biological vigor.

In the United States, the interplay between technology and biology informed and energized an already racialized idea of nationalism. In discussing the role Spanish-Cuban-American War shorts played in the development of early American cinema in *The Anarchy of Empire in the Making of U.S. Culture*, Kaplan suggests that the conflation of technological progress and U.S. imperialism was so great that the projection machines used to show war shorts "such as Edison's Kinescope, were renamed as War-Graph, or Warscope."[20] A bionational chauvinism was strengthened by this synthesis: the films contributed to Anglo-Saxon racialist superiority by providing spectacular displays of American geographical mobility and active American troops while depicting the Spanish and Cubans as static and immobile. As the United States was debating the annexation of Hawaii prior to the wars against Spain and the Philippines, African American newspaperman Edward E. Cooper expressed dissatisfaction with black anti-imperialism, which, in his thinking, unnaturally restricted the geographical enlargement necessary for black maturation: "The wolf cry of imperialism," he wrote in the *Colored American*, "cannot keep us in swaddling clothes forever. Expansionism is the natural order of things in nations and individuals."[21]

It is therefore important to emphasize that Steward's and Gilmore's ascription of technology to the black male body will occur within a cultural milieu where "expansionism" and "industrialism" had accrued physiological meanings. In an American epoch more often called the "machine age" than the "age of empire," manufacturers touted varied innovations in technology—electric irons and cash registers, even the simple fountain pen—as the solution to the human body's physical limitations. The rapidity of factory industrialism only encouraged their consumption; these devices appeared endlessly available, each model advertised as better, and more necessary, than the last.[22] While a great many Americans seemed to embrace these products as progress, scholars of the period also have suggested that the increasingly unclear meaning of flesh and bone in a society rapidly surrendering to the lure of things inanimate gave rise to a reactionary antitechnological physical culture consumed by reaffirming the natural body's primacy: the need to demonstrate that the body was as capable—and valuable—as the machines it produced. There is certainly little evidence that African Americans at the turn of the century harbored these kinds of anxieties, welcoming machines as labor-saving devices (replacing the black body as laboring machine) but also envisioning a connection to advancements in technology as "supplementing" a body the dominant culture deemed deficient. During this same period, in 1897, the American Negro Academy was founded, a heady collective of black male intellectuals that included Grimké, Steward, Du Bois, and Dunbar among others considered the "talented tenth" of the race.[23] Founded in part to counterbalance the hegemony of Booker T. Washington's "cast your buckets where you are" politics, which progressive blacks viewed as little more than retrogressive neoplantationism, the academy was imagined in martial terms. Describing itself, in fact, as an organizational self-defense against "vicious assaults," it first convened on the same date Crispus Attucks fell in the Boston Massacre, "an event especially sacred to the Negro,"[24] wrote academy founder Alexander Crummell, a prominent intellectual and Episcopalian priest. At that inaugural meeting, Crummell delivered an address defining the spirit of the organization: "Civilization: The Primal Need of the Race." "To make men you need civilization," he declared, describing civilization nearly expressly in terms of science and industrialism: "Civilization . . . uplift[s] the crudeness of laws, giving scientific precision to morals and religion, stimulating enterprise, extending commerce, creating manufactures, expanding mechanism and mechanical inventions . . . meeting the most minute of human needs, even to the manufacturing needles for the industry of seamstresses and for the commonest use of human fingers."[25]

Like his great admirer Du Bois, who would argue later in *Black Reconstruction* that the black race could only be accurately documented through an "objective," scientific method of historiography, Crummell expresses faith that a rational society governed by enlightened scientific detachment in all of its spheres will allow blacks to emerge as they may, properly disinterested in the outcome. This industrialized, scientific civilization will run predictably, like the machines it produces, impervious to human weaknesses and passions; it will unfailingly "make" black men who express and embody what Crummell calls "the impulses of irrepressible progress"[26] (rather than those who exhibit the irrational mind and body of the primitive made, alternatively, by nature).

Steward's and Gilmore's reimagining of black masculinity rests on a similar belief: that a military shaping and shaped by an industrial and scientific society can make the irrepressibly progressive black body Crummell envisions. By the late nineteenth century, American military strategists had more fully adopted the thinking of their European counterparts, insisting that a distinction be drawn between war as an art and war as a science; the latter thought to have more reproducible methods and foreseeable outcomes than wars conducted by brilliant but idiosyncratic military leaders. Officers trained at West Point were introduced to "scientific" principles of warfare, "the science of administration" in arsenal weaponry; the ordinary soldier was drilled by "scientific" disciplinary techniques and engaged in a "scientific" practice of the skills he had acquired.[27] But even before the military sciences had become fully institutionalized across the armed forces, the army had undergone a profound structural shift that Steward and Gilmore use to make an argument for the army's unrivaled ability to aid in black uplift. Because blacks were not part of a standing army before or during the Civil War, the male bodies that underwent "rearrangement" in the Union army in black American Civil War fiction—Robert Johnson, John Salter, and Harry Leroy in Harper's novel; "Nigger Ed" in Dunbar's—were sent "home" after the conflict ended. In 1866, however, the American government made provisions for blacks to join the regular army in eight segregated regiments that were eventually merged into four: the Ninth and Tenth Calvary and the Twenty-fifth and Twenty-fourth Infantry, the units that would be called to serve in the wars against Spain and the Philippines. This was the first step in institutionalizing the military as a viable profession for black men. Despite the racism and discrimination they still encountered, most pronounced in the limits placed on upward movement (only a handful during this period became commissioned officers), they were paid the same salaries as whites; they were fed, clothed, and housed, and they were also offered opportunities for educational improvement.[28] Joining one of these four units gave African American men a relatively assured means of social advancement. In the same vein, it allowed Steward and Gilmore to herald black men's transformation into "proper" black subjects—into citizens—in a space *apart* from domestic settings. Emphasizing the military's industrial structure, these writers describe a soldier who has been "manufactured" by the military (rather than "raised" in a home), implying that the military can produce a better model of black masculinity. And importantly, this model can be easily reproduced.

In sum, *Colored Regulars* and "The Problem" glorify a black military-industrial masculinity improved and produced by the nineteenth-century scientific "genius" that allowed the United States to move abroad, a black imperial soldier who is "expansionist"—able to transcend prescribed racial, geographical, and social boundaries. In analyzing and describing the way each writer constructs and deploys this body in his work in this chapter, I will also consider the implications of their exultation of the role of U.S. military technology in imperialist warfare waged against populations of color. First, however, it is necessary to examine the racial contexts that led Steward and Gilmore to envision that technology as corporeal redemption.

Race and Nostalgia: Domestic Immobilization

With the passage of the Fifteenth Amendment, black men had become legally enfranchised, however fictionally, before the Spanish-Cuban-American War. This "right," coupled with black incorporation into the standing military, allowed some African Americans to more easily imagine interracial fraternity and a shared national identity as the nation moved into foreign territory than during the regionally and racially divisive Civil War. Herschel Cashin and Charles Alexander, the editors of the black military history *Under Fire with the U.S. Calvary* (1899), declared that with "the destruction of the Maine. . . . Instantaneously, there was no North, no South, no black, no white. We were at once a compact national force marching forward on a high mission."[29] The editor of the Washington, D.C., *Colored American* used strikingly similar terms to argue that the Spanish-Cuban-American War would "cement the races into a more compact brotherhood through perfect unity of purpose and patriotic affinity."[30] To become "compacted" into a narrow American "patriotic" identity required, therefore, relinquishing or reining in an expansive diasporic subjectivity, configuring a relationship to subjects of imperialism that could somehow justify these wars of conquest. In the main, blacks implemented two strategies. As one, they adopted a paternalistic attitude toward the Cubans and Filipinos by playing the part of the global "leader" of "darker races"—the hierarchical racial schema in which black Americans would assume a "civilizing" role to people of color in other, less "advanced" nations, the same rationale that had guided nineteenth-century black missionary work. For example, two of Steward's colleagues in the American

Negro Academy, the prominent black journalist John W. Cromwell and Kelly Miller, a professor at Howard University, believed that an American victory over Spain in both wars provided a means for African Americans to exercise a positive influence over "weaker races," that is, people of color outside of the United States. Miller in fact advocated a program to "Americanize" young Puerto Ricans, Cubans, and Filipinos.[31] Others saw territorial acquisition as another opportunity to advance emigration schemes that had all but failed in Haiti and Africa. Even Du Bois would find in empire an opportunity for black Americans to "guard and guide . . . the teeming millions of Asia and Africa," as he hopefully states in "The Present Outlook for the Dark Races" (1900), though later he would adopt a stance that was radically anticolonial.[32]

Other proimperial black Americans simply denied any kinship to darker Cubans and to the Filipinos. Ascribing both groups the status of "foreign" or "other" allowed African Americans to dismiss any notions of relatedness altogether, rendering them "alien": the very status and language the writers of Under Fire disaffirm for black Americans. An uncompromising editorial from the Indianapolis Freeman expresses impatience with the idea that Filipinos are part of a dispersed family of dark peoples: "It is quite time for the Negroes to quit claiming kindred with every black face from Hannibal down. Hannibal was no Negro, nor was Aguinaldo. We are to share in the glories or defeats of our country's wars, that is patriotism pure and simple."[33]

While the outright rejection of "familial" ties to Cubans and Filipinos—both populations that included peoples of African descent—might seem startling to racial sensibilities conditioned to accept contemporary notions of diasporic and transnational identities, the othering of non-Americans by some nineteenth-century black Americans was part of a well-established habit of seeking assimilation through an identification with hegemonic norms. During the era leading to Spanish-Cuban-American War, black infantry and cavalry distinguished themselves militarily as part of the violent expansionist enterprise that led the United States westward. Nicknamed "Buffalo Soldiers," an appellation rumored to have come from Native Americans, they gained a mythical status due in part to the racialism influencing white officers' perceptions: "The most utterly reckless, daredevil savage . . . stands literally in awe of a Negro and the blacker the Negro the more he quails."[34] Capitalizing on myth, legend, and documented "successes," Steward and Gilmore describe a black imperial soldier who has cut his war teeth by fighting Mexicans and "hostile" or "savage" Indians on the ever-broadening frontier, implying that he was aptly conditioned to execute his task abroad—aligning himself with the United States as the nation mobilized to suppress equally hostile foreign "enemies," be they the "hot tempered" Spanish or the "barbaric" Filipinos. The black soldier becomes, then, not the "domesticated" but the domesticator.

In portraying a black imperial male who is "the domesticator," both civilized and civilizing, Steward and Gilmore repudiate the racial nostalgia that influenced representations of national and domestic life at the turn of the century, a subject I will treat in some detail before exploring the writers' works. This nostalgia greatly contributed to the continued production and consumption of retrogressive images of black Americans. Tom shows still abounded; just prior to the wars, a plump, smiling Aunt Jemima had been unveiled at the World's Fair as the icon for a new line of food products. While the marketing of black bodies as easily consumed commercial articles was clearly another containment strategy capitalizing on the threat posed by black civic advancement—something I have already pointed out—the desire to recede ever more deeply into the nation's former interior life might also be understood as a response to the United States' forward, outward thrust into the racially uncertain world of empire. For instance, in *Tender Violence: Domestic Visions in an Age of U.S. Imperialism*, Laura Wexler suggests that much of the work by white women photographers at the turn of the century constructed images of peaceful domestic scenarios that, in part, concealed antagonistic racial relationships at home—and their relationship to racial strife abroad—by capturing "harmonious" portraits of blacks and whites together that recalled the plantation imaginary.[35] In discussing black responses to southern reconciliation narratives, I noted Walter Benn Michael's suggestion that white nationalists used depictions of a rapacious black masculinity for an anti-imperialist agenda, calling attention away from ill-conceived enterprises abroad back to what they considered the more pressing problem of racial disorder at "home." This disorder, as I mentioned, was quieted only by the reestablishment of the plantation hierarchy. In both examples raised here, imagining domestic interracial peace requires the return to an ostensibly simpler time when racial delineation was allegedly clear. Set against the backdrop of U.S. overseas empire, they may be interpreted as a cautionary against the direction the nation was taking—mixing with the affairs of people of color abroad, and even more dangerously, bringing them into the national household. Calvin Chase, an outspoken black writer for the *Washington Bee*, described southern anti-imperialism in related terms: "the same old fear of 'nigger domination' albeit . . . 8000 miles away."[36] In one sense then, imperialism inspired the familiar horror—it was political miscegenation, taken to an exogamous extreme.

The move to revive the racial dynamics of a bygone era was also intimately tied to preserving the uncontested authority of the white male body as it found itself battling a seemingly endless stream of dark male others: blacks, Indians, Mexicans, Filipinos. Many literary historians have noted that alongside those novels celebrating the restoration of the southern "master," white American historical romances featuring chivalric heroes modeled after Scott's *Ivanhoe* or rugged men based in frontier mythologies were among the best-selling novels at the turn of the century.[37] This phenomenon must be read, at least partly, as another manifestation of an antitechnological impulse, a reclamation of white manhood in the era of industrialism and machines. Too, however, the reading public might have been drawn to an idealized white masculinity from prior historical moments as a way of creating racial coherence in the face of the nation's increasingly heterogeneous imperial identity, and as a means of imagining safety in a world of bellicose dark others.

The extent to which these fear-driven needs informed one another was evidenced in the figure of Theodore Roosevelt, who presented himself as a man made vital by his years raising cattle on the closed western frontier. As Kaplan's insightful analysis of Roosevelt has shown, his successful reinvigoration of a white imperial masculinity drew much of its energy from a strategic and effective denigration of the black male body. After the Spanish-Cuban-American War, Roosevelt, who had fought alongside the Tenth Cavalry as a Rough Rider, buoyed his own appeal as a vice presidential candidate by diminishing black participation in the Battle of San Juan Hill.[38] Infamously describing the black soldier as "peculiarly dependent" in the serialized version of *Rough Riders* first published in *Scribner's* in 1899, Roosevelt attempts, in Kaplan's interpretation, to transpose the master/slave relationship onto white officers and their African American subordinates:

> None of the white regulars or Rough Riders showed the slightest sign of weakening; but under the strain the colored infantry (who had none of their officers) began to get a little uneasy and to drift into the rear, either helping wounded men, or saying they wished to find their own regiments. This I could not allow, as it was depleting my line, so I jumped up, and walking a few yards to the rear, drew my revolver, halted the retreating soldiers, and called out to them . . . that I should shoot the first man who . . . went to the rear.[39]

Imagining their reaction as a performance, a "comic opera," Roosevelt writes that his gun-waving threat sufficiently disciplined the men: the " 'smoked Yankees'. . . flashed their white teeth at one another, as they broke into broad grins, and I had no trouble with them."[40] More than a matter of political expediency, Roosevelt's flip-flop (he had praised these soldiers as "an excellent breed of Yankees" during the war) denied the black male body the full "manhood" it was demanding outside the arena of war and became a way of resilencing a body that had dared enunciate itself within a national historical narrative.[41] The most powerful weapon Roosevelt uses against black men is not the pistol he fantasizes brandishing in *Rough Riders*, then, but a combative discursive strategy: scripting black men at war as little more than participants in a traveling minstrel show on a tour abroad. As Kaplan claims, Roosevelt's rendering of a confusing battle fought on foreign soil alongside black troops becomes framed within a domestic racial order; a circumstance made less "strange" when given the familiar comforts of "home."

The *Scribner's* article ran counter to those depictions describing the Tenth Calvary as rescuing the Rough Riders from annihilation, accounts that included numerous eyewitness testimonies from white soldiers. Its publication unleashed a deluge of counterevidence and objections in the black press, the most biting from black soldiers incensed that their contributions had been trivialized within racist caricature. Not surprisingly, Steward and Gilmore also take issue with Roosevelt's representation of the battle and black soldiering, Gilmore going so far as to lampoon Roosevelt's masculine bravado. But it is essential to note that Roosevelt's version of black service in Cuba was hardly idiosyncratic; instead, it was part of the larger set of images of black soldiering that had gained popularity during the Civil War as black citizenship seemed imminent, and that continued to influence perceptions of black military participation.

These portrayals were so powerful and ubiquitous that they managed to find their way into some cultural products generated by African Americans. The aforementioned *Under Fire with the U.S. Calvary: Being a Brief, Comprehensive Review of the Negro's Participation in the Wars of the United States* stands as one example. Just after the Spanish-Cuban-American War ended, Cashin, a prominent Georgia Republican, and Alexander, a newspaper reporter and later the publisher of *Alexander's Magazine*, enlisted the help of three black men who had served in the conflict, Sergeant Horace Bivins of the Tenth Cavalry, army chaplain William T. Anderson, and military surgeon Arthur M. Brown to assemble the "Negro's story of the Cuban campaign."[42] Like other African Americans who published historical accounts of black military service, the editors state that their work was necessitated by "the tendency of the average historian to either entirely ignore or very grudgingly acknowledge the courage, valor, and patriotism of a so-called *alien race*, in their efforts . . . to court the popular."[43] As in Susie Taylor's autobiography, however, the seemingly singular purpose of Cashin and his coauthors' work is complicated by a white officer's prefatory material. Written by General Joseph Wheeler, who commanded the cavalry units in which Roosevelt served, the remarks appear to undermine the very spirit of the project:

The men of the South know that the prominent characteristic of the old Negro slave was loyalty—a loyalty touching in its beauty and simplicity. How few examples we have of treachery compared with the many instances of unselfish devotion exhibited by the slave in his loyalty to a loved master or mistress. Who has not seen a thousand times the counterpart of Sam in "Mars' Chan," a story so touchingly true to life that one can scarcely read it with dry eyes. Is it then any wonder or any matter of surprise that the colored troops true to their inborn spirit of loyalty went forth full into battle with a foreign foe. . . ?[44]

Taking a page from Thomas Nelson Page's book, almost literally, Wheeler simply laterally transfers depictions of black masculinity from contemporary southern nationalist literature about the Civil War into his own commentary; like Roosevelt, he effectively transforms the foreign battlefield into a domestic space: this time, into an overseas southern plantation. And while borrowing fictive scenarios from racist white men about one war to frame a nonfiction work compiled by black professional men about another makes for an incredibly messy move—historically, generically, and racially incongruous—it was also culturally easy and politically expedient. By transfiguring black soldiers into slaves genetically predisposed to be "loyal," the general reinforces the idea that African American men were not inclined to fight for any self-interested, self-determining purpose, conflating service to the military or nation with domestic service to whites. As such, Wheeler accomplishes what Roosevelt did—he is able to write white male officers into their master-full command, forcing a text bursting with black masculine self-assertion to submit to his authority. The general's tearful sentimentalizing might not parallel Roosevelt's detached disparagement precisely, but both men describe blacks as dependent—and peculiarly so—in other words, in a way that makes sense of black masculinity within a white supremacist framework. Extending his scope of control even further, Wheeler goes on to divide the black soldier from the nation's "foreign foe" by bestowing upon the black body a default status of "American" by comparison, disallowing the possibility that black soldiers may have felt any affinity with the Cuban natives or the Filipinos, racially or politically. Loyal to both whites and nation, black *American* men are incapable of "treachery," incapable of turning against their governors like the unruly insurgents they so very much physically resemble.

Wheeler's anachronistic interpretation of the black male body was certainly misguided and possibly damaging. Nonetheless, it is useful to note that in invoking the slave body to suggest black fidelity and an authentically *native* black identity, the general was really doing little to blacks that Booker T. Washington had not done to them already. Washington's much-maligned 1895 address to the

Atlanta Exposition, given only four years before Under Fire was published, makes political use of the very same nostalgia-ridden, revised version of the master-slave relationship to shape an argument for black inclusion in the American socioeconomic system. The speech also revealed Washington's anxiety about foreign "others." He implores southern businessmen not to forsake the loyal African American for immigrant workers: "As we have proved our loyalty to you in the past, in nursing your children, watching the sickbed of your mothers and fathers . . . in our humble way we shall stand by you with a devotion no foreigner can approach, ready to lay down our lives, if need be, in defense of yours, interlacing our commercial, civil life . . . with yours."[45] In much the same way that Washington believed empire would distract the nation from the plight of blacks within the United States, he viewed the increase in immigration in the latter half of the century as a threat to the economic livelihoods of black businesspeople and laborers. If his disinclination to become involved in the affairs of darker races abroad might be characterized as a kind of racial isolationism, his attitude toward foreign labor within the United States can be accurately described as black nativism. Washington was by no means the only black feeling the panic betrayed by his nativist response (nor the only African American expressing nativist sentiment generally). The fear of losing economic ground was only heightened by the efforts frequently made to acculturate these new workers (who were mainly European), a stinging reminder of the efforts on behalf of blacks the government all but abandoned after the fall of Reconstruction. Placed in this context, General Wheeler's preface can be reinterpreted. While his comments and Cashin and Alexander's history do seem to offer wildly divergent and competitive versions of the black male soldier's body, the writers of Under Fire might have welcomed any sentiment that could destroy the image of blacks as a "so-called alien race," in the words of the authors. Like Washington, they perhaps believed that social and economic well-being was contingent upon securing a stable, identifiable position within the nation, even if gaining that position meant transferring the status of "alien" onto another kindred group of people, or, more problematically, even if it meant allowing themselves to be written into a domestic racial narrative that propelled them historically backward.

It is of course ironic that Washington would call forth images of plantation life to argue for blacks' inclusion in a political economy driven by industrial capitalism. Yet Washington's appeal implicitly recognizes that much of the "New South" only reluctantly accepted the shift from the slave-based agrarian economy as an inevitable consequence of the permanent loss of unpaid labor. To many southerners, the Civil War was not a victory that confirmed the North's superior racial ideals or moral purpose; it was simply proof that industrialism and technology could force even the most resilient and righteous people into submission. As Grimké wrote nearly forty years after the war in a paper published by the American Negro Academy, "It is the age of industrialism and democracy, aye, industrialism and democracy are destiny. Try ever so hard, we shall not escape our destiny, neither the Negro, nor the South, nor the nation."[46] Grimké's remarks suggest that a simplification of the war into a struggle between (northern) industrialism and (southern) agrarianism would prompt many African Americans like him to define industry as liberation.

The attribution of the North's victory to industrial superiority and southern defeat to its agrarianism is also ironic, then, when one considers that the justification for southern racism gained its greatest power from aligning the black body with "nature" in a hierarchical dichotomy divided along an axis of culture/nature or, in its more pernicious rendition, civilization/barbarism. As I have argued, the need to escape such designation will lead Steward and Gilmore to project the "natural" onto those "primitive" Afro/Asian bodies who will be violently and forcefully introduced to "civilization." Yet, as a final introductory point, I will suggest that the writers are also attempting to configure a black male subjectivity emerging wholly differentiated from of all manner of "natural" bodies, a differentiation that will emerge as a phobic response to the female body, the "feminine," and domesticity.

The authority Roosevelt assumed in his narrative of San Juan Hill depended on an implicit self-designation as the body of civilization exercising dominion over the black natural body (the "Buffalos," the "Immunes"[47]). As Gail Bederman points out,[48] in *The Winning of the West*, Roosevelt had positioned himself similarly to Native Americans during the Indian wars and later articulated his belief in empire within this corporeal taxonomy. His iconic status as the representative of white masculinity nonetheless resulted from a successful negotiation of the nature/culture divide, drawing power from both. He boasted, after all, of being a naturalist, his "manliness" a product of the "strenuous life." Roosevelt's conceptualization of white masculinity is ultimately both natural and cultural, linking the past and present, valorizing those necessarily aggressive "masculine" traits inherited from premodern Anglo-Saxon forefathers and tempered by civilization. The benefits of nature and civilization are thus a matter of quantity (and kind): a little nature infuses the blood with a warrior spirit; too much will cause degeneration. Civilization saves men from barbarism, but an "overly-civilized" man is lazy and ineffectual. Within his rather cobbled construction of the "manly," white aggression is altogether distinct from the base savagery of the "unmanly" Native Americans, whose congenital cowardice prompted them to rape helpless women and resort to "cunning" tactics in battle.[49] In *Rough Riders*,

Roosevelt does not accuse black troops of demonstrating the "unmanly" barbarism he ascribed to Native Americans, yet he does unman them. They want to be spared the scene of masculine civilization, marked by Roosevelt's fetishistic descriptions of automatic Colts, Mauser bullets, and Gatling guns. They "drift to the *rear*"; they want to care for the fallen; they long for the company of their black male companions. In others words, they retreat so far back from masculinity that they become women. Weak and dependent, clinging and fearful, they need the protection and guidance of "real" (white) men, brought into line only by an awesome and threatening display of the phallus. The feminine and the racial are mutually constitutive. As such, for Steward and Gilmore, the substitution of a domesticized citizenship centered on the home for an expansionist/imperial citizenship may be interpreted as a reinstitution of manhood through a process of "de-naturalization," exchanging what was understood to be a "womanly/natural" space for a masculinized domain—not simply that of war, which can be "primitive"—but also of technology and science. Not only is this industrialized, civilized imperial black male body defeminized, but by implication, it surpasses the white male "naturalist/primitive" body, for it reflects *only* "forward" movement. In Gilmore's work particularly, white men will be depicted as both feminine and socially "degenerate," falling helplessly backward into nature.

Technology and the Black Body Politic: Steward's *Colored Regulars*

In 1889, the *Christian Recorder* proudly reported that Steward had "secured promise of a space [that year] at the Paris Exhibition for the colored people of the country."[50] Steward held a deep and sustained interest in science, having published a book arguing for evolution, *Genesis Re-Read* (1888), and married Susan McKinney, the first black female physician in New York State. Though the minister's plan for the Paris Exhibition was eventually reduced in its scope, Steward had developed an "ambitious design to display diverse examples of blacks' scientific and technical skills."[51] Even earlier, Steward had supported efforts to include a display at the 1888 Maryland Industrial Exposition exhibiting the advancements African Americans had made since the end of the Civil War. Ever desirous of gathering evidence of black elevation, he would lobby to be granted temporary leave from his duties after he had become chaplain for the Twenty-fifth Infantry to attend the 1893 Columbian Exhibition in Chicago, a request that was ultimately denied.[52] Taking place just five years before the Spanish-Cuban-American War, the exposition had offered a good opportunity to glimpse what course the United States would take in terms of domestic and international racial politics. Boasting that the Chicago Fair was both larger and more costly than the Paris Exposition, the organizers envisioned the fair as an opportunity to show the world the modern genius of American industrial and technological ingenuity. Building upon building was devoted to demonstrating the latest developments in transportation, electrical engineering, and industrial machinery. Also of great interest to those touring the midway were exhibits from "exotic" far-away locales. A visitor could stroll through a Javanese village, see Algerian theater, or shop at an East Indian Bazaar. The exposition—grander than its Parisian predecessor, more expansive in its collection of "others"—is a powerful symbol for one of the primary American aspirations at the turn of the century: the desire to outdo European imperial and technological endeavors. If the Columbian Exposition did indeed reflect the nation's increased awareness of how it wished to define itself in relation to the world outside of its borders, the exposition also reflected the unabated racial strife within the United States' own boundaries. Originally, African American exhibits were excluded from the Chicago Fair, and only after great agitation on the part of African American leadership were black Americans allowed space, a relatively restricted amount, within its sprawling grounds.

The racial controversy did not end with the belated decision to include African Americans, however. In 1891, the black-owned newspaper the New York Age published an editorial critical of the exposition's Board of Lady Managers' decision to give a white woman, Mary Cecil Cantrell, control of the exhibits to be staged by African American women: "We have no doubt that MRS. CANTRELL is an estimable lady. But we are sick of being represented by white folks, whether they are 'ladies' or 'gentlemen.' We are plenty old enough and big enough to represent ourselves, in the Columbian Exposition, and in most other things, social, religious, political and industrial."[53] Black Americans had apt reason to reassert the ability of people of color to represent themselves, particularly politically. The editorial's argument—that blacks were both "old enough" and "big enough" to be self-determining—would be disputed by domestic and colonial practices that would have the cumulative effect of barring people of color in nearly all parts of the globe from the rights of self-governance. The same year the Age was making an argument for an evolved black body, John Burgess, a former Confederate soldier and a professor who once instructed Roosevelt, argued that less developed populations had "no human right to the status of barbarians. The civilized states have a claim on the uncivilized populations, as well as a duty towards them."[54] The editors of the Age implicitly understood that demanding black self-representation within the World's Fair's spectacular displays of modernity—in other words, claiming a black modernity—was essential to claiming all other manners of self-representation.

Quite similarly, the interest Steward took in supporting "science and technical" exhibitions at fairs such as the Columbian Exposition reflects his growing belief that science and technology were quickly supplanting other fields of endeavor, such as arts and letters, as the hallmark of an advanced civilization. As if to confirm Steward's inclination, Nelson Miles, the commanding general of the U.S. Army during the Spanish-Cuban-American War, implies in the preface to *Colored Regulars* that if African Americans were going to present an image of themselves that had caught up with whites, this image needed to be absolutely in synch with a culture that was defining itself increasingly in terms of its industrial and technological acumen. Miles expresses confidence that after black Americans "have experienced as many years of growth and development" as whites, they might very well match the "Anglo Saxons who now dominate the thought, the inventive genius, the military prowess, and the commercial enterprise of the world" (6)!

The work that follows Miles's preface is Steward's extended argument for black soldiers' technological viability. In the introduction to his book, Steward offers a standard assimilationist take on civic inclusion, stressing that most blacks will accomplish advancement and enfranchisement through a gradual yet inevitable psychosocial simultaneity. "Once filled with the common national spirit," Steward writes, "partaking of its thoughts, entering heartily into the common movements, having the same dress, language and manners . . . we may hope that the Afro-American will ultimately win and hold his proper place" (16). But Steward claims acceleration for black military men, heralding the black soldier's modern body as having already achieved technological synchronicity. These men are ready for full citizenship rights, fit to represent the less evolved members of the black body politic.

To begin to make his case, Steward divides blacks into two categories, distinguishing between the evolutionary course taken by the black civilian and the course taken by the black military man. Influenced to a great extent by notions of history that appear to be derived from both Hegel (Africa as a historical void) and Darwin (expanding nations as organisms naturally growing), Steward creates a mélange of emerging "scientific" discourses—biological, social and, most importantly, mechanical—to narrate a tale of blacks' emergence in the New World. "Marching from nowhere to somewhere," (14), "dug" from a "pit," "hewn" from a "rock," African slaves were reborn as the "Afro-American" from a "heterogeneous protoplasm," (13) and were "looking toward organic life" (12). While helped along by the "partially civilizing control" of slavery, according to Steward, blacks as a whole are still in preparation for a day "not yet come" (13, 14). The black soldier, however, stands apart from other blacks in America, and as such, has a somewhat differing story. Steward writes that his mission in documenting a history of black military achievement is to prove that black evolution has taken place—at least in military quarters—and to present "the portrait of this new soldier" (19). He repeats the military creation narrative: "knowing nothing of the spirit and training of the soldier" (16), the slave nonetheless took up arms in the Revolutionary War, performing admirably. He furthered his experience in the War of 1812 and in the wars against the Indians helping the fledging nation combat its enemies. It was participation in the Civil War, however, the first time African American men had been trained formally for the field of battle in "important numbers," that "secured" the black man's "standing as a soldier—the evolution was complete" (18). Absolutely sleek and modern, the new black soldier had arrived:

> The American Negro has evolved an active, aggressive element in the scientific fighting men he has produced. Individual pugilists of that race have entered all classes, from featherweight to heavyweight, and have remained there; receiving blows and dealing blows; showing a sturdy, positive force; mastering and employing all the methods of attack and defence allowed in such encounters, and supporting themselves with that fortitude and courage so necessary to the ring. . . . The soldier stands for something far higher than the pugilist represents, although he has need of the same qualities of physical hardihood—contempt for suffering, and coolness in the presence of danger, united with skill in the use of his weapons. (17)

The soldierly black body is aggressive but restrained, a body that while prepared to inflict violence by no means lapses into retrogressive notions of black male physical power: the hulking, brutish slave; the predatory rapist. At the time Steward was writing, pugilism—boxing—had emerged recently from a barefisted, "savage" fight to a sport characterized by intelligence, skill, technique, and rules. In the parlance of sports, it had become a game of science, and it had, in 1904, become a game in which black men were beginning to excel in the same arena, quite literally, as whites. As a trained pugilist warring for the greater good of his nation, the black soldier then is no longer the semicivilized savage, object of racialist science, but the product of American scientific genius, collected, efficient, a machine-man ready for his age.

Part of Steward's strategy in mechanizing the black body is to transpose onto black American male bodies the kind of mobility that Americans flocked to see in the Spanish-Cuban-American War films Kaplan describes. The lengthy descriptions F. Grant Gilmore's novel offers of the "transport 'America' . . . one of the products of American genius" sailing across "angry waves . . . in defiance" show, albeit awkwardly, how the personification of the ship (as U.S. forces) and the waves (as the Filipinos) associates Americans with machines that easily over-power those people who are still on the plane with nature (55). Steward's ma-chine metaphors differ from Gilmore's in that Steward is less interested in primitivizing the "other" than he is in showing black fighting men as "a moving force, capable of disturbing the currents of history and making a channel for the stream of their own actions" (17). Steward sees black participation in the Spanish-Cuban-American War, like the exhibitions he advocated, as a welcome opportunity for both display and inspection: black regiments "became more and more the mark of observation by foreign military men who were present, and by the great throngs of correspondents who were the eyes for the people of the civilized world," giving "the world a striking exhibition of the effect of military training" (238, 240). Again, what Foucault characterizes as disciplining observa-tion is precisely what Steward wants. But here, the publicity and "objectivity" of journalistic observation is made to rescue the black body from the dominant culture's privately scripted narratives of blackness. What did the civilized world see? "Active" men, rapid and energetic in their movement. Within Steward's conceptualization of a nation as a "machine," black men are well-oiled working parts of a grand mechanical system.

Throughout his book, Steward deepens the machine-body connection by em-phasizing the black soldier's skill and accuracy with weapons. More specifically, in a chapter offering an overview of the Black Regulars, he attempts to counter prevalent notions that the black soldier was simply not smart enough to handle newer, more exacting forms of artillery that required an understanding of what Steward dismisses as only the most rudimentary concepts of physics. Rudimen-tary perhaps, but because the specious argument had been forwarded already—the artillery is complex, and therefore requires a complicated mind to operate it—Steward is able to use black soldiers' deft handling of weaponry to point to their mental acuity: "Several of the best rifle shots known on this continent are Ne-groes; and it was a Negro who summerized [sic] the whole philosophy of rifle shooting in the statement that it all consists . . . in knowing just what value to assign to gravitation, drift of the bullet and the force of the wind" (105).

In the concluding pages of this chapter, Steward attempts to refute yet another claim of black deficiency: that black soldiers are not capable of commanding their own troops. After making his case, he ends the chapter with a footnote from Stephen Bonsal, a white military historian, commenting on the "remarkable physique" of American soldiers (105). The placement of this footnote merits attention. Most other notes—marked by an asterisk—are where they should fall, logically: at the bottom of the page where the asterisk has been inserted. This one, however, is marked on page 103, but the note at the bottom of the page asks the reader to see the end of the chapter, page 106. There we find Bonsal's comment. Purposeful or not, Steward ends his discussion of African American intelligence by a forceful assertion of the magnificent black male body.

Thus Steward's division of African Americans into two evolutionary paths—one for civilians, the other for soldiers—is predicated on a belief that all blacks must implement into their civilian lives the kind of structure the military has perfected, so that they too, can be looked upon and judged worthy of horizontal assimilation. In a section of the work tracing the rise of Spain as an imperial power, Steward suggests that during the sixteenth century the country was able to become "a machine of power" because its people came forward to organize like "soldiers," a theory that recalls eighteenth-century military theorist Sevran, who believed that the French nation and the military should collapse into one entity. Foucault explains that in Sevran's vision, the military nation-machine would indoctrinate children into militarism at a young age, teaching them "the profession of arms in 'military manors.' "[55] He continues: "it would end in these same manors when the veterans, right up to their last day, would teach the children, exercise the recruits, preside over the soldiers' exercises, supervise them when they were carrying out works in the public interest, and finally make order reign in the country, when the troops were fighting at the frontiers."[56] While Steward proposes nothing as dramatic as a total national military machine, the soldier is "drilled to efficiency by the military," while the average black citizen has not benefited from such structural and bodily rigor. Frank Schubert, who edited the most recent volume of Colored Regulars,[57] writes that Steward suggested, in Schubert's words, "that all schools for blacks employ ex-soldiers to teach drill and military matters to all male students," and argued that "military programs" be an essential part of black educational institutions.[58] In an editorial to the Indianapolis Freeman, Steward made his feelings plain: "Soft men cannot carry on a hard fight."[59] Even the pugilist, while effective as a model of physical and mental scientific evolution, is not as effective as the soldier, Steward argues, for an individual fighting by himself cannot compare to those who "subordinate" themselves to the "high lessons of obedience" of a commander within an organization structured to ensure both discipline and reproduction (17). John Brown's raid on Harpers Ferry, which "was military in character and contemplated the creation of an army of slaves," is "noble"; Nat Turner's insurrection, while heroic, was the "mad violence of revenge" (66).

In both of these instances of effective black masculine power—armies led by John Brown, black soldiers led by white generals—the black body is in the custody of whites. Nevertheless, given that Steward spends the entire final chapter advocating for black military officers, what is most significant here is not so much that these black bodies were led by whites as that those bodies were organized. Indeed, he appears to regret that Turner's efforts were thwarted by his lack of discipline. Though a "misguided slave," Steward says, Turner possessed "the elements of a vigorous captain" (68). Later in his work, Steward interweaves instances of blacks successfully taking command within white organizations (General Dodd and General Dumas, father of Alexandre Dumas, in the French Army) and successfully taking command to lead revolutions for their own people (L'Ouverture and Maceo).

Steward's approval of Brown's and Turner's insurrections makes it tempting to argue for subversion—to claim that Steward is proposing two alternatives for black militaristic organization: integrationist, like Dodd and Dumas, or revolutionary, like Brown, Turner, and L'Ouverture, the latter necessary if the former is not permitted. In fact, though he claims that the "Cuban campaign has forced the nation to recognize the completion of the Negro's evolution as a soldier in the Army of the United States" (327), his assertion is as contradictory as William Wells Brown's statements that the black Civil War soldier was both recognized and yet in need of recognition. Steward admits he is "weary" of the "patronizing paean 'the colored troops fought nobly'" (327), rejecting the language that casts the black subordinate's relationship to his white superior in domesticating terms. Having earlier noted and dismissed Roosevelt's accusation of dependence, here, he asserts that the black soldier does not "glow . . . when told of his 'faithfulness' and 'devotion' to his white officers, qualities accentuated to the point that they might well fit an affectionate dog" (327). In reward for his participation, the soldier simply wants his civil rights: "He lays claim to no prerogative other than that of a plain citizen of the republic, trained to the profession of arms. The measure of his demand—and it is the demand of ten millions of his fellow-citizens allied to him by race—is that the full manhood privileges of a soldier be accorded him" (327).

With his evolved, strong physique, his professional training, his "manifest capacity to command," "the colored soldier . . . speak[s] for the entire body of citizens" (327). Steward argues, therefore, that this civically denied black body of people finds embodiment in the soldier-representative. In his vision, this nation (or army) of millions is prepared to align with him as he leads the crusade for enfranchisement. The body of the soldier thus subsumes other, and, it is implied, less evolved black bodies.

This subsuming act finds Steward committing the very kind of error that Taylor—who was his contemporary, publishing in 1902—attempts to correct in her autobiography by giving her own female body a representative status. Arguing against the notion that bodies placed under political erasure are at last completely liberated when "spoken," Sánchez-Eppler cautions that, to the contrary, any form that body is given will necessarily bind it. Even in those "political or literary texts" that are liberational in their aims, "representing the body" can "exploit and limit it."[60] If, in "speaking" for the black body politic, Steward limits the black body, he does so most obviously by gendering the black public body as male; he does so most seriously by repressing all manner of black heterogeneity.

Repressing heterogeneity might have been his point. The model provided by the late nineteenth-century factory industrialism, as Mark Seltzer has suggested, had influenced perceptions of social organizations to the degree that organizations such as the Boy Scouts were admired for their unfailing ability to produce and reproduce "types." For African American men, institutions such as the army, or Gilmore's beloved Prince Hall Masons, became black versions of the "man-factory."[61] But in relying on a military-industrial model for black corporeal "typing," Steward runs the risk of lapsing into the manner of objectification that the speaking body attempts to undermine. Even if African Americans did not share white cultural anxiety about machines and sought to master them as a sign of being civilized, the very necessity of using machines for certain tasks, even rudimentary ones, acknowledges the body as needing compensation to complete its endeavors, the manner of compensation I noted in writing of Taylor's male performative, one necessary for the edification of masculinity.[62] Of course, this bothersome detail often goes unacknowledged: in his description of San Juan Hill, Roosevelt uses a revolver to discipline back men; yet he implicitly ascribes his power to his white masculinity. For black male ethnic bodies, the notion of a masculinity needing to be propped up "prosthetically" poses a set of specific problems that serve to compound any perceived threat technology poses to masculinity more generally.

In *Men and Machines*, written at the beginning of the twentieth century when racialist conceptualizations of national characters continued to dominate the American imagination, the social theorist Stuart Chase presents an odd hypothetical situation involving a poor Russian peasant who encounters "modern technology" upon arriving in the United States. The discovery of machines, Chase suggests, enables the "peasant youth" to transcend his "biological limitations" and "grow in all directions."[63] The illusion of an able body, magically overcoming natal ethnic "crippling," is created through a prosthetic extension. Steward, looking for an instrument to beat back the ever-present accusation of deficiency, slander he labels "violent" (97), offers the black male warring body as both full and able; however, the illusion is not complete without the extending weapon (his "arms," as Steward writes), nor is it complete without Bonsal, the white male (or the "world") in the powerful position of spectator. It is important here, then, to consider the prosthetic in its visual rather than physical capacity. If an actual prosthetic is typically used as a means of "normalizing" a body after it has become wounded or disabled, ostensibly making the body both more functional to its user, it also makes the body more acceptable to those who might be disturbed by the sight of profound physical alteration. The prosthetic can nonetheless be as revealing as concealing: the very attempt to "disguise" disability through devices that visually and mechanically mimic the human body calls attention to its vulnerability, the body's ability to experience loss. If Steward's prosthetic weapon renders the black body whole to the viewer, it may also inadvertently signal deficit.

Whatever problems Steward's biomechanical masculinity presents theoretically, Steward's black audiences hardly saw men he exalted as vulnerable. His narrative was acclaimed by contemporary black audiences for its portrayal of brave, intelligent black men and for countering the misrepresentations of black troops' service in the hands of whites, a treatment so egregious that one reviewer referred to these tales as nothing less than "pen murder."[64]

Civilization, Miscegenation, and Incest: "*The Problem*" (with Domesticity)

To return to a point I made in my introductory chapter, the highly influential German military strategist Karl von Clausewitz, a contemporary of Sevran, posits war as a "duel on a larger scale." In other words, war is a contest between two people, the "self" and the "other," enlarged into a battle between multiple "selves" (the same as you) and multiple "others" (different from you but indistinct from one another). Knowing who one is fighting with and against is of course necessary; however, in modern imperialist warfare, distinguishing that "other" and degrading that body becomes an essential step in exercising dominion with impunity. "We," Fussell writes, "are visible; he is invisible. We are normal; he is grotesque. Our appurtenances are natural; his, bizarre. He is not as good as we are."[65]

War may demand that these distinctions be made, but where the (always shifting) boundaries between self and other lie is not always readily apparent. As I have mentioned, the Spanish-Cuban-American Wars and the wars against the Philippines prompted some politically cognizant Africans Americans to undergo a process of racial reorientation, examining their identities not only to white Americans, or blacks from the Caribbean and Africa, but to darker races in the Pacific, a geography removed both psychically and geographically.

Any confusion that black Americans felt about who these "others" were—same as or different from "us"—was only multiplied by the dominant culture's own confusion. During the wars about which Gilmore was writing, the Filipinos had undergone a radical metamorphosis, from ally to enemy. As the "enemy," the Filipinos were "othered" to the point of being unrecognizable. They were "part-Spanish," "niggers," "Malays," and "Mongols"; Roosevelt referred to them as "Apaches" and "Oceala." One report declared that the Filipinos were "spotted" and "striped."[66] Ideas about the Cubans were equally fluid: depending on the source, they were "white," "mongrel," or "negros." As our allies, they were often called competent people; under our "protectorate," they were just as often infantilized.[67] In general, an identification with "us" as allies afforded "others" more generous representations in the American imagination than an allegiance to another nation or, most tellingly, an allegiance to themselves.

In a novel that lauds imperial warfare and black participation within it, it is exactly this—the distinction between sameness and difference—that appears to obsess Gilmore. His depiction of Cubans, Japanese, and Filipinos in particular is one means of differentiation: categorizing ethnicities in terms of those who are civilized and those who are not. The Japanese, who approved of the U.S. occupation of the Philippines, are a "civilized," "progressive" race (as are Americans);[68] the Filipinos, by contrast are a "semi-civilized," "illiterate" nation of people who demand guidance. Running the gamut from military alliances to romances between races, Gilmore has produced a novel replete with interracial couplings of all manner that taken together serve as a kind of (flawed) blueprint to distinguish between "good" interracial alliances and "bad" ones: those that reinforce order and connote progress and those that create disorder and threaten retrogression. While Gilmore does indeed attempt to create a hierarchal racial schema dividing races and nations abroad along the axis of civilization and progress, my reading of his novel will suggest that the dominant culture's idea of American military imperialism as a force capable of bringing order to a racially chaotic, heterogeneous world provided Gilmore with a model for structuring domestic racial relations. I will argue that in creating a plot in which military intervention stops the dual crime of incest and miscegenation from occurring—an unspeakable "interracial alliance" and a crime that Werner Sollors, quoting Richard H. King, describes as a (degenerative) "collapse back into nature" made possible by the legacy of slavery[69]—Gilmore demonstrates faith that the military will beat back a history of unequal racial power relations, acting as a defense against the African American's greatest enemy: the past. He opens his novel with a prefatory statement of intention:

DEAR READER: It is no purpose of mine to make an appeal to your sentimental nature in lauding the exploits of the principal characters. . . . You will note, in depicting the scenes, that the actual time and date are given to guide you through the career of the principals. The scenes are natural, and brought to your notice daily . . . the description of the action of the soldiers and the noble display of bravery are all too true. In all, as you follow through the many perilous scenes and incidents of this romantic novel, may the lesson taught bring us closer to mankind and that we may be charitable in thought and deed. As time passes, we are slowly drawing to the place where there is no race, no creed, no color. (4)

Gilmore first distances himself from the genre of the sentimental novel, adopts the verifying strategies of the historical novel ("actual time and date"), and claims a realistic mode ("the scenes are natural") only to, in the end, claim that the novel will be a romance. I would like to suggest that this generic crisis acts an index of multiple, multileveled crises of racially related representations within the novel. More specifically, Gilmore's refusal (or inability) to enact a strict, conventional mode of realism stems from his unwillingness (or inability) to segregate that which might be "true" about racial relations from that which might be ideal. For instance, his expectation of a "place where there is no race, no creed, no color" is spoken within a decidedly heterogeneous world where imperialism and Jim Crow dictate the categorization, separation, and surveillance of bodies. Moreover, while he needs the reader to believe that his descriptions of black valor are not, in his words, "exaggerated," he also presents a romanticized version of equalized racial relations in the military.

This generic tension extends well beyond any friction between realism and romanticism. At one particularly messy narrative moment, the point at which a tangled plot of confused kinship and mistaken racial identity will be resolved, Gilmore halts the narrative completely to insert a chapter offering a brief history of black American military history topped off by a five-page ballad, "The Troopers of the Ninth U.S. Calvary" (65). The novel then moves toward a quick, happy end. This invasive discourse—which I read as a "military occupation" of the narrative—signals the way in which Gilmore will conceptualize military presence throughout a work he explicitly subtitles *A Military Novel*. I speculate that Gilmore hardly envisions this seizure of narrative space as disruptive, interrupting the imaginary temporal movement within the world he has created in the novel; rather, I imagine that he sees the insertion of black military history as a necessary intrusion, restoring order to both the racially chaotic world he has created in his novel and the narrative itself, advancing his work toward closure.

Like Steward, F. Grant Gilmore was invested in drawing a portrait of black men as evolved soldiers. Cognizant, of course, of Roosevelt's rewriting of the Battle of San Juan Hill, Gilmore's description of the battle reestablishes black presence on that historic terrain. Even more like Steward, Gilmore invests the black male body with military-industrial masculinity, presenting "a man of indomitable, physical . . . construction" as his hero (27), and remarking on the smart "scientific character" of the drills and contests African American soldiers stationed in Manila perform before their white general (55). Steward's scientific fighting men stood in contrast to ordinary black Americans who had not benefited from the discipline and organization of the military machine. Gilmore, however, juxtaposes the science of these public exhibitions against the "guerrilla" tactics of the Filipinos to draw another distinction altogether: between American blacks and the "barbarous" other.

Guerilla warfare had been practiced for centuries—republican patriots had flummoxed the British by their irregular and unexpected tactics—however, during the American war against the Filipino insurgents, guerilla warfare became known as the method of the savage. Associated with hiding within the jungle or countryside, stealth animal movement, and primitive brutality, guerilla practices were the opposite of the "civilized" warfare derived from Europeans. The section of the novel set in the Philippines details the guerilla's "depredations" of property in Manila, their "ambush" of unsuspecting soldiers, and their threat to women walking alone in the streets (58). Gilmore implies that their ability to wreak havoc in the city lies in their ability to protect themselves within the country. He moves then to a description of the American headquarters in Manila, graced by a "modernly equipped hospital" and "efficient nurses and doctors" who are "under supervision" (58). Similar to the technology/nature or culture/nature dichotomy inherent in the image of the massive modern American ship silencing the angry (Filipino) waves, the guerilla's ability to cause destruction to culture—the city—then disappear into nature—the country—stands in contradistinction to the American military headquarters firmly and openly stationed in "enterprising" Manila (30). Metonymically displacing the whole of which it is a part, the restorative symbolism of the hospital obscures the other destructive technologies of American imperial occupation in the Philippines. In this manner, Gilmore diverts attention away from the main purpose of any army, which is not efficacy in healing but in killing.

To disguise further both the intent and effects of the American military presence, he tempers the active acquisitiveness by which the United States took the Philippines with that of passive receivership: "we find ourselves, through the conquest of war, possessors" (29). In Gilmore's estimation, what the United

States received was nothing more than an empty geography. Allowed to "map out its own destiny" under the lax control of the Spanish, the Filipinos languished in a state of retardation: the Philippines is an "unexplored" and "uncultivated country" where "idolatry reigned" immune to the civilizing forces of the Japanese and missionaries (29–30). Gilmore's assessment once again evokes the Hegelian notion of destiny and history that informed much nineteenth-century imperialist thinking: that lesser races had evolved as far as they could and, as such, belonged to the past. "Present and future," Seamus Deane observes, became the "temporal territory" of white Europeans.[70] As a disseminator of "progress," the American military machine moves in to protect international and domestic spaces from nature or "retrogression."

As my interpretation of "The Problem": A Military Novel will show, Gilmore manifests an unwavering faith in the military's ability to have the same "civilizing" effects on the home front as it does abroad. But he rewrites the de facto racialist assumptions of American imperialism when he brings it back to the United States. In Gilmore's work, the bodies that need to be policed—those bodies that are disorderly, disobedient, degenerative—are not black, but white. In one sense, then, he has deracialized imperialist discourse by making it a process in which bodies are judged, not by racial affiliation as an absolute term of categorization but according to those bodies' ability to move along the now-familiar evolutionary trajectory away from the past. Gilmore has recalled imperialism from its task abroad, making it operative in a domestic space.

In order to explain the significance of this relatively unknown work, it is first necessary to summarize the plot in some detail. At the forefront of the novel is the story of two blacks: William Henderson, a valiant sergeant who joins the military after his father's death, and Freda, a white-skinned mulatta, who is the illegitimate daughter of Colonel Fairfax, a married wealthy Virginian and former member of the Confederate army. After a well-to-do black landowner, Hezekiah Williams, dies, his wife is forced to sell her assets. Colonel Fairfax, a friend of the family, takes what Gilmore calls a "deeper interest" in the household (6), which leads to a single rapacious sex act with the Williams's young daughter, Amanda. Amanda gives birth to Freda. Upon discovering he has a child, Colonel Fairfax persuades Amanda that their daughter should be raised with the privileges his life could provide, taking her into his home as an "orphan," her roots unknown to her and his family. He convinces his wife that the "waif" would make his "lonesome boy," Henry, a good "companion" because of her "marvelous beauty" (7). His wife begins to love Freda like her "own . . . child" (10). The colonel dies without revealing his secret, although he has provided for Freda in his will, information Mrs. Fairfax withholds from her. Henry Fairfax falls in love with

Freda and vows to take her as his wife, unaware of their blood relationship. Putting off the prospect of engagement, Freda joins the Red Cross as a nurse and is stationed in Cuba during the war. There, she meets and attends to a wounded Henderson, who has distinguished himself in battle under the command of the benevolent, white General Funston (a recasting of the notoriously racist Frederick Funston)[71] and by "rescuing" the Rough Riders, led by a grateful Colonel Roswell (a stand in for Roosevelt), from annihilation. Henderson and Freda develop a love that both understand cannot be consummated because of social and cultural law against miscegenation. When her "foster-brother," who has followed Freda to war as a surgeon, overhears the two, he becomes enraged, likening the pair to Othello and Desdemona. To get rid of his rival, he unsuccessfully attempts to poison Henderson; Henderson, unaware, dismisses the affliction as a feverish delirium.

After the war, Fairfax, Henderson, and Freda return stateside; Freda takes with her Quito, a widow of a Cuban soldier who subsequently falls in love with Funston's black servant, Pete: "cupid playing pranks with the unlettered" (19). Unable to forget Freda, Henderson disguises himself and goes to the Fairfax Estate to give her a note expressing his gratitude for her kindness and to inform her he is leaving to fight in the Philippines. Fairfax discovers Henderson and accuses him of attempting burglary, a crime to which Henderson confesses in order to spare Freda's honor. The case is delayed when Roswell arrives and pleads for Henderson, losing his "manly composure" while a still "manly" Henderson remains calm (49). When Fairfax, Henderson, and Freda find themselves together once again in Manila, the surgeon, who has, at this point coerced Freda into becoming engaged, enlists Pinto, a Filipino insurgent to help him attempt to kill Henderson a second time. Pinto eagerly agrees: "Me do it! Me do it!" (61). The novel ends when all matters legal, racial, sexual, and familial are resolved: Amanda reveals her identity to her daughter; Freda is reinherited; the charges against Henderson are dropped; General Funston and Sergeant Henderson arrest Fairfax for treason; and the lovers are united.

This brief synopsis should make evident my earlier claim: that Gilmore attempts to separate "good" and "bad" interracial alliances. Pete, an African American "house servant," and Quito, a Cuban woman who "wait[s] upon" the white nursing corps, might be of differing races, but they belong to the same servile class; thus theirs is an appropriate coupling (18, 19). Quito also blossoms under Freda's "tutelage," which, Gilmore writes, introduces her to "modern customs" —another appropriate alliance (31). General Funston, Colonel Roswell, and Sergeant Henderson are united in service to their country—also appropriate. Inappropriate, however, and in fact dangerous, are the conspiracy of silence between

Amanda and Colonel Fairfax and the murderous conspiracy between Henry Fairfax and the Filipino insurgent.

The Domestic Past: Miscegenation and Incest

The interracial relationships that generate the most disorder, however, are the two relationships driving the plot—the rivalry over Freda. These cross-racial relationships will become the site where Gilmore expresses his complex ideas about the nation's racial past and its future, about domestic racial politics and imperialism. Henry Fairfax, initially called a "promising young man" becomes treacherous, treasonous, and possibly incestuous while unknowingly attempting to marry a woman who is black and his sister. Henderson, reduced to longing for a white woman from afar, is labeled a "slave" to love; he is forced to don a disguise to see her, become something other than himself; he is temporarily jailed (Roswell laments that he is "darken[ing] the prospects of his race"); and his life is put in peril (49). While the threat to Henderson's life might appear the most grave situation he faces, the others carry an equally damaging potential: each is an assault on the sanctity of his racial identity. Amidst this confusion, Freda turns to the Bible for solace and runs across a fitting verse: "The sins of the fathers shall be visited upon the children unto the third and fourth generations of them that hate Me" (53–54).

Although Colonel Fairfax is dead, all are paying the price for the sin of one "father" who has refused to transmit what Simone Vauthier calls The-Name-of-the-Father, borrowing a psychoanalytic framework from Lacan. Transmission of the surname, she argues, institutes the "universal Law that prohibits incest"; "the silence of the Father" permits that law to be violated.[72] Thus, in loosing his daughter from her origins, allowing her to remain unnamed, the colonel permits the mulatta body to perform a dangerous act of racial identity, much in the same way it has done throughout the early history of American literature. The only way to relinquish the power this patriarch exercises from the grave is through patricide: here, the act of speaking, naming the unnamed, inscribes Freda's "blank" life with an identity (24).

As Werner Sollors's fairly exhaustive study of interracial literature convincingly demonstrates, this deceptive body of the mulatto/a, a corporeal trompe d'oeil of sorts, often acts as a catalyst in plots where "miscegenation" and incest intersect.[73] Sollors also finds the intermingling of the two dissimilar forms of conjugal union, marrying "too far" and marrying "too close," in discourses outside of literature. He offers a rough division of the "trajectories" in which this conflation appears: " 'pragmatic' state-interventionist," " 'paranoid' racialistfascist," and " 'realistic' abolitionist-liberal."[74] The first elision is more or less hyperbolic. Laws against miscegenation categorize it as a "crime against nature" *like* incest, often lumping the two together in statutes listing the types of marriages legally prohibited. In the second, race nationalists such as Dixon create mildly incestuous scenarios (for instance, the brother-sister couples from *The Clansman*), in what I earlier referred to as a "quarantine" against black sexual contamination.

The final category—" 'realistic' abolitionist-liberal"—is most appropriate for explicating Gilmore's novel. Sollors argues that abolitionists used interracial incest as a means of showing the extent to which patriarchal chattel slavery deformed morality and confused natural kinship systems. The patriarch who does what he would like with his female slave property, including his own offspring, and then denies it creates a situation in which further "accidental" incest can, and does, occur. Sollors remarks that within literary narratives where incest and miscegenation intersect, the house of the patriarch disintegrates, falling "back into nature." The punishment for a crime against so-called natural law is, then, ironic: the return to nature itself.

This "return" is a significant point of intersection between degenerative white domestic bodies and dark degenerative bodies abroad. In Gilmore's military novel, the return to nature threatened by the possible convergence of incest and miscegenation parallels the same kind of retrogressive backward movement as the guerilla's effortless reabsorption into the countryside. Bound to the idea of disorder and nature, retrogressive activity demands an ordering, technological, progressive rectifying force to move in and enact stability: the military. Gilmore attempts, then, to link disorderly spaces, domestic and international—a neoplantation household where the miscegenation-incest possibility originates, and the Philippines, where "savages" fight the influence of civilizing Americans.

Sollors further notes that stories exploring the superimposition of incest on top of miscegenation often take place in a plantation setting where the white master can impose his will onto the bodies under his control. Blacks—men and women—could offer whatever form of household they were able to maintain within the system little real protection from external violations. Gilmore has tied his incest-miscegenation plot to a household that signifies a backward movement: a return to the plantation. Colonel Fairfax, a veteran of the Civil War, is able to commit the crime of miscegenation because the black patriarch of the Williams household has died, leaving the house of his wife open and vulnerable to exploitation. "Like one of the family," Gilmore writes, the colonel institutes himself as the de facto head of the household, plantation style, by offering the remaining Williams financial support, and by helping himself to Williams's young daughter, "his moral instinct paralyzed" (85, 86). He then takes her away, exercising yet another prerogative of the slave owner—and her mother, Amanda, takes a position to her own daughter that, too, recalls slavery: a nurse.

Gilmore's decision to have Fairfax place Freda in proximity to his son and offer his wife a bizarre rationale for why she would make his son a good playmate —her "marvelous beauty"—ascribes to the patriarch an unconscious desire to allow incest to occur, an unconscious desire to return to the era of the plantation. Gilmore has thus replicated the very type of dangerous scenario created by abolitionist writers in which the repetition of the sin of the father becomes a perverse way of extending not simply sin, but power relations "unto the third and fourth generations."

His task, then, is to show how the exportation of past power relations into the present can be prevented, which requires, as Vauthier suggests, killing the father. Amanda must therefore break the vow of silence and give her daughter a name. Toward the end of the novel, Amanda sends for Freda from her deathbed, writing her a letter explaining that she was Freda's nurse and would like to see her once more before she "leaves this world" (72). Having known nothing of this "nurse," Freda is anxious to meet the woman whom she surmises must know information about her origins. Freda goes to Amanda, begging information, but Amanda, dictated by the "voice of the dead"—echoes from the plantation past—will reveal nothing (72). At this point, Freda receives a letter from Sergeant Henderson saying that he will seek her out at her former nurse's home. Awaiting his arrival, she writes General Funston, "who had taken a fatherly interest in her," to ask him to help clarify her identity (74). Gilmore writes: "Amanda seemed to improve with the arrival of the new guest, and she laughingly remarked that the soldiers had taken possession of her home, but she was a willing prisoner with Freda on guard" (75). Once again we see the military's domestic function parallel its imperialist operations: like the United States, which began "a war for the elimination of despotism and tyranny, supplanting the same with the new reign of law" and whose job is "rebuilding . . . re-establishing" the Philippines under its protectorate, "cleaning up" (17, 30), the military occupation of the neoplantation household signifies a restoration of order. Among the military men who have inhabited her home and rendered it safe, Amanda reveals Freda's heritage. Freda becomes, therefore, "Miss Williams," the matrilineal act of naming thereby killing the white master.

To completely sever the past from the present, the son, who carries the legacy of degeneration, must also be killed. Henry Fairfax, fearing Freda will not return, heads for Amanda's. His mother accompanies him. When the two arrive, Henderson makes his accusation. Informing Fairfax that he was "sent here by the government of the United States to arrest" him "for treason," he gives Fairfax two options: a duel or court-martial (81). Henderson claims that he does not fear the result of the duel, "for one so despicable, who will sell his birthright to a hostile tribe, cannot hope for success in an equal contest" (81). He announces to the other officers: "You need not restrain him, officers, he's before his master now" (81). As with the hostile tribe with whom he conspired, Fairfax is rendered in bestial terms: "Like a wild animal held in leash, it seemed as if Fairfax frothed at the mouth" (81). If the killing of something is the changing of it, as Burke maintains, then the changing of something might be the killing of it. If so, it is not only the dead white father who is killed (again), so, too is his son, reduced to the status of an animal.

The narrative ends with two marriages in which the father's and son's positions in the courtship trope are usurped by representatives of the military. Funston, it is implied, will marry Mrs. Fairfax; Amanda will marry Henderson, both women entering into military domesticity.

The Domestic Future: Military Domesticity

Gilmore's alteration of the domestic space into a military zone is more than a matter of "cleaning up," of sweeping the household clean of the past; it is also, as I suggested, a means of usurping the primacy of the household for the production of a proper black American subjectivity. Gilmore introduces the reader to the hero of his novel after his father has died, leaving his mother to raise four children alone. Henderson, who becomes a troublemaker, is sent away to live with an uncle. The uncle, who has no better luck than Henderson's mother, allows him to join the army: "a tall, active colored man applied to the recruiting station" (14). It is there, in the military, that he becomes disciplined, rapidly advancing through the ranks. The military has thus done what a father should do—make a boy into a man. Indeed, Gilmore has given his reader a novel full of dead fathers: Freda's, Henderson's, and Fairfax's fathers all vacate a subject position that is then filled with either a representative of the military or the military itself as a surrogate father.

In making a military domesticity, Gilmore rejects the possibility of a functional maternally led household. The women in Gilmore's novel, who are alive, nevertheless fail their children miserably. Mrs. Henderson's son is a "marauder"; Williams's daughter is a victim of rape; and Mrs. Fairfax's son a would-be murderer. Although Gilmore's novel invokes domesticity, then, it shows African American war literature further moving away from the "domestic"—the home and the nation—as sites capable of ordering racial relations or producing "good" citizens, white or black. Both spaces must become synthesized with the military to become stabilized. Just as significantly, when the hero and heroine unite, marriage does not follow immediately; the text eschews a typical and important convention of the domestic novel. Rather, Henderson issues a lengthy speech telling Freda that he must serve his first love, the army, before he serves her. He then leaves and is never heard from again, his voice swallowed into a single hurried, disjointed sentence issued by the narrator: "A village church, a noble gathering, a perfect day, solemn words, prompt responses, the pealing of the organ" (93). If the (failed) domestic space is recuperated by the military, the military is also prioritized as the first site where fidelity is pledged, before the household, and is, in this work, the only site where a functional black male subjectivity can be depicted. If we return to the idea of the military as a machine, this makes sense. Theorizing about the "naturalist machine," the relay between the natural body and machines in naturalist literature, Seltzer argues that "the mother and the machine are, in the naturalist text, linked but rival principles of creation . . . such a counterposing of 'male' and 'female' powers or principles . . . displays the 'culturalist' desire to devise an anti-natural and anti-biological coun-termode of making, a desire to 'manage' production and reproduction."[75] While Gilmore's text does not neatly fit into the category of naturalism, it has naturalist elements; most specifically, the idea that the natural body is subject to passions, most prominently lust, that will ultimately be a source of its descent. As we have seen, the act of military intervention, an industrial-patriarchal "managing" of the female-led domestic site, stops incestuous and interracial sex from occurring. That a black child could have been "made" from these circumstances only con-firms the real threat of "bad" reproduction and, therefore, the need for the military to compensate for both the limits of the feminized domesticity and the vulnerability of the black female body.

Domestic Violence

Henry Fairfax's violent transformation—the foaming dog before his master—is as close as the works covered by my study thus far have come to depicting black violence against the white body. Many critics have argued that the very act of representation is, in fact, violence. As such, it logically follows that the farther the representation is removed from the "thing itself," the more violent that act of representation is ("pen murder" as the reviewer of Steward's work wrote). Roo-sevelt's conflation of Filipino bodies with Native Americans and Senator John Daniel's visions of "striped" "zebra" men are violent, certainly; these acts of unnaming also create the rationale for further violence against those bodies as they become so far from what they are that they become, in essence, nothing. Or perhaps the opposite occurs: these bodies become so overcharged with meaning, so shot through with competing discourses, that they become the corporeal equivalent of babble—in other words, grotesque. Either way, they are bodies marked for injury or death.

Henry Fairfax is not the only figure in the novel who suffers death by (mis)representation. Both Roswell and Funston bear no discernable resemblance to their historical counterparts. Of paramount importance, however, is Gilmore's presentation of the fictionalized Roosevelt. Gilmore's depiction of Roswell as a weeping "child" alters the aggressive racist: Roosevelt's supremacist masculinity becomes an infantile attachment to a black subordinate. We could speculate, then, that Gilmore is using his novel to exact retribution for Roosevelt's "murder" of the black soldier by narrative diminishment.

Gilmore's use of transformation as violence against the white male body once again points to the degree to which the expression of black male rage has been limited within the African American war novel. Imagining a Henry Fairfax as a dog or a Roosevelt as a child is one matter; imagining a black man killing a white man is another, as I suggested in my reading of *Iola Leroy*. The relationship first depicted in Brown's *Clotelle* and repeated in "The Problem"—a pathologically racist superior and a black soldier-hero—will recur in later war novels, and with more violent resolutions. This recurring narrative construct is as much tied to issues of political representation as Roosevelt's subjugation of the black soldier who fought on San Juan Hill, pointing to a need for black men to wrest leadership from a people who have been psychologically disabled by racism to the point that they are no longer able to abide by military or national law. Standing as the antithesis of the disabled white military leader, Henderson's power as a black soldier derives from a strict adherence to the spirit of the military's newer "civilizing" function. The (historical, repeated) violation of the (historically) innocent black body—first committed by Colonel Fairfax, then continued by his son's murderous intents—is initially displaced in the narrative by imperialism's necessary subjugation of the disorderly Filipino body abroad. I see Gilmore's valorization of imperialism's disciplinary function as a clever syllogistic argument to which he gets his reader to consent before performing a quick substitution: disorderly bodies demand discipline; the Filipino insurgent is a disorderly body; therefore, the Filipino insurgent deserves discipline. When he recalls imperialism home, replacing the Filipino body with the disorderly white body, we have already agreed, in effect, that Henderson should punish it—logic demands it.

In examining why white bodies deserve punishment in Gilmore's text, we can see that one of the primary problems to be solved in "The Problem" is the unrestrained desire for the "other." More often than not, war is about wanting something someone else has and using violent means to get it. Imperial warfare overseas is an exaggerated form of that desire, its satisfaction requiring traveling over great distances. And yet, if we read imperialism alternatively as an attempt to turn "others" into representations of or extensions of "self," the desire turns incestuous. That Gilmore embeds Colonel Fairfax's excuse for raping Amanda— "We have no control over ourselves" (87)—within a narrative intertwining the vicious war against the Philippines and incest again raises questions about the nature of Gilmore's "patriotic" imperial rhetoric. If unchecked (white political) desire is the prerogative of the dominant, then why, within the bounds of the domestic, is this unchecked (white sexual) desire characterized as so transgressive that it needs to be ended in violent means? 1915—the year *"The Problem"* was published—was the same year D. W. Griffith's *The Birth of A Nation*, a film adaptation of *The Leopard's Spots* and *The Clansman*, caused a national controversy, sparking riots in Boston; a slew of articles and letters denouncing the film appeared in black newspapers and periodicals. Several years earlier, in a self-published book of poetry, *Masonic and Other Poems* (1908), Gilmore writes of an event I discuss in the next chapter, the 1906 Brownsville incident, in which black soldiers in Steward's Twenty-fifth Regiment were accused of disrespecting the town's white women, resulting in a riot whose outcome was the dishonorable discharge of over one hundred black soldiers. Dedicating the poem to his "Soldier Chum,"[76] he suggests that the disgrace brought upon the infantry was an unjustified result of an irrational race hatred directed at black men. It does not seem unreasonable, then, to conjecture that the tried and true representation of an aggressive, rapacious black masculinity in the hands of whites might have prompted Gilmore to invest white masculine desire with an equally destructive quality, even if, by metaphoric association, that representation contradicts the "benevolent" form of U.S. imperialism heralded in the novel.

We must also ask ourselves what it means for an African American writer to use the "dual crime" that, intentionally or not, serves as a warning against racial mixing, especially within a social milieu in which the lynching of African American men was the dominant culture's "warning" against the same sexual trespass, real or imagined. Gilmore purposefully evokes this punishment. When Henry Fairfax trumps up the burglary charges against the hero as a means of exacting revenge against the man Freda desires, Henderson is forced to appear before Judge Lynch, a name borrowed from the historical figure after whom the practice is named. For most of the novel, the reader believes that Freda is white; therefore, what Henderson and Freda are feeling for one another (though not acting upon) is both illicit and illegal in Gilmore's fictional world and in the world into which he published. As a "historical" fiction, the outcome of the real political conflicts involving Cuba and the Philippines had already been decided. The unresolved "war" in the novel thus finds itself expressed in the struggle between a black man and a white man over the white female body. In *Race, Rape, and Lynching*, Sandra Gunning notes that "the interracial male struggle over the terrain of the public would always be figured finally in terms of the domestic—the privatized expression of the nation's political anxieties. White American's conflation of the public and the private as the twin targets of black designs meant that the figure of the black as beast threatened to become a totalizing symbol of a race war many felt was already in progress."[77] The white female body is hardly a sexual being, but a political space: the struggle is over power. Freda's "blackening" merely allows Henderson to take that power from Fairfax: "She can be mine!" he exclaims (84). Her body territorialized, Henderson takes her from the defeated surgeon (who has, recall, been made "Filipino") in the manner that the United States seized islands in the Pacific and Caribbean geographies to begin building its overseas empire.

The Pacific and the Caribbean, the imperial "elsewhere" and the site of the United States' future, provided both Gilmore and Steward a space for imagining a black masculinity apart from the stereotypes dominating the national consciousness, a body that is industrial, expansionist, postslavery, and postagrarian. Even more, it was, as I argued in the introduction to this chapter, "postdomestic": an endeavor to find an alternative way "out" of the restrictions of the domestic in all of its forms, including the functions of the idealized (but also confining and feminized) black home. After completing *Colored Regulars*, Steward would publish a series of articles he wrote while stationed in the Philippines, "Two Years in Luzon" (1901–2), noting how well black men fared socially during occupation, including photographs of a black soldier and his Philippine "bride" as proof.[78] Domestic interracialism can work, apparently—if that home is away from home.

Returning to a major claim of this book, that African American war writers have avoided critiquing war on its own terms, here, we see that the need to imagine the military and imperialism as creating various zones of egalitarianism prevents these writers from connecting what African Americans were experiencing domestically to the violence people of color abroad were being subjected to at the hands of U.S. troops. By supporting the war, Steward broke with the position adopted by the A.M.E. ministry, who vehemently opposed black participation (as it did during the Civil War), citing the incessant domestic violence leveled against blacks as one reason: "The Negro has no flag to defend. . . . He is only regarded as entitled to powder and lead and the burning fagots. . . . If we had the voice of seven thunders, we would sound a protest against Negro enlistment till the very ground shook beneath our feet."[79] Ida B. Wells asked blacks to denounce imperialism on the same (shaking) grounds. In his 1899 novel *Imperium in Imperio*, African American novelist Sutton E. Griggs links two simultaneous historical events—the lynching of a black postal worker in Waco, Texas, and McKinley's call for American citizens to support U.S. efforts against the Spanish—to illustrate the dilemma facing black Americans at the turn of the century. His novel crescendos as the Imperium, a government of black men formed literally underground, congregates to meditate on solutions to "the negro problem." The war in Cuba confirms, in the words of the president of the Imperium, that Anglo-Saxons "have apparently chosen our race as an empire" and brings the congress to a point of crisis: "I deem this, my fellow countrymen, as an appropriate time for us to consider what shall be our attitude, immediate and future, to this Anglo-Saxon race, which calls upon us to defend the fatherland and at the same moment treats us in a manner to make us execrate it."[80] Griggs's evocation of the war in his novel draws attention to African Americans' difficulty in navigating an unmanageable terrain of inclusion and expulsion, where a black man might either end up fighting for his nation or hanging from a tree, or fight for his nation and still wind up on a tree, depending on the circumstance. However, this statement does not ask whether the same system that rationalizes violence internally is the same system rationalizing the use of violence externally. The question to ask of Griggs's text is this: if blacks were no longer victims of lynching and other forms of violent physical intimidation within the boundaries of nation, would that then solve the problem of whether or not to participate in warfare for the "fatherland," no matter what race it chose as its "empire"? Even the A.M.E. ministry's denunciation of black enlistment was based largely on its inefficient exchange value, asking if "the Negro should enlist in great numbers and go to the Spanish islands and help to subjugate the territory . . . and subordinate it to the dictatorial whim of the United States. . . . What right, what privilege . . . will he be the recipient of ?"[81] Five years later, the A.M.E.'s book concern would publish Steward's work, apparently finding political value in its content.

In black Civil War literature, lynching appeared as a way of demonstrating white America's commitment to using any means, however horrendous, to keep blacks from entering the body politic. Somewhat differently, the centrality of lynching in African African American debates over empire registers a heightened anxiousness, a recognition of the real, material vulnerability of their own black bodies as they watched the nation wield violence against others like them with impunity. For Steward and Gilmore, the ascription of technology and the materials of industry (iron, steel) to the black soldier's body, a process of "denatural-ization," might have therefore arisen from a desire to imagine a body capable of escaping its very humanity—in other words, the ability of human flesh to be altered through violence. Read in that way, the industrialized body may represent more than an infallible warrior, or a black embodiment of progress and civi-lization. It may serve perhaps as Steward's and Gilmore's need to conceive of a black masculinity immune to the "rope and faggot," not simply the shot and shell. Too, this body could have provided them another kind of defense al-together: a transubstantiated body, displacing the human one, could deflect black anti-imperialists' accusations that black soldiers were participating in the mur-der of their kindred. This is similar to Gilmore's use of a military hospital as a signifier of the army as diversionary strategy, in which imperial violence and occupation signal healing rather than destruction and oppression. Metaphoriz-ing the black male soldier into one simple part of the military "machine" conve-niently deanimates the institution and its human components. People don't kill people; machines do.

However, safeguarding a move that might have been, however expedient, the results of celebrating the black military-industrial soldier—as I argue both writers do—might have less obvious, but potentially more serious, implications. In the same essay in which Benjamin analyzes technology as a cause of imperialist vio-lence, he warns of the consequences of aestheticizing any aspect of warfare, ulti-mately arguing that the two are connected. He quotes from a Futurist manifesto on the colonial war against Ethiopia to make his point: "we Futurists have re-belled against the branding of war as anti-aesthetic. . . . War is beautiful because it establishes man's dominion over the subjugated machinery by means of gas masks, terrifying megaphones, flame throwers, and small tanks. War is beautiful because it initiates the dreamt-of metalization of the human body."[82] Using tech-nology, dominating it, then becoming it: the ends, the dream of "metalization," is perhaps most troubling here, precisely because it inures the injuring party to the destruction of what Benjamin calls "human material." The beautifying of killing in artistic replication, the beautifying of the killer, the move further and further away from the nature of war itself, in other words, allows for war's easy and pleasurable consumption, and therefore, its endless earthly reproduction.

In 1900, Kelly Miller, who had trumpeted black colonial ventures abroad, made the connection that Steward and Gilmore, in their efforts to make imperial warfare politically useful to African Americans, would not: "Acquiescence on the part of the negro in the political rape upon the Filipino would give ground of jus-tification to the assaults upon his rights at home. . . . For how, with consistency, could the despoilers of the brown man's rights in Manila, upbraid the nullifiers of the black man's rights in Mississippi? The pill of imperialism may be sugar-coated to the taste, but the negro swallows it to his own political damnation.[83]

In an analysis that again critiques the ease with which imperial violence can be deceptively packaged and consumed, Miller argues that instrumental violence is merely a sweet bit of quackery, not a real cure for internal ills. Steward and Gilmore swallow the pill nonetheless; later black American war writers will refuse. Many of the African American World War I and World War II novelists I will discuss in the next chapters—Victor Daly, Claude McKay, Chester Himes, William Gardner Smith, and John Oliver Killens—will interrogate the rhetoric used to galvanize support for the United States' continuing military intervention-ism to critique the ongoing domestic violation of African Americans.

5 INNOCENCE, COMPLICITY, CONSENT

Black Men,
White Women,
and Worlds
of War

It was a tall time. And of course my blood was
Boiling about in my head and straining and howling
    and singing me on.
Of course I was rolled on wheels of my boy itch to get
    at the gun.
Of course all the delicate rehearsal shots of my child-
hood massed in mirage before me.
Of course I was child
And my first swallow of the liquor of battle bleeding
    black air dying and demon noise
Made me wild.

It was kinder than that, though, and I showed like a
    banner my kindness.
I loved. And a man will guard when he loves.
Their white-gowned democracy was my fair lady.
With her knife lying cold, straight, in the softness of
    her sweet-flowing sleeve.

But for the sake of the dear smiling mouth and the
    stuttered promise I toyed with my life.
I threw back!—I would not remember
Entirely the knife.
—Gwendolyn Brooks, "Negro Hero / to suggest Dorie Miller," 1945

A mess attendant on the USS *West Virginia* at the time of the Japanese
attack on Pearl Harbor, Private Dorie Miller was on laundry detail when
startled by the sound of explosions coming from the deck of his ship.
Recognizing it was under fire, Miller climbed to the top, removed his
wounded captain from the bridge, took control of a machine gun, and
shot down at least two Japanese warplanes. While this might sound

like nothing more than what any well-prepared sailor would do in a crisis of war, many African American men like Miller had been barred from formal combat training in the Navy as part of the ongoing practice of assigning many military duties by race. So unwilling was the military to recognize Miller's accomplishment that it initially denied him public accolade. It was only after the African American press expressed outrage over the military's negligence that he did in fact receive the Navy Cross.[1] In a move both crass and ironic, the War Department then appropriated his image for military propaganda, issuing a poster featuring a drawing of the brawny Miller from the chest up, the slogan "above and beyond the call of duty" floating loftily above the sailor's head.[2] His story was told in a Frank Capra short film, The Negro Soldier, a documentary Chief of Staff George Marshall asked the director to create as a means of promoting patriotism among blacks.[3] The belated fanfare accompanying Miller's name might have indeed impressed some, but in 1943, when this "hero" died in active service, he died as a steward, in a deeply segregated military within a deeply segregated nation.

Brooks included "Negro Hero" as a part of her collection of poems, A Street in Bronzeville, published in 1945, just after the end of the war. Deploying the familiar trope of woman-as-nation, Brooks gives the nation's duplicitous treatment of Miller a corporeal form, transforming the United States into a figure of white feminine treachery. She is the "Terrible Goddess," the "White Witch," the "Bitch Goddess," a Janus-faced temptress who has the power to both seduce and destroy.[4] Commenting on the repeated use of this archetype in African American literature, Felipe Smith argues that an embodied, female representation of the United States "becomes a key figure in a tradition that examines the ambivalent attachment of the black male to the 'dazzling opportunities' of the white world that might partially result in the spiritual death of black America."[5] As Brooks's poem indicates, in the case of war, that death might be quite literal.

Brooks's repetition of the Terrible Goddess figure operates within this tradition by ascribing the white female body a capacity for seduction and violence, pushing it, therefore, outside the realm of the "pure." Brooks thereby challenges the powerful psychosexual narrative circulated by the dominant culture: the mythic innocence of the white female body. In the previous chapter, I pointed out that the dominant culture's most pernicious use of this "pure" body has indeed been to wield it as a weapon against African American men—the same argument African American war writers have made in direct response to the historical omnipresence of a body that has inflected all manner of political discourse involving black men. And the eternal accusation this body makes is, of course, rape. If a white woman and a black man have contact, sexual or not, the black man stands culpable of a crime no matter what the circumstances of that contact might be. It is also important to reiterate that the standing pronouncement of absolute and irrefutable guilt has had profound implications in the realm of the symbolic. If the chaste white female body is the sign of nation, as Brooks's invocation suggests, any desire on the part of black men to access citizenship becomes an act akin to violation, nothing less than a political rape.

But the task that Brooks and other black writers have taken on—sullying the innocence of the white female body—has had the effect of creating yet another innocent body: the body of the innocent black male. In her scorching critique of lynching, *Southern Horrors* (1892), Ida B. Wells issued her notoriously frank remark regarding the "chastity" of white women: "Nobody in this section of the country believes the old threadbare lie that Negro men rape white women. If Southern white men are not careful they will over-reach themselves . . . and a conclusion will be reached that will be very damaging to the moral reputation of their women."[6] Later, she adds: "White men lynch the offending Afro-American, not because he is a despoiler of virtue, but because he succumbs to the smiles of white women."[7] The first statement, initially published earlier that year in the black-owned *Memphis Free Speech*, outraged whites enough that Wells received death threats and was forced to relocate in the North. Questioning the integrity of white women proved dangerous for Wells but lent necessary force to a vein of antilynching discourse that sought to safeguard the black male body by relocating sexual agency onto the white female body. The activist's uncompromising honesty was not solely reserved for white women, however; she did quietly concede that black men could be, in a few instances, guilty of rape. Of course, as Wells was quick to note, this was not to suggest that great numbers of African American men were in actuality forcing themselves on white women—and certainly not to suggest that lynching was an appropriate response to violation. But because African American communities were intent on exposing the innumerable false claims of rape that cost thousands of black men their lives, very few within those communities were willing to entertain publicly the possible veracity of some claims of rape. One mythology of innocence—white female chastity— inadvertently gave rise to another.

In the twentieth century, this mythology was mobilized perhaps most visibly in defense of the astonishing number of black servicemen who faced such accusations. In 1944, the *Crisis* ran a full-page advertisement asking its readers to contribute to a legal fund for three black soldiers who had been convicted of raping a white woman while stationed in Alexandria, Louisiana.[8] The accompanying photograph is staged simply: the three men stand in a military-erect posture, fully uniformed; they face the camera directly, hands placed behind their back. The names and ranks of each are printed below the figures; the caption printed above making an urgent appeal: "HELP SAVE THESE SOLDIERS!" In describing their plight—they were sentenced to death—the advertisement states that they "did not have a fair trial." It does not, then, expressly claim that they are innocent of the crime, yet the composition of the photograph implicitly makes that argument. In particular, the military uniform, as a sign of honor, integrity, and, of course, discipline (as it snaps their bodies into posture) also represents the judicious, restrained use of force (hands behind their backs), which expresses, in turn, libidinal regulation, and, therefore, the unlikelihood of their guilt.

In the vocabulary of war, the terms "innocent" and "innocence" have, arguably, two primary definitions. The first, "nonthreatening," refers to the status of civilians and noncombatants, often characterized as "innocent" victims of war. The second refers to a lack of guilt, the absence of war crimes on the part of governments, armies, and military personnel who have, ostensibly, followed the theories of "just" warfare and the stipulations of related documents, such as those laid forth in the Geneva Convention.[9] The black male narrative of sexual innocence inherently connotes both: a nonthreatening status and the absence of guilt. It is not my intention here to imply that any specific number of black men did or did not commit the crimes of which they were accused; the use of the charge as a method of racial terrorism precludes any accurate assessment of the "facts," as the *Crisis*'s call to action makes abundantly clear. Too, of course, the sheer number of claims points to the probable innocence of many, if not most. However, in this chapter, I wish to explore the implications of embedding the narrative of black male sexual innocence (connoting a lack of violation) within narratives of black participation in warfare (a necessarily violent space). To consider this relationship, I will analyze several novels by African American men in which World War I or World War II plays a significant role in shaping narrative events: Victor Daly's *Not Only War: A Story of Two Great Conflicts* (1932),[10] Chester Himes's *If He Hollers Let Him Go* (1945),[11] and William Gardner Smith's *Last of the Conquerors* (1948).[12] Although written about wars thirty years apart and taking place in vastly differing settings, each of these works hinges upon the unjust consequences of black male sexual or nonsexual contact with the white female body. By highlighting prohibitions against interracial male-female contact between black men and white women, these writers intentionally draw upon the metaphorical relationship between interracial sex and political integration used to imagine black male citizenship as a violent intrusion. In their hands, the meaning of that tropology is altered, invoked to protest an exclusionary U.S. citizenship and to expose the disingenuousness of a nation fighting wars for democratic or egalitarian principles when those principles were not applied to African Americans.

Yet I will suggest that calling upon this trope, even if to reinscribe it, hides a problematic narrative bound to the mythology of black male sexual innocence. I return to Brooks's poem to elucidate my point. In "Negro Hero," Miller's confessions about being aroused by war—feeling "wild" from "swallowing" battle blood—is subsumed into a gentler love story, the narrative of a man's love of his nation, his love for his beautiful "fair lady." The fact of the hero's "innocent" posture in relation to the white female body also allows Brooks's hero to assume a posture of innocence in relation to war by naturalizing the "boy itch to get / at the gun," as Brooks words it, into an impulse of a "kinder" sort.

"Love" is certainly one kind of innocent contact with the white female body. In *Last of the Conquerors*, Smith's soldier begins a mutual, consensual "love" relationship with a white German woman in occupied Berlin and is duly punished for it. However, there are others. In Daly's novel, the protagonist's contact with a white French woman is merely companionship, ostensibly nonsexual. He nevertheless ends up court-martialed. Himes's treatment of the sexual power dynamics between black men and white women is more complex than Daly's or Smith's; Himes allows aggressive sexual contact to occur between his black hero and a white female character. But by no means does that contact result in an actual rape. Arrested and sentenced for a crime he did not commit—though at one point did consider—he is sent to serve his time in the army.

What I call the "narrative of innocence" was not solely the product of public antilynching discourse that aimed to reframe the accusation of rape, but also stemmed from black men's own desire to protect their bodies from the often-fatal consequences of engaging in consensual sex with white women. In a fascinating analysis of how black men viewed interracial sex during the Civil War, "Wartime Dialogues on Illicit Sex: White Women and Black Men," Martha Hodes writes of abolitionists James Redpath's and Richard Hinton's efforts to gather information about black life in the South for the newly formed American Freedman's Inquiry Commission. Although she does not specify why the sexual behavior of the black population was deemed pertinent enough to document, Hodes notes that black men who admitted to having consensual sex with white women "may have crafted their narratives as stories of coercion to present themselves as innocent participants in such legal and social transgressions."[13] Leery of the implications of any kind of interracial sex, the men to whom Hodes refers assumed innocence to avoid any repercussions for their liaisons, even if the contact had been mutual and even if it had taken place many years prior. However, unlike these men, the protagonists of the novels in this chapter do not manage to stave off the consequences of their acts.

Indeed, the meaning of these works lies in the inevitability—and injustice—of punishment. In examining the centrality of the punished black male body within this literature, I will attempt to complicate the use of the corresponding "narrative of innocence" by arguing that it ultimately gives violence the appearance of originating exclusively from white men, rendering the black male body as the recipient rather than the instigator of aggression. Given the works' shared historical context, wartime America, that narrative warrants exploration. In my analysis of *Iola Leroy*, I noted that although many black men volunteered for service during the Civil War, others were forced or coerced. Here, I will emphasize the opposite. While many African American men were drafted into World War I and World War II, many others volunteered to go to war to fight the United States' "enemies," often articulating a desire to protect and preserve "the American way of life." In short, they were nationalists.

In *Violence, Identity, and Self-Determination*, Hent De Vries and Samuel Weber imply that the validation offered the "self-determining" nationalist violence of the First World War not only gave ideological grounds for World War II but also for later anticolonial nationalist movements, such as those currently erupting in post-Soviet Europe and Asia.[14] They also suggest that the idealization of self-determination and the blood shed in its name tacitly sanctioned the use of violence for *individual* identity formation. Often conceptualized as revolutionary or defensive acts, such self-determining aggression on the part of the oppressed seeking a recognized, autonomous existence nonetheless relies on reinstituting the very binary of self/other that brought about imperial violence in the first instance. The "ascription of violence to *either* the self *or* the other," they caution, is "facile."[15] More than facile, it allows the recipients and victims of aggression, whether oppressor or oppressed, to imagine themselves as spaces of "pure non-violence,"[16] even as they generate it themselves. De Vries and Weber's point is particularly well-taken in light of the fundamental premise of this study: that before the desegregation of the military, African Americans, although victims of violent racist practices in the United States, clamored for an opportunity in each and every war to use a "self-determining" violence against a common external "enemy," not simply for national preservation but for individual identity formation, to remake themselves as "citizens."

World War I, Segregation, and Black Male Sexual Regulation

When Woodrow Wilson announced that the United States would go to war against Germany, those African Americans who wished to enter the military on an equal basis as whites were once again up against tremendous odds. The years of "peacetime" between the wars at the turn of the century and the beginning of World War I had not been ones of respite for racial tensions in the military, and reform-minded blacks and whites failed to change military policy substantially. The Wilson administration's final decision to maintain a segregated armed forces was informed in part by two events, one preceding and one during the war: the "Brownsville Incident" and the Houston Riots.[17]

In brief, the Brownsville Incident occurred in 1906 after the First Battalion of the Twenty-fifth Infantry, a black regiment stationed in that small town in Texas, was purportedly involved in several racially charged events. Although historians disagree on the precise detail, in one, a white customs officer accused black soldiers of jostling a white woman in the street; in another, a white woman accused a black soldier of attempting to attack her; in a third, another white customs officer pushed an intoxicated black soldier into the Rio Grande, deeming it a just response to public drunkenness. On August 14th, approximately two weeks after the first "offense," a group of unidentified men took to the streets of Brownsville after midnight. Congregating across from Fort Brown, where the Twenty-fifth was housed, the group randomly opened fire, killing one civilian man and wounding others. Several townspeople claimed to have seen or heard blacks within the crowd of raiders. Although the evidence unearthed by an investigation seemed to defy the possibility of black involvement, Theodore Roosevelt supported repeated investigations into the matter, eventually sanctioning the dishonorable discharge of 167 soldiers, comprising the entirety of three companies within the regiment.[18]

Eleven years later, African American soldiers found themselves yet again in conflict with white residents of a Texas town. As in Brownsville, the mere presence of a black regiment angered whites, who did little to hide their dissatisfaction. On August 23, 1917, a black soldier from the Twenty-fourth Infantry happened across a white police officer beating a black woman during an arrest and attempted to intervene. He was clubbed and jailed. A second black soldier from the same regiment who went to the jail to check on the first was treated to similar abuse by the same police officer. Not only was he beaten, however—this time with a gun over the head—he was also fired upon as he tried to run, was beaten again, and, finally, he too was jailed. Although the second soldier was released, rumors of his murder had spread during his incarceration; and while his return dispelled the false reports, his battered appearance infuriated his regiment. By dusk of the same day, approximately one hundred armed soldiers left camp and headed toward the police station intent on retaliation. In the chaos that ensued, more than a dozen whites were killed, including four police officers. One hun-

dred and eighteen of the "rioters" were charged in the two separate court mar-
tials that followed. A total of nineteen black soldiers were hanged, including six
whose executions were approved by President Wilson.[19]

For whites who had been against black military participation, Brownsville and
Houston served as proof of a complete lack of self-discipline and control among
African American men within the military. Even more than that, it raised the fears
that surfaced when blacks took up arms in the Revolutionary War—that arming
an oppressed group of people could have dangerous ramifications. Hence, Wilson's insistence in denying blacks full participation in the military was partly
punitive but was also informed by the deeply ingrained belief that black men were
fundamentally incapable of governing their impulses. Given that truth, they
could never be trusted to lead themselves. Blacks leading themselves, after all,
meant slave rebellions, mutinies, uprisings, riots. Therefore, if blacks were to
fight under their nation's flag in World War I, they were to do so only under white
leadership.

Not Only War: Black Men, White Women, and Les Zones Interdites

The reluctance of the U.S. Army to use black troops resulted in only two
combat divisions being sent to France: the Ninety-second and the Ninety-third,
the latter coming into existence after the Wilson administration concluded that
African Americans would support the war more heartily if an increased number
of blacks served. Accompanying these two divisions were expeditionary forces
and labor troops. As a whole, the regiments were hastily formed and poorly
trained, and as a result, their performance was compromised. The Ninety-third,
in fact, was given over to the French, who offered additional training, gave them
equipment, and outfitted them in French helmets. The Ninety-third Division
performed so well—particularly the 369th—that the French government awarded
the Croix de Guerre to three of the four regiments formed.[20] The appearance of
total and effortless integration ultimately alarmed the U.S. Army enough to ad-
monish the French for their relatively egalitarian treatment of black Americans.[21]
Not surprisingly, the idea that France might not be as virulently racist as the
United States appealed to African Americans. In one of the many prowar editorials *Crisis* editor W. E. B. Du Bois published throughout the war before reversing his position, he urges African Americans to join the Allies, calling France
"the most kindly of all European nations in her personal relations with colored
folk. She draws no dead line of color."[22]

World War I veteran Victor Daly's first and only novel turns on the hysteria generated over that very possibility—that French women, like their nation, would draw "no dead line of color." Eventually, pressure from the U.S. Army over the absence of strict segregationist regulations in the French forces did prompt Colonel Linard of the French Military Mission to issue an internal bulletin, "Secret Information Concerning Black American Troops," specifying how French officers and civilian officials were to treat black soldiers.[23] One of the "conclusions" Linard reached was that the French "cannot deal with" black officers "on the same plane as whites without deeply wounding the latter. We must not eat with them, must not shake hands or seek to talk or meet with them outside the requirements of military service."[24] He next asked that the French "not commend too highly black American troops," especially in front of white Americans. The final conclusion was the most telling: "Make a point of keeping the native cantonment population from 'spoiling' the Negroes. [White] Americans become greatly incensed at any public expression of intimacy between white women and black men."[25] Daly, a lieutenant within the Ninety-second, was not a member of the division for whom this directive was written. The Ninety-second was nevertheless included in the flurry of regulations spawned by the fear of contact between black soldiers and white French women. Noted historians of black army participation in World War I Arthur Barbeau and Florette Henri argue that this "neurotic terror" gave rise to a "promulgation of orders" giving "the impression that every black man was a potential rapist."[26] One order drafted for the Ninety-second claimed that "on account of the increasing frequency of the crime of rape, or attempted rape, in this Division, drastic preventive measures have become necessary . . . there will be a check of all troops of the 92nd Division every hour daily between reveille and 11:00 p.m."[27] They were also forbidden to stray more than one mile from camp unless granted "exceptional" status.

Daly's novel takes place in two locales: Spartanburg, Virginia, the site of a training camp for army enlistees, and northern France, the site of Allied offensives against the German forces. Creating a political continuum across the novel's two settings, Daly shows that Anglo-Saxon patriarchal control of women's bodies, a defining characteristic of white supremacy domestically, becomes integral to an assertion of U.S. imperialist military power abroad, transforming foreign geographies into national spaces. This becomes quite apparent in the pivotal moment in the novel: a white lieutenant, Robert Lee Casper, finds a black sergeant, Montgomery "Montie" Jason, accommodated in the home of a young woman in a small village in France. Enraged that the two might be involved, he has the sergeant court-martialed. What neither Robert nor Montie know, however, is that in Spartanburg, the two had been involved with the same woman, a black schoolteacher named Miriam Pinckney. Recognizing, in her words, that white men only desire "a social equality that existed after dark," she hides the affair from her friends and family, and, importantly, from her black suitor (40).

Not Only War appears to engage the two men in a tug-of-war over the female body, whether that body is black or white. In Spartanburg, Daly presents Robert in very much the same manner in which F. Grant Gilmore presented Colonel Fairfax—as a sexually exploitative southern patrician whose historical sense of entitlement extends to black women. Montie, in contrast, stands as the honorable suitor whose interest in Miriam is ostensibly genuine. In France, the two take on roles even more familiar to African American war literature: the racist superior and black subordinate. One of the only extant interpretations of the novel, J. Lee Greene's assessment in his 1996 book *Blacks in Eden*, envisions the two men engaged in a "miscegenetic triangle."[28] He also writes that the pair first conflict over the black female body in a psychosexual battle prompted by Montie's "erroneous belief that Robert is sexually exploiting a black woman."[29] I find Greene's decision to label a character who believes "in the supremacy of the white race," refers to Miriam as a "nigger," and uses economic coercion to appeal to her as a lover as *not* exploitative troubling (13, 17). But Greene manages to further this serious misreading by committing two factual errors: Robert and Montie do not meet until in France and do not engage in a psychosexual battle over a female body until that female body is white.

We must indeed wonder what Daly is attempting to convey by having an unsubstantiated "violation" of a white female body bring Robert and Montie in contest while an actual violation of a black female body creates little consequence. The triangularity that Greene mentions invites a discussion of interracial homosociality, which differs from the same-race homosocial bonding I explored in relation to *The Clansman*. Dixon's homosociality, predicated on a fear of political and racial miscegenation, attempts to use interregional same-race heterosexuality to bring together white men who were previously divided over the Civil War. In the African American war novel, interracial homosociality does signify political integration (rather than the racialist term—"political miscegenation"), but its relationship to heterosexual union is more ambiguous. Recall, for instance, that while the bonding among Sergeant Henderson, Colonel Roswell, and General Funston on the battlefield did make "military domesticity" possible in *"The Problem,"* Gilmore's presentation of that domesticity was truncated: a perfunctory gesture within the tradition of sentimentality. When loosed from that genre altogether, interracial homosociality in the African American war novel becomes even less tied to heterosexual production, and in fact, might preclude it altogether.

In an oft-cited early analysis of Don Quixote's admiration of the legendary knight Amadis of Gaul, René Girard explores the concept of "'triangular' desire,"[30] positing a configuration in which men of unequal stature, "the model" and the "disciple" create a lopsided power formation based on the disciple's wanting to be whatever the model is, to have whatever the model has. Whatever object the model possesses or deems estimable becomes the object the disciple wants. That object becomes "mediated," Girard suggests, a desire dictated "*according to Another*."[31] But when that object is a woman, the dynamic is altered; what men want is not the woman at all, but each other, a desire that can only be expressed through a heteronormative dual possession of (or duel over the possession of) Woman. Grafting interraciality onto the triangular, Leslie Fiedler later complicated the notion of homosocial desire by dropping the mediated woman altogether and, importantly, endeavoring to erase the asymmetry essential to Girard's model/disciple relationship.[32] Arguing instead that interracial "homoeroticism" (the term for which I substitute the more public "homosociality") takes place in spaces away from civilization (war, the forest, the sea), and apart therefore from the constraints of heterosexuality, Fiedler calls the unmediated, nonsexual union of two men from different races "a marriage of equals": "To emphasize the purity of such unions, the fact that they join soul to soul rather than body to body, they are typically contrasted with mere heterosexual passion, the dubious desire which threatens always to end in miscegenation."[33]

While forgoing an in-depth discussion of the "dubious desire" and the threat of "miscegenation," Fiedler does imply that the fear lies within white men who wish to maintain a "pure" civilization whose image is perfected in "pale genteel women busy in schools and churches."[34] Miscegenation is defined therefore as black men and white women; the flip side of interracial heterosexual desire— white men and black women—remains shrouded in silence. As Robyn Weigman notes, Fiedler writes with a certain degree of consciousness that his work, published first in 1960 and revised in 1966, is being unleashed into a nation being fundamentally altered by the civil rights movement.[35] If segregation meant the separation of black and white bodies, to Fiedler—and to America—desegregation came to be understood as a unidirectional black "penetration" of white spaces, and not the inverse. Correspondingly, black male penetration of the white female body became the corporeal (and sensational) equivalent of desegregation, at least within a white masculinist purview. The opposite was hardly imagined.

With Girard and Fiedler in mind, then, I would like to revisit the manner in which Daly constructs his two instances of triangularity. The first involves a white man possessing a black woman; the black man does not know of this possession, nor does he attempt to discover why the woman he desires is being pulled away from him or try actively to prevent it. In the second, which supercedes the first, a white man has de facto imperialist control over the body of a white woman; the black man knows this, pursues contact with her nevertheless, and ends up in direct confrontation with the white possessor. My reading of *Not Only War* will argue that Daly's use of the homosocial triangle does give primacy to the (would-be) bonds between men of different races, with the mediated woman of secondary consideration. I will also interpret Robert's easy, unimpeded access to Miriam and Montie's willingness to risk court-martial to be close to a white woman (and risk nothing to be close to a black woman) as Daly's critique of the sharply contrasting historically and politically determined values accorded these female bodies within a fraternally organized nation based in the "male traffic of women."[36] To be sure, Daly is not offering a repudiation of the trafficking process that objectifies women, but of the resulting fetishization of what the white man has—white women. That fetishization represents a misdirected integration-ist desire and a misplaced political energy: a substitution for the more conse-quential interracial fraternity based in egalitarianism.

However, for Daly, even the concept of "egalitarianism" bears interrogation. It is important to note that this is one of the first instances in the African Ameri-can war novel where black men quite clearly give voice to resistance politics—refusing to enlist, dreading the draft—unwilling, they say, to go to war for an undemocratic nation. Placing Daly's work within commentary about black con-scription in World War I, I will argue that Daly not only questions integrationist desire as expressed through an overemphasis on gaining unpunished access to the white female body, then, but as expressed through the continued pursuit of white men across their segregated battlefields.

Fallen Nation: Devaluing Black Womanhood

As I suggested in my analysis of Gilmore, the inability of black men to protect black women within the African American "protest" literature often acts as an evocation of the past, a reminder that black American men historically have been robbed of a "rightful" patriarchal power over "their" women's bodies. The ab-sence of a black patriarch signals a racial distress that can be rectified by the creation of racially recuperative households led by young black men; in the case of African American war novels such as Harper's and Gilmore's, that young black man has distinguished himself as a military hero. Daly appears to be re-presenting the racial rescue narrative by mentioning that Miriam would not be "strolling leisurely out on Vine Street at eight-fifteen one night" to meet Robert if her father—a black patriarch provocatively named Toussaint—had still been living, and by sending the novel's hero to meet her at the same time (39). Daly nevertheless resists this narrative, upsetting any expectations that Montie will reach her in time to intervene.

If the black "nation within a nation" has raised a female to a figurative status matching the larger nation's "pale genteel" woman "busy in schools and churches," it very well might be the nurse/schoolteacher/wife, a woman who epitomizes public service and charity, chastity and domesticity. In other words, she is Freda, Clotelle, Iola: the literary expression of the nation-building black woman that so many African American writers and political leaders in the late nineteenth and early twentieth century imagined as a companion to the African American man. Harper, Delany, Washington, and Du Bois, among others, have offered versions of this nationalist ideal. Though in no way monolithic, she possessed certain standard characteristics, such as an impeccably developed spiritual faculty and an unwavering duty to the betterment of her race. Du Bois paid particular attention to the foundation for nation building: a patriarchal dictate of the womb, expressing dismay over what he perceived as increasingly lax morals among black women and the resulting "illegitimacy" of their black children. In the *Philadelphia Negro* (1899), Du Bois argued that to ensure female chastity, young girls needed to be kept "off the street at night."[37]

Although a 1932 review of *Not Only War* in Du Bois's *Crisis* makes no mention of Miriam's scandalous behavior,[38] Daly has put Miriam exactly where Du Bois says she should not be: in the street. In doing so, Daly also places her squarely outside of the realm of the black ideal that would allow her emblematic status. Her nationalist symbolic possibilities nullified on multiple levels, Miriam simply will be removed from the text. In one of the final events of novel before the setting shifts to France, Montie attempts to call on Miriam and finds that she has unexpectedly left town. Daly has this narrative event fall upon the heels of a discussion Montie and his friend have after witnessing "gaudily dressed Negro girls" socializing with white soldiers (57). Remarking on the lack of "self-respect among that type," they then proceed to Miriam's to discover her gone (57). The conflation of Miriam's body with those of the flirtatious "Negro girls" signals her definitive descent. Though Daly graces Miriam with the name of the woman who helped lead the Jewish exodus from Egypt, Daly makes his character her antithesis, derailing the familiar narrative that would have her joined with the soldier-citizen at the forefront of the black nation.

Daly's refusal to draw Montie into Miriam's sexual "errors" allows him to bestow upon Montie a kind of naiveté that will serve an important function later in the novel. When Montie thinks he sees Miriam with a white man, he believes he is mistaken. When she is repeatedly unavailable, he can not fathom why.

COLORED MAN IS NO SLACKER

"The Colored Man Is No Slacker," G. H. Henesch, 1918. The vision of the military as a site for black nation building had accrued such powerful meanings within the African American community that it was propagandized in this World War I recruitment poster. Gilder Lehrman Collection, courtesy of the Gilder Lehrman Institute of American History.

When he finds she has left town, he assumes she has "quit him cold," refuses to pursue her or even write her, though he claims to be "very much in love" with Miriam (60, 58). Rather, acting upon an earlier notion he had to join the army, he enlists in the military, hoping to become a noncommissioned officer.

Montie's persistent "naiveté"[39] suggests that Daly presents it as a *willful* state of unknowing, a self-imposed blindness. Daly, a Washingtonian who wrote periodically for the *Crisis*, published an article in 1939 taking the district's African Americans to task for what he perceived as a quiet acceptance of Jim Crow. Having achieved a bit more than other African Americans socially and economically, he argues that the black bourgeoisie of Washington have been "lulled into a coma of complacency" by a growing sense of satisfaction "with the status quo."[40] They live in an "artificial sleep" that prevents them from taking the actions necessary to ensure their civil rights. The same could be said of the college-educated, ambitious man Daly chooses to be the protagonist of his novel. He is one of the young race men that Du Bois implored to fight to secure the betterment of black people: "Forget our special grievances and close our ranks shoulder to shoulder with our white fellow citizens and the allied nations that are fighting for democracy."[41] Allowed to join the army, though not on the terms he originally expressed—as a bona fide trained commissioned officer—Montie "forgets his special grievances," takes what the military will give black men, and vows to work his way up through the ranks.

When Du Bois in fact discovered that the army initially had no plans for training African American men as officers, he spearheaded the effort for segregated camps, in what became a much-criticized public acquiescence to Jim Crow practices. He rationalized segregated camps as opportunities for black men to show that their loyalty exceeded the nation's determination to keep them subjugated. Not all shared his view. As Lee Finkle words it in his examination of the origins of the modern black press, others of the African American print media "choked over the idea" of putting aside their grievances,[42] arguing that Du Bois's position amounted to asking blacks to suppress their domestic fight for civil inclusion, a risk they could not afford, even temporarily. Du Bois later added in answer to the negative response his call engendered, "*first* your country, *then* your Rights."[43] Accordingly, I read Miriam's aborted "racial rescue" as Daly's warning against racial abandonment, a demonstration of the consequences of a "*then* your Rights" philosophy. Montie's adherence to that philosophy results in a negligence stemming from being seduced by the " 'dazzling opportunities' of the white world," a negligence that, as Smith points out, might hasten the death of the black nation.

My interpretation is derived in large part from the historical context in which the novel was produced. If Montie's decision to join the army represents the sway of Du Bois's early thinking about the war's potential to help black men secure citizenship rights, Daly's novel, published thirteen years after the war ended, is in accordance with a profound shift in the Du Bois's thinking, a shift shared by many African Americans. By the time the Armistice was reached in 1919, Du Bois had become angry over the United States' "contemptible nastiness" toward African Americans:

> For the America that represents and gloats in lynching, disenfranchisement, caste, brutality and devilish insult—for this, in the hateful upturning and mixing of things, we were forced by vindictive fate to fight also. . . . But by the God of Heaven, we are cowards and jackasses if, now that the war is over, we do not marshal every ounce of our brain and brawn to fight a sterner, longer, more unbending battle against the forces of hell in our own land.
> We return.
> We return from fighting.
> We return fighting.[44]

The year of the Armistice was also the year of the Red Summer, so named because of the astounding level of racist violence against blacks. Looking back upon that year in his 1940 memoirs, Dusk of Dawn, Du Bois writes that the "facts concerning the year 1919 are almost unbelievable. . . . During that year seventy-seven Negroes were lynched, of whom one was a woman and eleven were soldiers; of these, fourteen were publicly burned, eleven of them being burned alive."[45] Encouraged by white conservative leadership to believe that, in the words of a Mississippi senator, "French-women-ruined Negro soldiers" were a threat to white southern women, some attacks specifically targeted returning soldiers,[46] a subject both Walter White and Claude McKay will treat in fiction. That summer, over twenty riots occurred in cities across the nation in reaction to the violence and out of African Americans' sheer frustration over the lack of civil redress and the lack of civil rights more generally.

By the time Daly first presents his writings on war and on the politics of integration in the Crisis, it was led by the more radicalized Du Bois, whose vision, which had always been informed by an understanding of the importance of racial solidarity and group cohesion in the battle for civil rights, had grown more insistently nationalist. Additionally, in the years before Daly published Not Only War, the NAACP, the parent organization of the Crisis, had come under the control of Walter White, an antilynching activist and the author of Rope and Faggot: A Biography of Judge Lynch (1929).[47] White had also published The Fire in the Flint (1924),[48] a novel in which a black doctor who served in World War I returns to

Georgia only to be lynched by the Klan for attending to a sick white woman. Additionally, 1932—aside from being among the worst years of the Great Depression—was the era of the infamous Scottsboro Trial, in which nine black youths, ages thirteen to twenty-one, were accused of raping two white women in Scottsboro, Alabama. A doctor's examination of the women uncovered no evidence of violation. Eight of the men were found guilty.

Dazzling Opportunities: Those Things Worth Fighting For

Daly dedicated Not Only War to "THE ARMY OF THE DISILLUSIONED"; undoubtedly, the antiblack sentiment that marred race relations in the United States before, during, and after the war soured Daly's attitude toward military service. The two short stories Daly published about World War I in the Crisis, though characterized by a bleak humor not found in the novel, share Not Only War's ambivalence about black participation in the "war to end all wars." The protagonist of "Private Walker Goes Patrolling" (1930) is a country draftee from Arkansas who "hated a fight";[49] in "Goats, Wildcats and Buffalo" (1932),[50] a black regiment realizes a chilling lesson in "equality"—that the German forces were just as ready, quite naturally, to kill blacks as they were to kill whites. Daly's sobriety distinguishes him from those African American war writers guided by sentimentalism; the second half of the novel begins with a vivid portrayal of warfare unmatched in realism by any of the novels in my study that have preceded it. In describing Montie's regiment as it advanced toward the German front, Daly strives to create the psychological horror and physical decimation Allied troops faced as they were made to walk unprotected directly into machine gun fire: "They advanced by inches, seeking imaginary shelter behind each twig or stump. . . . The incessant tapping of the riveting machine guns was interspersed only with the anguished groans of the dying. . . . A burst of bullets carried off a leg. A sudden hail of lead punctured a chest. A single bullet hurried on its way through a jaw and out by the way of the temple. A heart was shattered. But the line pushed on" (70).

Surviving the advance, Montie and members of his battalion seek reprieve in the small town of Laval, where the "remnants" of the regiment were to be accommodated (74). He leads his men to the house of a young French woman, Blanche Aubertin, who informs him that her home was to be reserved for commissioned officers—white men. After hesitating, she decides to house the black soldiers, and Montie and his men take shelter. Blanche embodies the imaginary France, savoring Montie's exotic blackness and expressing indignation over racist military policies. Robert, a lieutenant within another company, has been stationed three kilometers away, in another town. Robert and Montie meet when Robert agrees to accompany a drunken fellow officer who wants to go to Laval to find a woman who had earlier rebuffed his advances: Blanche Aubertin. Upon discovering Montie housed with Blanche, the lieutenant is obviously more enraged at the possibility that Montie and the young woman might be romantically involved than he is at the fact that Montie disobeyed military housing regulations. He has Montie court-martialed.

In this section of the novel, Montie is once again positioned as an innocent. While Daly presents Blanche as an object of desire—a proud, fiery blonde, wanted by white men—we never learn whether or not the sergeant had any intimate contact with the French woman. To Daly, that seems hardly the point. Rather, he allots primary attention to the young soldier's reaction to the accusation in the aftermath of the court-martial. Although Montie knowingly eschewed army regulations, having "chided" himself prior to being discovered for "intruding" in a house "reserved for . . . white men" (79), his self-admonition is partially mitigated by a meditation on the larger racial injustices the war has brought to the foreground:

> Could he ever forget that look of exultation that came over Casper's face when [the] sentence was pronounced? . . . Then his mind traveled to the war itself, to destruction, and suffering, and death . . . to the hundreds of other black boys who had died and were rotting up there [in the trenches]. For what good purpose, he asked himself. Came in answer all the high-sounding phrases that lull men's reason to sleep, and allow them to be led off like sheep to slaughter—to make the world safe for democracy—war to end war—self determination for oppressed people. But they didn't mean black people. Oh no, black people don't count. They only count the dead. They are not even fit to be officers in their own regiment—not even non-commissioned officers if they are going to be friendly with white girls. (93)

It is significant that this interior monologue falls on the heels of Montie's trial. He went to Laval having been promoted to a corporal for his bravery in battle; in one single move, a white officer is able to strip away all that he has earned. Montie's agonizing renunciation of war therefore stems from its failure as an instrument in securing freedom and "self-determination" for black people—and himself—which is several steps from a renunciation of war on the basis of war itself: what war is and what war does apart from its ends.

I raise the basis of Montie's disillusionment not to imply that Daly, as a war novelist, should issue any specific critique of war, but to emphasize the exact terms Daly has his hero use to determine war's futility—its failed instrumentality.

In particular, I find the passive language Montie wields to speak of his own participation in warfare a telling aspect of the novel because it so greatly contradicts the character's initial attitude. Early in the novel, Montie announces his desire to enlist, believing the "government will reward the race for its loyalty" (20). He is shouted down by his college buddies, who deride him as an Uncle Tom: "I read somewhere that the loyalty of a slave to his master is a vice" (20). They attempt to talk him out of serving by pointing out that no matter how valiantly he serves, he will "ride in a Jim Crow Car for the rest of" his life, "live in a segregated neighborhood," and be lynched "whenever they get ready" (20), Montie ignores them, adding, "I, for one, will never wait to be drafted" (21). In the wake of his court-martial, he no longer remembers himself as the discrete "I," the "one," who enlisted of his own volition; he sees himself as one of a nameless many black men lulled to sleep and led to slaughter.

His construction of himself as a passive victim of war and of military racism is bound, in his mind, to the senseless repercussions he endured for being "friendly" with a white girl. This requires ignoring that he enlisted willingly, and as I have pointed out, chose to take accommodations at Blanche Aubertin's with full understanding that his decision might subject him to punitive action. The white female body, first a symbol offering integrationist possibilities, then a symbol of disenfranchisement, alternates between becoming a location of inclusion and one of exclusion. Either way, that body—both mediated and controlled by white men—gives it proportions it would not have otherwise. Indeed, much of the correspondence from African American soldiers stationed abroad cite the French's comparatively relaxed attitude toward interracial dating between black men and white women as evidence of France's more civilized attitude toward blacks generally. As Walter White writes in *Fire in the Flint*, the black soldiers' "most vivid memories" of the war "were of . . . brief adventures with the *mademoiselles*" (43). Meanwhile, within the American military, black men were being tried and convicted on allegations of raping those very same "mademoiselles." While I will not attempt to dismiss the role basic libidinal desire must have played in bringing black men to French women, there is also evidence that black men flouted interracial contact as a means of defying white American authority—in spite of the possible repercussions.

I would like to suggest, then, that the elision Montie makes in his speech—his expression of despair over the lost promises of democracy, self-determination, and white women's bodies—is a purposeful move Daly makes to emphasize the paucity of an integrationist-egalitarian vocabulary that finds its most vocal articulation in a wish to be able to associate freely with "white girls."

In fact, in spite of the fact that Daly presents the reader with two instances of interracial heterosexual contact, in *Not Only War* the most powerful integrationist images are between black and white men. Daly frames the section of the novel taking place in France—the war section—with two interracial moments. Several paragraphs into the first battle scene, the men in Montie's battalion are stunned by their first encounter with war. After a shell explodes near them, Daly writes, "they huddled there together, the black man and the white, each seeking the protection of the others [sic] body. Fifteen minutes later, when the shelling had subsided, they climbed out, and the column moved on" (66). The novel closes when Montie, sent back into battle, finds Robert lying wounded in the bottom of a trench, his left leg shattered by bullets. Though dazed, Robert recognizes him: "You're Jason, aren't you?" (103). After grappling with thoughts of leaving the lieutenant to die, Montie's anger becomes "pity" and he tries to drag the man to safety: "Once more, they set out on their slow, painful journey. Twice more they stopped to rest. . . . Again they resumed the struggle. Then came a sudden riveting of maxims. Two bodies slumped as one. They found them the next morning, face downward, their arms about each other, side by side" (106).

In a novel which examines a black male effort to secure political integration through a fraternal organization in a patriarchal society, it is safe to assume that Montie's willful decision to place himself within dangerous proximity of a white female body merely substitutes for meaningful egalitarian contact with its male counterpart in the institutions of democracy: fraternal, not sexual, assimilation—the need to be recognized in the eyes of the dominant other. So strong is this desire that he risks death to save his oppressor, dying in the arms of a white supremacist who had him court-martialed. This is Fiedler's vision of a mythic interracial elsewhere gone woefully awry.

This ending could, of course, be given a patriotic turn; in the end, the African American soldier is more committed to the welfare of his fellow man than his white superior officer. Montie, not Robert, embraces the essence of a democratic humanism. I suspect, however, that Montie's death is intended to ask the question that Brown posed in writing of the attack on Port Hudson but then partly withdrew: "But had they accomplished anything more than the loss of many of their brave men?" In other words, does black men's participation in war add up to little more than more black men dying in war?

I have argued that Daly constructs his hero as innocent or naive. He is blind to Miriam's affair with a white southerner; he joins the war believing a display of loyalty will grant him entrée into the institutions of democracy; and he is unjustly accused of "inappropriate" contact with a white woman. These situations are no more than repetitions of historical circumstances: white southern control of black women's bodies, the perpetual punishment black men suffer under claims of various forms of "rape," the continued deferment of citizenship rights to people willing to kill and die for their nation. Brooks writes that Dorie Miller's "love" of "his fair lady . . . white-gowned democracy," requires not "entirely" remembering the knife hidden in her sleeve. Montie's actions are also dependent upon a mode of black forgetting that permits him to proceed while forgoing an assessment of whether African American service had substantially altered black civil status. His desire for integration demands, therefore, that he consent to take the memory of the state as his own, rejecting a black collective memory of betrayal to invest in the promises the U.S. government and its military made black servicemen. Montie's friends warn him that black remembering will inevitably follow black forgetting. The Jim Crow existing before the war, they argue, will be the same Jim Crow existing thereafter. Montie volunteers nevertheless. Daly, however, was drafted.

If He Hollers Let Him Go: Lynching and Democracy

As the United States began mobilizing for World War II, African Americans as a whole were less enthusiastic about the prospect for fighting for a racially segregated nation. The discriminatory hiring practices in the defense industry offered blacks an early indication of how they would be treated in the military. Foreseeing a "crisis in democracy" in 1941, A. Philip Randolph issued a call in the *Black Worker* asking for support for a march on Washington to demand that the government issue an order ending discriminatory practices in defense work and all branches of the armed forces.[51] Roosevelt capitulated, issuing Executive Order 8802, a fair employment initiative; Randolph called off his proposed march. The next year, the *Pittsburgh Courier* initiated the famous "Double V" campaign after *Courier* correspondent James Thompson penned a piece urging blacks to "adopt the Double VV for a double victory. The first V for victory over our enemies from without, the second V for victory over our enemies from within."[52] The subsequent issue of the *Courier* was emblazoned with a "V" across the front page. The editor of the New York edition remarked that the "two wars were inextricably intertwined."[53] Rather than asking blacks to put aside "special grievances" during wartime, in the main the mainstream black press urged fighting on all fronts: fighting for nation, fighting for the right to fight on an equal basis as whites, and fighting for civil inclusion. While such defiant rhetoric might seem to signal the beginnings of a movement to wholly resist military service, few proposed coordinating an all-out rebellion to the draft for fear of being accused of undermining the war effort and being branded as "traitors." Moreover, while the mainstream black press reported on the many "race riots" and racial disturbances on military sites at home and abroad, most African American newspapers and periodicals tended to downplay those racial disturbances initiated by black soldiers, most likely for a similar reason—so the men would not be labeled "non-cooperatives" during a national time of crisis. The Militant, the organ of the communist Socialist Worker's Party, ran several editorials castigating the campaign's mission, particularly disturbed that many in the black left had joined the Courier's cause.[54] Arguing that the "Double V" is "far from a radical or antiwar slogan . . . only a cover for unqualified support of the war," the Militant railed against thinking blacks had anything to gain from positioning Hitler as "their main enemy" while "poll taxers, lynchers and advocates of white supremacy" were having their way at home.[55]

If members of the mainstream black press wished to avoid being labeled infidels in a time of war, they did relentlessly question the nation's commitment to democracy. Articles covering the war "against fascism" appeared alongside those criticizing racism within the war industry—the segregated military, inequalities in selective service registration, the discriminatory treatment of blacks in defense plants. Reports covering and tallying lynchings acted as a barometer indicating the "real" state of racial relations, particularly after the lynching of a black private at Fort Benning, Georgia, in 1941, early in the war. The soldier was found hanging from a tree with his hands tied behind his back, yet the military initially labeled his death a "suicide" and did little to investigate.[56] The absolute disregard for black rights signified by the routine and indifferent obliteration of black life became increasingly central to the movement for civil rights gaining momentum under the Double VV program.

For instance, a 1944 issue of the Crisis included an editorial by army chaplain Grant Reynolds railing against policies limiting the upward mobility of African American soldiers. In it, he argues that in a war "to maintain the white man's right to keep the colored man in social and economic bondage," the army refuses to recognize black "manhood," instead classifying African American men "as morons incapable of attaining the intelligence of the most ignorant southern cracker." The chaplain drives home the point by accusing the army of "lynching" the black soldier's "ability."[57] But a single fact made the repeated coverage of lynching (and even its metaphorical invocation) especially potent. Lynching continued to occur within a white nation whose belief in its own ethical superiority brought it in violent confrontation with another white nation; that specific white nation was attempting to exterminate an ethnic "other." Returning to a point I made in the introduction to this book, lynching positioned within the context of white-generated violence served as a powerful indictment against the primary rationale for white global dominance: that whites have proven themselves to be the most "civilized" race. Trudier Harris's analysis—that the ritual of lynching aligns white supremacists with practices they have assigned to those dark, "uncivilized others" with whom they have associated ceremonial violence—also deserves emphasis here.[58] Just as Gilmore uses established white male patricians who rape and attempt murder to question white claims to civilized behavior, the black press's repeated insertion of lynching into discussions of the ostensibly "civilized" practice of modern warfare can be seen as an effort to confuse what "civilized" means and whom that word can truly characterize.

The use of lynching as a tool to intimidate black Americans into sociopolitical submission would emerge repeatedly as a concern in Chester Himes's writings during the war. In "Democracy Is for the Unafraid," a 1945 article included in Bucklin Moon's collection of essays about World War II, *Primer For White Folks*,[59] Himes raises the issue of lynching three times, while making scant mention of other assaults against black citizenship. For Himes, lynching is a telling act of violence committed by a people whose insecurity about their alleged racial superiority prompts them to "prove" it. The Klan, he writes, and "storm troopers" share a similar cowardice; this fear demands that they "destroy" the " 'minority.' "[60] Himes's fictional work from this period would make the "one crime" that "justified" lynching—rape—more central to his analysis. During the latter years of the war, Himes was a regular contributor to *Negro Story*, a fiction magazine that advertised itself as printing "Short Stories By or About Negroes for All Americans."[61] It circulated only briefly, from 1944 to 1946. Many of the stories he published in the magazine deal directly or indirectly with the war, often returning to a similar theme: a black man who is punished for real or imagined associations with white women. In "A Night of New Roses" (1945), a black defense worker loses his deferment for an unnamed offense involving a white "degenerate slut";[62] in "A Penny for Your Thoughts" (1945), a black soldier faces lynching for allegedly raping a "thin, sun-burned" woman who "had beat a murder rap";[63] in "One More Way to Die" (1946), two police officers shoot a black man in cold blood for accidentally hitting a "juiced-up" "old wino."[64] She, of course, is white.

Arguably an expansion of "A Night of New Roses," *If He Hollers Let Him Go*, Himes's first novel, tells the story of Bob Jones, a worker in a California shipyard who finds himself accused of raping Madge, a white female coworker, and is subsequently offered two alternatives as punishment: joining the army or going to jail. He chooses the army. The events that transpire between his first encounter with Madge and his entrance into the military illustrate Himes's conceptualization of the United States as a giant factory in which the government, civilian capitalist businesses, the police, and the judicial system act in unison for the single purpose of feeding black bodies into a military machine. After Bob agrees to the judge's terms and consents to join the army, he is led through a corridor of the court and unceremoniously handed over to the policeman on duty: "The sergeant didn't even look at me; he called over to a cop by the door in a bored, indifferent voice, 'Here's another soldier' " (203). In Bob's assessment, what has happened to him is quite clear. When Madge made the accusation of rape, there could be but "one conclusion—that I was guilty. . . . The whole structure of American thought was against me; American tradition had convicted me a hundred years before. . . . I was innocent and I didn't have a chance" (187). Several pages later in the novel, he dreams of an encounter with a white American marine who brags, "Hell, I've raped all kinda of women, white women, black women, yellow women, and the only reason I ain't raped no green women is 'cause I couldn't find none" (199). Then the marine points to a dazzling array of medals decorating his chest. Obviously, Bob believes that if anyone is guilty of "rape," it is a nation that has historically practiced and rewarded violence as a matter of course.

Ultimately, this ending—this repetition of the narrative of innocence—falls into what De Vries and Weber label a "facile" understanding of self/other within a context of violence, ascribing violence to the dominant other while imagining the black self a site of "pure non-violence." Early in the narrative, Bob recognizes that even looking at a white woman's body would be enough to get him lynched, and, sure enough, that is what occurs, if not literally, then legally, in an undeniable exercise of judicial violence set in motion by a vicious, retaliatory, and utterly false accusation of sexual violation. It must be noted, nonetheless, that Bob does think to himself, "What I ought to do is rape her" (126). He does vow to "make her" a "whore" (123). And, finally, he does arrive at her motel room uninvited, where he "[breaks] her down to the floor" (147). De Vries and Weber warn that real violence stems from the attempt to forge a difference between self and other "geographically . . . politically, religiously, sexually,"[65] and, I will add, racially. Bob's impulse to rape, understood as an attempt to create himself as the more powerful "masculine" to Madge's "feminine," and Madge's accusation, understood as the need to lord her more powerful whiteness over his weaker blackness, is about finding supremacy in delineation, and doing so quite violently. It is critical to remember that delineation—drawing boundaries—is a precursor to war.

I will demonstrate that throughout this novel about that subject—war, and wars within wars—Himes seems to be moving toward capturing the profound ambivalence about bodily locations of violence, an ambivalence that blurs distinctions between perpetrator and victim and raises issues about African American complicity in maintaining a culture of aggression. After all, if Madge capitulates to the white patriarchal dominant's means of creating the abject black male subject, transforming Bob into the black "rapist," Bob uses the same tools of destruction, hoping that intercourse with Madge will render her an untouchable to white men, "as low as a white whore in a Negro slum" (123). But I will also question whether Himes, in the final analysis, undermines this uncertainty by allowing the brutal assertion of power by the state—the lynching—to reinforce Bob's status as "innocent."

From the opening chapters of the novel, Himes has Bob vacillate between feeling as though he were at the complete mercy of the white world, awakening "scared" as though he would "have to get up and die" (2), yet experiencing surges of aggression that offer him momentary feelings of power: "all I wanted in the world was to push my Buick Roadmaster over some Peckerwood's face" (14). And from the moment Bob meets Madge, they perceive each other in over-determined, racialized terms, initiating a dangerous sexual and racial power struggle of which they are both aware. Each time they met, she would "put on that scared-to-death act," Himes writes; "we would both perform" (19, 27). The first ritualized encounter is a volatile, wordless one: she backs away from him "as if she was a naked virgin" and he "was King Kong." He is nonetheless stricken with "lust . . . like an electric shock" (19). Needing the assistance of a coworker later that morning, he asks Madge to work with him, approaching her as though she were "a vicious dog" (27). Becoming suddenly "tight-lipped and brutal," she exclaims that she will not be made to work with a "nigger." In a move that will prove catastrophic, he calls her a "cracker bitch" (27). She reports him to his supervisor; he is demoted; and, as a result, he loses his army deferment. That same day, Bob is further humiliated when white coworkers accuse him of cheating in a game of dice and refuse to give him the money he has legitimately won. A brawl ensues, and one man, Johnny Stoddart, steps forth and knocks Bob out cold. When he comes to, he searches the ship for the man; upon finding him, the two begin a bloody fight. Bob suddenly stops, knife in hand, overcome by a moment of clarity: "It was then I decided to murder him cold bloodedly, without giving him a chance. What the hell was the matter with me, running in there to fight him? I thought. What did I want to fight him for? I wanted to kill the son of a bitch and keep on living myself. I wanted to kill him so he'd know I was killing him and in such a way that he'd know he didn't have a chance. I wanted him to feel as scared and powerless and unprotected as I felt every goddamned morning I woke up" (35). The two plots symbolically converge into a single quest for Bob to redeem his manhood. After work, running his hand over the gun he keeps in his beloved Buick Roadmaster, he initiates a vague plan to kill Stoddart, and after a white male coworker insists on giving Bob Madge's address, he decides as well "to have her" (123). Even though he realizes that either course of action could result in his death—killing Stoddart could get him "hanged"; being caught with a white woman could get him "lynched"—he goes forward. He will give up his designs to murder Stoddart before anything consequential happens, however; his rage becomes focused on the sheer control Madge was given over his life. It eats at him: "I'd forgotten about the white boy I'd wanted to kill. It was just Madge and me in an empty world" (71). As the novel reaches its conclusion, a character will comment on Bob's ravaged body: "Looks like this man has had a war" (203). Madge will become the site on which he attempts to wage this war. He will come to the conclusion that to recover his masculinity he must rape her.

Society Must Be Defended: Race Wars and Rape

In a series of lectures given at the Collège de France in 1976, Michel Foucault attempted to determine to what extent power relations in a society were governed by the principles of war, focusing a great degree on how external, imperialist "race wars" came to define the dynamics of internal national racism.[66] In *Critique of Violence*, Foucault scholar Beatrice Hanssen summarizes the hypothesis underlying his exploration:

> War, during the course of modern history, had changed from being a strategic, military principle—the fare of martial experts—to becoming part of the inmost fabric of civil society where . . . it was wired into the filigree of peace. As it gradually left its position at the nation-state's outer periphery, where it served to sub-tend state boundaries, protecting the nation against external foes, war migrated inward, culminating in an "internal colonialism" enacted in the state-sponsored regimes of "bio-power," which aimed to control, eventually to eliminate, the inner social enemy, or other.[67]

Hence, the title of Foucault's lectures: "Society Must Be Defended." For order to be maintained within a nation—to achieve "peaceful coexistence" among individuals and groups—quite paradoxically, he argues, a warlike environment had to be instituted. Even more paradoxically, peaceful coexistence meant that the "inner social enemy" had to, by some means, *cease* to exist, a condition most efficiently brought about by "elimination," or, I will add, expulsion. If we consider American society during the time Himes was writing, white America's defense of itself against minorities took many forms: expulsion could mean being shuttled away into the penal system or being disenfranchised from the realms of civics and politics. Extermination could be effected through the imposition of poverty, forced sterilization, or intentionally poor health care; and, of course, it could be effected through overt forms—racially motivated murder, particularly lynching.

Somewhat differently from Foucault's emphasis on the inward migration of racism, Himes's novel implies that during World War II, ethnic antagonism against external others exploded outward from an inner core of white nationalism. The marine in Bob's dream confesses that when he was young, he carried around a "rifle looking for a nigger to kill"; the hunt for black men stopped, he says, when he joined the marines and began "killing all kinda of sonabitches" (199). The outwardly directed violence of nationalist warfare nevertheless returns inward, invariably. The war, Bob notes, has aggravated existing racist conditions: "It was that crazy, wild-eyed, unleashed hatred that the first Jap bomb on Pearl Harbor let loose in a flood. All that tight, crazy feeling of race as thick in the street as gas fumes" (4). The list of domestic racist affronts Himes mentions in his novel—Japanese interment camps, white American anti-Semitic literature, the Zoot Suit Riots,[68] lynching—positions Americans of Japanese, Jewish, Mexican, and African descent in conflict with the same internal Anglo oppressor. Though Himes's focus differs from that of Foucault's lectures, Himes conceives of the United States as a nation engaged in interior racial warfare very much in the terms Foucault would lay out more precisely thirty years later. And as Foucault's conceptualization implies, while it is the dominant culture that imagines itself under some form of attack from within—as the victim, as it were—it becomes the aggressor "defending" itself by taking offensive, "protective" measures. In *If He Hollers*, Himes's protagonist imagines blacks in a similarly defensive/offensive position: while numerically, socially, and politically disadvantaged, if mobilized, they could nevertheless prove formidable enemies against the state, with the ability to infiltrate and weaken the foundations upon which the nation stands. In "Negro Martyrs Are Needed," an essay written during the war, a radicalized Himes in fact outlines the rationale and strategy for black revolution, forwarding the American Revolution as an object lesson and invoking Friedrich Engels's goals for a communist state to frame his own arguments for overthrowing a white supremacist government.[69] Claiming that whites have become "barbarians," and therefore "can no longer govern themselves," he advocates meeting might with might, quoting Engels's declaration that communists were "to recognize no means of carrying out these objects other than a democratic revolution by force."[70] Although Himes acknowledges that "many Negroes will be shot"—just as Bob realizes he will be "hanged" for raping Madge—Himes asks blacks to put aside their fears, as he says, "Negro martyrs are needed."[71] Himes does not in any way advocate rape as a revolutionary exercise of "force," nor as a means of creating one of the "incidents" he argues are necessary to bring matters to the point of confrontation. But I will suggest that within a black revolutionary "army" as Bob imagines it, the rapist is indeed the martyr-terrorist; his target, white women—a declaration Black Panther Eldridge Cleaver would later make without apology.[72]

The primary justification offered for acts of terrorism is, in the main, fourfold. The terrorist feels precluded, or is in fact precluded, from participation in the "democratic" resolution of his or her grievances against a more powerful entity. Second, without military resources and the backing of a state, groups seeking power or political redress are thus "forced" to resort to "illegitimate" forms of violence as a means of destabilizing the targeted government, its apparati, and its populace. The third justification argues that the very distinctions made in categorizing violence are false; there is no such thing as "illegitimate" violence to begin with. Violence, whether the violence of "legitimate" warfare or the violence of "revolutionary" causes, has the same goals, purposes, and effects. In this way of thinking, the illegitimate/legitimate distinction is characterized as an ideological tool wielded to keep the dominated helpless and compliant, afraid to aggress against the oppressor, and, in a related goal, is intended to coalesce sentiment against the "revolutionary," thought to operate outside the laws of civilization the rest of "us" abide by. Finally, the use of violence leveled against civilians is justified by drawing an analogy to the inevitable and "acceptable" death and injury of civilians in state warfare; moreover, these civilians, as citizens of the offending state, are claimed to necessarily support structures of domination simply by participating in a given society's operations. In other words, there are no "innocents."

> It wasn't that Madge was white; it was the way she used it. She had a sign up in front of her as big as the Civic Centre—KEEP AWAY NIGGERS, I'M WHITE! And without having to say one word she could keep all the white men in the world feeling they had to protect her from black rapists. That made her doubly dangerous because she thought about Negro men. . . . I could imagine her teasing them with her body. . . . Then have them lynched for looking. . . . I felt castrated, snake bellied, cur-doggish, I felt like a nigger being horse-whipped in Georgia. Cheap, dirty, low. I wanted to grab some bastard and roll down the stairs. My face felt tight. The taste of white folks was in my mouth and I couldn't get it out.
>
> What I ought to do is rape her, I thought. That's what she wanted. (125)

In this passage, rape, the very crime through which Madge can exercise control over Bob's body by simply making an accusation, also becomes the means through which he can exert control over her body by destroying her sexual agency. The risk-reward factor in this particular desire to rape becomes then an act akin to going into battle, where the possibility of both killing and dying exists simultaneously; and within the context of war, either alternative translates into a glorious expression of masculinity. Stoddart, in confronting Bob, prepared to fight, is said to be "ready to die for his race like a patriot" (128). In the war between blacks and whites, this is Bob's corresponding gesture: even if he will be "hanged" after raping Madge, as he notes, such is the sacrifice a soldier makes for his nation. In a discussion taking place in the novel about the "Negro problem," Bob echoes Himes's language from "Negro Martyrs," suggesting that the only solution "is a revolution . . . the only thing white people ever respected is force" (84). Bob's violence against Madge will be, in his mind, revolutionary.

With this understanding, he goes to her motel, unannounced. After initially asking him to leave and threatening to call the police, she relents and allows him in. In her room, the power struggle that began at the shipyard takes a physical form:

> She jerked to one side, turning, and went half across the room . . . She was big strong and quick and it was all I could do to hold my own. . . . We stopped for a moment by common accord, resting. . . . I relaxed my hold and she snatched a hand loose and hit me in the face. . . . I took a deep breath and bore down. . . . She was almost as strong as I, but not quite. I slowly broke her down to the floor, and she looked me right in the eyes, hers buck wild.
>
> 'All right, rape me then, nigger!' Her voice was excited, thick with threads in her throat.
>
> I let her loose and bounced to my feet. (146, 147)

Bob leaves and climbs into his car. Madge has him wait and asks to get in his car, referring to him as she does as a "scary nigger" (148). He insults her in return. The next day, he runs across her at the shipyard, where she is napping in a cabin. Flustered, he tries to apologize for his behavior the previous evening and leave, but she blocks the doorway. He attempts to push her out of his path; instead, she grabs his head and moves to kiss him. Bob reiterates that he no longer wants her. Hearing men's voices at the door, he quickly calls out that he will open it. Panicked at what might be inferred if she were discovered behind a locked door with a black man, Madge throws him to one side of the room and screams out that she is being raped.

Juxtaposed against one another, these two scenes demonstrate an abrupt, startling reversal of power. When Bob goes to Madge's motel, he has thought about raping her—a thought that is in part constructed by a society that has labeled him a rapist—and she responds as though being raped, perhaps being similarly informed that interracial sex between a black man and a white woman can only be conceived of as assault. Or, in an interpretation that momentarily subordinates issues of race, perhaps Madge uses the word "rape" to describe the contact because being overpowered and held to the floor feels indeed a lot like rape. Either way, the second scene is a brilliant inversion of the first: Himes creates a dynamic and wields a language that makes it appear that Bob is being violated by Madge, setting the tone for the institutional rape that Bob will endure later.

Bob's dream about the marine demonstrates that Himes understands that "legitimate" war involves rape, both metaphorically and literally. Summarizing Susan Brownmiller's early and influential understanding of rape within a "context of war and other violent conflicts," philosopher Ann Cahill explains that according to Brownmiller rape is not, from the perspective of the rapist, "an act against the woman herself. Indeed, such a formulation would demand that the woman is someone herself, which she clearly is not. Rather, the act is a direct threat to the ownership of the man who is the rapist's enemy."[73] That Bob first gives voice to his impulse to sexually degrade and/or assault Madge after he feels humiliated by a white male coworker, and goes to her apartment after he sees his African American girlfriend in the company of a white man, would give credence to Brownmiller's theory. Like the objectified white female body that becomes "mediated" in interracial homosociality, a substitute for the man himself, Madge is indeed on one level the enemy by "proxy," a thing to be destroyed in the adversary's absence. Having said that, it is also critical to stress the degree to which race complicates that paradigm, both within the world of the novel and without.

As crucial as Brownmiller's positioning of women as "objects" was in the creation of a viable feminist definition of rape, Angela Davis issued an important critique of her analysis, exposing Brownmiller's inadequate theorizing when it comes to racial matters.[74] This insufficiency, Davis claims, borders on racism. Davis notes that in discussing the Scottsboro case, Brownmiller characterizes the nine men as "semi-literate fellows . . . who only wanted to beat the rap," while drawing a more sympathetic picture of the white women who perjured themselves and ruined those men's lives.[75] They were, in Brownmiller's own words, "corralled by a posse of white men who already believed a rape had taken place. Confused and fearful, they fell into line."[76] Brownmiller refuses to attribute agency to these women and, as Davis notes, prefers to absolve them "of the responsibility of having collaborated with the forces of racism."[77] The overarching paradigm in Brownmiller's work—that women are always already objects within a patriarchal, sexist system—extends so far that Davis argues that the Scottsboro women become, to Brownmiller, inanimate female "pawns," which comes uncomfortably close to Brownmiller's denying that they had any ability to refuse cooperation.

Looking at Madge in this light, she is not the enemy by proxy, an "innocent," but the enemy herself. She is not a weapon of war, powered, controlled, and directed by white men, but a woman who willingly chooses to make her body instrumental in the internal racial war against black Americans. Thus, although a woman, inhabiting a marginalized subject position, Madge's whiteness gives her a compensatory political power that Himes depicts in her physical ability: in the motel, Madge is "big, strong and quick," "almost as strong as" Bob; in the cabin, she comes at him, flinging him toward a bunk and leaving him "sprawled face down on the mattress," prone (146, 179). She is America's Sweetheart, the woman idealized in Norman Rockwell's muscular rendition of Rosie the Riveter on the celebrated 1943 cover of the *Saturday Evening Post*; but here, she has come to life in a most monstrous form. In fact, Himes once described the United States as a "big overgrown idiot of a nation with an underdeveloped brain," whose idea of solving social issues was to "build hydrogen bombs and build horror stories to scare themselves into screaming nightmares."[78] Himes's many references to Madge's "awkward" size and unusual strength—when coupled with her readiness to conjure the phantasmal black beast—transforms Madge into an image of the United States itself.

We Are All Guilty

Davis's invocation of the word "collaboration" in describing the Scottsboro women is particularly helpful in thinking about how Madge operates within Himes's novel. To think of Madge as a collaborator rather than an instigator would not make her any less responsible for her actions, it would merely mean she has participated in a system that she did not have a hand in constructing. However, as collaboration implies, she could not act alone. Her battle cry, her screaming of "rape" at the top of her lungs, is enough to mobilize every white man in the vicinity to come to her "rescue," and is enough to get all repressive state apparati, to use Althusserian terms, acting in concert against the black male body. It becomes, as Himes writes, a war.

I noted in the introduction to this work that Clausewitz writes that a duel is not a war; a war is a duel on a larger scale. To have a war, one must have forces operating together against the "enemy." There must be, in other words, complicity, if not agreement and accord. Himes's war writings tend to position African American men outside of the arena of war, as objectors, if not with the detailed philosophical rationale a conscientious objection would imply. In "A

Night of New Roses," Himes writes that the "colored fellows" in the bar his protagonist frequents "were the usual run, mostly army age but keeping out by hook or crook, drugs and poison, lies and trickeration" (12). They resist, it can be inferred, by any means available. In *If He Hollers*, Bob thinks about what might happen if African Americans collectively decided not to participate in the war effort: "I wondered what would happen if all the Negroes in America would refuse to serve in the armed forces, refuse to work in war production until the Jim Crow pattern was abolished. The white folks would no doubt go right on fighting the war without us, I thought—and no doubt win it. They'd kill us maybe; but they couldn't kill us all. And if they did they'd have one hell of a job burying us" (115–16). Shortly thereafter in the novel a character argues that any black man fighting in a Jim Crow army was fighting against himself: "If Bob lets them put him in the Army he's a coward" (121). Bob assents: " 'That's right, I said' " (121). Bob's brief fantasy of resistance is interesting because he sets up a dichotomy between the choice of killing (if not directly) and being killed. It is even more intriguing because the idea of the mass slaughter of African Americans by its government invokes, of course, the extermination of Jews in Nazi Germany. Bob imagines the United States quite capable of committing the kind of human atrocity that it so vehemently decried. In a comically perverse commentary on the United States' ironic position as "liberators," Himes wrote a short story in which an African American dreams he is trapped by Hitler in Germany and that the U.S. forces have come to rescue him.

Of Bob's ultimate fate, then, we can say that he was "forced" into the army, given the alternative—entering the penal system—or we can say that he "chose" to join the military, given the alternative. In that same way, we can say that Madge chose to cry rape to stave off the punishment sure to befall a white woman who appears to have "compromised" herself with a black man. The two are not exact parallels, but the point I wish to make is this: in a society oriented toward war, in a nation whose very structure has been determined by the organizing principles of warfare, it is uncertain who can remain "innocent," that is, outside of the machinery of violence. Bob does not want to fight for the United States, but he participates in the war industry and profits from it. He opts to place himself in the position to kill or injure rather than suffer the violence of incarceration. And while he does not rape, he considers it.

Himes would write a later novel, *A Case of Rape* (1963),[79] that would lend more insight into how he viewed the interconnectedness of war, violence, racism, and the myth of the black male rapist—or its inversion, what I have labeled the narrative of black male innocence. In this work, a group of black men living in Paris are accused of raping and killing a white woman who was once the lover of one of the men. Having conceived of the novel while living as an expatriate in that city, Himes wrote the story with an awareness of racist attitudes exacerbated by the French-Algerian War. Technically, the accused are innocent—though one gave her a drug that accidentally killed her. A black American writer turned detective attempts to prove the guilty verdict erroneous. He fails. Later, he considers what would have occurred if he had found information that might have exonerated the men. In this final chapter, entitled "Speculation," he wonders:

> Whatever would have been the outcome, one assumption may be drawn. . . . No one would ever be able to point an accusing finger at all Negro men and think: They are potential rapists. Men would have then been influenced to consider whether the greater crime was rape or the conviction of innocent men on trial for rape on racial preconceptions. Perhaps this might have forwarded the precept of all men of whatever race to bear some measure for mankind's greatest crime, man's inhumanity to man.
>
> And that's how it should be. We are all guilty. (105)

Last of the Conquerors: "Negroes, Nazis, and Jews"

Chester Himes compares the Klan to storm troopers; he imagines white America capable of mass slaughter; he has a character dream he is held prisoner by the Nazis. In doing so, he enters into a very particular rhetorical moment in which African Americans began comparing and conflating the bodies of black Americans to that of European Jews. Grant Reynolds, the army chaplain who spoke of the "lynching" of black male ability, asserted that it had been performed by "domestic nazis"; Thurgood Marshall's 1943 Crisis article on the Detroit Riots was entitled "The Gestapo in Detroit."[80] A black soldier liberating Dachau said that he could only make sense of the human waste by comparing it to the disregard of life during American slavery.[81] William Scott III, a black journalist, accompanied an African American engineering corps charged with the task of burying the dead from Buchenwald. He wrote:

> I saw in front of me the walking dead. There they stood. They were skin and bone. They had skeletal faces with deep-set eyes. Their heads had been shaved. They held each other for stability. I couldn't understand this. . . . I went to a building where they stored body parts from "medical experiments." I saw the fingers and eyes and hearts and genitals. . . . If this could happen here, it could happen anywhere . . . and I thought about how many times my people were lynched and mistreated across this country and nobody raised a voice.[82]

And there it is: African Americans' own experience in their native country had sensitized them to the effects of a racism that ran so deeply that it could move some members of a society to wish to annihilate others, and in the process of justifying that annihilation, transform the others' bodies into objects of corporeal explorations that would ultimately declare them strange, unnatural, repulsive, worthy of the desecration and destruction that would befall them. As early as 1938, a *Crisis* editorial, "Negroes, Nazis, and Jews," explained the connection in this manner: "It is doubtful that any section or race has sympathized more whole-heartedly and keenly with the Jews than Negro Americans, for he has known the same kind of persecution . . . reviled and misrepresented in textbooks, from the kindergarten to the research seminar."[83] Years after the war, in 1951, William Patterson would produce a petition for the United Nations cataloguing antiblack violence and label the list of atrocities *We Charge Genocide: The Crime of Government Against the Negro People.*[84] What happened to Jewish bodies in Nazi Germany offered African Americans one means, however horrendous, to position their issues within the broadened context of human rights, rather than within the local geopolitical space that "civil rights" denotes.

The black press did make an effort to cover the Nazi's attitudes toward blacks and kept watch on the Third Reich's antiblack practices and propaganda, to the extent that was possible. Yet the connections most African Americans made between black American and Jewish bodies often had little to do with Hitler's specific antipathy for blacks themselves—the disgust he expressed for the *schwarze* in *Mein Kampf*, or the fact that Nazis had held a number of blacks born or residing in Europe in "labor" camps, including the American woman jazz trumpeter Valaida Snow and the African Leopold Senghor, who would become the first president of Senegal after its decolonization.[85] Even less considered was the relationship of the black body to the evolution of Aryanism. In a relatively unknown *Opportunity* article published in 1939, "Once More the Germans Face Black Troops," Claude McKay attempts to convince his African American audience that the terror over German race-mixing began when France stationed black colonial troops in the Rhineland after World War I.[86] Indeed, as Paul Gilroy reminds us in *Against Race*, Eugen Fischer, a German anthropologist, conducted studies of the *Rhineland-bastarde*, the mixed-race children of these black men and German women. The children were eventually sterilized.[87] However, before the *Rhinelandbastarde* became a problem to the Germans, Fischer had published work on the offspring of the Dutch and the Hottentot, under the title "The Rehoboth Bastards and the Problem of Miscegenation among Humans."[88] Prior to Fischer's studies, the French Count Gobineau's *Essay on the Inequality of Races* had drawn on French colonial contact with Africans for its theories of Nordic superiority. Both Fischer's and Gobineau's speculations on ethnic hygiene became highly influential in the racial component of Nazi fascism and the plans for Jewish extermination. Nonetheless, blacks were not singled out for elimination, in part because of their relatively small presence. However ironic, Hitler felt extreme measures leveled against blacks might spoil racial relations in an imperial design that was to include the eventual domination of Africa.[89]

Thus while a spectrum of phobic responses to the black body played a critical role in Nazi ideology, William Gardner Smith dedicates much of his first novel, Last of the Conquerors, to exploring what the writer views as a great irony: that, despite the influence of Aryanism, the "average" citizen of Germany held no particular prejudices against black Americans. Set in occupied Berlin, where Smith himself had served as a clerk typist after being drafted in 1946, the novel tells the story of a troop of African American men who explore their attitudes about racism within one context, the American military, which is superimposed upon another—post-Nazi Germany. To be certain, Smith's depiction of German attitudes is never simplistic: not every German character denounces Hitler in one speech and extols the virtues of a racially blind society in another. But his portrait is, as a whole, sympathetic. With the exception of the character of Randy, who reminds the other men about Hitler's commentary on blacks in Mein Kampf, most of the others—the "Professor," Homo,[90] Murdock, and the protagonist, Hayes Dawkins—note the relative lack of racial antagonism directed toward them and express ambivalence, even anguish, about returning stateside after demobilization. Homo, in fact, chooses to disappear into Berlin's Russian Zone before being shipped out; and after being discharged, Smith's hero vows to return to Germany. A statement the Professor makes toward the novel's conclusion summarizes the men's sentiment: "I'll always remember the irony of my going away to Germany to find democracy. That's bad" (216).

Smith has most of the men make their analyses of comparative racial politics through a familiar site: the white female body. Most of the novel is in fact given over to exploring the sociopolitical dimensions of a love affair between Hayes and his white German lover, Ilse Muller. They meet on the army facilities in Berlin, where she, along with many other German women, is employed as a secretary. A relationship develops, and after Hayes is quite suddenly transferred to Bremberg, Ilse makes a long, dangerous trip across Germany that includes a two-day, one-night walk to the British zone—just to reunite with her lover. The danger does not end with her journey, however; in Bremberg, Ilse is forced to contend with a white military police force whose primary duty appears to be an imposition of the domestic racial order on black soldiers abroad. Nicknamed "nigger hell" because it housed black troops nearly exclusively, Bremberg became a site where illegal regulatory measures specifically directed at African American soldiers could be issued without reference to race, and therefore without legal repercussions. Additionally, because Bremberg was under U.S. control, the military could do as they wished with German civilians there. Predictably, the greatest restrictions were instituted to reinforce sexual segregation. Hayes's white commanding officer is said to "hate to see one of the boys with a white girl" (121); black soldiers and German women were consequently punished for these relationships by being subjected to random "VD checks" often accompanied by periods of incarceration.

As a result, one evening as the two are walking home after a date, an M.P. picks Ilse up for a "VD check," takes her away, and throws her in a building with other German women "caught" socializing with black men. There, she is told that black American men are deficient, diseased, "not like everybody else," outside of humanity proper, a contaminant (176). The officers tell the women that they can be released in exchange for sex. When they refuse, they are told they are "nigger lovers" no longer good enough for white men. Ilse is held for two weeks. African American soldiers are also detained there.

It is in this episode that Smith comes closest to linking American and Nazi regimes of racism. The parallel he attempts to draw between a concentration or labor camp and the all-black army camps where white authority can, in isolation, enact a total domination is evident. What also becomes evident in the act of sexual regulation is the essential role of what Foucault calls "biologizing" eugenics in the development and maintenance of the modern nation-state:

> Beginning in the second half of the nineteenth century, the thematics of blood was sometimes called on to tend its entire historical weight toward revitalizing the type of political power that was exercised through the devices of sexuality. Racism took shape at this point (racism in its modern, "biologizing," statist form): it was then that a whole politics of settlement (peuplement), family, marriage, education, social hierachization, and property, accompanied by a long series of permanent interventions at the level of the body, conduct, health, and everyday life, received their color and their justification from the mythical concern with protecting the purity of the blood and ensuring the triumph of the race. Nazism was doubtless the most cunning and the most naïve (and the former because of the latter) combination of the fantasies of blood and the paroxysms of disciplinary power.[91]

In an essay that in part looks at the "fantasies of contagion and disease within German culture of 1939," Sander Gilman reiterates that Hitler often expressed his racist ideas in terms of bodily invasion: he warned against the "syphilitic Jew" weakening the Aryan fiber, of polluting pure German blood through racial inter-marriage, and expressed further anxiety over the *Mischling*—the Jew hidden by a Germanic surname "just waiting to corrupt the body politic."[92] As I pointed out in my examination of disease in Harper's novel, a very similar rhetoric posited that the "virulent" black body would infect and weaken the American body politic. In fact, like McKay and Gilroy, Gilman reads these accusations against the Jewish body within the context of the German empire in Africa to conclude that racialist science's admonishments against blood-mixing made Jews, in effect, "black"[93]—the empire once again moving inward, as in Foucault's theory of internal racial war. A particularly bizarre theory circulated among Nazis theo-rized that Jews were the degenerative "hybrids" of Asians and Africans.[94] Smith, however, redirects the connection between Jews and blacks: in placing the segre-gation and stigmatization of black soldiers within the context of post-Nazi Ger-many, Smith makes black bodies Jewish, an association that stands as an accusa-tion against American racial nationalism.

The ideas about body and race raised by the relationship between Hayes and Ilse are one reason this neglected novel makes an unexpected appearance in Paul Gilroy's aforementioned work, *Against Race*. *Against Race* is, in Gilroy's own words, a rather "utopian" meditation on the possibility of freeing a human consciousness overdetermined by "race-thinking."[95] He argues that while coun-terhegemonic identity politics might have been a necessary phase of racial libera-tion, that moment has passed, and now, "epidermally" based political and social logic merely leaves human beings divided from one another by distinctions that do not exist beneath the skin. His book positions the moment of unchecked Nazism as an object lesson: this is precisely what happens, he says (as have many others), when an oppressive force such as fascism takes the "fact" of ethnic "differences" as an opportunity to radically embody a horrifically destructive politics. Gilroy sees *Last of the Conquerors* as an especially valuable text, not only for Smith's willingness to link "antiblack racism . . . to antisemitism," but for the manner in which the interracial affair comes to express the potential "value of love and the possible significance of common humanity sexual desire brings into focus."[96]

As seductive as Gilroy's utopian reading may be, Smith's novel complicates the potentially transcendent power of interracial sex; his complication is not simply a matter of the kinds of punishments to which interracial couples were subjected from "above." One soldier in particular, Randy, stands out as an in-triguing character because he sees the interrelatedness among gender, race, and nation differently from the other men and seeks to trouble the black soldiers' relationships with white German women. Called "patriot" by Homo for his

sometimes nationalist assertions about the United States and his wholesale denunciation of the German people as "savages" (28), Randy dismisses the other
men as "dumb" for believing that women exist exterior to the political system, or
as Homo says, that "the women don't have anything to do with it" (14). "It" is,
ostensibly, many things: Hitler, Nazism, genocide, and war. Observing that the
men have been confused by the ready availability of "white chicks," Randy later
comments that the German women are making "fool[s]" of the men: "You don't
know it but they're laughin' at how dumb you are behind your backs. . . . They
play you for all they can get while you're here and then as soon as you go they just
get another soldier and play him the same way. . . . I'll bet you give your girl all
your cigarettes every week" (60). Randy's implication that these women are using
the men to try to survive in a country decimated by war corresponds to his
perspective on Germans' attitudes toward the American taking of Berlin. He
argues that the Germans "cheered" not because they truly welcomed the American forces, but "because they wanted cigarettes and chocolate and they were too
scared to do anything else. Damn right they cheered" (28).

Within his novel about black men participating in the American occupation of
Berlin, it seems then that Smith uses Randy's cynical assessment of the evils of
German women to show us that their "desire" is intertwined with the power that
these black men's status as Americans affords them. Indeed, while Berlin was
militarily occupied by American forces sent in for a political purpose—a "de-
nazification" program—the goals of occupation are also economic. Smith notes
the rapid introduction of Woolworth's, Coca-Cola billboards, and American cinema. One line, embedded in a throwaway conversation about dating, illuminates
how the U.S. interventionist presence also spills over into matters sexual: Hayes
refers to two women who are already dating other men as "occupied chicks"
(131). The territorializing of German women's bodies inherent in this phrase
places their relationships with black soldiers within a complex system of com-
pliance and dependency fostered under American military governance.

Far from "cheering," many Germans in fact resented the occupational forces,
a resentment that often articulated itself in derisive portraits of German women
who "fraternized" with American GIs against specific policies the German government had instituted in part to prevent what was perceived as an increasing
sexual opportunism on the part of the occupying forces.[97] These portraits frequently depicted the German women as "prostitutes" who were all too willing to
exchange their bodies for the "chocolate and cigarettes" Randy mentions, a
transaction from which German men were largely excluded.[98] These women's
bodies thus became part of a larger underground "cigarette economy" that permitted American servicemen to trade U.S. commodities for meals and other

services with the German population, for whom certain goods, such as sugar—and of course, cigarettes—were in short supply. Susanne zur Nieden claims that the trope of the "cigarette" emerges repeatedly in the antioccupation literature published after the war, operating dually as a metonym for U.S. material goods and as a metaphor for the phallic power given the American servicemen possessing those commodities.[99] Not a few of the stories take up the issue of black soldiers specifically, whose access to German women was viewed as an especial affront to German masculinity,[100] posing a problem similar to the black French troops stationed in the Rhineland after the First World War. These relationships sparked rumors that black men had been specifically instructed to ethnically pollute the "pure" German race.[101] The policing of German women Smith describes was not only a result of the U.S. military's desire to enforce racial-sexual segregation, then, as it did during World War I, but also reflects the strategies Germans implemented to punish German women, characterized as "traitors" willing to betray their nation for nothing more than a bit of coffee. Beyond incarceration, German military authorities attempted to desexualize the women by cutting their hair off; in some other instances, they raped them—an act intended to intimidate German women and to operate as a form of retaliation against the occupying armies.[102] For German women, who had already been targets of rapes by the Allied forces,[103] this tactic proved especially psychically damaging.

I would like to return, then, to the analytical frame of this chapter, black male innocence. It seems that Gilroy's idealistic reading is necessarily influenced by his implicit understanding that black male/white female relationships are fundamentally fraught with racial anxiety; to complement his larger argument, he chooses to perform an interpretive intervention of sorts, rereading a culturally overdetermined relationship as an example of a potentially revolutionary form of human contact. I have suggested, however, that the narrative of innocence—the emphasis on the unjust consequences for interracial contact between black men and white women—becomes problematic within a wartime setting because it has the effect of diverting attention away from the role African American men often willingly played within the military machine and a culture of violence.

Yet it is crucial to remember that killing and injuring are not the only violating forms militarism can take. The women in the novel who date black American soldiers—the "occupied chicks"—are presented, as Randy implies, as aggressors. They attach themselves with a certain purpose or desperation to these men; the Professor, who ostensibly loses his virginity to one of these aggressive women, tells the men the story of a German woman who "loved" a black soldier so much she killed him rather than see him leave. So while they are largely depicted as forward, "loose," hungry, it is important to point out that their neediness had been created to a great extent by the very American forces that quite purposefully blasted their city to pieces. But let us assume that Gilroy is correct: that Hayes's and Ilse's desire for one another just might be emblematic of a human impulse that has the potential to operate outside of the racial. Even if that were so, there is another determining difference between the two—the one that Randy pinpoints—the imperial. Thus, in considering what I referred to as other violating forms of militarism, I will suggest that depicting the women as the aggressors while at the same time focusing on the punishment meted out by white authority for interracial contact obscures the sexual opportunism on the part of the black soldiers and thus separates them from the U.S. occupationist/ imperialist ethos. Smith's novel might ask whether desire can circulate outside of the racial, but the book leaves us with another question altogether: whether it can circulate outside of the "imperial," particularly within unbalanced power relations created by American military occupation.

The marketing of the novel brings out some of the elements I wish to bring to the forefront in relation to this issue. When the young novelist first presented his manuscript to Farrar and Straus, it bore the title *Dark Tide Over Deutschland*. Unimpressed with Smith's choice, and with his second attempt at naming the novel, *The Hammer and the Nail*, his editor decided it should be distributed under another title, *Last of the Conquerors*.[104] The final title—with the idea of conquering—places the hero within a history of belligerent territorial invasions that had become a defining characteristic of U.S. "foreign policy" despite its stint of "isolationism." The United States had exercised military governance in at least ten exterior locations in the relatively short period from the end of the nineteenth century to just before World War II.[105]

The paperback edition, published by Lancer in 1965, has a startling cover:[106] a black man, brawny, clothed in army fatigues, has his mouth opened onto the neck of a white woman, who appears to be nude from her waist; he is clutching her tightly. Her head is tossed back in what seems to be passion, her blonde hair flowing down her back. On the front cover, in black capital letters above the title, the publisher labels the novel a "SENSATIONAL BEST SELLER ABOUT LOVE AND HATE—BLACK AND WHITE." The back cover summarizes the novel in an equally provocative manner, again in black capital letters: "WHITE MEN CALLED HIM A NIGGER—IT TOOK A WHITE WOMAN TO MAKE HIM SEE THAT HE WAS A MAN." Quite obviously, the cover reinforces a problematic representation of black male/white female sex. That she is unclothed while he is dressed evokes rape; that the publisher attaches "love and hate" to the image implies that interracial sex necessitates a pathological psychic split in the black male (in the manner that a writer such as Himes purposefully depicts); and last, the publisher's marketing plays on the commonly held idea that the black male is forever in search of his denied masculinity in the white female body.

Although Smith sought to create a work in which his hero was divorced form stereotypes of black masculinity, even going so far as to make Ilse the pursuer (she asks Hayes out, she seduces him, and it is she who follows him), the cover externally imposes the very narrative on the novel that Smith was attempting to undermine. But the effect is intriguing. The title and the image below it combine to frame black predatory masculinity in terms of imperial conquest, creating a kind of sameness between the two in which this racialized sexual power is merely an extension of a nationalist drive that finds its political expression in domination. The black male body suddenly becomes very American.

I find this accidental reinscription of national/imperial conquest important precisely because of the manner in which the novel, in the end, attempts to recuperate that difficult issue in relation to gender, negating Randy's earlier observations. For example, Ilse and Hayes are introduced to a young biracial boy in Berlin named Sonny who is the product of a black American soldier and a white German woman. The boy is "beautiful," and unlike many other Germans after the war, the mother has money. Nor has she been ostracized for having a black child; many men want to marry her (though historically many women in a similar position were indeed considered undesirable). Sonny is fawned over by the Germans, and in a romantic moment, Ilse and Hayes are walking in the park with the handsome boy child and are delighted to see that others believe he is theirs. His lovely presence serves to obscure the conspicuous absence of the black soldier who is his father. In another episode that demonstrates the way gender and imperialism intersect in the novel, Hayes criticizes Russian soldiers for what can accurately be called territorial intrusion: "We did not like them to dance with our girls. If they danced with our girls they swung them about in wild Russian dances which were too much for those not used to the tempo, and afterwards the girls would be sore and worn out and not up to what we wanted to do later after we got home . . . the girls were no good after dancing with the Russians" (48). In Smith's narrative of innocence, interracial love is romanticized without examining the uncomfortable fact that the politics of U.S. occupation often meant viewing sex as an imperial prerogative, the prerogative of the dominant—and in this instance both categories, imperialist and dominant, include black men. Hayes sees himself as a racialized subject seeking freedom from oppression, but he does not know himself as an already nationalized subject; even if he exists only in the margins of that nation, he carries within him ideologies shaped by his emergence within its boundaries.

In general, the centrality of the narrative of innocence renders Smith's otherwise provocative insights less convincing and overshadows more pressing racial politics. Two very different race-based violations that occur in the novel elucidate this point. The night Ilse is taken from Hayes for the "VD check" he becomes enraged: "In bed that night I killed the MP's many times. I smeared paint over their faces and pushed my fingers into their eyes. I killed them slowly, pushing their eyes out and then beating them and pouring gasoline over them and lighting the gasoline and then hanging the charred bodies to trees as had been done to many Negroes in the South. I had the desire, very strong to do the same to them. Because I knew why they had taken Ilse. And it was not because they thought she had venereal disease" (172). He imagines lynching white men over the white female body—which, in itself, gives the strange impression that disrespecting the white female body indeed demands a hanging—but when a military "lynching" of black men occurs, our hero does nothing. In one of the most compelling parts of the novel, Smith depicts the results of the Gillem Plan, a controversial army initiative that sought to reduce the number of black soldiers deemed "undesirable" and "ineffective" in a now-notorious effort to shrink its peacetime personnel and to keep black soldiers at a maximum quota corresponding to their percentage of the general population.[107] As a result, blacks were discharged for any and all reasons, including a "blue" discharge for venereal disease. As Hayes's friend Steve observes: "Ain't many white soldiers getting the discharges. But the commanders of nigger outfits is having a ball. Discharging everybody" (183). Rather than refusing to participate—though Steve does resist—Hayes types the discharges until he has helped write out "seven hundred and sixty four of them" (184). Smith biographer Leroy Hodges calls Hayes's participation a "character flaw,"[108] and indeed the depiction of his complicity is curious when measured against the rage Smith has the character display when Ilse is snatched away from him. More telling than what Hayes thinks in the latter situation, however, is what he does: he goes directly to his commander and demands action.

This should not be surprising. This is how the white female body ultimately functions in all of the novels in this chapter, bringing the black man into direct confrontation with the system that oppresses him. The body becomes a site where black men seek either recognition (to be seen by the white man), reckoning (to go to battle with the white man), or reconciliation (to find fraternity). *Black Skin, White Masks*, Frantz Fanon's brilliant meditation on the effects of colonialism on the Antillean subject, uses Hegel's philosophy of acknowledgement and recognition within the master-slave dialect to argue that a "consciousness of self" is achieved first through the desire to be recognized by the other.[109] To desire moves one from the status of object to subject; to desire recognition is asking "to be considered."[110] Fanon also argues that this recognition can only be brought about forcibly, imposed on the settler violently: "a conflict, a riot."[111] He turns to African Americans as an example of a group of blacks who wage war upon their oppressors relentlessly, forcing recognition, bringing about changes in law and status. Imagining a black male subject, he frames black resistance in terms of regaining a denied masculinity: "On the field of battle, its four corners marked by the scores of Negroes hanged by their testicles, a monument is slowly being built that promises to be majestic. And, at the top of this monument, I can already see a white man and a black man hand in hand."[112]

Fanon's dream of fraternal egalitarianism ends with a beautiful homosocial moment: black men and white men "hand in hand," black men holding the same hand that had "hanged" them "by their testicles"—very much like Montie in death embracing the man who had him court-martialed for interracial sexual contact. Within Daly's, Himes's, and Smith's works, the quest for manhood—the process of recognition, reckoning, or reconciliation (the desire, the battle, the final moment of fraternity)—is enacted through a displaced desire for the white female body, substituting for the white male's. Accordingly, the internal sexual/racial war through which that manhood will be lost or found takes on a greater significance than the external war waged by the nation because fighting *with* the white man in his wars has not brought about the swift, permanent acknowledgement of manhood participation in war has promised; he must, therefore, fight *against* him. The subtitle of Daly's novel, *A Story of Two Great Conflicts*, underscores the importance of this second, internal war.

As a result of this emphasis, these novels have much less to say about the ways in which nations have come to relate to one another during periods of conflict. In Smith's novel, Hitler's racism is problematized; his violent expansionism is not. The hypocrisy of American "democracy" is questioned; the bombing of civilians in Germany is not. The narrative of innocence, the familiar chorus ("we are not guilty of a sexual crime"), and the accompanying depiction of the many forms of physical and psychic violence leveled against black men by white authority becomes yet another way African American writers end up skirting around the issue of war, resisting a head-on analysis of the United States' use of violence as a means of solving problems on a national or international level.

In that way, the narrative of innocence results in a black male ethos that approximates U.S. claims to innocence in its own historical narratives of war. The Spanish-Cuban-American War, World War I, World War II, Vietnam, the "freeing" of Kuwait and Iraq: the stories are both similar and familiar. Drawn into conflicts against its will, the United States is, as Edward Said writes, "a righter of wrongs around the world, in pursuit of tyranny, in defense of freedom no matter the place or cost . . . overseas American interests have insisted upon American innocence."[113] In the next chapter, I will argue that Jamaican-born writer Claude McKay's assessment of World War I will insist upon American guilt.

6 DIASPORA AND DISSENT

World War I,
Claude McKay,
and *Home to Harlem*

Any effort to understand what distinguishes Claude McKay's first published novel, *Home to Harlem* (1928),[1] from the World War I fiction produced by the black American writers explored in the previous chapter might begin, not in Harlem, but by mapping the ideological and geographical route that brought McKay to the Soviet Union in 1922. Before immigrating to the United States in 1912, the Jamaican-born poet and novelist had already developed a sustained interest in socialist ideology. As McKay critic and biographer Wayne F. Cooper has noted, the writer had dedicated an early book of poetry published in Jamaica to Sir Sydney Oliver, who was the country's governor at that time and also a Fabian socialist.[2] This interest only deepened after McKay left his original destination, Tuskegee, for New York, where he was energized by the daring political commentary of radical publications such as the *Masses*. Later reborn as the *Liberator*, the magazine first published McKay's acclaimed antilynching poem, "If We Must Die," in 1919. Its appearance led to his celebrated friendship with the *Liberator*'s editor, Max Eastman, and to an immersion in the world of the New York left. Merely months after the publication of "If We Must Die," however, McKay unexpectedly accepted an invitation that afforded him the occasion to visit England. After a brief stint in London writing for the communist weekly the *Worker's Dreadnought* in 1920, he returned to the United States in 1921, eventually securing work on the *Liberator*'s staff and rising to the position of coeditor.[3] He used the *Liberator*'s office in 1921 to hold meetings for the African Blood Brotherhood for African Liberation and Redemption, a small, underground Black Nationalist organization founded in 1919 by the West Indian radical Cyril Briggs, who also edited the group's official publication, the *Crusader*.[4] Formed independently of the Communist Party, the Brotherhood was nevertheless deeply sympathetic to the party's aims, attracting numerous influential black radicals, including Hubert

H. Harrison, Otto Huiswood, and Grace Campbell. While it is unclear how deeply involved McKay was with the Brotherhood, he was among its charter members, and his affiliation certainly offers evidence that McKay's skepticism of the white American left's commitment to African Americans had begun to intensify.

In fact, in another characteristically abrupt move, McKay unceremoniously resigned from the *Liberator* in 1922, later admitting he had become disenchanted with white American radicals' reluctance to deal frankly with the particular racial problems facing blacks in the United States. Quitting the *Liberator* once again freed McKay to leave New York City, this time, to travel to Moscow. In *A Long Way Home*, his 1937 memoirs of life abroad, McKay writes that he had finally surrendered to a "dominant urge" to visit Russia, but without resources he was forced to rely almost wholly on friends and political acquaintances for financial assistance.[5] McKay arrived in time to attend the Fourth Congress of the Third International, which had convened in part to assess realistically the prospect of a united, international revolutionary movement and to rectify prior Internationals' nearly exclusive focus on radicalizing white European workers.

Although McKay alleges in his memoirs that the American delegation "resented" his unofficial status, by all accounts, including his own, he was warmly embraced by the Russians and the other participants, who, McKay believed, took his ideas on racial matters and standing as a poet more seriously than anyone in the United States, black or white, had previously. The writer's acceptance in fact sufficiently emboldened him to formally address a special session dedicated to the discussion of the "Negro Question."[6] In 1923, the *International Press Correspondence* published the speech McKay delivered before the congress, ensuring that his remarks would reach a wider audience than those present at the International's proceedings. Undoubtedly influenced by the Comintern's speculation that the recently ended "Great War" had signaled the beginning of the end of capitalist empire, McKay used this opportunity to raise an issue he would return to throughout his career—the involvement of African Americans in U.S. warfare. In accord with Lenin's reading of imperialist conflict as the "armed struggle between the 'great' powers for the artificial preservation of capital,"[7] McKay argues that the United States has had a long history of coercing black Americans into undermining their own economic interests. It was able to do so, he claims, by trading on African Americans' faith in military service as an avenue to civic recognition: "The Northern bourgeoisie knows how well the Negro soldiers fought for their own emancipation, although illiterate and untrained, during the Civil War. They also remember how well the Negro soldiers fought in the Spanish American war under Theodore Roosevelt. They know that in the last war over

400,000 Negroes who were mobilised gave a very good account of themselves . . . fighting for the capitalists."[8]

As much as the Third International and Leninism might have shaped McKay's interpretation of World War I, it is essential to note that the African Blood Brotherhood's original call for membership elicited inquiries from a "disproportionate number of black veterans from the First World War" who,[9] it seems, envisioned "African liberation and redemption" as a way to liberate and redeem themselves from white imperialist warfare and its ideological imperatives. It seems unlikely that the flood of letters from black veterans would have gone unnoticed, and it possibly buoyed the Brotherhood's sense that black autonomy was an appropriate response to the exploitation of blacks under empire, be it in the realm of labor or of war. The Comintern's resolutions concerning blacks, the "Theses on the Negro Question," was drafted in part by members of the Brotherhood—McKay among them—who also traveled to the congress separately from the American delegates.[10] Much of the document's content bears the unmistakable imprint of Black Nationalism:

> i) The Fourth Congress considers it essential to support *all forms of the Negro movement* which aim to either undermine or weaken capitalism and or to prevent their further expansion.
> ii) The Communist International will do all it can to force the trade unions to admit Negro workers. . . . If this proves unsuccessful, it will organize Negroes into their own unions. . . .
> iv) The Communist International will immediately take steps to convene an international Negro conference or congress.[11]

As Winston James claims in his study of U.S. Caribbean radicalism during the first decades of the twentieth century, Lenin was receptive to the idea of allowing "self-determining" political strategies that might emerge from independent nations as a transitional phase before absorption into a global, international socialist structure.[12] Nevertheless, the inclusion within the resolutions of a recourse to separatism and the call to support independent, *black* agitation, whether communist or not, appears at odds with the International's ultimate goal of creating raceless revolutionary tactics. The point I wish to make here is that while McKay's association with the Brotherhood was brief, and his relationship to Black Nationalism probably no more than a flirtation, his attraction to that organization indicates that his primary allegiance may not have been to Communism but to black liberation—however that liberation proved feasible. McKay's interpretation of imperialism in his Comintern address does not simply offer blacks as an example illustrating imperialism's sphere of destruction; quite to the contrary, he cautions against their being wielded as a "symbol" by the Party. Neither does McKay explicitly finger imperialism as the root cause of antiblack subjugation. It appears that for McKay, European and American imperialism and warfare merely have allowed already-existing racist practices to be exercised in their most deceptive, deadly, and widespread form. Thus, McKay seems to view Communism, like the Black Nationalism he would later relinquish, in utilitarian terms, as the best solution to black oppression and annihilation the West had yet offered. As such, he pledged himself—at least temporarily—to propagandizing its message through his fictional works and essays. The main reason McKay repeatedly revisits "the Great War" in his writings, particularly in *Home to Harlem*, might therefore lie outside of an inherent desire to promote socialist philosophy. Rather, the scope and scale of the war's destruction may have offered McKay a site to meditate on the specific racial injuries it inflicted; injuries experienced by blacks from nearly every point across from the diaspora.

McKay's decision to explore World War I's fallout in expressly racial terms would prompt him to write his first-known fiction about its consequences, "The Soldier's Return," produced sometime between 1922 and 1923 during his stay in the Soviet Union. The story appeared as part of a larger collection of short fiction, *Sudom Lincha* (*Trial by Lynching*), translated from English into Russian and issued by a Moscow publishing house in 1925.[13] Perhaps because McKay was not fully under Marxism's sway, or because he understood he was "preaching to the converted," McKay forgoes exposing the imperialist aims of World War I in "The Soldier's Return." Yet, it is more probable that the claim he makes in his memoirs—that the well-meaning but often uniformed Russians needed to be educated about the deeply pathological nature of racism in the United States—led McKay instead to create a work illustrating white American supremacists' use of antiblack violence to "manage" African American soldiers in the postwar nation.

Very much, then, like Daly's *Not Only War* and White's *The Fire in the Flint*, "The Soldier's Return" also centers on white men's use of white women's bodies as weapons in the domestic war raging against black men in the United States. Even more like White's narrative, the story focuses on a demobilized black American veteran who returns to his southern hometown only to be wrongly accused of rape. White's protagonist, recall, is killed at the hands of a mob; McKay's is threatened with lynching. Too, as I mentioned in the previous chapter, both writers published their works in the years following the Red Summer of 1919 and register the outrage generated by several postwar lynchings that claimed former soldiers as victims, their murders understood as a backlash against black veterans' demands that white Americans treat them with the full respect they felt they had earned and offer them the full citizenship rights they felt due. The mayor in McKay's story will inform the black soldier that his very uniform is a both an affront to white men and a masquerade of masculinity: "we don't like it when niggers wear soldier's uniforms . . . won't put up with even one of them . . . putting on airs" (40–41).

Home to Harlem, a novel detailing the experiences of Jake, a black veteran who deserts the American military after becoming disillusioned with the institution's entrenched racism, may seem thematically quite similar to Not Only War and The Fire in the Flint. However, McKay's novel represents an important deviation from the critique of the white, anti-integrationist tactics so crucial to those novels' political projects. Even more significantly, McKay eschews the critique of those measures he issues in his own earlier story. I will suggest that this shift, a move away from detailing the impact of white supremacy on black existence, emerges from McKay's growing sense that an excessive focus on the white world's acceptance or rejection of blacks was primarily a "bourgeois" concern. From McKay's point of view, this obsession not only interfered with a necessary analysis of capitalism but also diverted political energy from the urgent problems of the black working class, proving ruinous to the prospects of an authentic racial solidarity across class lines. This is not to say McKay rejected integrationist goals in their entirety. In "For Group Survival," an article appearing in the Jewish Frontier in 1937, he makes his position on the matter clear: "all sane Negroes want integration."[14] In that same article, however, he rails against African Americans who simply wish to become part of "the present set-up of capitalist society" without analyzing "the economic issue," "neglect[ing] their own group" while hopelessly pleading for white acknowledgement.[15] A consideration of McKay's position on integration suggests that Home should be read as more than a condemnation of white structural racism or even an indictment of what Marxist Antonio Gramsci characterized as the most coercive apparatus in a capitalist state—the military—but as a novel that uses a black man's voluntary service to underscore African Americans' willful participation in their own debasement. The far-reaching consequences of sustaining the imperial machine are equally troubling for McKay, who argued that those blacks who support U.S. military endeavors unavoidably bring about the degradation of all people of color impacted by the spread of American empire. This stance was not entirely unique among black intellectuals; nevertheless, as I have shown, the bulk of the imaginative literature produced about the war tended to restrict itself to the circumstances and outcome of African American service: exposing the injustices of a segregated armed forces and the failure of military participation in effecting the wholesale and permanent changes necessary for black advancement. This chapter will conclude that McKay uses *Home to Harlem* to disseminate a more radical reading of blacks' relationship to "the Great War"; one meant to complicate the myopic nationalist perspective that, in McKay's mind, prevented African Americans from viewing the war in a more expansive political context.

As my introduction to this chapter indicates, interpreting *Home to Harlem* as a revision of black integrationist politics and a departure from black American fiction about the First World War requires making a counterintuitive gesture—dislocating McKay from Harlem and the Harlem "Renaissance," the geographical and literary milieu that has until very recently framed most critical analyses of McKay's novel.[16] McKay did live in the United States for the duration of World War I, working, like his protagonist, on a railroad, where he gathered the experiences that would serve as the basis of his novel. However, it was during the postwar years spent in France that McKay conceived of, began, and completed *Home to Harlem*, based on a short story of the same name, quite likely a revised version of "The Soldier's Return." Having failed in his previous attempts to get longer works of fiction published, McKay was convinced by his American literary agent that the short story could be expanded into a successful novel about Harlem life.[17] That is precisely how the novel has been characterized since its publication: as a quintessentially Harlem novel, produced by a black New Yorker at the end of the Renaissance. Certainly, as many critics have claimed, the novel's appearance during the "Harlem Vogue" contributed to its great financial success. Yet, when writing about the work in *A Long Way from Home*, McKay makes a comment regarding its creation that I see as critical to supporting recent interpretations of the novel as a transnational, rather than national, text: "I had done my best Harlem stuff when I was abroad," he writes, "seeing it from a long perspective."[18] I would like to suggest that the visual and spatial metaphor that McKay chooses to characterize his relationship to his Harlem literature—his "long perspective"—encompasses more than geographical distance. McKay's status as a Jamaican British subject, his encounters with non-American blacks living outside of the states, and his interest in both Marxist internationalism (however expedient) and Black Nationalist thought (however tentative) all cooperated in instituting the gulf he felt separated him from many of his African American literary and intellectual counterparts. Just as significantly, the reflexive comparisons often drawn between *Home to Harlem* and other prominent works of this period, most typically Carl Van Vechten's novel *Nigger Heaven* (1925), further circumscribe the text, making the war content in the novel secondary to McKay's rendering of the novel's Harlem setting. Such readings miss the influence of important World War I fiction writers on *Home to Harlem*: in particular, the French naturalist novelist Henri Barbusse, to whom McKay refers in the narrative, and

Ernest Hemingway, whose oeuvre McKay had consumed before completing his novel. Thus, similar to Jake's observation that the boundaries of Harlem have expanded in his absence—and appear to grow with every passing moment—I will explore the numerous and complex ways McKay's "long perspective" on World War I moves the novel beyond the limits of "Harlem proper."

Of course, stretching the novel's interpretative limits is not to dismiss Harlem as irrelevant to McKay's project. To the contrary, the varied elements comprising McKay's "long perspective" are articulated through his imaginings of that location. Nonetheless, a transnational reading of the novel will interpret Harlem as representative of other Western geographical spaces where blacks have been "lumped together" under white nationalist or imperialist reign.[19] Drawing energy from Paul Gilroy's observation that "neither political nor economic structures of domination" are "co-extensive with national borders,"[20] my discussion of *Harlem* will therefore situate the work within McKay's other writings about the war to argue that the novel draws conscious parallels between Harlem and Africa and between Harlem and the West Indies, two locations often submerged in Western histories of the events. More specifically, I will read this spatial, political, and racial correspondence as part of McKay's effort to bring the vast (and black) geography of the war "home to Harlem," suggesting that *Home* alludes to the manner in which World War I complicated the ethnic and racial affiliation of those blacks serving in white imperial and national militaries. In his controversial 1923 essay, "Soviet Russia and the Negro," published in the *Crisis* as part of McKay's self-proclaimed mission to spread propaganda among blacks, he warns the audience that joining these militaries merely facilitates the dominant's strategy of division and conquest. The "conscript slave-soldiers of Imperial France," he argues, ". . . can in no wise help the movement of Negroes" globally.[21] As Tyrone Tillery explains in his study of McKay, the writer had issued a similar analysis three years earlier in the *Dreadnought*. Responding to a German officer's praise of black soldiers who fought under his command in East Africa, McKay characterizes their service as a capitalist ruse: "England also used her black troops, and the whole nasty business shows to what depths Capitalism will descend to maintain its supremacy. Ignorant black men were pitted against their brother in a cause that was alien to them. . . . The exploiting classes world wide would set black against black."[22] Examining *Harlem* as a rearticulation of these concerns, I will theorize that the images McKay offers of a Harlem ravaged by physical and psychic violence among blacks—"yellow against black and brown" (34)—purposefully evoke the violence and disunity within and among black populations both engendered and exacerbated by World War I. McKay's assessment of the war's impact on blacks is nevertheless a complicated one. While McKay did believe that World War I and colonialism had divided blacks on many fronts, his writings also reveal that he saw postwar black immigration and migration as having an unintentional effect: the creation of black transnational contact zones, places such as McKay's beloved Marseille—and of course, Harlem—where blacks from the diaspora could interact and exchange ideas, the creation of sites where they could develop what McKay refers to in his writings as a "group soul."[23] Toward the end of the war, McKay remarked that World War I had proved "the real hollowness of nationhood [and] patriotism."[24] This rupture in white, Western ideas of nation allowed McKay to conceptualize a black identity emerging from beyond the realm of empire: a black subjectivity brought into being outside of the reach of colonial powers and outside of the boundaries of "big nations" (154). Yet, in the end, this very rupture—and the devastation left by its making— would leave McKay wondering where, if anywhere, that "beyond" might be.

White Folks' Business

In Daly's *Not Only War*, a friend of the soldier-protagonist summarizes the feelings of many American blacks who denounced the war: "It's a white man's war. He started it. Let him finish it" (20).[25] In some ways this assessment is quite accurate—it remains true that World War I was fought primarily for the interests of those "big nations"—yet nearly all countries used black troops and manpower to achieve their military aims, including Germany, France, Great Britain, the United States, and Portugal. These black troops came from the Caribbean, the United States, and, of course, Africa, the site of the longest campaign between the Allieds and the Germans in the entire course of the war. Africa, however, was not the only black geographical area outside of the European theater that became a site of contestation between the Allieds and the Germans. In a little-publicized incident of the war, the United States invaded and occupied Haiti in 1915 to defend against an alleged threat by the Kaiser. American forces remained there five years instituting a period of violent military rule.[26]

Some of the leading black Western intellectuals, including Du Bois and James Weldon Johnson, commented on the significance of an international war that had unexpectedly affected such a large number of blacks and black nations.[27] At the 1919 peace conference in France leading to the Treaty of Versailles, Woodrow Wilson made his famous self-evident proclamation: "New nations are to be formed. Old nations are to be recreated."[28] What McKay quickly learned while living in Europe in the years following the war was that the project of European nation building unleashed a torrent of racist attitudes directed toward colonials, many of whom were demobilized soldiers, and others who had migrated to

Europe to fill labor vacuums during the war. In the 1939 piece McKay published in *Opportunity*, mentioned in the previous chapter, he would link the descent of Western empire to the rise of internal racism: "The Great War had shot Europe to pieces, increasing and nourishing all the petty national and racial hatreds."[29]

The *Opportunity* article, "Once More the Germans to Face Black Troops," seeks to root Hitler's ability to carry out his "mad onslaught against the Jews" in the racist campaign against the French black colonial servicemen stationed in the Rhineland after the First World War. This strategy, as McKay explains, depended on generating fears of "hybridization" between black soldiers and German women, eventually taking the form of a "crusade" against the allegedly rapacious Africans whose wanton sexual violence both threatened the nation's racial purity and raised the specter of "*Neger-regierung* (Negro-rule)."[30] McKay theorizes that the belief in "Nordic superiority" emerging from the campaign allowed Hitler to capitalize on the distrust of the ethnic "other" that lingered well after the hysteria over black troops had ended. McKay was made aware of the "Black Horror" when British labor propagandists wielded the German accusations for altogether different purposes. His time in London coincided with the French occupation, which had been sanctioned by the Treaty of Versailles as a necessary step in securing the reparations the Germans owed the French government. When the French were permitted to advance further into a more heavily industrial territory, the Ruhr, the international Left condemned the move as an antilabor imperialist maneuver designed to wrest the region's resources from the hands of the German working class. McKay suggests in his memoirs that an "almost congenital" English prejudice against black colonials found its raison d'être in this event, resulting in a series of sensational newspaper reports that repeated German claims of the sexual atrocities committed by French Africans. McKay castigates the British labor movement for running the articles, labeling one of the sources of the rumors a "prurient-minded white man."[31] He assesses the situation in these terms: in the fight over "which white gang should control the coal and iron of the Ruhr"[32]—the French or the Germans—British sympathy lay with the Germans, whose Socialist-Democratic government was prolabor. During a dispute over some industrial plants, the French sent in troops. Gathering support for the German government was a difficult task, McKay explains, so the issues became couched in racial terms; "African" forces, it was rumored, "had acted to dislodge German workers" from one of the plants in dispute.[33] According to McKay, the British press chose to focus on "the erotic implications of the occupation," running headlines such as "Appeal to the Women of Europe" and "Sexual Horrors Let Loose by France,"[34] a tactic made possible by the antiblack propaganda circulating in Germany. In this environment, racial relations in

Britain quite predictably deteriorated. For England especially, competition for jobs after the war had already created tensions between native whites and blacks, erupting in the summer of 1919 (the same year as the Red Summer in the United States) in a series of riots across England, primarily in major industrial cities such as Liverpool and Manchester. McKay contends that labor used this coverage to help the British justify and encourage racial attitudes that would render blacks unemployable. Placed within the interpretation of Foucault's paradigm I offered in the chapter prior, this purposeful economic disenfranchisement and the threat of violence would act in concert to create internal warfare; if colonials were not "eliminated" in riots, they would be pushed to the national periphery or outside of its boundaries altogether.

In an episode in the first chapter of Home to Harlem, McKay puts his hero, Jake, who has deserted the American military, in the East End of London during that explosive summer, working on the West India docks, where he witnesses "a big battle staged between the colored and white men" (7). Wearied by the violence, Jake makes his decision to return the United States. Nine pages into the novel, those three events that will determine the course of the narrative occur. He deserts the military, rejecting what he calls "a white folks' war," abandons his British girlfriend, calling her a "creature of another race—of another world," and leaves Europe behind (8). While McKay gives Jake's relationship with his white lover only a few lines in the narrative, her abbreviated appearance is in exact proportion to the political importance McKay feels the white female body and what that body symbolizes should be granted in the world outside of the novel's pages. Throughout his memoirs, McKay expresses a certain exhaustion as he repeats instance after instance in which white women are used by blacks and whites alike as tools in political, national, and racial struggle. Detailing his experiences in Marseille toward the end of his work, he describes an exchange involving a Senegalese veteran who claimed "it was an international gesture for him to be married to a white woman, especially since white chauvinists objected to intermarriage."[35] The "strange conversation," McKay writes, leaves him "lost."[36] By allowing Jake a decidedly carnal affair, however short, with a white woman in Home to Harlem, it seems that McKay is playing with his readers' expectations, raising the possibility that he will activate the highly charged set of meanings interracial sex between black men and white women has accrued. Having Jake rather indifferently terminate a relationship that has inspired little more than his desire to go home is McKay's blunt refusal to do so, a signal that he is unwilling to articulate racial matters in the cultural and social vocabulary made available to him.

Later in the novel, Jake will reflect on the "interracial sex skirmishes" between black and white men across Europe, calling them "blunderers" in "pools of blood" who "didn't know what they were fighting for, except it was to gratify some vague feeling about women." (70). Like Jake, who compares himself to "a man charged up with dope every day" for believing he could live in Europe instead of Harlem (9), the "vague feeling" for which these black men risked being "hurt, wounded, killed" (70) is the psychoemotional manifestation of an unnamed and unrecognized internalization of white valuation. I imagine, then, that McKay originally viewed the substance of his earlier story—a decorated black soldier falsely accused of rape by an undesirable, "half-witted" white woman—as a smart reversal of the dominant culture's narratives of interracial sexual contact. I also imagine that he later reconsidered his effort as an equally blundering foray into an equally useless fight. Thus, while Daly's and White's novels might reach a similar conclusion, Home to Harlem will not deploy the white female body in its usual capacity: as the corporeal representation of restrictive white spaces, of the alluring promises of the white world, of things worth killing and dying for, of black protest and black innocence, or of the power white men hold over black in a world where the mere claim of sexual violation held disastrous consequences. Neither then will the military, as a "white space," serve as a site where a black man attempts to struggle his way into American society. Jake's (and McKay's) disengagements clear the way for a protagonist who will traverse the limits of a Western ideological terrain and begin to "find" himself within a broadened racial and political geography.

Quite immediately in the novel, McKay exposes as misguided the fantasy that prompted Jake, and many black men like him, to enlist in the army—the opportunity to prove their manhood by braving the nation's "enemy" in battle. Most black military enlistees, like Jake and his Harlem buddy Zeddy, were assigned to labor battalions, unloading and loading ships and working as stevedores.[37] The work conditions in Brest, where Jake is stationed, were brutal. These black men often worked sixteen-hour shifts in mud and rain. During a single day, they collectively unloaded 5,000 tons of cargo. They slept on dirt-floor tents or on the ships' decks to escape the suffocating sleeping quarters below; they were denied passes allowing them to leave camp; they were improperly outfitted and therefore dangerously exposed to accidents and the elements.[38] Prowar African Americans, once again hoping that black participation in the war would rehabilitate the dominant culture's notions of a degraded, backward black masculinity, scrambled to recuperate the back-breaking labor as both important and empowering. In 1919, Booker T. Washington's former secretary, Emmett Scott, published a history of the war that included a report describing the crucial nature of the work and the "cheerfulness" of the troops, following the assessment with a poem celebrating the stevedores as "lusty and virile and strong."[39] But *Home to Harlem* resists this revision, ending with Jake's defense of his decision to liberate himself from the oppressive circumstances: "I didn't run away because I was scared a them Germans. But I beat it away from Brest because they wouldn't give us a chance at them. . . . They didn't seem to want us niggers foh no soldiers. We was jest a bunch a despised hod carriers, and Zeddy know that" (331).

Jake's determination to go AWOL in the first chapter of the novel marks the onset of an awakening but not solidified racial consciousness. He will question why he became involved in the war, asserting that blacks are "always thinking they got something to do with white folks' business" (8). The term "business" as implemented here is polyvalent, denoting the interdependent operations of war, white hegemony, capital, and the state. McKay intends that Jake's original patriotic sentiment, articulated as a desire to destroy the Germans, be read as a mystifying, received nationalist ideology that confuses his ability to discern the "enemy" in his American incarnation. As McKay quite accurately points out in the *Opportunity* article, the intensity of American bigotry may have given the Nazi regime apt reason to believe the United States would share in Germany's "gospel of racial superiority."[40] During World War I—before the French occupation—the Germans felt so certain that blacks had been demoralized by American racism that they dropped leaflets among black units inviting them to desert the American army, asking blacks why they would fight for the United States, a country that would not allow them basic human freedoms and where they were subject to cruelties such as lynching. Jake's girlfriend will raise similar questions: "What right have niggers got to shoot down a whole lot of Germans for? Is they worse than Americans or any other nation of white people" (331–32)?

Jake's willingness to align with one racist imperialist nation to fight another is also reminiscent of the "unreformed" consciousness of colonized subjects. That is, Jake's position evokes the reasoning used by many African leaders to justify defending the Allied empires against the Germans. The rationale was simple: the colonists they knew were preferable to the colonists they did not. Therefore, a people such as the Congolese, as Du Bois wrote early in the war, were fighting against the Germans "to protect the wives and daughters of the white Belgians, who have murdered and robbed his people."[41]

McKay was fascinated by the peculiar position of black colonials in European armies. During his stay in London, the writer frequented the Drury Lane Club, where he met "a host of colored soldiers . . . from the West Indies and Africa, with a few colored Americans, East Indians and Egyptians among them."[42] He published articles on these soldiers in the *Negro World* sometime between 1919 and 1922, although none has yet been recovered. In his later *Opportunity* article, he notes with some irony that during the Victorian Era, black West Indians who conscripted into the British Army under the Queen were used to conquer black West Africans. Similarly, World War I pitted Africans against Africans and blacks against blacks, dividing those mobilized for the Allied forces from those enlisted to support the Kaiser. Like many African Americans in the United States, many Africans and West Indians actively resisted service, citing their unwillingness to support nations that kept them subjugated. Others desired conscription, hoping that aligning with colonizers might raise their status. In "Once More the Germans to Face Black Troops," McKay challenges the latter belief, implying that Africans fighting for the empire were mainly viewed as colorful exotics.[43] Referring to Le Feu, the celebrated 1916 World War I novel written by French pacifist Henri Barbusse, he quotes a passage in which a white French soldier labels black African soldiers as somehow "other." Barbusse was an outspoken critic of French officials, who, he claimed, made "use of black cannon fodder."[44] McKay's original mention of Le Feu in Home to Harlem—when Ray, the Haitian intellectual Jake will befriend on the railroad, praises the novel as an "anti-romantic" treatment of war (227)—creates an intertextual moment in the work that lends outside support for McKay's own beliefs.

As I have mentioned, McKay viewed the placing of blacks in armed conflict with blacks as one the most damaging aspects of the war. But in addition to the fact that blacks were forced to fight each other by way of their willful or coerced allegiances to Germany or the Allies, the war fueled other forms of racial animosity. West Indian conscription into imperial armies, for instance, only intensified racial hierarchies already present in that region. Mixed-raced "coloureds" in Trinidad and Barbados particularly did not want to serve in the same capacity as blacks, and often blacks resented the fact that some light-skinned men were allowed to serve with whites. After the war, the imperial forces drew national boundaries in Africa that forced tribes who were historically hostile to one another to coexist in one new nation, sparking new conflicts or renewing old ones.[45]

While World War I quite obviously affected black subjects within the old colonial empires, Haiti, the first black republic in the Western hemisphere, felt the impact of a newer empire testing the range of its powers. Although the United States claimed only to want to position itself strategically in the West Indies lest the Germans use the Panama Canal for military gain, the American government allowed the marine corps to seize the island, beginning a reign of terror in which by some estimates 3,000 Haitians were murdered.[46] Moreover, like the European imperialists who created internal conflict in Africa by unmaking indigenous structures of authority and encouraging strife among ethnic groups, Americans in Haiti fomented intraracial dissension among Haitians by demonstrating favoritism toward mulatto leadership.[47]

The African American critics who denounced *Home to Harlem* when it first appeared frequently cited the violence permeating the novel as especially objectionable, distressed that McKay was perpetuating the most pernicious stereotypes about blacks simply for popular consumption and profit. Read differently, within McKay's "long perspective," the violence hardly appears as gratuitous but as central to the novel's examination of the war's effects on black nations and communities. Everywhere in Harlem, Jake notices turmoil and is repulsed by it: "Niggers fixing to slice one another's throats. Always fighting" (287), even characterizing a skirmish between black men as "war" at one point in the narrative (165). Yet he also slaps a lover who expects to be abused as a normal, natural part of lovemaking before ultimately recoiling from her demands. Jake's conflicted and contradictory response to the self-defeating violence surrounding him offers evidence that McKay is doing more than adding sensational scenes to his work to gratify his potential readership. Rather, placing Jake within a black war zone gives McKay the opportunity to replicate and interrogate simultaneously the intraracial violence that Fanon argues emanates from the "native's" contact with white imperialist cultures. The key to this interpretation lies in a pivotal moment occurring at the end in the novel. In this episode, Jake allows himself to engage into a fight with his buddy Zeddy over Jake's girlfriend Felice, threatening Zeddy's life with a gun. Sickened and ashamed by his behavior, Jake admonishes himself for acting like the white men he met during the war and postwar years in Brest and London: "Oh, he was infinitely disgusted with himself to think that he had just been moved by the same savage emotions as those vicious, vile, villainous white men who, like hyenas and rattlers, had fought, murdered and clawed the entrails out of black men over the common, commercial flesh of women" (328). Fanon would analyze this scene as descriptive of the recognizable symptoms betraying the profound effect of colonial violence on the colonized's psyche. In *The Wretched of the Earth*, the groundbreaking anticolonial manifesto published after *Black Skins*, Fanon characterizes the "autodestruct[ive]" impulses of "native" populations as a stage preceding externally directed, revolutionary violence. "The colonized man," he writes, "hemmed in" by "apartheid," "will first manifest the aggressiveness which has been deposited in his bones against his own people. This is the period where the niggers beat each other up."[48] While Jake is not "technically" a colonized subject, throughout the novel, McKay has endeavored to graft colonized black geographies onto Harlem, situating the protagonist within a milieu evocative of the repressive environments arising from white imperialist rule. As Jake leaves Europe at the onset of the narrative, he imagines Harlem as a space of pure blackness that he will claim as his own: "Harlem for mine" (9)! The place he returns to, however, is anything but a space of uncontaminated blackness, and anything but his. McKay shows Harlem as a place victimized by "foreign exploitation" (29). The spots Jake frequents, places whose names are reminiscent of Africa—Congo, Sheba Palace, Queen of the Nile—are often operated by whites who wish to make money off of black customers and are frequented by whites seeking the "primitive" experience of black jazz venues and cabarets. Black Harlemites are also made to feel the more intrusive nature of state power. The party crowd lives in dread of police sent to Harlem to raid their clubs; "draft-dodging" black men live in fear of military agents sent uptown to smoke them out. A friend of Jake's comments on the toxic atmosphere resulting from this physically and psychically "hemmed in" existence: "Wese too thick together in Harlem. Wese all just lumped together without a chanst to choose and so we nacherally hate one other" (285).

Part of the thickness of Harlem was due, of course, to the Great Migration to the North, a mass movement instigated in part by African Americans' desire to escape the violence and oppression of the South. Many who migrated to New York during the war years hoped to fill the industrial labor vacuum created by the loss of white male workers to the military. However, a great number arrived only to face unemployment, and segregation made it difficult to live anywhere in Manhattan other Harlem. But as much as McKay understood the deleterious effects of blacks' being "lumped together," he also saw promise in its circumstance. Part of McKay's purpose in bringing together Jake and Ray, two black men from separate nations, within Harlem—a black transnational contact zone— was to show the potential diasporic interchange had to give rise to a "new group orientation."[49] Before the two men recognize that their blackness should foster a mutuality of feeling, Jake expresses his Yankee antipathy for blacks from outside of the United States: "as an American Negro, he looked askew at foreign niggers. Africa was jungle, and Africans, bush niggers, cannibals. And West Indians were monkey-chasers" (134). Similarly, Ray acknowledges his distaste for Yankee "coons," questioning why he should "have and love a race" (155, 153). Jake dislikes foreign blacks because *he* is a Yankee; Ray dislikes American blacks because *they* are. In McKay's vision, a new consciousness would unmake such artificial divisions erected by national, class, and cultural affiliations. These promising spaces, "the map of the world in colors" as Jake muses (134), stand therefore in direct opposition to the "national" space opening the novel—"the freighter . . . [that] stank between sea and sky"—depicted as a physically, psychically, and racially confining site, where Jake mimics the anti-Arab sentiments he has adopted from the white American sailors (1–2).

Though McKay's version of an international racial solidarity might seem a historically recognizable, and perhaps derivative, notion of black collectivity, it resists neat classification within the many ideologies grouped under "Black Nationalism." While World War II had indeed led McKay to denounce the tribalism and exclusivity of white ideals of nationhood, ultimately, he also rejected traditional conceptualizations of pan-Africanism, which possibly accounts for his fleeting association with the African Blood Brotherhood (the exact circumstances of his departure are unclear). McKay targeted Marcus Garvey in particular, dismissing his "back to Africa" movement as colonialism at worst, and at best, as a retrogressive racial naiveté. Africa, McKay believed, had been too irrevocably altered by contact with the West to be a place where one could discover racially unadulterated blacks. Instead, he preferred his own idiosyncratic utopian vision, shaped in great measure by Lenin's emphasis on interracial solidarity and by McKay's tendency to mythologize the migratory existence he led for most of his life. As McKay imagines them, these black contact zones, although products of the black dispersal caused by Western imperialism, can be reconfigured as empowering spaces where transcendent notions of a black identity strong enough to withstand the racial and economic challenges of the twentieth century have an opportunity to emerge. When Jake asks Ray why he is in the United States working "on a white man's chu-chu," he attributes his displacement to the American military occupation of Haiti: "Uncle Sam put me here . . . during the World War Uncle Sam grabbed Hayti. My father was an official down there. He didn't want Uncle Sam in Hayti and he said so and said it loud. They told him to shut up and he wouldn't, so they shut him up in jail. My brother also made a noise and Americans marines killed him in the street. I had nobody to pay for me at the university, so I had to get out and work. Voila!" (137–38). In spite of the fact that Ray's migration was forced, it has tossed him among the black American working class, where he begins to grapple with his own cultural chauvinism. Moreover, it is through a friendship with Ray that Jake begins to understand that there exists a world beyond his experiences. "Hayti . . . ?" he asks Ray, not knowing where it is. Most significantly, Ray inadvertently causes Jake to realize that his power as a black man could be harnessed for greater purposes than it was in the U.S. military. After Ray regales him with the tale of Haitian revolutionary Toussaint L'Ouverture, Jake responds: "A black man! A black man! Oh, I wish I'd been a soldier under sich a man" (132). "He plied his instructor with questions. Heard of Dessalines, who carried on the fight begun by Toussaint L'Ouverture and kept Hayti independent. But it was incredible to Jake that a little island of freed slaves had withstood the three leading European powers" (132).

In Fanon's description of the "new" black man who will emerge from the ruins of empire, it is the true revolutionary such as L'Ouverture who stands as the emblem of black manhood, having successfully and violently forced the oppressor to acknowledge him.[50] In this moment of revolution, the Haitian has something the citizen of Fanon's Martinique does not: the necessary instance of forced recognition that solidifies selfhood—Martinque's "freedom" was proffered from without. In *Home to Harlem*, revolutionary violence used to achieve a decolonized black subjectivity is decidedly romanticized. Jake imagines the revolution as "dramatic and picturesque," a "strange, almost unimaginable eruption of the beautiful ideas of the 'Liberté Fraternité, Egalité' of Mankind" (130). The Haitian Revolution may have been the most "dramatic" and fruitful instance of black self-liberation, but McKay was attracted to the success of slave resistance from sites across the diaspora as models of racial solidarity, collective action, and correctly directed violence. In her unpublished study of literary representations of maroonage, Randi Gray Kristensen presents compelling evidence that McKay gained inspiration for "If We Must Die" from the English writer Aphra Behn's fictionalized depiction of a Surinam slave uprising in her 1688 novel *Oroonoko; or, The Royal Slave*, which had been reissued in 1915, just three years before McKay's poem appeared.[51] Kristensen astutely notes the nearly exact parallel between lines in McKay's work ("If we must die, O let us nobly die,") and the cry Oroonoko issues to his army in the face of defeat: "Come, if we must die, let us meet death in the noblest way."[52] McKay was also quite familiar with Karl Marx's analyses of U.S. slavery and certainly knew that Marx had credited blacks' unofficial warfare against the institution with forcing the issue to crisis. After Lincoln formally declared war against the Confederacy, Marx was also adamant in insisting that slave populations participate in their own emancipation, arguing for the formation of black regiments.

It is difficult to ascertain from McKay's work whether his celebration of black spaces and the self-determining role blacks played in dismantling white structures of domination ever *seriously* tempted him to envision a black political destiny apart from white civilization. His short membership in the African Blood Brotherhood and his participation in drafting the "Theses on the Negro Question" only confuse matters even more. It is likely that any thinking along separatist lines was deadened, not simply by his own belief in the irreversible heterogeneity of the modern world, but once again, by his decision to accept the tenets of Marxism. Before wholly repudiating Communism later in his life, McKay would declare black liberation as inseparable from the interracial and international war against capitalism. After the close of the Comintern, Trotsky published an open letter to McKay cautioning him against separatist ideology:

. . . One of the most important branches of this conflict consists in enlightening the proletarian consciousness by awakening the feeling of human dignity, and of revolutionary protest, among the Negro slaves of American capitalism. As stated above, this work can only be carried out by self-sacrificing and politically educated revolutionary Negroes.

Needless to say, the work is not to be carried on in a spirit of Negro chauvinism, which would then merely form a counterpart of white chauvinism,— but in a spirit of solidarity of all exploited without consideration of color.[53]

Yet, McKay's memoirs recount an instance in which he expresses distrust in a party leader's eagerness to enlist black men "in the cause of Communism" because they would "make splendid soldiers."[54] He goes on to describe his reaction: "So many other whites had said the same thing—that Negros make good cannon fodder when they were properly led—led by whites to the black slaughter. That filled me with resentment." What truly disturbed McKay was that this sentiment came from the "mouth of a Communist," forcing him into the discomfiting position of doubting the sole ideology which had made egalitarian interracialism appear feasible.[55] During the course of the congress, Trotsky managed to convince McKay otherwise, alleviating his fears that black bodies would only be sacrifices to the overthrow of capitalism. Thus assured, McKay chose to conclude his address at the International with the prediction that "we shall soon see a few negro soldiers in the finest, bravest and cleanest fighting forces in the world—the Red Army and Navy of Russia—fighting not only for their own emancipation, but also for the emancipation of the working class of the whole world."[56]

Unlike Du Bois, who became a pacifist in the wake of World War I, and despite believing that the war had transformed the world into "a vast international cemetery," McKay remained capable of embracing the *idea* of revolutionary violence (227). In the final analysis, however, McKay admitted that he was not a joiner, an organizer, or a leader, and would not, therefore, lend his body to the work that would help bring about the revolution he advocated. Attempting to explain his unexpected welcome at the Third International in his memoirs, he acknowledges that the militancy of "If We Must Die" may have substituted for more concrete radical credentials. Although McKay therefore saw himself first and foremost as a poet and a "propagandist," a soldier in what Gramsci calls the ideological "war of position,"[57] Marxism's positivistic belief in the transformational power of knowledge may have added to his sense that his interventions into the discourses of capitalism were vital contributions to the Communist cause. For McKay, Marx himself stood as the most persuasive example. In the Comintern speech, he asserts that Marx's public condemnations of U.S. slaveholders amounted to a fight "against chattel slavery."[58] McKay also argues that as Communist propaganda made twentieth-century black Americans aware of Marx's sustained interest in antebellum emancipation, they had begun to demonstrate increased faith in Marxism's liberatory promise.

But if McKay's role in revolution was to engage in a war of words, those words were perhaps more shield than sword. McKay scholars have observed that the writer continually sought refuge from the political and personal demands the world placed upon him. He shifted philosophical allegiances, moved constantly, resisted the obligations of friendship, and even abandoned his own child. Most attribute his inability to commit himself completely to anything other than his writing to a profound failing of character or a need to outrun racism. More provocatively, some have speculated that McKay was attempting to find a space where he could repress or enact a black queer identity.[59] Any or all of these might be true. Nonetheless, these assessments can be complicated further if we reconsider McKay as part of World War I's collateral damage. It seems almost unnecessary to reemphasize here that McKay did not simply write about the First World War but lived through it, an experience that left many of his generation psychically unmoored. Yet that analysis—so common when considering the white cultural production of that era—is rarely extended to blacks, who are placed somehow outside of the realm of territorial and emotional devastation. This is the very misapprehension that I have claimed McKay endeavors to correct. A brief but telling moment in his memoirs finds McKay confessing that the war had indeed spiritually and intellectually ungrounded him, leaving him with "no reason to think that world I lived in was permanent, solid and unshakable."[60] It would be hard to imagine that McKay's sense of the world's instability had no impact on his fiction, and I will conclude this essay with a consideration of that possibility. The success of *Home to Harlem* was followed by a critical and financial failure, *Banjo: A Story without a Plot*, published in 1929.[61] Although the work does not as overtly engage World War I as *Harlem*, McKay nonetheless infuses the narrative with lengthy discussions of the conflict that both repeat and expand those positions he had expressed within *Harlem* and his political essays. It also repeats the "picaresque style" McKay uses in the first novel.[62] *Banjo*'s poor reception motivated McKay to try other fictional modes, yet he was thwarted by what he describes as a near compulsion to write in that genre, worrying—as did his critics—that his incapacity stemmed from the limits of his talent and imagination. It seems significant nonetheless that McKay found himself almost helplessly drawn to the picaresque, a genre distinguished by geographical migrations and a fragmented, episodic narrative structure. McKay never explicitly links his urge to produce this form of fiction to a consciousness shattered by the war, and certainly the genre provided a structure receptive to his exploration of one of the major themes of these novels: the black dispersal World War I created. Looked at from another angle, however, McKay may have been using migration as a metaphor for the spiritual dislocation and rupture the war engendered.

Perhaps the fates of Jake and Ray best exemplify my point. The first novel closes with Jake escaping from Harlem to Chicago with Felice, who says she is more than willing to "slack" and "desert" with her lover (331). In Banjo, we discover Jake has slacked and deserted Felice. McKay has him leave the United States to join Ray in Marseille, a place of transnationals, immigrants, and exiles. Ray and Jake are also joined by Banjo, an African American who fought for the Canadian forces. As the subtitle of the novel makes clear, very little by way of formal narrative structure occurs in the story. Three blacks set adrift by warfare, the characters move from place to place, wander from one experience to another, and drink heavily. They are not unlike (yet very much unlike) "the Lost Generation" of Hemingway's classic 1926 World War I novel, The Sun Also Rises. While it is not my intention to push a comparison with Hemingway, McKay had read the author before writing his own longer works of fiction, lauding him for his refusal to produce "false romantic realis[m]."[63] McKay also gives Jake the same name as the protagonist of Sun; and in his memoirs, McKay takes time to blast those contemporary critics who (accurately) discerned the influence of Hemingway on his fiction. Yet if there are parallels to be made between the works, I see the most important not as textual but psychic. Both writers attend to the manner the war has rendered its characters spiritually depleted and emotionally paralyzed. Haunted by its memory, they are unsure of what to do, and as result, are able to do little. Indeed, for Jake and Ray, the war is a spectral presence; throughout the narrative, Jake wonders if his AWOL status will catch up with him in Harlem and struggles to justify his desertion to himself and others; Ray attempts to grasp the implications of a life undone by imperial warfare. It may have been comforting for many black Americans to believe that their soldiers had returned from the war "fighting," as Du Bois famously suggested, and that armies of black civilians had rallied to their cause—all miraculously healed by their political commitment to bring about democracy at home. But McKay's wandering figures ask us to consider otherwise, allowing us to acknowledge those blacks who were left unanchored by the most disastrous war the world had ever witnessed.

At the end of Banjo, Jake and Ray "beat it" out of Marseille, unclear of what they are looking for.[64] McKay, too, was looking. It was in fact his search for meaning in the war's aftermath that solidified his relationship to communist ideology. I return here to a statement McKay makes in his memoirs: "I had no reason to think that world I lived in was permanent, solid and unshakable: The

World War had just come to a truce. So I started reading Marx."[65] Aside, then, from Marxism's potential to free blacks from racial and economic oppression, it is also likely that Marxism's rational, scientific explanation of historical rupture helped McKay make sense of the war; the possibility of a world where socialism reigned offering him hope for a more predictable future. Eventually, McKay would "beat it" from Marxism, turning elsewhere for answers, a quest that in an ironic turn led him to Catholicism. Before, however, under Marxism's influence, part of his long (and infinitely complicated) perspective, he produced *Home to Harlem*—not simply one of the most celebrated novels of the "Renaissance"— but a singular and significant fictional interpretation of blacks and the First World War.

7 IF WE COME OUT STANDING UP

Gwendolyn Brooks, World War II, and the Politics of Rehabilitation

The final chapter of Gwendolyn Brooks's 1953 novel *Maud Martha*, entitled "back from the wars!," begins with the eponymous heroine taking joy in her brother's return from World War II: "There was Peace, and her brother Harry was back from the wars, and well. And it was such a beautiful day!" (177).[1] It is for Maud Martha a long-awaited moment of relief; however, her respite will prove brief. Just as she dashes out of her kitchenette in "exhilaration," her mind is invaded by brutal images of bodies transformed by war: "They 'marched,' they battled behind her brain . . . the men with two arms off and two legs off, the men with the parts of faces. Then her guts divided . . ." (ellipses original) (179). These descriptions—explicit, unsparing— openly refuse any glamorization of war, serving as bodily reminders of war's inevitable consequences. This kind of frank corporeal imagery also structures Brooks's presentation of war in an earlier twelve-poem meditation on World War II, "gay chaps at the bar." Published in the 1944 book of poems *A Street in Bronzeville* and initially labeled "The Soldier Sonnets,"[2] these poems were based on letters Brooks received from servicemen abroad, including her brother Raymond Brooks, to whom she dedicates the sequence. It begins with a quotation from a letter in which a soldier remarks on the state of men returning from the front, "crying" he writes, "and trembling" (64).[3] It is this understanding of war, culled from the "stuff of letters," as she writes in her autobiography,[4] that will shape her imagining of the soldier's body.

Brooks's "realistic" representations of psychic and corporeal wounding mark an important turning point in the way both forms of injury will be presented in African American war literature. Throughout this study, I have argued that many black American war writers have used a variety of textual strategies to enact "damage control," arising from their hesitance to offer graphic descriptions of black bodies and minds physically and psychically wounded in warfare. Of particular importance to this chapter, I located this reluctance in the dominant culture's persistent conflation of blackness and "disability," suggesting that any depiction of the injured black body could invoke the ascription of "disability" that has been used to exclude those considered "disabled," and thus the congenitally "disabled" black American, from the national body politic. I further suggested that the tendency to routinely attribute psychic damage to injured bodies compounded this risk; well beyond the formal end of slavery, I claimed, African Americans endeavored to escape beliefs that a myriad of "disabilities" acquired within that institution had irrevocably compromised blacks' ability to function in civic and social arenas. Drawing on Henri-Jacques Stiker's contention that the "rehabilitative" technologies emerging in post–World War I France were intended to allow the war-wounded to reenter society easily, undetected, I theorized that black war writers' "damage control" was rehabilitation's literary equivalent, giving rise to a "black politics of rehabilitation" dependent on omission and minimization. If the conspicuous, "abnormal" black body could disappear within a fantasy of "sameness," it might also be fully "integrated" into national structures. In that light, Brooks's detailed depictions of decidedly unrehabilitated black male bodies in "gay chaps at the bar," produced before the desegregation of the military, and in Maud Martha, written before the larger desegregation of the nation, would appear to wholly undermine these aims.

Even more, the appearance of these injured bodies at the close of Maud Martha, a work exploring a black woman's struggle to make her domestic life conform to the heteronormative ideals of marriage and family, continues to perplex the novel's readers. War is merely alluded to prior to this final chapter, seeming no more than a historical referent, and certainly not as central to Maud Martha's life or the novel's purpose. As Brooks herself has stated, the semiautobiographical Maud Martha stands as her blunt response to blacks' subscription to the "second cult of true womanhood" of the 1950s. This "cult" emerged in part as a postwar backlash against women workers, who, after helping sustain the American economy, were nonetheless coerced, and sometimes forced, to relinquish their jobs to demobilized male veterans. The government-led campaign to return women to the home was further fueled by the specter of communism, that "other," "unnatural" way of being, lending new urgency to constructing oppositional ideologies of "Americanism." This incarnation of "Americanism" idealized a homogeneous, patriarchal vision of the domestic that could resist those disruptive political forces—both internal and external—that threatened the foundation of American society: a capitalist economy dependent on gender, racial, and class stratification. Yet the domestic ideal reigning in the 1950s ran counter to African American familial configurations and labor patterns necessitated by economic exigencies. In an insightful reading of James Baldwin's rendition of the domestic space in his 1950s gay bildungsroman, *Go Tell it on the Mountain*, Roderick Ferguson explains that the question of whether a black heteronormative family was possible (or, for that matter, desirable or "natural") for African Americans was lost in sociological discourses that rescripted the domestic variations in black communities as voluntary transgressions or signs of moral deficiency: "The heteronormative household was practically a 'material impossibility' for people of color as the U.S. 'family wage' in the early twentieth century defined the American home as white, heterosexual, and American, and thereby excluded people of color on the grounds that they were incapable of, or uninterested in, constituting heteronormative families and adopting their regulatory demands."[5] These "regulatory demands" had particular implications for black women. Because they were, from the onset of slavery, needed as both laboring machines and "sexual latrines"—to use bell hooks's disturbingly apt characterization[6]—the dominant culture generated an amalgam of cultural, medical, scientific, and sociological "evidence" declaring black women's gender and sexual "abnormality" to preclude them from fully inhabiting the category of "woman."[7] Depicted as physically malformed, genitally excessive, and sexually deviant, many black women sought to destigmatize their bodies by adopting the dominant culture's "feminine" paradigms, striving to present themselves as physically and morally fit for domesticity, the desire that guided Harper's idealized description of Iola Leroy. Thus, in very much the same way that the military (and war) had become a site where black men could "rehabilitate" their bodies, the domestic served as a space where black women could also rehabilitate theirs. Indeed, Maud Martha, dismissed as an uncomely "old black gal" in the novel (34), believes that her worthiness as a woman can be validated through procuring a husband and a home, the prizes presumably only offered those women considered desirable enough to deserve them.

Quite clearly, this model of black rehabilitation required that African Americans capitulate to a range of normalization processes set forth by white America. For black women, the most evident and detrimental concessions were corporeal in nature—skin lightening and hair relaxing, as two examples. Noting that Maud Martha's mind turns to the "pale" female faces peering off of the pages of "the Negro Press" just after she pictures the stream of wounded soldiers (179), Harry B. Shaw rightly interprets the novel as expressing "the specific war that black women wage with . . . standards of beauty."[8] However, this battle with bodily image comprises only part of Maud Martha's struggle. Brooks paints a portrait of a woman whose psychic damage comes from the "failure" of her body, to be sure, but also from the manner in which her "gray" domestic life has stifled her autonomous desires and limited her world to the confines of her dingy kitch-enette, leaving her, Maud Martha realizes, "with her hungriest lack—not much voice" (176). Two years prior to the publication of the novel, the *Negro Digest* ran Brooks's editorial addressing the sources of black wives' domestic discontent, "Why Negro Women Leave Home."[9] A rebuke of an article appearing earlier in the magazine, "Do Black Women Make Good Wives?," her brief but biting commen-tary suggests that the economic independence wage work provided black women during World War II had made them less equipped to submit to their husbands in household affairs. These newly empowered women could, she writes, "buy their child a new overcoat without planning an elaborate strategic campaign, or under-going the smoke and tire of a semi-revolution."[10] The language Brooks chooses here is revealing, supporting an interpretation of *Maud Martha* as a work imagin-ing black women's resistance to patriarchal norms as a form of domestic warfare.

It hardly needs to be said that the invocation of war rhetoric in relation to black women's engagements with white supremacy and heterosexist practices is not to be taken literally. "The war with beauty" and the domestic "war" Brooks explores in *Maud Martha* and her editorial are obviously metaphorical; the war she refers to within her novel and her sonnet sequence is "actual." But the fact that the two "wars" are elided within *Maud Martha* offers evidence that Brooks is inviting her audience to forge some form of comparison. And so, rather than isolate *Maud Martha* as a novel about black women and the domestic, and "gay chaps at the bar" as poems about black men and war, I will argue that the two should be read coextensively, as texts informing one another's content. I will suggest that Brooks in fact uses both to explode the myth of racial "rehabilitation": exposing as false the allegedly redemptive properties of the national and nationalist institutions black women and men had come to see as their racial salvation. Interpreted in this way, "gay chaps at the bar" and *Maud Martha* can be analyzed as corresponding statements meant to intervene into discourses that herald the military, warfare, and the domestic as means of black "normalization."

Brooks's distrust of normalization was certainly well founded. As Stiker as-serts, the most deleterious effects of positing social reintegration—or "normal-ization"—as the outcome of rehabilitation were multiple and complex. First and foremost, it assumed that there was a recognizable and objective "normality" to which all should strive, thereby instituting nothing less than a tyranny of homo-geneity. This tyranny did not content itself to reforming bodies perceived as visibly or functionally "disabled"; it extended itself to remaking interiors. As a long-term result, an increasing number of people marked "different," from the poor to the unemployed, have been labeled "disabled," becoming targets of rehabilitative practices implemented across institutions meant to prod the (allegedly) "maladapted" into behaving like the (ostensibly) "adapted."[11] Refusing to characterize this coercion as simply domination in its most obvious form, Stiker notes that the "other" will accept rehabilitation—like Brooks's Maud Martha—to gain whatever a given society markets as the benefits of sameness, colluding in an illusory performance of assimilation that attempts to efface difference and the myriad of difficulties difference creates. More problematically, this cosmetic fix allows the inequities created by the very political, social, and ideological practices that relegate certain bodies to economic, gender, sex, physical (and racial) alterity to conveniently recede from view. In short, Stiker believes that through "naturalizing" socially produced disability, naming all difference "disability" and claiming all "disabled" capable of "rehabilitation," preventative measures are judged unnecessary: "there was nothing to be done."[12] Societal transformation halts; social destruction proceeds unimpeded.

I detail Stiker's assessment of the stance Western culture has taken toward disability to illumine my penultimate claim: that Brooks's war literature endeavors to correct this very posture. I invoke the language of rehabilitation here intentionally, for I believe that Brooks does, in the final analysis, forward an argument for rehabilitation's potential. Her version, however, neither begins nor ends with the reconstruction of bodies and minds violated by the destructive forces of racism, sexism, heteronormativity, capitalism, or war. Instead, Brooks's insistence in calling attention to these forces themselves and their debilitating effects on black Americans suggests a revisionary understanding of African American disability—and the value in its presentation—what I will call a "black womanist politics of rehabilitation." Articulated through Brooks's deployment of "damaged" and imperfect figures in "gay chaps at the bar" and Maud Martha, I see this alternative set of politics accomplishing several aims. It 1) forces socially produced disability into view (disallowing the disappearing acts "normalization" encourages); 2) takes society and its harmful institutional practices as the objects in need of repair; 3) acknowledges the reality of specifically racial and gendered injury while resisting institutional rehabilitation as a "corrective"; 4) envisions black male and female injury as bound; 5) and, finally, refuses to exempt black Americans from the destruction done to self or other.

In 1944, when Brooks published her series of sonnets, racialist concepts of the subhuman and diseased body still persisted: white soldiers circulated the preposterous myth that black soldiers had tails, given as an explanation for why these men could not be aviators.[13] More notoriously, the War Department insisted that black blood donations not be given to white soldiers in spite of the American Medical Association's and Red Cross's protestations that theories of "tainted" black blood had no basis in science.[14] In "the white troops had their orders but the Negroes looked like men," Brooks reveals the fundamental absurdity of using theories of black congenital deficiency to rationalize military segregation. Although the white soldiers in this poem have a "fixed" "formula" for "remember[ing]" the "Congenital inequities that cause / Disfavor of the darkness" (70), Brooks imagines this formula quickly falling apart in the face of war. If they had "obeyed instructions" and "boxed / Their feelings properly, complete to tags— / A box for dark men and a box for Other—" they also found "the contents had been scrambled. / Or even switched" (70).

In an image as ironic as it is disturbing, both black and white bodies are radically integrated as both are radically disabled, obliterated beyond recognition. Brooks's poem points to yet another irony, however, one beyond exposing the superficial nature of race. The political and social "recognition" black men sought through service, a recognition they hoped might finally, definitively, negate racist characterizations of "congenital defects," as Brooks names them, is complicated by what their bodies could become in violent death—unrecognizable in relation to what they were before. In discussing the meaning of the black soldier Jerome's decapitation in Brown's Clotelle, I noted Elaine Scarry's important claim: that a particular civilization embeds itself in the body, expressing itself in culturally specific gestures, such as a handshake. That civilization's corporeal manifestation, she writes, is perhaps most heightened in the bodily rituals of the military: the step, the salute.[15] The irony, she theorizes, of "dying for one's country" lies in the deconstruction of the body in violent death; when "the chest is shattered," the nation empties from the body; "the civilization as it resides" in the body is unmade.[16]

This "unmaking" is critical to Brooks's project. The unmaking of the black soldier's body, the focus on its ability to be disabled, is also the unmaking of the ideological assumptions that accompany those presentations of the black warring body as whole, able, heroic. Yet, if Brooks is specifically "correcting" many of the black war writers who have preceded her, she is also writing against visual military propaganda that used idealized constructions of the black male body as a recruitment tool and as a means of appeasing African Americans incensed both by policies that drafted blacks into segregated forces and by the scant acknowledgement they received for their services. Very much like the Office of War Information's poster depicting a brawny Dorie Miller,[17] the ability of Miller's body, its size and its strength, was also afforded great attention in the press (who perhaps picked up on the emphasis in military releases).[18]

Of course, the same body that was now being recognized, admired, even claimed, had kept Miller from being legitimately introduced to military weaponry prior to the incident. In "Negro Hero—to suggest Dorie Miller," a poem I also analyze in Chapter Five, Brooks invests the sailor with an understanding of how

"Above and Beyond the Call of Duty," David Stone Martin, 1943.
Library of Congress, Prints and Photographs Division.

beliefs in congenital difference/disability marred his achievement: "Still—am I good enough to die for them, is my blood / bright enough to be spilled, / Was my constant back-question—are they clear / On this?" (49).

But it is in the experimental, off-rhyme, strained poems of "gay chaps at the bar" that her exploration of these issues becomes more complex as she attempts to give voice to a range of "nonheroic" bodies: anonymous, "crying and trembling," and most important, visibly physically broken. The decision to render the physically catastrophic potential of war in the sonnet, a form that is distinguished by the control the writer exercises over language, permits Brooks a space to consider the uses and limits of language, juxtaposing them against the uses and limits of the body. One speaker laments that he has no "smart, athletic language for this hour" (64), language and the body needing the same strenuous ability athleticism implies—both failing to find it. Even more specifically, in her apparent attempt to bring war under the ordering properties of the sonnet, Brooks parallels the manner in which the official, mythologizing language of the state also tries to contain the destructive nature of war. This official rhetoric influences the language most early African American war writers adopt to describe the black warring body (the soldiers are "courageous," "valiant"; they are "patriots" who "love their country") precisely because it encourages denial. But the truth of war, Brooks appears to say, will threaten any language—official or poetic—that seeks to regulate it. This is where the disabled body becomes central to Brooks's presentation of war: this tension is explored most provocatively on that site. In choosing to "alter" the physical, human form of the black soldier, she is forced to alter the poetic form structuring the sequence.

The sonnet "still do I keep my look, my identity" demonstrates how deftly Brooks brings together the ideas of recognition, the body, language, and poetic form to rescript mythological presentations of war. In this piece, the speaker mediates on what might happen to his body during battle. It might easily be mistaken for a Shakespearean sonnet and indeed follows that rhyme scheme perfectly for the first octave:

Each body has its art, its precious prescribed
Pose, that even in passion's droll contortions, waltzes
Or push of pain—or when a grief has stabbed,
Or hatred hacked—is its, and nothing else's.
Each body has its pose. No other stock
That is irrevocable, perpetual
And its to keep. In castle or in shack.
With rags or robes. Through good, nothing, or ill. (65)

The last six lines allude to the Petrarchan sonnet (Lentino's thirteenth-century version of the sestet):

And even in death a body, like no other
On any hill or plain or crawling cot
Or gentle for the lilyless hasty pall
(Having twisted, gagged, and then sweet-ceased to bother),
Shows the old personal art, the look. Shows what
It showed in baseball. What it showed in school. (65)

In merging the two forms, Brooks achieves a striking effect. The reader's expectations for one form—the Shakespearean sonnet—are ruptured just at the precise moment Brooks turns from the subject of a body's life to, instead, its death. In this poem, the "pose" struck before war becomes a posture of a different kind: a "twisted" one. Even though the speaker wishes to imagine his body unaffected, Brooks twists both the body and the form that "writes" that body, forcing both the reader and the sonnet to respond to the ability of war to alter what it touches. The speaker's need to conceive of a death that lacks the power to transform him physically can be read as a somatic metaphor for the intended effects of American mythologies of war, which attempt to turn the nation away from the unstructuring or deconstructive aspects of war to war's ostensible capacity to "preserve" (ways of life, for example) or to "save" (people, resources). If Brooks's poem seeks to remind us of the vulnerable nature of the body, it might also ask us to note the fragility of rhetorical illusion. On its surface, her sonnet appears whole, undisturbed. Upon closer inspection, it is two fragments pieced together. Brooks's disability politics have given rise to a disability poetics.

A passage from her novel further illustrates the extent to which the disabled body troubles claims made by governments about the rectifying power of war. After Maud Martha finds her exhilaration disrupted by images of disfigurement, she momentarily meditates on the possibility of "man . . . completely succeed[ing] in destroying the world" (179). She then quickly turns to the subject of flowers, assuring herself that they would "come up again in the spring . . . if necessary, between or out of—beastly inconvenient!—the smashed corpses lying in strict composure, in that hush infallible and sincere" (179). Flowers growing out of corpses: Maud Martha's insistence upon turning destroyed bodies into fertile, life-giving ones is more than a hopeful vision of regeneration. Rather, it seems that Brooks is alluding to the absurd manner in which death wrought by war can be narrated in any manner the living see fit. The "hushed" and silent dead, forced into the state of calm and decay that "composure" dually implies, have no choice but to cooperate in this reading. Sharon Holland's observation merits repeating here: "The ability of the emerging nation to speak hinges on its correct use of the 'dead' in the service of its creation."[19] The dead do not speak, but are "spoken for." The dead can be regulated.

However, the very material existence of disabled bodies, in their visibly irregular state, refuses the cooperation that memorializing so readily offers. David Gerber's examination of disability imagery in World War II films notes that many major "newsreels and news magazines, most significantly *Life*, had a policy against publishing images of dead, dying or severely wounded combat forces."[20] Gerber theorizes, in part, that these organizations believed the American public entirely unprepared to accept that warfare could produce such extraordinary disfigurement and such high rates of casualties[21] (a position that the Bush administration has taken during the current war against Iraq, banning images of coffins containing dead soldiers being returned to the United States). But an attendant anxiety stemmed from demobilization after World War II—that these very same "deformed," "disfigured," disabled men would return "abnormal," their psyches as irrevocably altered as their bodies, the parallel that kept African American war writers from depicting images of damage. Inspiring even more fear in the public was the prevalent notion that these men would no longer "fit" into society, would become disruptive: "menaces," parasites, or wanderers (like McKay's figures), operating in a realm outside of any proper social order. Gerber argues that many of the films produced after World War II are recuperative responses, focusing on the disabled veteran's successful reintegration into his community. As such, they offer narratives that depict the veteran as successfully rehabilitated—not just physically, the aspect Stiker emphasizes, but emotionally, the emotional recovery signaling his readiness to reenter society. That reentry was frequently finalized by marriage, the establishment of the domestic space, where heteronormative behavior, the ultimate signifier of masculine regeneration, will thrive.[22] The underlying assumption giving rise to the demobilization anxieties that Gerber argues these films were meant to alleviate was the fear that the veteran's losses might cause him to harbor anger and resentment toward the nation that, in sending him to war, caused him to make such great sacrifice.

Gerber's analysis can be productively applied to recuperative narratives seeking to minimize the particular difficulties attending black "homecomings." For demobilized African American soldiers disabled in service, any anger that may have been caused by their wounded bodies and minds was often reinforced by the racism they endured serving in a segregated, discriminatory army. Numerous letters from black men serving in the war document the degree to which physical disability and institutional racism operated in tandem to create unbearable, often inhumane conditions. Disabled black men were frequently left unattended, made to work through injury, threatened with discharges for not returning before recovery; they were punished, very simply, for the failings of their bodies, and the greatest "failing" was evidently being black.[23] In a letter to the *Pittsburgh Courier*, one soldier pleaded for help: "I am a sick disabled man in the Army. . . . If I don't get out of here alive very soon I'll end it all by killing myself. I am tired of suffering. . . . Since I've been here I've seen many cripple Negroes. . . . They keep our men in the army disabled until they die I know; it has happen [sic] here last week."[24] Another, claiming to write on "behalf of myself and 60 other men like me," complained that "the sick and disabled soldier is treated worse than a Jap. . . . The punishment we get for being disabled is extra duty."[25] The psychologically disabled seemed to fare no better. One soldier suffering from an unspecified psychological condition described being forced to undergo shock treatment in a southern army hospital. In a letter written to the editor of the *Baltimore Afro-American*, whom the soldier apparently knew before service, he claims that he had no recognizable mental illnesses prior to duty: "You know . . . when I left you I was well."[26] After detailing the process step by step, he writes that he "ran away from the hospital" to avoid additional treatments, only to be "caught" and subjected to "the treatment more often. . . . Remember all of this is happening in 'Kentucky' where nobody can help me." Out of despair, he continues, he tried to kill himself by drinking lye. He adds: "I forgot to tell you they used to beat me up while I was unconscious . . . sometimes my jaw was swollen and hurt, and other times I would have a mouse under my eye, you know, a lump," blaming his compounding miseries on "the way those crackers treated me."[27]

There is much evidence confirming that correct diagnoses of blacks with disabilities were all too frequently precluded by military physicians' attachment to the "congenitally afflicted" theory or other theories suggesting that blacks were somehow naturally predisposed to physical and mental illnesses.[28] Accordingly, disabilities were often downplayed in medical reports or dismissed as fakery, resulting in the denial and reduction of benefits. Alternately, black soldiers' disabilities were exaggerated. In an illuminating article analyzing the experiences of disabled black World War II veterans, Louis Jefferson points out that black men were claimed to have abnormally weak psychological conditions, making them more susceptible to "nervous disorders."[29] Thus, whether any specific black servicemen's belief that his recovery from disability was hindered by racist practices was accurate or not, a clear picture emerges from the totality of such complaints. The mere *perception* of racism—that the soldiers may have been neglected or even persecuted—played a definite role in worsening their experiences of physical and psychological injury. In the particular instance of the case of the soldier subjected to shock treatment and beatings, another, more disturbing image arises: psychological disabilities may have provided an opportunity to exercise racial discipline, perhaps even sadism, within the bounds of "therapy": "I have two black burns on each side of my temple, and you know they were never there before."[30]

Some forty years after the war, an article published in *Military Affairs* suggested that the military was, in fact, ill-prepared to handle the "magnitude" of "psychiatric casualties" emerging from combat or any preexisting psychological illnesses predictably exacerbated by warfare and military life.[31] In the main, the author argues, men suffering from "battle fatigue" were offered therapies insufficient in method and duration, and then, if possible, they were returned to service as quickly as they could be: an imperative created by the numbers of bodies needed to fill the military's depleting ranks. Referring to surveys conducted among servicemen during the war, he notes that a number of covariants could reasonably determine the severity of posttraumatic stress, such as the men's emotional proximity to those they may have witnessed being killed and injured, or the redeployment to camps located in isolated areas.[32] Not surprisingly, racial discrimination was among these covariants: "The morale-destroying effect of racial prejudice was demonstrated by the relatively high BF [battle fatigue] rates of the 92nd and 93rd Infantry Division—black units led primarily by Caucasian officers. These divisional soldiers were often treated with derision by the civilian population during mobilization and contempt by members of other combat units when committed to battle; they received little recognition for their combat accomplishments."[33] Recognizing discrimination and prejudice as covariants in "psychiatric casualties" goes part way to understanding the nature of war-related racial injuries. Yet it seems that the prevalence of racial terrorism within the armed forces—murders, beatings, extreme and cruel forms of punishment—produced its own racially specific traumas. In another letter written to the *Pittsburgh Courier*, a black soldier stationed in Arkansas details what happened to a member of his unit who went AWOL: "Our Bn. Commander threatened to take a hammer and a beat a soldier's 'Head in to your shoulders.' Everyone stood by waiting for action. The same soldier left Sunday absent without leave and returned after being gone about 8 hours. On his return he was chained to a tree as though he was some killer or even worse. The morale of the whole outfit changed."[34] Summarizing the effect of continued racial degradation, a soldier in Louisiana writes, "Our nerves are being shattered. They stay tense waiting to see what's next. It's enough to drive anybody psycho."[35]

Still, very few in the military sought to ascertain what black veterans demobilizing might require to reenter society "successfully," with or without psychological and physical injuries. Well aware of this oversight, African American political leaders rallied to the cause of returning black veterans, publishing numerous articles in black periodicals instructing black veterans how to secure benefits under the GI Bill, including information for those men who had acquired disabilities.[36] In a 1943 article published in the *Journal of Negro Education*, "Problems of Demobilization and Rehabilitation of the Negro Soldier After World Wars I and II," Rufus E. Clement offered an assessment of the needs of disabled black World War II veterans more specifically. Primarily, Clement asserts that black men deserve equal access to medical care, job training, employment, and education, arguing that the increased number of blacks being drafted and returned— many more than during World War I—meant that they could not and should not be neglected in the same manner black men were after the former war concluded. Yet his "equal access" argument stops short of evaluating whether these rehabilitative measures adequately address the particular problems attending disability. Without suggesting that black leadership completely failed to grasp the complexity of issues facing the war disabled, it does appear, however, that these issues became subsumed within the more general struggle for black veterans and the larger, continuing agitation for black civic equality. The conclusion of Clement's essay further exemplifies this tendency. Rather than reiterating the problems and solutions outlined earlier, the article ends as a jeremiad, figuring the returning veteran as someone to be feared: "Any planning which envisages the peaceful settlement of the problems the Negro soldier will face at the end of World War II must take cognizance of the state of mind in which this soldier is likely to be found. If he comes out of the war feeling that the Negro race has lost ground in its attempt to gain full citizenship status, he is likely to be bitter. On the other hand, if he feels that definite gains have been achieved . . . he can be expected to be cooperative and patient."[37]

Clement apparently understood that the black veteran's "state of mind" was very much on the mind of white Americans. Screenwriter Carl Foreman's 1949 film version of Arthur Laurent's 1946 play *Home of the Brave* is a good case in point.[38] Released just before the Korean War began in 1950, *Home* indicates the depth of the desire to quell fears that racially injured, embittered black veterans had been loosed upon society unrehabilitated, or more accurately, into a society that itself had yet to rehabilitate itself racially (neither Laurent, Foreman, nor the film's director, Mark Robson, were black). In Foreman's interpretation, an African American soldier who is psychologically impaired by rage and resentment after a traumatizing racist incident suffers partial amnesia and temporary paralysis from the waist down. During sessions with a therapist, the patient speculates that he is suffering from guilt over experiencing a brief burst of joy when a white soldier, an old boyhood friend, calls him a racial epithet and is killed in action promptly thereafter. The psychiatrist's job is to convince the black soldier that he did not, in fact, experience happiness when the racist was leveled; his emotion was simply the relief all soldiers feel when they realize that they have been spared the fate of their comrades. Anger at racism (an illegitimate and threatening psychological disability) is successfully relabeled as survivor's guilt (a legitimate one), a condition the patient is told he shares with many other soldiers, black and white. Stiker's contention that rehabilitation depends on the illusion of identical-ness bears out in these scenes. As part of the soldier's therapy, the psychiatrist makes him repeat the mantra "I am the same. I am the same," which he does, robotically. The most frightening implication of this moment arises from the full rehabilitation of the black soldier's psyche. Disciplined into submitting his inte-rior, his physical and his *social* mobility will require that he unthinkingly parrot the state's assuaging messages regarding both warfare and racial relations.

In a related move, Foreman directly parallels the black soldier's psychoso-matic disability to the injury of a white soldier whose arm has been amputated; the two men become fast friends, leaving the military to open a bar together. Foreman places the black soldier's racial injury in a metaphorical relationship to the white soldier's bodily injury as an instructive lesson in healing. Just as the white soldier will be offered a prosthetic and will be "good as new," the black soldier has been given a new white friend, a human prosthetic, to replace the one who betrayed him. He is also socially corralled; the black patient is discharged into the care of a white custodian rather than set loose on his own. This scenario fulfills the prescription given by at least one Veteran's Administration physician: "Guardianship arrangements for Negro patients are the best way to insure that all personal affairs are handled according to the high standards of civilization established by white men."[39] A contemporary review in the *Nation* remarked that blacks were bound to laugh at the absurdity of the film, particularly as the soldier is cautioned not to be too sensitive about racial matters.[40] However, it also can be imagined that many others in the film's audiences experienced their own relief as they witnessed a black man's autonomous thoughts slowly disintegrate before them, his disruptive potential diminished. The film went on to become a hit, even receiving a positive review in the *Chicago Defender*.[41]

A product influenced by the culturally hygienic Cold War,[42] the reinterpreta-tion of *Home of the Brave* acts as a racial retro-fix, asking its audiences to forget that the racist conditions under which blacks served their nation may have created a circumstance leaving legions of black men full of rage toward whites. It did, of course: that rage in fact led many black veterans to become politicized, their mobilization on the home front (buoyed by a black solidarity forged in service, an ironic by-product of a segregated armed forces) has been credited with playing a critical role in energizing the civil rights movement. Disabled black veterans had no small part in this. Forming their own organizations to support each other emotionally and in their collective and individual efforts to procure compensation, these groups also became sites facilitating political change on other fronts.[43] This context might further illumine the film's closure. If the interracial fantasy concluding *Home of the Brave* is partially remedial, it might also be anticipatory, expressing anxiety that increased agitation would result from the coming of the Korean War—in spite of the fact that the military had been desegregated a year before the film's release. Perhaps *Home* recognizes that the deep entrenchment of military racism and the intractability of the racism residing in those who served could not be easily legislated out of existence.

Origins notwithstanding, these varied framings of the black disabled soldier's demobilization tend to employ him as a symbol within highly politicized narratives of social and political "mobility," effectively obscuring these servicemen's more "personal" experiences of their disabilities. Many, in fact felt psychically *immobilized*; not knowing what to expect upon returning "home," they worried about whether they would be able to "adjust" and whether the individuals in their lives would adjust to them. "My marital life is curtailed," one soldier lamented, ". . . the damage done to me is quite beyond repair."[44] Similar to *Home to Harlem*, Brooks imagines her disabled figures in existences outside of any of the predominant, and ultimately containing, narratives. In "gay chaps" Brooks devotes several sonnets to the subject of the soldier's return, none of which ease existing concerns about black veterans' mental, physical, or political "state of mind." In the poem "my dreams, my works must wait till after hell," a soldier finds himself "hoping that" he can "resume" bodily and emotion stability in spite of the "hurt" he has suffered: "I bid, Be firm till I return from hell" (66). He wonders, whether, "On such legs as are left me, in such heart / As I can manage, remember to go home" (66).

It is important to note that in this sonnet, Brooks does what African American writers before her have not: not only does she explicitly foreground the subject of pain, she risks associating a failing body with a failing heart. The soldier "keep[s] eyes pointed in" toward his wounded interior. Physical and psychological transformation are bound here; damage to the body *is* damage to the mind. And as the speaker also acknowledges, that physical and psychological transformation might make reintegration difficult, if not completely impossible; the soldier is not certain that he can "remember to go home," relearning to "love" the "honey and bread" awaiting him. Instead, he might do what was dreaded when demobilization began: become socially unmoored, unable to be regenerated by the comforts of the domestic.

Brooks thus expressly challenges narratives positing a completed reentry into the social order, leaving her soldier in transition, unhealed. By "disabling" the black bodies in her poetry without any wishful recuperative sentiment, she creates an "othered" space where these bodies might give voice to an alternative view of war, rather than "lying" as she will write later in Maud Martha, "in strict composure." In the final sonnet of the sequence, ironically named "the progress," Brooks has her soldiers speak in a unified "we," their voices also collectively expressing doubt as to their capacity to hold up physically and mentally after the war concludes. As their "initial" nationalist "ardor" wanes, they must rely on performance of nationalism to keep them steadied: "still we wear our uniforms . . . applaud the President's voice and face . . . remark on patriotism, sing, / Salute the flag" (75). Yet, "inward grows a soberness . . . a fear" (75). "For even if we come out standing up / How shall we smile, congratulate: and how / Settle in chairs?" (75). The final question the speakers ask is critical for understanding how Brooks addresses how war affects the body. If, they wonder, if we are not dead or disabled to the point of not being able to "stand up," if they can "doctor" their "sallow" interiors, if they can "comb and brush" the "pride" of service, the body still might not "settle" (75). The lingering internal, psychic injury will, they fear, manifest itself in physical discomfort that will not allow them to forget what the war has done to them. Further, no ceremonial language or ritual gesture will prevent them from being haunted by, as the sonnet continues: ". . . The step / Of iron feet again. And again wild" (75).

Although the goal of Brooks's politics of rehabilitation in her war writing is the prevention of the "again"—the repetition of the circumstances that makes socially produced disability appear an inevitability—she ends her sonnet sequence with her soldiers' anticipating war's psychic return in the form of a disordering posttraumatic "syndrome." She is also raising the probability that another war, "real" and material, will actually occur. This probability is indicated in the way the speakers conceptualize the warring body as "iron" in this final line, dehumanizing the soldiers into part of the machine of war. To make war, in other words, soldiers must conceive of the body (whether one's own or the "enemy's") as inanimate entity, a immunizing rhetorical maneuver that removes human beings from the discomfiting fact that they will both inflict and receive injury, as I suggested in my interpretation of Steward and Gilmore. But there is a pronounced pause in the last line, rendered as a visual gap between the words "And" and "again." The speakers' verbal hesitation is then followed by the vocalization of a radically opposing idea: the body made "wild" by warfare, a being who is not "iron" at all but who devolves into a state of utter savagery.

As much as we might admire Brooks's corrective, "realistic" constructions of human bodies and human minds who are neither infallible nor inured—who can be debilitated and damaged by war—it must be acknowledged that there is danger in deploying images of disability in the service of a political agenda, a danger other than black war writers' anxiety that war damage and "congenital" racial damage could be conflated. Most evidently, no matter how "accurate" the "ableist's" representations might be, they may nevertheless obscure the disabled's acts of self-representation, whether these acts of self-portrayal are for political purposes or for reasons more private or personal in nature. Further, as Rosemarie Garland-Thomson has claimed, the proliferation of "realistic" visual images of disability in the service of politics, "charity" photography in particular, often invites false identification between the able viewer and the disabled subject.[45] Any ensuing political or social action in such instances, Garland-Thomson argues, is motivated by a fear that we could end up like the subject, a "warn[ing] . . . against becoming disabled" that reinscribes disability as a horrific condition without engendering an understanding of what the disabled him or herself may feel.[46] Too, I will add that realistic images of disability meant to inspire action just as commonly rely on disidentification, a point Garland-Thomson also makes. We express "pity" for the poor "other," while distancing ourselves as we take comfort in our own good fortune. The very act of representation, no matter how "authentic," aids in this estrangement precisely because the disabled are mediated, not actually present as real bodies and real minds. If we do act, then, it is frequently taken from a safe emotional, psychological, and physical proximity: a check in the mail, for example, or a letter to a representative.

While Brooks therefore enters into potentially explosive territory as she uses disabled bodies as emblems of the catastrophe of war, her writing displays an acute awareness that simply exhibiting broken bodies was not, in itself, enough for her readers to apprehend war's devastation or compel them to preventative action. "Pity," an intellectual distancing reaction, must be supplanted by "sympathy," which, in Brooks's literary vocabulary, denotes a corporeal (and connecting) response that reduces the estrangement between the "able" self and the disabled "other."

Between the publication of *A Street in Bronzeville* and *Maud Martha*, Brooks produced her Pulitzer Prize–winning book of poems, *Annie Allen*. Appearing in 1949, this work opens with a poem memorializing her close friend Ed Bland, killed in battle four years prior. In the first of the three other poems, grouped under the title "loose leaves from a loose-leaf war diary," Brooks implies that there is a manner of visual apprehension that will inspire a bodily sympathy in the able viewer—referred to alternately as "watch[ing] and "[see]ing" (110).[47] Beginning with a quotation we imagine she has reproduced from the media "('thousands—

killed in action')," the piece accuses a "you" of refusing the ways of looking that may lead to an appropriate response to war: "You need the untranslatable ice to watch. / You need to loiter a little among the vague / Hushes, the clever evasions of the vagueness" (110).

In this poem, "watch[ing]," "see[ing]," and subsequently feeling the emotions "proper" to warfare—"horror" and uncontained "grief"—are foreclosed by an "intellectual damn" that permits the "you" to only "half-hurt" (110). "Quickly you are well," she writes, "But weary" (110). Brooks indicates that the clarity that comes with looking with "untranslatable ice," a looking not easily recuperated into the obscuring, "vague" rhetoric surrounding war, would inherently disallow the "you" to become "well" so "quickly." This "loiter[ing]" manner of looking is also spatial, given the potential to bring the "you" in closer proximity to war, forcing her to engage other senses: "The purple and black to smell" (110). ". . . How you yawn, have yet to see / Why nothing exhausts you like this sympathy" (110). I will not propose here that Brooks has neatly solved the many problems arising from asking the able-bodied to "falsely" identify with the disabled person or his or her circumstances. Yet her poem makes the implicit claim that identification, however fabricated, may be a necessary step in arousing a somatic correspondence (the "you" *should* feel a sympathetic illness and recognize its symptoms as such). As Toni Cade Bambara once wrote of Brooks's own literary style: it "cause[s] internal bleeding."[48]

Although Brooks avoids specifying the gender of the "you" in this first poem, I have sexed her as female because of Brooks's insistence in binding black male and black female injury in her later work, Maud Martha, and because the writer critiques her character's inability to do just that—failing to envision her own "feminine" debilities in connection to the "masculine" wounds of the disabled men who momentarily insinuate themselves into her imagination. In large measure, this incapacity emanates from Maud Martha's profound need to imagine herself unharmed (relatively) by the sexist and racist violence endemic to a white heteropatriarchal culture. It is also due to a related need to believe she plays no part in abetting the culture's social dysfunction, particularly war, an event that asks women to see themselves outside of its primary functions. She sees herself as neither "victim" nor "perpetrator."

Nor is she altogether insulated from the cultural violence surrounding her. Her half-sight into its workings allows her to experience "half-hurt," contributing, in the end, to her fundamentally divided sense of self. Hence, while the character recognizes the social ills that plague her family, her friends, her race— and of course, Maud Martha herself—she condemns herself to inaction, claiming she has neither the capacity to "resolve nor dismiss" (176). Unable to lull herself

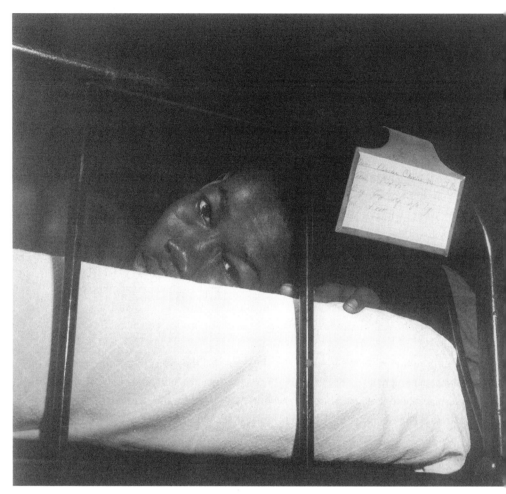

"Charlie Dunston, S1/c, Amputee Case at the Naval Hospital, Philadelphia, PA," Ens.
Thomas Binford, 1945. The photograph of this amputee does not reveal his injuries.
National Archives at College Park, College Park, Maryland.

into complete amnesia, and equally unable to shake her paralysis, Maud Martha looks, assesses, but ultimately tries to repress reality—which she describes in one scene as "ungauzed, self-assertive, cancerous" (20)—by pushing it to the periphery of her consciousness. In this way, the character embodies the very cultural response to socially produced harm that I have suggested Brooks wishes to expose. Like the speaker in "loose leaves," Maud Martha will far too "quickly" become "well."

A darkly humorous scene from the chapter "brotherly love" elucidates Brooks's belief that repression—the will to be well—can have disastrous political implications: a expeditious yet perilous psychic gesture that relieves one of the moral and ethical responsibility to act. Cleaning out the insides of a chicken she is preparing for dinner, Maud Martha becomes increasingly resentful that the meat scarcity caused by the war has given butchers the luxury of selling customers chickens without doing this work themselves. Calling herself "brave," she sets about this "stomach-curving" task:

> People could do this! people could cut a chicken open, take out the mess, with bare hands or a bread knife, pour water in, as in a bag, pour water out, shake the corpse by the neck or by legs, free the straggles of water. Could feel that insinuating slipping bone, survey that soft, that headless death. The fainthearted could do it. But if the chicken were a man!—cold man with no head or feet and with all the little feath—er, hairs to be pulled, and the intestines loosened and beginning to ooze out, and the gizzard yet to be grabbed and the stench beginning to rise! And yet the chicken was a sort of person, a respectable individual, with its own kind of dignity. The difference was in the knowing. What was unreal to you, you could deal with violently. If chickens were ever to be safe, people would have to live with them, and know them, see them loving their children, finishing the evening meal, arranging jealousy.
>
> When the animal was ready for the oven Maud Martha smacked her lips at the thought of her meal. (152)

In this scenario, Maud Martha first only considers the war in terms of its inconvenience, inasmuch as it forces her to do something she would rather not: square off with a dead chicken. Having exposed Maud Martha's shallowness—so we think—Brooks then takes the passage in an unexpected direction, investing her character with insight into how objectifying the "other" makes violence possible (or possibly palatable). But to make this revelation, Martha must also dissociate herself from the act she is committing. "People" and "you" can do "this," not

Maud Martha, who after all needs to eat, and whose healthy appetite has not been in the least diminished.

More significantly, this form of repression permits Maud Martha to mistakenly believe that her hands are still clean, in a manner of speaking. "The bread knife had it all to do," she thinks, "for she had no intention of putting her hand in there" (151). This ability to exempt herself from the world's "nasty, nasty mess" (151) is crucial to Maud Martha's self-perception; moreover, as I have suggested, it is central to her method of survival as a black woman in a sexist, racist nation. Repeatedly within the narrative Maud Martha lauds herself for being "good." An early chapter, "you're being so good, so kind," finds a young Maud Martha feeling grateful that a white schoolmate will visit her home; accordingly, she frantically scrambles to make her house look proper for her little guest, covering tears in the family sofa, even opening windows in case the rumor that "colored people's houses necessarily had . . . an unpleasant smell" were actually true (17). He is "benefactor," she tells herself, she "recipient" (18). Unveiling the depth of Maud Martha's double consciousness, "you're being so good, so kind" refers to how Maud Martha hopes the boy—whom she sees as a rudimentary embodiment of "the entire Caucasian plan" (18)—will interpret her performance of graciousness.

As this episode foreshadows, the adult Maud Martha will grow to meet the criteria for female "goodness" as defined within the 1950s heteropatriarchal lexicon. She is chaste, clean, well-mannered; an exemplary homemaker; a dutiful (if discontented) wife and mother; a loyal daughter. She is, in other words, both compliant and constricted. A fully disciplined black female subject, she dares not behave in an unruly or "unfeminine" manner, a trade-off she makes to be considered "normal" and lead a "normal," if mundane, life. However, Brooks shows us that her decision is hardly benign; the bargain that she has struck will inevitably affect more than Maud Martha's own dulled existence. In one of the most devastating and telling scenes in the work, her mother informs her that Maud Martha's sister, the light-skinned and delicate Helen, the object of Maud Martha's ceaseless envy, is to be married:

> "Helen thinks she is going to Marry Doctor Williams."
> "Our own family doctor. Not our own family doctor!"
> "She says her mind's about made up."
> "But he's over fifty years old."
> "She says he's steady . . . and will give her a decent home."
> "And what do you say?"
> "I say, it's a hard cold world and a woman had better do all she can to help

herself get along as long as what she does is honest. It isn't as if she didn't like Doctor Williams."

"She always did, yes. Ever since we were children and he used to bring her licorice sticks, and forgot to bring any to me, except very seldom."

"It isn't as if she merely sold herself. She'll try to make him happy, I'm sure. Helen was always a good girl. And in any marriage, the honeymoon is soon over."

"What does poppa say?"

"He's thinking of changing doctors." (168)

The conversation about Helen ends there; Maud Martha and her mother move on to another subject. But not before the institution of marriage is laid bare: exposed, in this case, as an economic transaction that permits men to prey on women who aspire to its ostensible comforts and "safety." Far from a site of "normalization," the domestic is ready to mask aberrant behaviors—is indeed receptive to them—even something as violent and destructive as a relationship that might have begun as pedophilia. Though Maud Martha recognizes this, she nevertheless colludes in her mother's and father's passive acceptance of her sister's situation. Once more, her insights do not lead to action; Brooks reveals that the "good" Maud Martha is actually a very bad girl: complicit in another black woman's damage.

The mother's faulty logic sheds light on the degree to which the performance of heteronormality is given (falsely) rehabilitative powers. If Helen is a "good girl" (like Martha), her marriage must also be a "good" one. The belief in the "normality" of Helen's marriage depends upon creating the illusion of wholesomeness; in turn, the illusion of wholesomeness rests upon the delusion that Helen herself is "whole." Any likely emotional and psychological problems arising from the implied pedophilia are less important, it seems, than the tantalizing prospect of black upward mobility. Marrying "well," as it were, will miraculously remedy any of Helen's inner damage.

Similarly, then, Maud Martha's investment in "donat[ing] to the world a good Maud Martha" (22), as Brooks writes, helps her to maintain her own illusion of psychic wholeness. Her self-named deficiency, "her hungriest lack—not much voice," is in fact reminiscent of the confession a black soldier makes in one of Brooks's war sonnets: "I am very hungry. I am incomplete" (66). Both Maud Martha and the soldier may be superficially whole, bodily intact, yet they also feel an interior insufficiency, something missing within their invisible insides. Immediately before acknowledging her "lack" of voice, Maud Martha characterizes the emotions she is loath to exteriorize as a faceless entity: "There were these scraps of baffled hate in her, hate with no eyes, no smile . . ." (176). Brooks's decision to personify Maud Martha's hate is critical to the way disability functions in the novel, as it suggests that the unwhole person dwelling within Maud Martha is actually a repressed image of self—her "disabled" double—the woman she will not let anyone see. While Maud Martha may consider the repression of her disabled self a private gesture, her desire to hide her disfigured "altered" ego parallels the manner in which those thought disabled were kept from public view (when not being made profitable spectacles) or rehabilitated into disappearing, normalized beyond recognition. That Brooks conceives of this figure without eyes or the capacity to smile underscores the socially and politically "danger" posed by the disabled's visibility: Maud Martha's disabled self is incapable of donning the mask so necessary to her "able" self's performance of the "good," the wholesome, the "normal."

Moreover, Maud Martha's physically and psychologically fragmented double, constituted by "scraps" of emotion, can be read as a representation of the fragmentation inherent to feminine subjectivity, a concept that Lennard Davis has provocatively interpreted within a disability studies framework.[49] Following Lacan, Davis reminds us that the mistaken belief in our bodily integrity, our wholeness, is a requisite for proper socialization—being accepted and desired by the Other, whose laws we must obey, whose institutions we must be permitted to enter. This means we must first regulate ourselves, a process that begins by denying the original experiences of our bodies as infants: the "turbulent" and erratic "movements" of our flailing arms and legs,[50] limbs that feel distinct, disconnected from one another. Lacan theorizes that this correct apprehension of our physicality is initially interrupted when we see ourselves in a mirror and identify these refracted images—which appear coherent—as "self." Here, I will also point out that Lacan suggests our ability to look in the mirror at this stage is only made possible by a prosthetic: "Unable as yet to walk, or even to stand up, and held tightly as he is by some support, human or artificial (what, in France, we call a 'trotte-bebé'), he nevertheless overcomes."[51]

Davis claims that "real" disabled bodies are therefore rejected as "the reminders of the whole" self "about to come apart at the seams,"[52] a rejection arising from the fear that we, like the disabled, will be expelled from the social order. This need to avoid these reminders, very much like Maud Martha's repression of her double ("*the imago of one's body*," Lacan writes, can manifest itself "in the appearances of the *double*"),[53] partly explains Western culture's attraction to the idealized human form. The ideal is epitomized in artistic renderings of the nude—the female nude in particular. The perfected female form in this instance offers something beyond the repression of our "real" fragmentation; it allows us to suppress the effects of the violent and violating objectification of women, most valued in terms of their individual parts: faces, legs, breasts. Davis theorizes that this valuation may explain the unlikely appeal of the Venus de Milo, a sculpture we know as an amputated figure. As a representation of disability and of our own tentative state, she should only inspire repulsion, yet she arouses desire as the spectator is allowed to consume a representation of a woman dismembered—and therefore allegedly helpless—fixed in the submissive state that makes femininity both appealing and socially useful. At the same time, the viewer can defer acknowledging the pleasure he feels in consuming a "mutilated" female body by reconstructing her as "whole," imaginatively retrieving the body parts that were once present, what Davis calls her "phantom limbs."[54] This reconstitution enables the cultural fantasy that women are not, in fact, mutilated subjects and that we do not, in fact, want them in this state.

The fragmentation arising from female objectification is of course compounded by race; if women are reduced to "parts," black women are split even further as they are asked to pry the signs of blackness from their bodies and as blackness is ripped from their bodies and reshaped into a myriad of cultural signifiers. This leads me back to the images of disabled soldiers in "back from the wars!" that have jarred critics, as Brooks employs stream of consciousness to maneuver Maud Martha's mind from "the men with two arms off and two legs off, the men with the parts of faces" to "the usual representations of womanly Beauty, pale and pompadoured," and finally to "the stories of the latest of the Georgia and Mississippi lynchings . . ." (179). The uncovering of male disability here is juxtaposed with the very manner of representation designed to mask feminine fragmentation and rehabilitate female blackness into something desirable: a social promise that can only pledge to bring about more debility. That the disabled soldiers and stories of lynched bodies surface seemingly from nowhere then just as quickly disappear can again be explained in terms of Maud Martha's repression of her own "disabled" double. As Lacan states, "imagos" of our fragmented bodies, such as "mutilation, dismemberment . . . bursting open of the body," frequently emerge in the expressions of the unconscious, in our "hallucinations, dreams."[55] Our unconscious therefore drives us in two directions: toward identifying with whole images of the body that allow us the charade of coherence, and toward identifying with those imagos we instinctively recognize as "us."[56] Accordingly, Maud Martha's unconscious begs her, albeit in vain, to make the crucial identification that her conscious mind will not—an identification that if recognized, would destabilize the social order. Thus, the *conscious* identification with disabled bodies I referred to earlier (the "untranslatable watching" and somatic sympathy that precipitates social action) reveals its subversive potential. Recall Maud Martha's immediate reaction: "Then her guts divided." This somatic correspondence, both a sympathetic response to their condition and a brief suggestion of hers, will nonetheless be promptly displaced by intellectualism: "and it was doubtful whether the ridiculousness of man would ever completely succeed in destroying the world" (179). Although her body, like those of the soldiers, is left in pieces, Maud Martha will not "loiter" among the wreckage long enough to "see."

Another soldier from the sonnets, exhausted by the apparent endlessness of the war, describes its perpetuity to his lover: "This morning men deliver wounds and death. / They will deliver death and wounds tomorrow. / And I doubt all. You. Or a Violet" (73). Part of the reason Maud Martha diminishes the impact of war in thoughts of natural regeneration—the flowers emerging from corpses, the very violet the soldier in this poem doubts—is rooted, we learn, in her pregnancy. "And in the meantime," she rhapsodizes, "she was going to have another baby" (180). The dichotomy is familiar. Men "deliver wounds"; women deliver life. I will nevertheless resist dismissing the conclusion of the novel as Brooks's reflexive capitulation to the ideologies attendant with gender inscription, or as a simple need to tack on a "happy ending" to convince us that "another baby" will finally replenish Maud Martha's malnourished insides. All prior evidence in the text points to the contrary. If Maud Martha herself romanticizes her first pregnancy, her childbirth, and her subsequent relationship to her daughter, Brooks does not offer Maud Martha a part within the cultural script her character fumblingly tries to follow.

Indeed, in a much-examined scene from the work, Maud Martha, big with her first child and feeling particularly unattractive, agonizes silently as her husband flirts with another, light-skinned woman at a social event. Secretly enraged, she declares (only to her "selves," of course) that she could "go over there and scratch her upsweep down. I could spit on her back. . . . 'Listen,' I could scream, 'I'm making a baby for this man and I mean to do it in peace!' " (88). When the anticipated moment of delivery does arrive, described in "a birth," Maud Martha's will to be well results in a denial of her own bodily experiences and in a refusal to consider the implications of "motherhood." The title Brooks gives this chapter immediately signals Maud Martha's dissociation, employing the abstracting article "a" rather than, for instance, the personal pronoun "her," or even the more specific article "the." Not even recognizing that she is about to give birth—her husband, Paul, must tell her what is happening—she afterwards declares that she feels "strong enough to go out and shovel coal" (98). "Having a baby," she exclaims to a neighbor, "is *nothing*. . . . Nothing at all" (98). Maud Martha can think of it as "nothing" because she decides not to think: "Maud

Martha's thoughts did not dwell long on the fact of the baby. . . . She preferred to think, now, about how well she felt" (98). To further empty the event of any romantic content, Brooks has Maud Martha compare childbirth to a "bowel movement" and Paul describe the newborn as "gray and greasy" (96, 97). Perhaps he sees what Maud Martha does not; that, in psychoanalytic terms, she has just given birth to the abject subject. Put plainly, she has "shit," has expelled all the "crap" she has heretofore quietly swallowed, has created another black human being the culture will treat as "dirt." As Brooks has Maud Martha muse, "Was it, she suddenly wondered, as hard to watch suffering as it was to *bear* it?" (97).[57]

In "Woman's Error and Her Debt," an essay the birth control advocate Margaret Sanger published just after World War I, Sanger in fact holds women responsible for war.[58] Their "error," Sanger claims, is continuing to populate a world already scrambling for resources: "While wringing their hands over each fresh horror, [women] submit anew to their task of producing the multitudes who will bring about the *next* tragedy of civilization."[59] Put in Brooks's language, women bear suffering; in Sanger's, they also bear the blame for it. We know, however, that Sanger was also a eugenicist (and racialist) who believed in sterilizing the mentally and physically disabled as a means of ridding the world of "defectives."[60] As she notoriously proclaimed in a later book, *The Pivot of Civilization*: "Every single case of inherited defect, every malformed child, every congenitally tainted human being brought into the world is of infinite importance to that poor individual; but it is of scarcely less importance to the rest of us . . . who must pay for these biological and racial mistakes."[61] For African Americans, Sanger's views on sterilization came dangerously close to advocating the eradication of races and ethnicities too frequently thought of as "biological and racial mistakes." Moreover, given that black women had often been tricked into "consenting" to sterilization and abortion, her position proved disconcerting,[62] especially in light of her instrumental role in the Negro Project,[63] a birth-control initiative aimed at black women in the South.

But Sanger's call for birth control as a solution to war, if aimed at all women, is no less troubling in its implications. Sanger endeavors to take an undeniably natural biological process that women should feel free to choose—or not—and frame it as pathological. The decision to bear multiple children contributes not only to woman's own "physical degeneracy," as she writes in *Pivot*,[64] but to the degeneracy of all humanity. Undoubtedly, women's ability to exercise control over their own reproductive decisions has benefits on multiple levels. Yet Sanger's inverted logic in relation to war and childbearing diverts attention away from the very *social* pathologies creating conflict (such as capitalist hoarding) that led her to characterize bringing children into the world as an unhealthy act to begin with. Stiker's historicism is especially pertinent here. Just as the injured soldiers demobilized in France became "objects of repair" after the same war, Sanger points to the body as the problem, thereby naturalizing war as an inevitable response to the "driving power of a population too large for its borders."[65] Certainly, Brooks's decision to complicate the male/female roles ascribed in warfare by making Maud Martha complicit in its continuance is meant to raise questions around similar issues, particularly her description of an obstinately gleeful Maud Martha using her pregnant body as a buffer against images of debility. And yet, I will suggest that Brooks's position is not to be interpreted as antireproduction (or even proreproduction). Rather, Maud Martha's "error" lies in her steadfast unwillingness to change the world the child will be forced to negotiate—or to make that attempt, at the very least. To make a baby "in peace," to make "peace" for her baby, Maud Martha would have to make "peace" possible, which requires more than surrendering quietly when confronted with injustice. For instance, when faced with her daughter Paulette's recognition that a low-rent department store Santa Claus has treated her differently from the white children—refusing to look at her or shake her hand—Maud Martha simply offers a flurry of excuses for his behavior. Not that we entirely blame Maud Martha for her stealthy evasions, but we wonder at their rationale. Her wish, she claims, is to "keep [for Paulette] that land of blue! . . . and Santa every winter's lord . . . who never looks grotesque, who never has occasion to pull the chain and flush the toilet" (176). Her wish, in other words, is to keep white American mythologies intact, and to keep her daughter from ever discovering whites are merely what blacks are: human, and sometimes grotesque ones at that.

What Brooks knew, and what Maud Martha does not, is that another war was imminent; World War I, the "war to end all wars" had done nothing of the sort, nor had the one that followed. This may account for Brooks's decision to explore Maud Martha's psychic and political limbo: resentful of war rations, she is hardly working for "V"; gliding over reports of lynchings, neither is she working for "Double V." Man may destroy man, or perhaps not. Like the disabled soldiers' minds and bodies in "gay chaps in the bar," Maud Martha's consciousness is unrehabilitated at the novel's conclusion, her wounds still open—Brooks's means of keeping matters unresolved: "What, *what* am I to do with all this life?" (178). And like those poems, *Maud Martha* is also a fractured text. We think we have been given Maud Martha's "whole" story, if episodically, but important parts are missing: her nuptials, for example, or the fact that her brother Harry had been sent to war, something we only learn in the same instance of his homecoming. In spite of these similarities, it bears repeating that the black soldiers' disabilities are not the "same as" Maud Martha's; the "masculine" debilities caused by war are not the "same as" the "feminine" debilities resulting from Maud Martha's "wars" with patriarchy, white supremacy, or heteronormativity. Neither does the spectator/reader "become" the disabled through "watching," "seeing," or somatic sympathy. There are no easy equivalents in Brooks's politics. But in closing the distances between masculine and feminine injury, the able and the disabled, and among the differently damaged, Brooks uses her war writing to argue that very few—if any—escape the effects of a society whose very structures engender destruction. It seems that the plural in "back from the wars!" also refers to Maud Martha's war.

Finally, in thinking about Davis's claim about the powerful role Western art plays in the denial of disability, I find it interesting, then, that Maud Martha is not only a repressed black female subject but also a repressed artist. The visual power Brooks gives her character, her gift of looking with an artist's eye, is nonetheless lost within Maud Martha's instinct to beautify what she apprehends. In "spring landscape: a detail," she remarks upon the "gray" sky, but notes that the "sun was making little silver promises up there"; assessing the day as a "rather bleak" one for June, "still," she insists, "there were these little promises, just under cover" (4). The kind of artist Maud Martha would become, had she let herself become one, would probably be at odds with the writer who created her: the writer who allows herself to traverse a cultural and corporeal landscape marked by damage, assess what she sees, and offer us the parts other black war writers preferred to bury "in a hush, infallible and sincere."

CONCLUSION: LET THIS DYING BE FOR SOMETHING

And Then We Heard the Thunder and the Military Neoslave Narrative

In March of 1942, a nine-day series of violent confrontations took place between white and black U.S. troops stationed in Brisbane, Australia. The report on the incident issued by C. H. Barnwell, the inspector general for the army's operations in the region, offers an uncertain assessment of its origins: "Opinions differ as to the causes of the clashes."[1] Nevertheless, he goes on to claim that the catalyst appeared to be white soldiers' barring African American soldiers from Australian-owned "dance halls and skating rinks," suggesting that "the initial fault lies not with negro troops." He also notes the root causes lay in the ongoing antiblack "harassment of negro troops by white troops."[2] The "negro troops," he writes, became "resentful toward the American white troops, culminating in disorders of greater proportions and involving the banding together of negro soldiers in the city streets."[3] Although the disturbances in Brisbane were unusual in their duration, racial disturbances were frequent occurrences during the war: "riots" prompted by racial tensions, mob violence against minority soldiers, mob violence by minority soldiers against whites, white civilians attacking black and minority soldiers, minority insurgences against white superiors, and all manner of lesser, interethnic skirmishes labeled "racial," accurately or inaccurately.[4] There was at least one documented mutiny led by fifty black sailors stationed at Port Chicago, a munitions facility in California, one of the largest events of its kind in naval history.[5] While Barnwell's official report on Brisbane fails to specify what actually happened as a result of "the banding together of negro soldiers," in unofficial accounts, the black soldiers had armed themselves, fearing that the white soldiers might use the occasion to slaughter them. John Oliver Killens chooses to end his Pulitzer Prize–nominated novel *And Then We Heard the Thunder*,[6] a sprawling meditation on World War II and the Jim Crow military, with a fictionalized version of that event.

Those contemporary reviews noting Killens's inclusion of the incident each use a quite different label to describe the conflict: it is "a mutiny" in one, a "battle" in another; in others it is a "race war" or a "bloody race riot."[7] These varying descriptors become critical to understanding how critics of the novel attempted to make sense of the clash some twenty years after it had occurred. None of these labels is inherently accurate, of course, but they do serve as important indexes of the politics critics brought to bear on the novel. On one end of the spectrum, a mutiny would imply planning, a perhaps necessary insubordination with a definitive target, coordinated and controlled; on the other end, "a bloody riot" makes the event appear a spontaneous explosion of violence, generalized and undirected: the allegedly "inarticulate" expression of the dispossessed. Ted Poston, calling it "the best kept secret of the war," writes that the black soldiers were not merely armed but "armed with weapons of mass modern warfare,"[8] transforming Brisbane (renamed Bainbridge in the novel) into an event that could have brought about a racially motivated apocalypse. Killens himself calls it a "racial war"; in other words, politics, as von Clausewitz writes, "by other means." While the deployment of the term "war" may seem an effort to legitimize the conflict—a material manifestation of the "two front war" of the Double V campaign—its appearance comes at the tail end of a novel that is, I will argue, an uncompromising critique of nationalist and imperialist warfare. In this concluding chapter, I will offer a brief reading of *And Then We Heard the Thunder*, reading this "racial war" within other acts of violence central to the narrative to determine how Killens himself makes sense of Brisbane within this larger context of U.S. warfare: the same question Killens's protagonist will ask himself when the tensions subside.

At the beginning of Killens's work, Solomon Saunders, a black army draftee from Harlem, vows to commit his experiences in the army to paper. Later in the narrative, as he is sailing from the United States toward the Pacific theater of war, he keeps the promise he has made to himself: "Some of his hours he spent getting a novel started. He wrote pages, he tore up pages. He tried realism, naturalism, he tried streams of consciousness. He tried to remember Creative Writing courses he had had at City College. He sweated over pages, till finally he wrote five pages to his liking and he felt like celebrating" (256). In 1963 Killens would publish that novel, unleashing it into a nation in racial turmoil. Although two political milestones had been reached prior to the appearance of Killens's work—the military had been desegregated in 1948 and *Brown vs. the Board of Education* had been decided in 1954—the critical civil rights legislation of 1964 and

1968 had yet to be enacted. While the 1963 March on Washington would present a unified black population engaged in peaceful protest, the mainstream civil rights movement was actually splintering, competing with emerging veins of Black Nationalism that were arguably more influential than its nineteenth- and early twentieth-century predecessors. Positioning themselves in part as alternatives to the larger movement's "assimilationist" aims and what was perceived as a concessionary "gradualism," they would question the movement's commitment to "nonviolence," a philosophy that would seem less convincing, even antiquated, in the aftermath of successful African independence movements that had used violence to "force the settler" to relent, in Fanon's words. The founding documents of the Organization of Afro-American Unity (OAAU) and the Black Panthers, published in 1964 and 1968 respectively, both include statements justifying a recourse to violence as a necessary means of "self defense." The OAAU's treatise contained the notorious phrase "by any and all means necessary";[9] the Panthers' was even more explicit, ending with a simple statement: "GUNS BABY GUNS."[10]

Killens's novel also appeared on the eve of one of the most bloody decades in the twentieth century—the assassinations of Medgar Evers, Martin Luther King, the Kennedys, Malcolm X; the murders of Schwerner, Cheney, and Goodman; the hosing, beating, and tear gassing of peaceful civil rights protesters in Birmingham; the church bombing in that city the following year; the Watts riots; the explosion of the Vietnam War into the American consciousness. Given this volatile environment, it would be logical to assume that Killens's treatment of violence would be substantially different from the black American war novels published before his work.

It is. But my reading of Thunder will suggest that the novel is not, as some have intimated, solely the product of a consciousness transformed by the violence of that era. More pointedly, neither is it only a product of the many forms of antiblack violence leveled at African Americans specifically or of the violent solutions some Black Nationalist organizations proposed to answer it. Though many Americans, black and white, were aghast at this "new" breed of revolutionary, the moral and ethical legitimization of violence as a tool of the oppressed black classes had much philosophical precedent. The early nineteenth-century advocates of Black Nationalism, such as David Walker, Henry Highland Garnet, and Maria Stewart, among others, had laid the same claims to violence as the later organizations. But even if we place the long legacy of Nationalist validations of revolutionary tactics aside, any reading that would frame And Then We Heard the Thunder's treatment of the political aspects of violence within a 1960s framework exclusively would also mean forgetting that there had hardly been a "quiet" decade in American history—wars, genocide, lynchings, labor clashes, anti-worker violence, riots, and assassinations were facts of a nation in constant social and political upheaval. Indeed, in *Black Man's Burden*,[11] a collection of essays published three years after his novel, Killens will issue that very analysis:

> We have always been a nation of violence. Our, rather, your proud forefathers killed off an entire race whom they arrogantly called Indians. . . . And when John Fitzgerald Kennedy was assassinated little white children cheered in Dallas schools, and as at least one newspaper morbidly pointed out, in the comparatively short time of our existence as a nation we have assassinated more of our leaders than any nation in history. . . . We also dropped the most devastating bombs ever dropped in a military operation, and we dropped them on civilians. (121)

Earlier in the work, he makes the case more succinctly: "There is much inhumanity, violence and brutality in our nation's history. We must face that" (54).

Even more significantly, *Thunder* was in fact begun well before the 1960s. As Keith Gilyard points out in his recent book on Killens's writings, sections of the novel were completed in the 1950s, drawing from Killens's dyspeptic 1952 short story about the Korean War, "God Bless America," his first published work of fiction.[12] Gilyard also provides evidence indicating that other parts may have been written as early as the 1940s, just after the writer was demobilized from the army. Like Saunders, Killens had been drafted in 1942, serving in an amphibian unit in the South Pacific, where he sets the second half of his novel. Before his conscription, Killens was studying law—also like Saunders—yet his stint in the military would irrevocably alter the direction his life would take: "With the stench of blood and shit still in my nostrils, I reasoned that a lawyer was not a revolutionary by the very nature of his position in society. . . . Right or wrong, this was my rationalization for not going back and completing my last year of law school."[13]

"The stench of blood and shit" would also provide his impetus for writing. Although Killens became an avowed Black Nationalist "revolutionary," a writer in the cultural arm of the movement, and while it is evident that the writer grafted Nationalist politics into earlier versions of the work, his profoundly dystopic vision of warfare was initially borne out of his firsthand experience as a battle soldier in World War II. This might not seem an altogether groundbreaking assertion, especially since it has been derived from Killens's own description of his "birth" as a novelist. It is nonetheless a necessary one. Similar to *Home to Harlem*, a novel whose content, I argued, has been circumscribed by its appearance during the Harlem Renaissance, the curiously little scholarship existing about *Thunder* tends toward a single issue: whether Killens's evisceration of the Jim Crow military leads him to adopt a stance more "nationalist" or "integrationist." Thus, while the novel is by all measures a semiautobiographical work, war becomes incidental in many analyses; the author's years in the South Pacific an interesting biographical detail when they are mentioned at all.[14] However, in terms of the integrationist-nationalist debate—not an unimportant one—it seems that Killens advocates neither, an observation Gilyard also makes.[15] Both are given hearings; both are determined to have their merits. In Black Man's Burden, Killens indicates that envisioning black political agitation in such starkly contrasting terms obscures its fundamental goals: "The thing that unites all black Americans is not our desire to integrate into this society, or to separate from it, but our undivided determination to be free men and women in this American society" (172). What becomes abundantly clear in reading Thunder is that his criticism of the military's racist practices is double-edged—an equally damning assessment of blacks who capitulate to its demands, of those who adopt an assimilationist/accommodationist mind-set that equates black progress with behavioral and ideological "identicalness." "We are not fighting," Killens frankly states in Burden's opening essay, "for the right to be like you" (12).

But even more crucial here is the way the writer binds his denunciation of accommodationism to his renunciation of warfare. Note the shift in his statements about U.S. violence. The accusation against the white "you," "your forefathers," is displaced by a "we"; the "we" who dropped bombs on Nagasaki and Hiroshima. This switch, one he will make throughout Black Man's Burden, is an acknowledgement of black participation in the "nasty, nasty mess" of war,[16] the discomfiting fact that I have claimed African American war writers have struggled to accept and have developed strategies to avoid. Thus in Killens's political imagination, consenting to war may be the greatest and most devastating accommodation of them all. It is partly for that reason that And Then We Heard the Thunder will extend beyond the comparatively safe political parameters of the novels produced by Brown, Harper, Gilmore, Daly, and Smith. In other words, Thunder must be read as more than an examination of how World War II affected blacks who served, a comparison of "external" and "internal" warfare, or even more broadly, as an exploration of how the war affected those blacks across the diaspora impacted by the war's geographical scope, the perspective McKay brought to World War I. Killens will take up those issues, certainly. However, in giving room to those concerns, he does not let them crowd out an analysis of war on its own terms.

The title Killens gives the novel—And Then We Heard the Thunder, borrowed from a haunting discursive image Harriet Tubman drew of the Civil War—offers an early indication of how the novel will represent warfare. Killens reproduces Tubman's description as an epigraph to the work: "And then we saw the lightning, and that was the guns. And then we heard the thunder and that was the big guns. And then we heard the rain falling and that was the drops of blood falling. And when we came to get in the crops, it was dead men that we reaped." It is important that he chooses words spoken by a former soldier and former slave. Even the Civil War—the object of romanticizing, sanitizing myth—is, for Tubman, blood, death, terror. In Killens's perspective, World War II, an event he labels "the Second World-Wide Madness,"[17] has merely brought more of the same.

Soldiers and Slaves

Following the cycle Tubman describes—in which war reaps death—Killens divides his novel into four books: "Planting Season," "Cultivation," "Lightning-Thunder-Rainfall," and finally, "The Crop." The novel begins as Saunders, married and middle class, prepares to leave his wife and his life in Harlem for the army. Although he expresses reticence, his social-climbing wife, Millie, implores him to make the most of his lot, convincing him that he can use his service to facilitate upward mobility: "I know you're not going into the army with a chip on your shoulder. Forget about the race problem at least for the duration. Be an American instead of a Negro . . . and while you're in the Army work for those promotions just like in civilian life" (6). He struggles with heeding her "upward and onward" racial mantra, questioning her desire to be "accepted" in the white "world" as a product of her "sheltered, bourgeois colored life" (6). But after having a disturbing dream in which the "white couple" who owns their apartment admonishes him for creating "a house divided" (domestically and nationally, it appears), he decides to pledge himself wholly to the military (7). Not wanting to seem unpatriotic in the eyes of white America, and equally unwilling to compromise the prospects of his race, he defers his misgivings. "Now," he says to himself, "I am a soldier. I'll be the best damn soldier in the Army of the United States of America" (7).

The work then focuses on a group of black soldiers as they move together from a training camp in Georgia to a shipping station in California and, finally, to the Pacific theater where they are deployed to the Philippines and Australia. Like Smith, Killens uses these men to voice a range of attitudes toward black military service: "Buck Rogers," an opportunistic "Uncle Thomas" (94); the voracious reader and "militant" Bookworm, who campaigns for a Section Eight by pretending to be gay ("I really don't look good in Khaki," he notes) (20); Scotty, a southerner who frequently goes AWOL as a means of resistance; the irreverent "Bucket-head," who issues sharp racial analyses of the war; "General" Grant, a radicalized Black Nationalist Trinidadian; Quiet Man, who simply attempts to stay out of the fracas. If this range falls rather narrowly into anti-establishment sentiments, the major white characters are nearly uniformly authoritarian and racist, with the notable exception of Samuels, a liberal Jewish commander with genuine respect for the men below him. Samuels's antithesis is embodied in the condescending Captain Rutherford, the ."Great White Father" (284), "the one that cracked the whip" (84): "The men of H company called it Hell company but the men of the other companies of the regiment called it 'Rutherford's Planta-tion,' and the men of H Company had earned the title of 'Rutherford's Slaves'" (84). The legion of lowly "cracker" MPs who watch, harass, and beat the black men regularly to keep them "in line" are, in Killens's version of the army, nothing more than overseers in military uniforms. In this metaphorical environ, perhaps best described as a military neoslave narrative, the favored Saunders is destined to become a "slave . . . in the Big House," as Scotty calls him, while labeling himself a "field hand" (88).

In the introduction to this study, I noted that black American war writers tend to make this move almost reflexively, invoking the dynamics of slavery to char-acterize relationships between black men and their white superiors. However much Killens's rescripting of the military into a plantation resonates with earlier writers' gestures, it just as greatly reflects his professed investment in black narratives rooted in the South, Killens's place of birth and his spiritual home. Yet the *manner* in which he transforms the military into a plantation scene parallels the particular way African American and other liberal and left historians were revising "standard" histories of slavery during the 1960s. These revisions com-plemented prior efforts to dispel notions that slaves were "contented participants in a pastoral fantasy," to return to Leonard Cassuto's words.[18] Aside from the discovery of the many narratives describing the innumerable instances of black flight, historians had also unearthed evidence pointing to the pervasiveness of other forms of disruption—rebellions, murders, work stoppages, the intentional destruction of machinery—that led them to reconsider slaves as dedicated sub-versives who attempted to undermine the system at each and every opportunity.[19] While the more insistent versions of this reinterpretation of slavery might appear overly corrective in hindsight, they added necessary dimension to the under-standing of "slave personality,"[20] discovering agency in those who did not suc-ceed in running away, or more pointedly, in those who never attempted it: all too often dismissed as passive victims of a system that had crushed their wills and constricted their spirits. In a similar fashion, most of the black soldiers in Killens's novel—"Rutherford's slaves"—are described as strong, capable, quick-minded, witty men; but drafted into service against their will, they are also shown as defiant "malcontents" who want out of a racially stratified and discriminatory institution by using whatever means at their disposal. Barring that possibility, they will disturb and trouble its operations. In "The Black Psyche," the celebrated essay from *Black Man's Burden* that riveted contemporary black critics and writers, Killens describes his discovery of this aspect of "slave personality":

> I did considerable research on that by-gone "utopian" era, and I got a very different picture, slightly less romantic. I found that the slaves were so happy that most of the plantation owners couldn't afford the astronomical rates of fire insurance. Those rapturous slaves kept setting fire to the cotton patches, burning down the plantation, every day the good Lord sent them. They organized countless insurrections, killed their masters, poisoned their mistresses, even put spiders in the Big House soup. They demonstrated their contentment in most peculiar ways. (6)

It seems evident that the writer's desire to link these men to an empowering legacy of black resistance to white oppression was infinitely more important to his project than presenting them as "patriots." As he remarks in that essay, "We don't break into cheers any more when the cowboys chase the Indians across the movie screen, or when the Army finally captures old John Brown" (6). Certainly, none of Killens's men will die like Daly's protagonist—embracing the white superior who persecuted him.

In what amounts to a political bildungsroman, *Thunder* will allow Saunders to escape his original destiny—to be a flunky for those who run the "Big House." The initial attitudes he held toward the military, racial mobility, and warfare will be tested, and, in the end, reworked altogether; the vague, abstract conceptualizations he has of all three disintegrating as he is forced to confront the actuality of each: white supremacist army structures, black men from classes and environments different from his own, and, not least of all, the reality of battle. Killens will deploy several narratives to trace Saunders's first evolution, his transition from an "assimilationist" Negro to an enlightened "race man." As it increasingly dawns on him that Captain Rutherford, who has promised to look out for him, relies on Saunders as a racial intermediary who will quell the black men's discontent, he will switch his allegiance to his fellow soldiers, finding himself especially, if inexplicably, drawn to Scotty, "chained" to him, as Killens writes. After he falls in love with a black woman who is not his wife—Fannie Mae, a self-described "militant" from Georgia, a person he comes to see as his "alter ego . . . the *I* that I aspire to be" (168)—he will question the basis of his bourgeois marriage. And when he later learns his wife has died giving birth to his son, he will resist entering into a relationship with a white Australian nurse desperate for him, holding out instead for a future with Fannie Mae. The kinship that Saunders feels for Scotty and Fannie Mae, both southerners, is hardly accidental. Killens also intends for Saunders's transition to mark the acceptance of a racial consciousness rooted in the South, black southern history, and the experience of slavery. This burgeoning awareness is articulated, quite literally, as a "verbal exchange." Analyzing the function of literacy in the novel, Gilyard observes that Saunders will dispense with patriotic rhetoric and parroting his superiors, instead finding himself remembering the black national anthem, "Lift Every Heart and Sing."[21] He will also recall the lyrics from the sorrow songs, whose words and grief tap into an ancestral memory he has repressed, conjuring images of black bodies toiling in the fields. He will realize that he is tied to his ancestors in all ways—historically, culturally, spiritually, and bodily.

Nigger Breaking, Nigger Making

The plantation-military analogy that Killens forwards throughout the novel would seem to position the novel's culminating event, the "racial war," as a slave rebellion, "an opportunity of settling with the 'ole boss' for a long score of cruelty,"[22] as Brown wrote of the Civil War. As might be ascertained from the pleasure Killens expresses at discovering slave resistance, the writer had a great admiration of slave rebels, whom he argued were the true heroes—and models— for black Americans. In *William Styron's Nat Turner: Ten Black Writers Respond*, he famously castigated Styron for using his novel, *The Confessions of Nat Turner*, to turn a "giant" into a "child of pathos."[23] Killens would also write a book about Denmark Vesey,[24] and participated in creating the screenplay for the 1969 *Slaves*, a reworking of *Uncle Tom's Cabin*. Disappointed with the final results, he later turned his ideas for the original script into a novel by the same name.[25] It is quite significant, then, that Killens forges a narrative path toward a "slave rebellion" only to abandon it, as I will argue, preventing the reader from celebrating the racial war as necessary black insurgency. Instead, as the last of one of a series of violent episodes in the novel, the clash becomes the destructive end point of a degenerative spiral downward rather than a moment of black ascension.

Saunders has been in the military merely weeks when he is first offered insight into its corrosive milieu. In this early scene, Bookworm returns to the barracks bloodied by a beating at the hands of "two cracker M.P.s" after a night of drinking in Ebbensville, the town closest to the army's training station. Bookworm explains that he was simply engaging in a little "R & R," when the MPs suddenly crashed the bar, for the sole purpose, he believes, of provoking African American soldiers. Outraged by his refusal to meekly accept their reference to him as a "boy" (58), they forced him into their jeep, carrying him to an isolated spot where they promptly pounded him: "Bleary-eyed, swollen face, sniffling and crying and snuffing his nose, he was a sorry-looking mess" (59). Hearing Bookworm's story shakes Saunders; he "felt like crying himself" (59). This event, to echo Douglass, was Saunders's entry into the "blood stained" gate of U.S. military culture;[26] over the course of the narrative, Saunders, like Douglass, will be "doomed to be a witness and participant."[27] Recalling Douglass even further, Saunders's original status as witness fails to bring about a full understanding of the institution and his position in it. Douglass, as we know, watched in horror as his Aunt Hester's master tied her to a joist and tore into her flesh with a whip. He writes that the bloody "exhibition" "struck" him, indicating that it physically resounded within his own body. Yet, while his sympathy of feeling forces him to recognize that his black body is like hers, he can not bring himself to wholly identify it as the same as hers. As a consequence, he expresses his terror in a self-reflexive statement, a fear, as he writes, that "my turn would be next."[28] Douglass again returns to this self-protective sentiment when describing his master's vicious treatment of Douglass's brother: "to give me a sample of his bloody disposition, [he] took my little brother by the throat, threw him on the ground, and with the heel of his boot stamped upon his head till the blood gushed from his nose and ears . . . well calculated to make me anxious as to my fate."[29] In much the same way, Saunders, spared being the object of violence thus far, remains corporeally divorced from "Rutherford's slaves": a distance he hopes might save him from their abjection. Indeed, when Bookworm says he wants to get a gun, or at least lodge a formal complaint, Saunders talks him down, endeavoring to persuade Bookworm that he was partly responsible: "You were wrong all the way. You were AWOL from the start" (59). Secretly, Saunders feels like "blowing a few M.P. brains out," yet checks these feelings by reaffirming his commitment to becoming an officer "in spite of the cracker M.P.'s in Ebbensville" (59). His self-interested rationalization requires denying Bookworm the opportunity to even fantasize revenge; in so doing, Saunders can resist being drawn into a narrative that will ask him to identify with black degradation and the murderous impulse it inspires.

Paralleling Douglass's final initiation into slavery and the blackness of his body—his stint with the "nigger-breaker" who transforms him into a "brute"[30]—Saunders will be forced into an understanding of his status when he is the victim of an assault similar to Bookworm's. Technically AWOL after visiting his girl-friend in Ebbensville, he is confronted by MPs at the town's bus station who patrol through a throng of black soldiers asking for their passes, a scenario quite clearly alluding to the systematic surveillance and policing of black bodies under slavery. When Saunders fails to produce one he is hustled to a local police station, where he protests its jurisdiction: "You can't hold me here. I'm a soldier" (127).

His status as a soldier is effectively disputed by a string of authority figures, including an army colonel, who summarily dismisses him as little more a "nigger" in spite of the uniform Saunders hopes will protect him. As one MP puts the matter after labeling Saunders a "monkey": "Thinks he's a soldier cause they let him wear a soldier suit" (128). To remind him of who, exactly, he is, they decide to "teach him a lesson," a process that seating him in a chair and asking him to spread his legs: "The colonel grabbed a nightstick from the big cracker cop, his gray eyes gleaming, and he began to beat Solly about his legs and thighs in the direction of his groins, but Solly closed his eyes and fell forward in self defense. . . . They forced him back into the chair again, and the colonel moved in with the nightstick and blow after blow fell upon Solly's thighs and almost in between his legs. . . . At the moment he feared for his manhood, and he had forgotten to fear for his life" (129). Similar to Bob's fate in *If He Hollers*, the military and police cooperate to execute a symbolic lynching, targeting Saunders's penis as the most visible, potent, and offending sign of his masculinity. Detailing a litany of contemporary assaults on "black manhood" in *Burden*—physical, but also political and social—Killens characterizes their aims as "psychological castration": "To grind down black men bit by bit and turn them into eunuchs is the very purpose of the process" (102). In the scene from *Thunder*, the MPs will try their best to beat Saunders out of his "manhood" and into a wretched form of blackness, demanding that he leave one body and inhabit another, imaginary one that can be easily read within a racialist semiotics: "So you're a man? . . . You are nothing but a nigger, nigger," the colonel informs him (128). It is at once an act of embodiment and disembodiment, materialization and abstraction. The "nigger," Killens notes in *Burden*, is an "invention" (11), a creature that may have been dreamed up in slavery but has continued to service whites politically. And therein lies the larger meaning of antiblack violence; it asks that its victims give up the useless masquerade of humanity. Like the goals of the torturer, its perpetuators want black bodies to "confess," to confess to being black, to being "niggers," even if that confession is false.[31] The brutalization of the body is a means to an ends; the ends is to destroy voice, to reduce it to grunts and groans, to make it ultimately say whatever the torturer wants to hear.[32]

This event, however, will not succeed in robbing Saunders of his voice; conversely, it gives him reason to exercise it. He and Bookman draft a letter detailing their experiences and send it off to major black newspapers. Raising his voice in protest marks Saunders's "moment of literacy." But rather than learning to read, as in Douglass's narrative, Gilyard claims that Saunders must learn to give his already extant literacy purpose. As such, the letter more aptly corresponds to the

abolitionist aims leading Douglass to create the narrative itself. Of greater importance to assessing the way violence operates in *Thunder*, the beating also fosters a
corporeal connection to Bookworm that takes shape in this act of black solidarity.
In her provocative meditation on the "Rodney King Incident," Elizabeth Alexander theorizes the potent effects of African Americans' identification with spectacles of black pain. Observing how Emmett Till's decimated body lingered in the
imaginations of black "writers of a certain age, and perhaps, of a certain proximity to Southern roots," she suggests that Till's "story is a touchstone, a rite of
passage that indoctrinated these young people into understanding the vulnerability of their own black bodies, and the way that their fate was interchangeable
with that of Till. It was also a step in the consolidation of their understanding of
themselves as black in America."[33]

Alexander reads the traumatizing effect of Douglass's forced voyeurism as
another instance of this consolidation. Somewhat differently, I envision this
forced voyeurism as a step, merely: it was not *witnessing* degradation but *experiencing* it himself that lead to his insertion into the black collective body. It is after the
"breaking" that we see Douglass brainstorming plans for escape with other
black men, a group that includes a cousin he has yet to mention before that point.
His narrative suddenly becomes peopled with bodies that have a purpose other
than symbolizing the atrocities of slavery and Douglass's anxieties surrounding
his own potential pain. He has entered the black community through the recognition of his own abject state, the bloody route Saunders will also take in entering
into the community of black soldiers. The structural relays between the works,
are, I believe, yet another way Killens leads his readers to (falsely) conceptualize
violence as an integral part of the making of a black male subjectivity. In that
logic, defensive violence would be a crucial aspect of emerging fully into manhood. Certainly, that is how Douglass presents his battle with Covey; in his
famous chiasmus, his victorious two-hour fistfight reverses his reduction to a
brute, the slave is made a man.[34] But here, I would like to return to the argument I
made regarding Brown's 1867 *Clotelle*. I suggested that Brown's retooling of his
prior versions of that work, structured by sentimental conventions, gave way to a
moment of realism when he turned to the subject of warfare. For the disillusioned writer, sentimentality simply could not contain the "truth" of war's "violent essence" or the uncertain results of blacks' acceptance of war as a political
instrument in racial uplift. Killens's novel follows a similar narrative trajectory;
the first half is a neoslave narrative and the second, a narrative of war. As the
latter engulfs the former, the subject of violence will be split from the metaphorical context of slavery, a rupture that necessitates understanding violence within
the specific context of warfare.

All the Evidence

As Saunders is aboard the ship approaching the Philippines, where he will engage in battle for the first time, Killens writes that he catches a glimpse of what awaits him: the "planes like ghostly buzzards circling their targets and going into their dives and laying their death eggs . . . set[ting] the goddamn world on fire" (298). At that moment, he realizes that he must decide what manner of war novel he will write:

> He wondered about the men hidden somewhere in the darkness on the island, dedicated to defend it with their flesh and blood. He musn't think these kinds of thoughts, he musn't write that kind of novel. Men like himself, frightened and courageous men with eyes and mouth and teeth and hearts and souls and penises and bowel movements and ears and thoughts and feelings and dreams and hate and laughter and tears and religion and desires and aspiration and love and mothers and fathers and wives and children. . . . What the hell did he have against these men he had never gazed upon? He musn't think like this. (299)

Saunders defends *against* producing something other than a patriotic narrative, a version where he could revel in the defeat of the enemy. To do this, his own nagging doubts about warfare will have to be drowned in affirmations of World War II as a war "for Freedom," something of which he must repeatedly remind himself (299). But Saunders's experiences as "both witness and participant" will make those affirmations impossible. As a meta-reference to the writing of *Thunder* itself, this passage signals the opening of Killens's war novel. What follows is a relentless series of scenes that unveil a panorama of war's destruction.

If Saunders's avowal to World War II has already begun to falter at this point, he will forswear it completely in the wake of his first killing:

> He held the man's wrist now and twisted his arm and he listened hard to hear it snap, both of them grunting and groaning and breaking wind, and he could see the young frightened face clearer now, much much clearer than any face he'd ever seen in all his life's brief span. . . . The man's arm finally snapped at the elbow . . . now Solomon Saunders held the dagger . . . and then Solly came down with a vengeance, and he felt the steel tear ruthlessly in human flesh like it was a chicken, and back and down . . . the man's chest was a dark bloody geyser gushing blood, his pleading eyes, his desperate eyes. (348–49)

This scene is critical for several reasons. It deglamorizes war as a loss of bodily control, like "breaking wind"; it shows the "enemy" as a person Saunders is quite literally forced to countenance; his reference to himself by his full proper name is a recognition that he is entirely present, committing this horrendous act. Afterward, crying and nauseous, he speaks to the dead man: "I don't hate you! I don't even know you—" and falls "forward on top of this very very dead young stranger from the islands of Japan, and all was peace and all was quiet, and brotherhood and all that crap" (349). The collapsing of bodies, enemy and other, the living and the dead, eradicates any ostensible distinctions between the two sets of "oppositions." Part of Saunders has died with this man; part of this man will live in Saunders, and he knows this. Earlier in the work, Saunders is nearly as shaken and torn when he discovers the bodies of a dead Filipino woman and her child, the "collateral damage" of a bombing: "Her face was so beautiful and sweetly calm in death as she lay there on the floor of the shack with a big hole in the back of her head and a gaping canyon in her side and a hollow where her young breast used to match the other one and another chunk from the thigh of her left leg, and that was all the evidence" (330). Another dichotomy, combatant and civilians, erected to spare "innocents" from falling victim to war, is an inadequate defense within a total war whose goals are, in Saunders's vision, "to bust" countries "wide open" (213). His solidifying repudiation of war will be further cemented as he listens to one of his friends, Jimmy, the soldier nick-named Quiet Man for his gentle demeanor, confess to having participated in a group "train" with Filipino prostitutes: "I didn't want to do it! But they kidded me day and night—they said I was a queer or something. Said I didn't like women. But I didn't want to take advantage of those starving women! . . . We were like dogs! We were worse than dogs!" (341). The character has been chided into performing what I have called a violent act of gender delineation, a violent reinscription of the masculine and feminine. But Solomon and Jimmy both view the rape in terms of what it has undone. Far from the reinscription or the "making" of black masculinity, Solly conceptualizes the violation as the unmak-ing of a human being: "Mothers and Fathers, that's the biggest lie in World War Two. . . . The Army'll make a man out of your darling boy. The Army takes a human being and makes him into an animal" (340).

In this novel, Killens will level all "self-determining" acts of violence—sexual, racial, national—into a sameness that he will assess as damaging and futile. The self/other differentiation that De Vries and Weber call "facile" comes apart in Killens's work as violence done to the other results in the annihilation of self and self-same. Captives of this environment, Saunders and his fellow black sol-diers turn on one another, fighting each other for reasons they cannot even name. As the violence surrounding them is internalized, "the taste of death" in their mouths (313), it threatens to implode their interiors. When Saunders kills, "he felt his stomach erupting and scalding lava spilling over eating up his insides" (349). Taking stock of his internal damage, he imagines his ever-present inner turbulence as mirroring the operations of war; his "throbbing head . . . seemed to have been converted into a busy rifle range, and a pounding heart in which blockbusters were continuously exploding. And his left arm was always burning. He lived in fear of the veins in his head bursting open, of his heart muscles, which always felt as though they were constricting and expanding like they were playing tug of war, and one day they would rip his chest wide open and tear his heart in two" (357).

Where the New World Is

The circumstances leading to the racial war begin when the commanding officer of the unit restricts all soldiers, black and white, from an Australian nightclub, the Southern Cross, because locals have complained of disturbances created by drunken Americans. Although the Australians appear to have made the complaints against white soldiers, blacks are nevertheless included in the restrictions. The Southern Cross is one of the few places blacks are allowed—the same is not true of whites, naturally. Incensed that they have been left with nowhere to socialize, a group of black soldiers decide to defy their orders and return to the Southern Cross. That night, white MPs invade the club and drag two soldiers into the station, one of whom is Jimmy. Outraged by what they perceive as an accumulation of injustices against them, a "delegation" of eight black men storm the station and demand his release, threatening the MPs with loaded weapons, Double V insignias emblazoned across their uniforms. The MPs release Jimmy, and the men take off in their vehicles. Just as they think they have made it safely away, they hear the sound of gunfire. Jimmy is killed. What begins as a battle turns into a war as each side calls in reinforcements. Captain Samuels chooses to fight alongside the black soldiers.[35] In the hours that follow, Saunders loses three more of his closest friends, including Bookworm: "And here they were ten thousand miles away from home fighting for their country and Democracy and Freedom and Manhood, and they were dead and dead and dead" (482). Standing above the bodies, he makes a vow in their names: "I will always hate war with all my heart and all my soul. I will always fight the men who beat the drums for war in the name of Holy Patriotism in any nation, any language" (482). In the aftermath, as he sits with his last standing buddy, two white soldiers join them. Thinking at first it is a "trick," they reach for their weapons, but the white men plea: "We ain't got nothing against nobody" (484). Solly then invites more soldiers to rest: "This is the place where the New World is" (485). Together, exhausted and depleted, they cry. Saunders wonders whether "all this dying was for something" (485).

Killens has already answered the question by purposefully conflating the ostensible differences between killing during legitimated American national warfare and racially motivated murder. Throughout his novel, he shows that within a system of values in which violence is sanctioned to regulate the body or bodies, individually or collectively, the moral or political legitimization for killing becomes dangerously arbitrary. Scarry concurs; in war, she suggests, the dead are buried within a bloody calculus of outcomes: "War . . . is the cost of freedom."[36] Saunders does in fact initially see the war in terms of "costs." He begins as an "assimilationist" black who believes war is the cost for "democracy," making his vow to be "the best damn soldier in the Army of the United States of America" (7). He enters the racial war believing it to be the cost for asserting a black manhood within a racist military embedded in a racist nation. He ends rejecting both forms of warfare, believing the price is far too steep, worrying that the "whole world" would become "like Bainbridge" (483).

And Then We Heard the Thunder marks a profound shift in the way war is both conceptualized and depicted in black American war literature, a precursor to the literature of Vietnam, when blacks' political stake in war would radically change. The large-scale drafting of black men, unprotected by their race or class, would empty working-class and poor communities, leading the affected to question the U.S. government's conscription policies and the purposes of the war itself. Martin Luther King would name the disproportionate number of poor black draftees as one of the reasons he felt compelled to speak out against Vietnam. In taking this stance, King ignored the advice of some within his circle who thought it would be counterproductive to the movement and believed that King risked politically dividing its members and distracting them from its primary endeavor. He was unswayed. To further justify his position, he also pointed to his anguish over blacks' growing sense that violence was a necessary catalyst for social change:

As I have walked among the desperate, rejected and angry young men I have told them that Molotov cocktails and rifles would not solve their problems. I have tried to offer them my deepest compassion while maintaining my conviction that social change comes most meaningfully through nonviolent action. But they asked—and rightly so—what about Vietnam? They asked if our own nation wasn't using massive doses of violence to solve its problems, to bring about the changes it wanted. Their questions hit home, and I knew that I could never again raise my voice against the violence of the oppressed in the ghettos without having first spoken clearly to the greatest purveyor of violence in the world today—my own government.[37]

By the time Killens wrote *Black Man's Burden*, the constant attacks on black Americans by their "own government" had wearied him. He would reject a fundamental principle of King's philosophy of Christian nonviolence: "He loses me and many other Negroes when he calls upon us to love our abusers."[38] Connecting the dropping of the atomic bomb and "the bitter fruit hung from Southern trees" as differing manifestations of the same destructive impulse,[39] Killens poses a rhetorical question to "America":

> How long, in this light of violence against me, can you continue to speak to me of non violence? The chasm widens steadily. Soon it will no longer be possible for me to hear you.
>
> For your black brother is spoiling for a fight in the affirmation of his manhood. . . . The more violence perpetuated against him, with pious impunity, the more he becomes convinced that this thing cannot resolve itself non-violently, that only blood will wash away the centuries of degradation. The burden is on White America to prove otherwise. But you had better get going in a hurry, for we are at the brink.[40]

Killens reminds his readers that the right to "self-defense" is authorized by the Constitution and that blacks are also its legitimate inheritors,[41] the American Revolution also their example—the very sentiments Phillis Wheatley expressed nearly two hundred years earlier and that others such as Himes would express after her. Using a metaphor of illness, Killens also argues that the nonviolent response to white brutality can only have a detrimental impact on the dominant culture. "There is no dignity," he claims, "in allowing another to spit on me with impunity . . . for him or for me. There is only sickness, and it will beget an even greater sickness . . . it encourages his bestiality."[42] What is interesting here is that Killens's stance is evocative of the anxiety Thomas Jefferson expressed over slavery's damaging effects on white masculinity. In *Notes on the State of Virginia*, Jefferson voices concern about the transformative nature of mastery, writing that slaveholders become overly dependent on the body of the slave, weakening their capacity for labor; they are given over to the "odious peculiarities" of tyranny (what Harriet Jacobs describes as "freaks" of despotism in *Incidents in the Life of a Slave Girl*), weakening their faculties.[43] Ever concerned with the health of the state (suggesting that integration would cause "convulsions" among the white populace),[44] Jefferson seems to be arguing that the unrestricted domination of the black body results in a loss of control over the white one; a mutual psychic and physical "degradation" that will ultimately prove deleterious to the national Constitution/constitution.

Of course, Jefferson also predicted that the continuance of slavery would bring about violent revolution, articulated in a language, Sterling Stuckey has observed, that anticipates the black jeremiad. Jefferson's concessions support Killens's ultimate point—not only has white America long understood the danger that oppressing blacks posed to all inhabiting the nation, it has also realized that it has perpetuated a circumstance that may culminate in violence. Killens's position may appear a stark reversal of the antiviolence statements he issues through *Thunder*, where Saunders states not that "blood will wash away the centuries of degradation" but that his tears might cleanse the earth of blood and pain. However, as Killens notes in *Burden*, there are proven peaceful means of change, and these strategies will first be exhausted before blacks turn to violent struggle. It is for that reason that I read Killens's Nationalist jeremiad as a restrained request, betraying a desire *not* to be further drawn into the United States' violent culture. If he was drafted into "the Second World War Madness" without his consent, he will have little choice but to volunteer for the Black Revolution. He seems a reluctant warrior nonetheless.

In the final analysis, Killens, like many of the African American writers in this study, appears uncertain about how and when violence can be used in the service of black liberation absent the clarifying circumstances of slavery. Even Du Bois, the war advocate turned pacifist, remained ambivalent about blacks' "passive resistance" to war and its alternative: participating in U.S. militarism to forward black civil rights. Writing just before the United States was poised to enter World War II, Du Bois offered his thoughts on the "price" of the war that had preceded it. In an uncharacteristically tentative voice, he admits his fear that a complete repudiation of war within a nation wholly given over to its operations would only imperil the African American population, making it vulnerable to further judicial and physical violence. To conclude, I will return to his words:

> I am less sure now than then of the soundness of this war attitude. I did not realize the full horror of war and its wide impotence as a method of social reform. Perhaps, despite words, I was thinking narrowly of the interest of my group and was willing to let the world go to hell, if the black men went free. Today I do not know. . . . Possibly passive resistance of my twelve millions to any war activity might have saved the world for black and white. Almost certainly such a proposal on my part would have fallen flat and perhaps slaughtered the American Negro body and soul. I do not know. I am puzzled.[45]

NOTES

INTRODUCTION

1. Quoted in William Cooper Nell, *The Colored Patriots of the American Revolution* (New York: Arno Press, 1968), 15–16. Originally published in 1855 (Boston: Robert F. Walcutt). *Colored Patriots* is an expansion of Nell's earlier pamphlet, *Services of Colored Americans in the Wars of 1776 and 1812* (1851).

2. Patricia Bradley, *Slavery, Propaganda and the American Revolution* (Jackson: University Press of Mississippi, 1998), 63.

3. Ibid., 61.

4. Bernard Nalty, *Strength for the Fight: A History of Black Americans in the Military* (New York: Free Press, 1986), 6. I will refer to this work throughout my study; one of the reasons this narrative history has been upheld as a standard is Nalty's consistent reliance on primary documents as source material.

5. Charles M. Christian, *Black Saga: The African American Experience* (New York: Houghton Mifflin, 1995), 13.

6. Ibid., 35.

7. Nalty, *Strength for the Fight*, 8, 9.

8. See Benjamin Quarles, *The Negro in the American Revolution* (Chapel Hill: University of North Carolina Press, 1996).

9. Nalty, *Strength for the Fight*, 11. Nalty quotes from "Minutes of a Council of War held at Headquarters, October 8, 1775." See Nalty's notes, 358.

10. Revere chose Christian Remnick to "colorize" his original black-and-white version.

11. For an assessment of the promotional materials surrounding the event, see Marcus Wood, *Blind Memory: Visual Representations of Slavery in England and America: 1780–1865* (New York: St. Martin's, 1991), 250–56. Wood also offers a discussion of the festival, whose attendees included abolitionist lecturers, writers, and activists John S. Rock (the name adopted by Harriet Jacobs's brother), Frances W. Harper, and William Lloyd Garrison.

    See poster and other promotional materials printed in Wood, *Blind Memory*, 252.

12. Bradley, *Slavery*, 63.

13. Ibid., 61.

14. Benedict Anderson, *Imagined Communities: Reflections on the Origins and Spread of Nationalism* (New York: Verso, 1991), 149.

15. See Nell, *Colored Patriots*, 323–42.

16. Phillis Wheatley, *Poems on Subjects Religious and Moral*, <http://digilib.nypl.org/dynaweb/ digs/wwm9728/úneric——BookView>, 19 (September 6, 2006). Originally published in 1773 (London: A. Bell). Also reprinted in *The Collected Works of Phillis Wheatley* (New York: Oxford University Press, 1988).

17. William Wells Brown, *Clotelle; or, The Colored Heroine, a Tale of the Southern States* (Miami: Mnemosyne Publishing, 1969). Originally published in 1867 (Boston: Lee and Shepard).

18. Frances Harper, *Minnie's Sacrifice*, in *Minnie's Sacrifice, Sowing and Reaping, Trial and Triumph*:

Three Rediscovered Novels by Frances E. W. Harper, ed. Frances Smith Foster, 3–92 (Boston: Beacon Press, 1994).

19. Frances Ellen Watkins Harper, *Iola Leroy; or, Shadows Uplifted* (New York: Oxford University Press, 1988). Originally published in 1892 (Boston: James H. Earle).

20. Chester Himes, *If He Hollers Let Him Go* (New York: Thunder's Mouth Press, 1945).

21. Claude McKay, *Home to Harlem* (Boston: Northeastern University Press, 1987). Originally published in 1928 (New York: Harper and Brothers).

22. Peter Aichinger, *The American Soldier in Fiction, 1880–1963: A History of Attitudes Toward Warfare and the Military Establishment* (Ames: Iowa State University Press, 1975), x.

23. Paul Laurence Dunbar, *The Fanatics* (Salem, N.H.: Ayer, 1991). Originally published in 1901 (New York: Dodd, Mead).

24. Susie King Taylor, *Reminiscences of My Life in Camp with the 33rd United States Colored Troops Late 1st S.C. Volunteers*, facsimile ed., in *Collected Black Women's Narratives*, ed. Henry Louis Gates Jr. (New York: Oxford University Press, 1988). Originally published by the author (Boston: 1902).

25. Herschel Cashin and Charles Alexander, eds., *Under Fire with the U.S. Calvary* (New York: Arno Press, 1969), 49. Originally published in 1899 (New York: F. Tennyson Neely).

26. Theophilus Gould Steward, *The Colored Regulars in the United States Army* (Philadelphia: A.M.E. Book Concern, 1904). Steward completed the manuscript in 1899; it was not published until 1904. A new edition, with an introduction by Frank N. Schubert, was retitled *Buffalo Soldiers: The Colored Regulars in the United States Army* (Amherst, N.Y.: Humanity Books, 2003).

27. F. Grant Gilmore, *"The Problem": A Military Novel* (New York: Arno Press, 1969). Originally published in 1915 (Rochester, N.Y.: Press of Henry Conolly Company).

28. Victor Daly, *Not Only War: A Story of Two Great Conflicts* (New York: McGrath Publishing Company, 1969). Originally published in 1932 (Boston: Christopher Publishing House).

29. William Gardner Smith, *Last of the Conquerors* (New York: Lancer, 1965). Originally published in 1948 (New York: Farrar, Strauss and Cudahy).

30. Gwendolyn Brooks, *Maud Martha* (Chicago: Third World Press, 1993). Originally published in 1953 (New York: Harper and Row).

31. John Oliver Killens, *And Then We Heard the Thunder* (Washington, D.C.: Howard University Press, 1983). Originally published in 1963 (New York: Knopf).

32. Gwendolyn Brooks, *A Street in Bronzeville*, in *Blacks* (Chicago: Third World Press, 1987). Originally published as *A Street in Bronzeville* (New York: Harper and Brothers, 1945).

33. Olivia Ward Bush-Banks, *The Collected Works of Olivia Ward Bush-Banks* (New York: Oxford University Press, 1991), 32–33. Originally published in Olivia Bush, *Original Poems* (Providence, R.I.: Press of Louis A. Bassinet, 1899).

34. Karen Sánchez-Eppler, *Touching Liberty: Abolition, Feminism, and the Politics of the Body* (Berkeley: University of California Press, 1993), 6.

35. Ibid., 4–5.

36. Wheatley, *Poems*, 64.

37. See Katherine Fishburn, *The Problem of Embodiment in Early African American Literature* (Westport, Conn.: Greenwood Press, 1997).

38. J. Lee Greene, *Blacks in Eden: The African American Novel's First Century* (Charlottesville: University Press of Virginia, 1996), 48.

39. Carla L. Peterson, *"Doers of the Word": African American Women Speakers in the North (1830–1880)* (New York: Oxford University Press, 1995), 17.

40. Quoted in Paula Giddings, *When and Where I Enter: The Impact of Black Women on Race and Sex in America* (New York: Bantam Books, 1984), 60.

41. For more on this debate over women's inclusion in the convention movement, see Shirley J. Yee, *Black Women Abolitionists: A Study in Activism, 1828–1860* (Knoxville: University of Tennessee Press, 1992), 136–44.

42. Frederick Douglass, "Colored Men, To Arms!" in *A Documentary History of the Negro People of the United States*, 5 vols., ed. Herbert Aptheker (New York: Carol Publishing Group, 1990), 1:478. Originally published by Douglass in *Frederick Douglass' Paper* (March 2, 1863).

43. Jim Cullen, " 'I'se a Man Now': Gender and African American Men," in *Divided Houses: Gender and the Civil War*, ed. Catherine Clinton and Nina Silber, 77 (New York: Oxford University Press, 1992).

44. Ibid., 87.

45. Ibid., 85.

46. David Walker, *Appeal to the Coloured Citizens of the World* (New York: Hill and Wang, 1995), 4. Walker's pamphlet was originally self-published in Boston in 1929.

47. Felipe Smith, *American Body Politics: Race, Gender, and Black Literary Renaissance* (Athens: University of Georgia Press, 1998), 37.

48. Anderson, *Imagined Communities*, 26.

49. Smith, *American Body Politics*, 35. For a full explanation, see "The Invention of White Space," 31–37.

50. Douglas Baynton, "Disability and the Justification of Inequality of American History," in *The New Disability History*, ed. Paul K. Longmore and Lauri Umansky, 33–35 (New York: New York University Press, 2001).

51. Douglass, "Colored Men, To Arms!" 478.

52. Quarles, *Negro in the American Revolution*, 15.

53. Ibid., 17.

54. Michel Foucault, *Discipline and Punish: The Birth of the Prison* (New York: Vintage Books, 1977), 138.

55. Ibid., 135.

56. For a discussion of these images, see Wood, *Blind Memory*, 266–71; and Maurice O. Wallace, *Constructing the Black Masculine: Identity and Ideality in African American Men's Literature and Culture, 1775–1995* (Durham, N.C.: Duke University Press, 2002), 52–81.

57. Foucault, *Discipline and Punish*, 136.

58. Richard Koenigsberg, "The Fantasy of Culture," <http://foucaltinfo/Foucault-L/archive/msg0942.shtml>, 3 (December 11, 2006).

59. Wood, *Blind Memory*, 267–68.

60. Michael Lee Lanning, *The African American Soldier from Crispus Attucks to Colin Powell* (Secaucus, N.J.: Birch Lane Press, 1997), 49. Dates, authorship, and content of this poem vary according to historical sources, but military historian Michael Lanning attributes it to a white writer named Miles O'Reilly.

61. Ibid.

62. Lerone Bennett Jr., *Before the Mayflower: A History of Black America* (New York: Penguin, 1988), 193.

63. Addie W. Hunton and Kathryn M. Johnson, *Two Colored Women with the American Expeditionary Forces* (New York: G. K. Hall, 1997), 232. Originally published in 1920 (Brooklyn, N.Y.: Brooklyn Eagle Press).

64. Amy Kaplan, *The Anarchy of Empire in the Making of U.S. Culture* (New York: Harvard University Press, 2002), 136.

65. Ibid., 127.

66. Martin Delany, *Blake; or, The Huts of America*. This novel was originally serialized in the *Weekly Anglo-African* (1859–62).

67. Frederick Douglass, *The Heroic Slave*, in *Autographs for Freedom*, ed. Julia Griffiths (Boston: Jewett, 1853), 174–239.

68. Thomas Wentworth Higginson, *Army Life in a Black Regiment and Other Writings* (New York: Penguin Press, 1997), 189, 44. Originally published in 1870 (Boston: Fields, Osgood).

69. Curiously, although Higginson writes that his expectation of discovering "Topsies" was not met, he references this character again in discussing what kinds of punishment worked on black soldiers: "We had to avoid all that was brutal and arbitrary . . . any such dealing found them as obstinate and contemptuous as was Topsy when Miss Ophelia undertook to chastise her" (201). The text is heavily influenced by romantic racialism, a subject I will briefly discuss in Chapter 3.

70. Charlotte Forten Grimké, *The Journals of Charlotte Forten Grimké* (New York: Oxford University Press, 1988).

71. Elizabeth Keckley, *Behind the Scenes; or, Thirty Years a Slave, and Four Years in the White House* (New York: Oxford University Press, 1998). Originally published in 1868 (New York: Carlton).

72. Hunton and Johnson, *Two Colored Women*, xviii.

73. Darlene Clark Hine and Kathleen Thompson, *A Shining Thread of Hope: The History of Black Women in America* (New York: Broadway Books, 1998), 263–64.

74. Ibid.

75. Hunton and Johnson, *Two Colored Women*, 5.

76. Margaret Sanger, *Woman and the New Race* (New York: Brentano's, 1920), 164, 165.

77. Alice Dunbar Nelson, "Why Must I Sit and Sew," in *The Norton Anthology of African American Literature*, ed. Henry Louis Gates et al. (New York: W. W. Norton, 1997), 916. The work was first published in 1920.

78. Quoted in Kim Field and John Nagl, "Combat Roles For Women: A Modest Proposal," *Parameters: The Quarterly of the U.S. Army War College* 31, no. 2 (Summer 2001): 76.

79. Ibid., 75.

80. See Margaret R. Higonnet, "Civil Wars and Sexual Territory," in *Arms and the Woman: War, Gender, and Literary Representation*, ed. Helen M. Cooper, Adrienne Auslander Munich, and Susan Merill Squier (Chapel Hill: University of North Carolina Press, 1989), 80–81.

81. Susan M. Schweick, *A Gulf So Deeply Cut: American Women Poets and the Second World War* (Madison: University of Wisconsin Press, 1991), 109.

82. Michael W. Schaefer, *Just What War Is: The Civil War Writings of DeForest and Bierce* (Knoxville: University of Tennessee Press, 1997), 23–40.

83. Interview with Alex Ryabov, *Democracy Now: The War and Peace Report*, WPFW, Washington, D.C., broadcast August 25, 2005. Transcript at <http://www.democracynow.org/article.pl?sid=05/08/25/1342233> (August 28, 2005).

84. See Schaefer, *Just What War Is*, 8–14.

85. For a discussion of Civil War photography, see Timothy Sweet, *Traces of War: Poetry, Photography, and the Crisis of the Union* (Baltimore: Johns Hopkins University Press, 1990), 78–137.

86. Schaefer, *Just What War Is*, 23–41.

87. See Karl von Clausewitz, *War Politics and Power* (Washington, D.C. Regenry Publishing, 1997), 55. He writes that "war . . . is composed of the original violence of its essence."

88. Ibid., 53.

89. Ibid., 55.

90. Ibid., 41–43.

91. Ibid., 42.

92. Paul Fussell, *The Great War and Modern Memory* (New York: Oxford University Press, 1971), 75.

93. Ibid.

94. Hunton and Johnson, *Two Colored Women*, 66–67.

95. Philip McGuire, *Taps for a Jim Crow Army: Letters from Black Soldiers in World War II* (Lexington: University Press of Kentucky, 1983), 5.

96. Joe Louis, "My Story," as told to Meyer Berger and Barney Nagler, *Life Magazine*, November 8, 1948, 139.

97. Lenwood Davis and George Hill, eds., *Blacks in the Armed Forces, 1776–1983: A Bibliography* (Westport, Conn.: Greenwood Press, 1985), 174–75.

98. Hunton and Johnson, *Two Colored Women*, 186–87.

99. Elaine Scarry, *The Body in Pain: The Making and Unmaking of the World* (New York: Oxford University Press, 1985), 81.

100. Ralph Peters, "In Praise of Attrition," *Parameters: The Quarterly of the U.S. Army War College* 34, no. 2 (Summer 2004): 28.

101. Quoted in "General Scolded for Saying 'It's Fun to Shoot Some People,' " *New York Times*, February 4, 2005, 115. General Mattis was not fired for his remarks.

102. Ted Poston, review of *And Then We Heard the Thunder*, by John Oliver Killens, *New York Post*, March 31, 1963, 492.

103. Daryl Michael Scott, quoted in Baynton, "Disability," 41.

104. Quoted in Suzanne E. Hatty, *Masculinities, Violence and Culture* (Thousand Oaks, Calif.: Sage Publications, 2000), 120.

CHAPTER ONE

1. William Wells Brown, *Clotelle; or, The Colored Heroine, a Tale of the Southern States* (Miami: Mnemosyne Publishing, 1969). Originally published in 1867 (Boston: Lee and Shepard).

2. William Wells Brown, *Clotel; or, The President's Daughter* (New York: Carol Publishing Group, 1995). Originally published in 1853 (London: Partridge and Oakley).

3. William Wells Brown, *The Negro in the American Rebellion: His Heroism and His Fidelity* (Miami: Mnemosyne Publishing, 1969). Originally published in 1867 (Boston: Lee and Shepard).

4. William Wells Brown, *The Black Man: His Antecedents, His Genius, and His Achievement*, <http://metalab.unc.edu./docsouth/brown.html>, 31. Originally published in 1863 (New York: Thomas Hamilton).

5. Ibid., 81.

6. Richard Yarborough, "Race, Violence and Manhood: The Masculine Ideal in Frederick Douglass's 'The Heroic Slave,'" in *Haunted Bodies: Gender and Southern Texts*, ed. Anne Goodwyn Jones and Susan V. Donaldson, 172–73 (Charlottesville: University Press of Virginia, 1997).

7. I am indebted to M. Guilia Fabi's work on the *Clotel* novels. See M. Guilia Fabi, "The 'Unguarded Expressions of the Feelings of the Negros': Gender, Slave Resistance, and William Wells Brown's Revisions of *Clotel*," *African American Review* 27, no. 4 (1993): 639–54.

8. Several of the South Carolina codes are reproduced in Deidre Mullane, ed., *Crossing the Danger Water: Three Hundred Years of African-American Writing* (New York: Doubleday, 1993), 301–2.

9. William Wells Brown, "St. Domingo: Its Revolutions and Its Patriots. A Lecture," in *Clotel; or, The President's Daughter*, ed. Robert Levine, 501–2 (New York: Bedford/St. Martin's, 2000). Originally published in 1855 (Boston: Bela Marsh).

10. Kenneth Burke, *On Symbols and Society* (Chicago: University of Chicago Press, 1989), 179.

11. William Wells Brown, *Clotelle: A Tale of the Southern States*, in *Violence and the African American Literary Imagination*, ed. Ronald Takaki, 289 (New York: Oxford University Press, 1992). Originally published in 1864 (Boston: James Redpath Publishers).

12. For another interpretation of this alteration see Nancy Bentley, "White Slaves: The Mulatto Hero in Antebellum Fiction," in *Subjects and Citizens: Nation, Race, and Gender from Oroonoko to Anita Hill*, ed. Michael Moon and Cathy Davidson, 195–216 (Durham, N.C.: Duke University Press, 1995).

13. William Wells Brown, "A Description of William Wells Brown's Original Panoramic Views of the Scenes in the Life of an American Slave, From His Birth in Slavery to His Death or His Escape to His First Home of Freedom on British Soil," in Levine, *Clotel*, 306. Originally published in 1850 (London: Charles Gilpin).

14. Brown introduces this document just ten pages into his work as part of a chapter on blacks who served in the Revolutionary War. He precedes it with Jackson's first 1814 letter imploring free blacks to participate in the 1812 conflict. "That colored men were equally serviceable in the last war with Great Britain is true," Brown writes, "as the following historical document will show" (9). The first letter, addressed to the "Free Coloured Inhabitants of Louisiana," promises black men who volunteer "the same in bounty, in money and lands, now received by the white soldiers of the United States" and freedom from "unjust sarcasm" (9). The second address, given three months later, lauds their service: "The President of the United States shall be informed of your conduct on the present occasion; and the voice of the Representatives of the American nation shall applaud your valor" (11). The exact wording of both speeches varies according to source; William Cooper Nell's reproduction in *Services of Colored Americans in the Wars of 1776 and 1812* (1851) differs from Brown's.

15. John Hope Franklin and Alfred A. Moss Jr., *From Slavery to Freedom: A History of African Americans* (New York: McGraw-Hill, 1994), 216.

16. Ira Berlin, ed. *Free At Last: A Documentary History of Slavery, Freedom, and the Civil War* (New York: New Press, 1992), 465–66.

17. For one of many works readings this figure, see Marina Warner's *Monuments and Maidens: The Allegory of the Female Form* (Berkeley: University of California Press, 1985).

18. Brown, *The Black Man*, 81.

19. Fabi, "The 'Unguarded Expressions,'" 648. This version was published as *Miralda; or, The Beautiful Quadroon: A Romance of American Slavery, Founded on Fact*, in the *Weekly Anglo African*, December 1, 1860–March 16, 1861.

20. Brown, *Clotelle: A Tale of the Southern States*, 340.

21. Robert Reid-Pharr offers a similar reading of Clotelle's racial reinterpellation and the significance of Jim and Dinah to the 1867 *Clotelle* in Robert Reid-Pharr, *Conjugal Union: The Body, the House, and the Black American* (New York: Oxford University Press, 1999). See the chapter on Brown, 37–64.

22. William Wells Brown, "Speech from William Wells Brown," in *A Documentary History of the Negro People in the United States*, ed. Herbert Aptheker, 1:470 (New York: Carol Publishing Group, 1990). Originally published in the *Liberator*, May 16, 1862.

23. Ibid.

24. William Wells Brown, quoted in *Clotelle: A Tale of the Southern States*, 227.

25. Brown was a product of his black slave mother and a white father, possibly a slave owner; it is believed Brown's father was related to her owner.

26. Elaine Scarry, *The Body in Pain: The Making and Unmaking of the World* (New York: Oxford University Press, 1985), 122.

27. Sharon Holland, *Raising the Dead: Readings of Death and (Black) Subjectivity* (Durham, N.C.: Duke University Press, 2000), 28.

28. Benedict Anderson, *Imagined Communities: Reflections on the Origins and Spread of Nationalism* (New York: Verso, 1991), 198.

29. Henri-Jacques Stiker, *A History of Disability* (Ann Arbor: University of Michigan Press, 1999). See 121–89.

30. Ibid., 124, 125.

31. Ibid., 124.

32. Ibid., 123.

33. Ibid., 123.

34. Ibid., 129.

35. See Michel Foucault, *The Birth of the Clinic: An Archaeology of Medical Perception* (New York: Vintage Books, 1994).

36. Claudia Tate, *Domestic Allegories of Political Desire* (New York: Oxford University Press, 1992), 125.

CHAPTER TWO

1. See John Limon, *Writing After War: American Fiction from Realism to Postmodernism* (New York: Oxford University Press, 1994). Limon argues, for instance, that William Dean Howell's *A Hazard of New Fortunes* (1889) is one of these belated responses.

2. Frances Ellen Watkins Harper, *Iola Leroy; or, Shadows Uplifted* (New York: Oxford University Press, 1988). Originally published in 1892 (Boston: James H. Earle).

3. Paul Laurence Dunbar, *The Fanatics* (Salem, N.H.: Ayer, 1991). Originally published in 1901 (New York: Dodd, Mead).

4. Harper, *Iola Leroy*, xxx–xxxi.

5. Ibid., xxxi.

6. See Martin Japtok, "Pauline Hopkins's *Of One Blood*, Africa and the 'Darwinist Trap,' " *African American Review* 36, no. 3 (September 1, 2002): 403–16.

7. For good overviews of this period, see Eric Foner, *A Short History of Reconstruction* (New York: Harper and Row, 1990); and W. E. B. DuBois, *Black Reconstruction in America : 1860–1880* (New York: Free Press, 1998) (originally published as *Black Reconstruction* [New York: Harcourt, Brace, 1935]).

8. David Blight, *Race and Reunion: The Civil War in American Memory* (Cambridge: Harvard University Press, 2001).

9. Ibid., 30–63.

10. Ibid., 122.

11. Ibid., 92–93.

12. Frances Harper, "A Duty to Dependent Races," in *Discarded Legacy: Politics and Poetics in the Life of Frances E. W. Harper, 1825–1911*, by Melba Joyce Boyd, 208–9 (Detroit: Wayne State University Press, 1994). Delivered February 1891 in Washington, D.C.

13. Paul Laurence Dunbar, "Recession Never," in *The Paul Laurence Dunbar Reader*, ed. Jay Martin and Gossie Hudson, 37 (New York: Dodd, Mead, 1975).

14. Blight, *Race and Reunion*, 24.

15. See Chapters 7 and 8 in Blight, *Race and Reunion*; also Paul H. Buck, *The Road to Reunion: 1865–1900* (Boston: Little, Brown, 1937); Nina Silber, *The Romance of Reunion: Northerners and the South, 1865–1900* (Chapel Hill: University of North Carolina Press, 1993); and Alice Fahs, *The Imagined Civil War: Popular Literature of the North and South, 1861–65* (Chapel Hill: University of North Carolina Press, 2001).

16. Blight, *Race and Reunion*, 84–85.

17. Amy Kaplan, "Nation, Region, Empire," in *The Columbia History of the American Novel*, ed. Emory Elliot, 242 (New York: Columbia University Press, 1991).

18. Quoted in Blight, *Race and Reunion*, 175.

19. Du Bois, *Black Reconstruction in America*, 713.

20. Ibid., 713–14.

21. Blight, *Race and Reunion*, 217.

22. In 1874, James Shepherd Pike claimed that in the midst of Reconstruction, South Carolina "lies prostrate in the dust, ruled over by this strange conglomerate, gathered from the ranks of its own servile population. It is the spectacle of a society suddenly turned bottom-side up." See Pike, *The Prostrate State: South Carolina Under Negro Government* (New York: Loring and Mussey, 1935), 12. Originally published in 1874 (New York: D. Appelton).

23. Felipe Smith, *American Body Politics: Race, Gender and Black Literary Renaissance* (Athens: University of Georgia Press, 1993), 56.

24. Thomas Dixon Jr., *The Clansman: A Historical Romance of the Ku Klux Klan* (Louisiana: Pelican Publishing Company, 2001). Originally published in 1905 (New York: Gosset and Dunlap).

25. See M. M. Bakhtin, *The Dialogic Imagination: Four Essays* (Austin: University of Texas Press, 1986).

26. Harper, letter to William Still, April 19, c. 1867, in *The Underground Railroad: A Record of Facts, Authentic Letters, &c., Narrating the Hardships Hair-breadth Escapes and Death Struggles of the Slaves in their Efforts for Freedom, as related by Themselves or Others, or as Witnessed by the Author, Together With Some of the Largest Stockholders, and Most Liberal and Aiders, and Advisers, of the Road*, ed.

William Still, 796. (Chicago: Johnson Publishing Company, 1970). Originally published by the author in 1872.

27. Ibid., 796.

28. Harper, "A Duty to Dependent Races," 209.

29. Ibid., 209.

30. Harper, in Still, *The Underground Railroad*, 796.

31. Ibid.

32. See Frederick Douglass, "Appeal to Congress for Impartial Suffrage," *Atlantic Monthly* 19 (January 1867): 113.

33. See note 26.

34. Harper, quoted in Frances Smith Foster, ed., *A Brighter Coming Day: A Frances Ellen Watkins Harper Reader* (New York: Feminist Press at the City University of New York, 1990), 134.

35. Charles M. Christian, *Black Saga: The African American Experience* (New York: Houghton Mifflin, 1995), 268.

36. Frances Harper, *Minnie's Sacrifice*, in *Minnie's Sacrifice, Sowing and Reaping, Trial and Triumph: Three Rediscovered Novels by Frances E. W. Harper*, ed. Frances Smith Foster, 3–92 (Boston: Beacon Press, 1994). The work was originally serialized in the *Christian Recorder*, but Foster notes that several installments are missing.

37. Harper, letter to William Still, February 1, 1870, in Still, *The Underground Railroad*, 801.

38. Harper, in Still, *The Underground Railroad*, 796.

39. See, for instance, William Andrews's essay, "Reunion in the Postbellum Slave Narrative: Frederick Douglass and Elizabeth Keckley," *Black American Literature Forum* 23, no. 1 (Spring 1989): 5–16. In part, Andrews argues that the "postbellum slave narrator seems almost determined to present these scenes of reunion as indicative of a progressive, forgiving spirit among blacks, born of their faith and hope in a God who delivers the captive and shows mercy on the sinner" (6).

40. Quoted in Blight, *Race and Reunion*, 126.

41. Houston A. Baker Jr., *Workings of the Spirit: The Poetics of Afro-American Women's Writing* (Chicago: University of Chicago Press, 1991), 30.

42. For Henry Grady's perspective on these matters, see Edna Henry Lee Turpin, ed., *Henry Grady: The New South and Other Addresses* (New York: Gordon Press, 1972).

43. Harper, "A Duty to Dependent Races," 209.

44. Harper, letter to William Still, March 29, 1870, in Still, *The Underground Railroad*, 803.

45. Ibid., 804.

46. Howard Zinn, *A People's History of the United States: 1492–Present* (New York: Harper Collins, 1999), 290.

47. See Walter Benn Michaels, "Anti-Imperial Americanism," in *Cultures of United States Imperialism*, ed. Amy Kaplan and Donald Pease, 365–91 (Durham, N.C.: Duke University Press, 1993).

48. Kaplan, "Nation, Region, Empire," 247.

49. Harper, letter to William Still, February 1, 1870; and December 9, 1870; in Still, *The Underground Railroad*, 801.

50. Harper, "Women's Political Future," in Boyd, *Discarded Legacy*, 224. Originally published in May Wright Sewall, ed., *World's Congress of Representative Women 1893 Proceedings* (Chicago: n.p, 1894).

51. Harper, letter to William Still, March 29, 1870, in Still, *The Underground Railroad*, 803.

52. Thomas Dixon Jr., *The Leopard's Spots: A Romance of the White Man's Burden* (New York: Doubleday, Page, 1902).

53. Kaplan, "Nation, Region, Empire," 247.

54. Charles Chesnutt, "The Future American," in *Charles W. Chesnutt: Selected Writings*, ed. SallyAnn H. Ferguson, 47–52 (Boston: Houghton Mifflin, 2001). Originally published in the *Boston Evening Transcript*, August 18, 1900.

55. Ibid., 51.

56. Harper, quoted in Still, *The Underground Railroad*, 785.

57. A Peaceable Man [Nathaniel Hawthorne], "Chiefly About War Matters," *Atlantic Monthly* (July 1862), 43–61.

58. Smith, *American Body Politics*, 65.

59. Robert Reid-Pharr, *Conjugal Union: The Body, the House and the Black American* (New York: Oxford University Press, 1999), 11.

60. Carla L. Peterson, " 'Further Liftings of the Veil': Gender, Class, and Labor in Frances E. W. Harper's *Iola Leroy*," in *Listening to Silences: New Essays in Feminist Criticism*, ed. Elaine Hedges and Shelley Fisher Fishkin, 99 (New York: Oxford University Press, 1994).

61. Harper, quoted in Still, *The Underground Railroad*, 797, 795.

62. Claudia Tate, *Domestic Allegories of Political Desire* (New York: Oxford University Press, 1992), 127.

63. See Elizabeth Young, "Warring Fictions: Iola Leroy and the Color of Gender," *American Literature* 64, no. 2 (1992): 272–96. A revision of this essay is available in Elizabeth Young, *Disarming America: Women's Writing and the American Civil War* (Chicago: University of Chicago Press, 2000).

64. Robert Lively, *Fiction Fights the Civil War: An Unfinished Chapter in the Literary History of the American People* (Chapel Hill: University of North Carolina Press, 1957), 46.

65. Quoted in Foster, *A Brighter Coming Day*, 168.

66. Ibid., 167.

67. James M. McPherson, *Ordeal by Fire: The Civil War and Reconstruction* (New York: Alfred A. Knopf, 1982), 471, 481.

68. Peterson has also made this observation; see Peterson, " 'Further Liftings of the Veil,' " 106–7.

69. C. Peter Ripley, ed., *The United States, 1859–1865*, vol. 5 of *The Black Abolitionist Papers* (Chapel Hill: University of North Carolina Press, 1992), 117.

70. Ibid., 331–32.

71. McPherson, *Ordeal by Fire*, 354.

72. Ira Berlin, ed. *Free At Last: A Documentary History of Slavery, Freedom, and the Civil War* (New York: New Press, 1992), 476.

73. Kali Tal, *Worlds of Hurt: Reading the Literatures of Trauma* (New York: Cambridge University Press, 2000), 6.

74. Ibid.

75. George W. Williams, *A History of Negro Troops in the Rebellion: 1861–1865* (New York: Kraus Reprint Company, 1969). Originally published in 1888 (New York: Harper and Brothers).

76. Ibid., xiii.

77. Don Dingledine, " 'The Whole Drama of the War': The African American Soldier in Civil War Literature," *PMLA* 115, no. 5 (October 2000): 1116.

78. Frances Smith Foster, *Written by Herself: Literary Production by African American Women, 1746–1892* (Bloomington: Indiana University Press, 1993), 131.

79. Paul Laurence Dunbar, *The Uncalled* (New York: Dodd and Mead, 1898); *The Love of Landry* (New York: Dodd and Mead, 1900).

80. Edmund Wilson, *Patriotic Gore: Studies in the Literature of the American Civil War* (Boston: Northeastern Press, 1984). See introduction.

81. Ibid., xx.

82. Peter Brooks, *The Melodramatic Imagination: Balzac, Henry James, Melodrama, and the Mode of Excess* (New Haven: Yale University Press, 1976), 15–16.

83. Ibid., 18.

84. Joanne Dobson, "Reclaiming Sentimental Literature," *American Literature: A Journal of History, Criticism and Bibliography* 69, no. 2 (June 1997): 207.

85. Ibid., 267.

86. Lively, *Fiction Fights the Civil War*, 62.

87. Harriet E. Wilson, *Our Nig; or Sketches from the Life of a Free Black, In a Two-Story White House, North. Showing That Slavery's Shadows Fall Even There, by "Our Nig"* (New York: Vintage, 1983). Originally published in 1859 (Boston: Geo. C. Rand and Avery).

88. Leonard Cassuto, *The Inhuman Race: The Racial Grotesque in American Literature and Culture* (New York: Columbia University Press), 128.

89. See ibid., 130–35.

90. Alice Fahs, *The Imagined Civil War: Popular Literature of the North and South, 1861–65* (Chapel Hill: University of North Carolina Press, 2001), 181.

91. Buck, *The Road to Reunion*, 198, 201–2.

92. Ibid., 201.

93. Martin Delany, *Blake; or, The Huts of America* (Boston: Beacon Press, 1970), 67.

94. See Saidiya V. Hartman, *Scenes of Subjection: Terror, Slavery, and Self-Making in Nineteenth Century America* (New York: Oxford University Press, 1997), 17–28.

95. Cassuto, *The Inhuman Race*, 156.

96. Lerone Bennett Jr., *Before the Mayflower: A History of Black America* (New York: Penguin Press, 1988), 278.

97. Quoted in John David Smith, ed., *The "Benefits" of Slavery* (New York: Garland), 169.

98. Ibid., 245.

99. Reid-Pharr, *Conjugal Union*, 90.

100. Ibid.

101. Paul Laurence Dunbar, *The Sport of the Gods* (New York: Dodd, Mead, 1902).

102. Ibid., 1, 255.

103. Dunbar, quoted in ed., Martin and Hudson, *The Paul Laurence Dunbar Reader*, 37.

104. Ibid., 36–37.

105. Joanne Braxton, ed., *The Collected Poetry of Paul Laurence Dunbar* (Charlottesville: University Press of Virginia, 1993), 221.

106. Ibid., 51.

107. See Orlando Patterson, *Slavery and Social Death: A Comparative Study* (Cambridge: Harvard University Press, 1982).

108. Homi Bhaba, quoted in Anne Cranny-Francis, *The Body in the Text* (Melbourne, Australia: Melbourne University Press, 1995), 52.

109. Braxton, *Collected Poetry*, 197.

110. Paraphrased in Paul Antze and Michael Lambek, eds., *Tense Past: Cultural Essays in Trauma and Memory* (New York: Routledge, 1996), 149. See Jack Kuglemass's essay in that collection, "Missions to the Past: Poland in Contemporary Jewish Thought and Deed," 215–34.

CHAPTER THREE

1. Susie King Taylor, *Reminiscences of My Life in Camp with the 33rd United States Colored Troops Late 1st S.C. Volunteers*, facsimile ed., in *Collected Black Women's Narratives*, ed. Henry Louis Gates Jr. (New York: Oxford University Press, 1988). Originally published by the author (Boston: 1902).

2. Darlene Clarke Hine and Kathleen Thompson: *A Shining Thread of Hope: The History of Black Women in America* (New York: Broadway Books, 1998), 126.

3. Ibid., 127.

4. Ira Berlin and Leslie S. Rowland, eds., *Families and Freedom: A Documentary History of African-American Kinship in the Civil War Era* (New York: New Press, 1997), 56.

5. Margaret R. Higonnet, "Civil Wars and Sexual Territory," in *Arms and the Woman: War, Gender, and Literary Representation*, ed. Helen M. Cooper, Adrienne Auslander Munich, and Susan Merill Squier, 80–83 (Chapel Hill: University of North Carolina Press, 1989).

6. Ibid.

7. Carla L. Peterson, *"Doers of the Word": African American Women Speakers in the North (1830–1880)* (New York: Oxford University Press, 1995), 15.

8. Ibid.

9. Ibid.

10. Sarah Bradford, *Harriet: The Moses of Her People*, ed. Butler A. Jones (New York: Citadel Press, 1989), 133–49. The letters are presented as an appendix to Bradford's self-published work; many letters, including those written by prominent abolitionist figures Gerritt Smith and Frederick Douglass, are also reprinted. Bradford published two versions of Tubman's biography; one in 1869 and an expanded version in 1886.

11. Quoted in Bennett, *Before the Mayflower: A History of Black America* (New York: Penguin, 1993), 207; from the *Boston Commonwealth*, July 10, 1963.

12. Quoted in Kate Clifford Larson, *Bound for the Promised Land: Harriet Tubman—Portrait of an American Hero* (New York: Ballantine, 2004), 214.

13. Catherine Clinton, *Harriet Tubman: The Road to Freedom* (New York: Little, Brown), 206–8.

14. Letter reprinted in Dorothy Sterling, ed., *We Are Your Sisters: Black Women in the Nineteenth Century* (New York: W. W. Norton, 1984), 260.

15. Ibid.

16. See Harriet Jacobs, *Incidents in the Life of a Slave Girl, as Written by Herself*, ed. Nellie McKay (New York: W. W. Norton, 2001). Originally published under the pseudonym Linda Brent as *Incidents in the Life of a Slave Girl, Written by Herself* (Boston: 1861); and William and Ellen Craft, *Running a Thousand Miles for Freedom* (Athens: University of Georgia Press, 1999). Originally published in 1860 (London: William Tweedie).

17. Sara Emma Edmonds, *Memoirs of a Soldier, Nurse and Spy: A Woman's Adventures in the Union Army*, ed. Elizabeth Leonard (Dekalb: Northern Illinois Press, 1999). Originally published as *Nurse and Spy in the Union Army* (Hartford, Conn.: Williams, 1865).

18. See Judith Halberstam, *Female Masculinity* (Durham, N.C.: Duke University Press, 1998), 2–

3. Halberstam argues this masculine "legibility" can be read through bodies other than those of the white bourgeois male, including marginalized male bodies.

19. Willie Lee Rose, "Introduction," in *Reminiscences of My Life: A Black Woman's Civil War Memoirs*, ed. Patricia W. Romero and Willie Lee Rose, 41 (Baltimore: Johns Hopkins University Press, 1995).

20. Joycelyn K. Moody, "Twice Other, Once Shy: African American Autobiographers and the American Literary Tradition of Effacement," *Auto/Biography Studies* 7, no. 1 (1992): 59.

21. Quoted in ibid., 48.

22. Ibid., 55.

23. Ira Berlin, ed., *Free at Last: A Documentary History of Slavery, Freedom, and the Civil War* (New York: New Press, 1997), 181.

24. Moody, "Twice Other," 55.

25. Jarena Lee, *Religious Experience and Journal of Mrs. Jarena Lee, Giving an Account of Her Call to Preach the Gospel*, facsimile ed., in *Spiritual Narratives*, ed. Henry Louis Gates Jr. (New York: Oxford University Press, 1988); and Julia Foote, *A Brand Plucked from the Fire*, facsimile ed., in Gates, *Spiritual Narratives*. Lee originally self-published her work in 1849 (Philadelphia); Foote's was published in 1886 (Cleveland: Lauer and Yost).

26. Elizabeth Young, "Warring Fictions": Iola Leroy and the Color of Gender," *American Literature* 64, no. 2 (1992): 276.

27. Ibid., 277.

28. Hine and Thompson, *A Shining Thread of Hope*, 131.

29. Halberstam, *Female Masculinity*, 2–5.

30. Peterson, "Doers of the Word," 178–80.

31. Ibid.

32. Charlotte Forten Grimké, *The Journals of Charlotte Forten Grimké* (New York: Oxford University Press, 1998), 494. Grimké's diaries were originally unpublished.

33. Ibid.

34. Sidonie Smith, "The Autobiographical Manifesto: Identities, Temporalities, Politics," in *Autobiography and Questions of Gender*, ed. Shirley Neuman (Portland, Ore.: Frank Cass, 1992), 187.

35. Robert Levine, *Martin Delany, Frederick Douglass, and the Politics of Representative Identity* (Chapel Hill: University of North Carolina Press, 1994), 4.

36. Bradford, *Harriet*. Bradford published two versions; see note 10.

37. Elizabeth Keckley, *Behind the Scenes; or, Thirty Years a Slave, and Four Years in the White House.* (New York: Oxford University Press, 1998). Originally published in 1868 (New York: G. W. Carlton).

38. Dr. L. S. Thompson, *The Story of Mattie J. Jackson*, facsimile ed., in *Six's Women's Slave Narratives*, ed. Henry Louis Gates Jr. (New York: Oxford University Press, 1998).

39. David W. Blight, *Frederick Douglass's Civil War: Keeping Faith in Jubilee* (Baton Rouge: Louisiana State Press, 1989), 102.

40. Alice Dunbar-Nelson, "Lincoln and Douglass," in *An Alice Dunbar-Nelson Reader*, ed. Ora Williams (Washington, D.C.: University Press of America, 1979), 131.

41. Ibid., 133.

42. William Wells Brown, *The Negro in the American Rebellion: His Heroism and His Fidelity* (Miami: Mnemosyne Publishing, 1969), 36.

43. Frederick Douglass, in *Frederick Douglass: Selected Speeches and Writings*, ed. Philip S. Foner (Chicago: Lawrence Hill Books), 618, 619. Abridged by Yuval Taylor from Foner's original five-volume series.

44. Ibid., 618.

45. Ibid., 615.

46. Ibid., 614.

47. Blight, *Frederick Douglass's Civil War*, 210.

48. Ibid., 239.

49. Thomas Wentworth Higginson, *Army Life in a Black Regiment* (East Lansing: Michigan State University Press, 1960), 10, 36, 39.

50. Ibid., 42.

51. For good overviews of black attitudes toward imperialism, see Willard B. Gatewood Jr., *"Smoked Yankees" and the Struggle For Empire: Letters from Negro Soldiers, 1898–92* (Fayetteville: University of Arkansas Press, 1987); and Gatewood, *Black Americans and the White Man's Burden: 1898–1903* (Chicago: University of Chicago Press, 1975); also, William Loren Katz, *The Black Press Views Imperialism, 1898–1900* (New York: Arno Press, 1971).

CHAPTER FOUR

1. Howard Zinn, *A People's History of the United States: 1492–Present* (New York: Harper Collins, 1999), 296.

2. John Hope Franklin and Alfred A. Moss Jr., *From Slavery to Freedom: A History of African Americans* (New York: McGraw-Hill, 1994), 298.

3. See Willard B. Gatewood Jr., *Black Americans and the White Man's Burden: 1898–1903* (Chicago: University of Chicago Press, 1975), 208.

4. Ibid., 206–7.

5. See Hazel Carby, " 'On the Threshold of a Woman's Era': Lynching, Empire and Sexuality in Black Feminist Theory," in *"Race," Writing, and Difference*, ed. Henry Louis Gates Jr., 301–16 (Chicago: University of Chicago Press, 1985).

6. See Gatewood, *Black Americans*, 187.

7. See Anne McClintock, *Imperial Leather: Race, Gender and Sexuality in the Colonial Contest* (New York: Routledge, 1995), 31–36.

8. See Amy Kaplan, "Manifest Domesticity," in *The Anarchy of Empire in the Making of U.S. Culture* (Cambridge: Harvard University Press, 2002), 23–29.

9. Quoted in Gatewood, *Black Americans*, 206–7.

10. Theophilus Gould Steward, *The Colored Regulars in the United States Army* (Philadelphia: A.M.E. Book Concern, 1904). Steward completed the manuscript in 1899; it was not published until 1904. A new edition, with an introduction by Frank N. Schubert, was retitled *Buffalo Soldiers: The Colored Regulars in the United States Army* (Amherst, N.Y.: Humanity Books, 2003). A prolific writer and outspoken race man, Steward was only the third black army chaplain commissioned after the Civil War. He delivered speeches as an active member of the Negro American Academy and published widely, including editorials, essays on theology, an autobiography, a book about the Haitian Revolution, and a Christian conversion novel, *A Charleston Love Story; or, Hortense Vanross* (1899, with F. Tennyson Neely), available on the University of North Carolina's website, *Documenting the American*

South. The novel's white protagonist served as a lieutenant in the Union army, but there are no major African American characters in this work.

11. F. Grant Gilmore, *"The Problem": A Military Novel* (New York: Arno Press, 1969). Originally published in 1915 (Rochester, N.Y.: Press of Henry Conolly Company). There is very little known about this author; I have only ascertained that he was a Mason from the author portrait in the novel and from his self-published book of poems, *Masonic and Other Poems* (1908). I have not been able to find him on any roster of black troops who served in the Spanish-American Wars. Although at least one of the few sources mentioning this author lists his year of death as 1915 (the same year the novel was published), I have located an "F. Grant Gilmore" in the 1920 Philadelphia census. His occupation is noted as "playwright," and New York State is listed as his place of birth. There is also some indication that a play version of the novel was mounted; see Bernard L. Peterson, ed., *Early Black American Playwrights and Dramatists and Dramatic Writers* (Westport, Conn.: Greenwood Press, 1990). That information coupled with the novel's Rochester publisher has led me to believe that the two are the same person.

12. Houston Baker, *Turning South Again: Re-thinking Modernism/Re-reading Booker T.* (Durham, N.C.: Duke University Press, 2001), 33.

13. Ibid.

14. See introduction.

15. James A. Field Jr., "American Imperialism: The Worst Chapter in Almost Any Book," *American Historical Review* 83, no. 3 (June 1978): 646.

16. Ibid., 668.

17. Walter Benjamin, "The Work of Art in the Age of Mechanical Reproduction," <http://bid.berkely.edu/bidclass/readings/benjamin.html>, 21 (September 6, 2006). Available in Walter Benjamin, *Illuminations* (Frankfurt, Germany: Suhrkamp Verlag, 1955).

18. See Walter Lafeber and Robert Beisner, comments on "American Imperialism: The Worst Chapter in Almost Any Book," by James A. Field Jr., *American Historical Review*, 83, no. 3 (June 1978): 669–78. In particular, Beisner seems rather troubled to discern whether Field might be approaching "a materialist . . . theory of history to explain American imperialism," charging him with an "almost total neglect" of the impact of "ideas[ideologies]" about empire and warfare in influencing military decisions. See 675–76.

19. See, for instance, arguments in Alex Roland, "Science and War," *Orisis: Historical Writing on American Science* 2, no. 1 (1985): 247–72; and Roland, "Science, Technology and War," *Technology and Culture* 36, no. 2 (April 1995): S83–S100.

20. Kaplan, *The Anarchy of Empire*, 148.

21. Quoted in Gatewood, *Black Americans*, 156.

22. See Mark Seltzer, *Bodies and Machines* (New York: Routledge, 1992).

23. For a study of the Negro Academy, see Alfred A. Moss, *The American Negro Academy: Voice of the Talented Tenth* (Baton Rouge: Louisiana State University Press, 1981).

24. Ibid., 35.

25. Alexander Crummell, "Civilization: The Primal Need of the Race," *American Academy Occasional Papers* 3 (Washington, D.C.: American Academy, 1898), 4, 6–7.

26. Ibid.

27. See Burton C. Hacker, "Engineering a New Order: Military Institutions, Technical Edu-

cation and the Rise of the Industrial State," *Technology and Culture* 34, no. 1 (January 1993): 1–27.

28. See Bernard Nalty, *Strength for the Fight: A History of Black Americans in the Military* (New York: Free Press, 1986), 47–62.

29. Herschel Cashin and Charles Alexander, eds. *Under Fire with the U.S. Calvary* (New York: Arno Press, 1969), 49. Originally published in 1899 (New York: F. Tennyson Neely).

30. Michael Lee Lanning, *The African American Soldier from Crispus Attucks to Colin Powell* (Secaucus, N.J.: Birch Lane Press, 1997), 84.

31. Franklin and Moss, *From Slavery to Freedom*, 302.

32. John Carlos Rowe, *Literary Culture and U.S. Imperialism* (New York: Oxford University Press, 2000), 203.

33. Quoted in William Loren Katz, *The Black Press Views Imperialism, 1898–1900* (New York: Arno Press, 1971), 150.

34. Edward Van Zile Scott, *The Unwept: Black American Soldiers and the Spanish-American War* (Montgomery, Ala.: Black Belt Press, 1996), 22.

35. Laura Wexler, *Tender Violence: Domestic Images in an Age of U.S. Imperialism* (Chapel Hill: University of North Carolina Press, 2000). See "Seeing Sentiment: Photography, Race and the Imperialist Eye," 52–93.

36. Quoted in Gatewood, *Black Americans*, 189.

37. For instance, see Amy Kaplan's chapter on late nineteenth-century historical romances and white masculinity, "Romancing the Empire: The Embodiment of American Masculinity in the Popular Historical Novels of the 1890s," in *The Anarchy of Empire*, 92–103. I am indebted here and elsewhere to Kaplan's many insights into this complex historical period.

38. For an extensive analysis of Theodore Roosevelt's depiction of racial hierarchy in *Rough Riders*, see Kaplan, "Black and Blue on San Juan Hill," in *The Anarchy of Empire*, 121–45.

39. Theodore Roosevelt, *The Rough Riders*, <http://www.bartleby.com/51/4.html>, 11 (May 5, 2006). Originally published in 1899 (New York: Scribner's).

40. Ibid., 12.

41. Though Roosevelt claimed he had to brandish a pistol to keep blacks from retreating to the rear, black soldiers challenged his version of events, arguing they had turned back for medical supplies and ammunition. As president, Roosevelt ordered the executions of two black soldiers for deserting their units in the Philippines, although whites deserted in far higher numbers.

42. Cashin and Alexander, *Under Fire*, iv.

43. Ibid., iii.

44. Ibid., xiv–xv.

45. Booker T. Washington, *Up from Slavery: An Autobiography* (W. W. Norton, 1996), 98–102. Originally published in 1901 (New York: Doubleday).

46. Archibald Grimké, "Modern Industrialism and the Negroes of the United States," *American Negro Academy Occasional Papers* 12 (Washington, D.C.: American Negro Academy, 1908),18.

47. They were referred to as "Immunes" because it was believed that blacks had a natural, biological resistance to tropical diseases because of their African origins.

48. Gail Bederman, *Manliness and Civilization: A Cultural History of Gender and Race in the United States* (Chicago: University of Chicago Press, 1995).

49. See Bederman, 180–215. *Winning* was published in four volumes (New York: G. P. Putnam and Sons, 1889).

50. William Seraile, *Voice of Dissent: Theophilus Gould Steward (1943–1924) and Black America* (Brooklyn: Carlson Publishing, 1991), 104.

51. Ibid., 104.

52. Ibid., 117.

53. "The Women and the Exposition (Editorial)," *New York Age*, November 7, 1891, <http://www.binghamton.edu/womhist/ibw/doclist.htm>.

54. David Healy, *U.S. Expansionism: The Imperialist Urge in the 1890s* (Madison: University of Wisconsin Press, 1970), 16; my emphasis.

55. Michel Foucault, *Discipline and Punish: The Birth of the Prison* (New York: Vintage Books, 1995), 165.

56. Ibid.

57. Frank N. Schubert, *Buffalo Soldiers: The Colored Regulars in the United States Army* (Amherst, N.Y.: Humanity Books, 2003).

58. Ibid., 19.

59. Ibid.

60. Karen Sánchez-Eppler, *Touching Liberty: Abolition, Feminism and the Politics of the Body* (Berkeley: University of California Press, 1993), 8.

61. See Seltzer, *Bodies and Machines*, 149–72.

62. Judith Halberstam, *Female Masculinity* (Durham, N.C.: Duke University Press, 1998).

63. Stuart Chase, *Men and Machines* (New York: Macmillan, 1929), 7.

64. Quote from the *A.M.E. Church Review*. See Seraile, *Voice of Dissent*, 136.

65. Paul Fussell, *The Great War and Modern Memory* (New York: Oxford University Press, 1975), 75.

66. Scot Ngozi-Brown, "African American Soldiers and Filipinos: Racial Imperialism, Jim Crow and Social Relations," *Journal of Negro History* 82, no. 1 (Winter 1997): 43.

67. Gerald F. Linderman, "American Imperialism," in *Interpretations of American History: Patterns and Perspectives*, ed. Frances Couvares, Martha Saxton, Gerald N. Grob, and George Athan Billias (New York: Free Press, 2000), 123.

68. Although this contradicts the dominant culture's idea of the Japanese at the time Gilmore was writing, many African Americans lauded a dark-skinned race's ability to become a formidable world power.

69. Werner Sollors, *neither black nor white yet both: Thematic Explorations of Interracial Literature* (Cambridge: Harvard University Press, 1997), 314.

70. Seamus Deane, "Imperialism/Nationalism," in *Critical Terms for Literary Study*, ed. Frank Lentricchia and Thomas McLaughlin (Chicago: University of Chicago Press, 1995), 355.

71. Among many other things, Funston is reported to have lynched Filipino soldiers.

72. Vauthier quoted in Sollors, *neither black nor white*, 317.

73. Ibid.

74. Ibid., 314

75. Seltzer, *Bodies and Machines*, 157.

76. See note 14.

77. Sandra Gunning, *Race, Rape, and Lynching: The Red Record of American Literature, 1890–1912* (New York: Oxford University Press, 1996), 21.

78. T. G. Steward, "Two Years in Luzon," *Colored American Magazine* 4 (November 1901), 4–10; *Colored American Magazine* 4 (January/February 1902), 162–67; *Colored American Magazine* 5 (August 1902): 244–49.

79. "The Negro Should Not Enter the Army," *Voices of Missions*, May 1, 1899, <http://www.boon docksnet.com/ai/ailtexts/vom0599.html>. In Jim Zwick, ed., *Anti-Imperialism in the United States, 1898–1935*, <http://www.boondocksnet.com/ai/> (December 7, 1999). The editorial states that "the Negro Minister of the Gospel who would encourage enlistment in the United States Army, in the conditions things are now, encourages the shedding of innocent blood for nothing."

80. Sutton E. Griggs, *Imperium and Imperio: A Study of the Negro Race Problem* (Salem, N.H.: Ayer, 1989), 207. Originally published in 1899 (Cincinnati: Editor Publishing Company).

81. "The Negro Should Not Enter."

82. Benjamin, "The Work of Art," 20–21.

83. Kelly Miller, "The Effect of Imperialism Upon the Negro Race," *Anti-Imperialist Broadside* 11 (1900), <http://memory.loc.gov/cgi-bin/query/r?ammem/rbpe:@field(DOCID+@ lit(rbpe07900600))> (December 12, 2006). Miller published this piece in the *Springfield Republican*.

CHAPTER FIVE

1. The Roosevelt administration was urged to recognize Miller in a series of letters written by the prominent black journalist Theodore Poston to government officials. Poston, who made his name covering the famous Scottsboro trial, was hired into the administration as a liaison to the black press. Letters from Poston to the administration officials are available in the National Portrait Museum Archives in Washington, D.C.

2. Issued by the Office of War Information in 1942.

3. *The Negro Soldier* was released in 1944.

4. Anna Maria Chupa, *Anne, The White Woman in Contemporary African American Fiction: Archetypes, Stereotypes and Characterizations* (Westport, Conn.: Greenwood Press, 1990), 1–11.

5. Felipe Smith, *American Body Politics: Race, Gender, and Black Literary Renaissance* (Athens: University of Georgia Press, 1998), 310. Smith's use of "dazzling" refers to James Weldon Johnson's description of the Ex-Colored Man's white wife in *Autobiography of an Ex-Colored Man*.

6. Jacqueline Jones Royster, ed., *Southern Horrors and Other Writings: The Anti-Lynching Campaign of Ida B. Wells, 1892–1900* (Boston: Bedford Books, 1997). The book includes *Southern Horrors*, *A Red Record*, and *Mob Rule in New Orleans*. These works were originally published in pamphlet form in 1892, 1895, and 1900, respectively.

7. Ibid., 54.

8. *Crisis* 50, no. 4 (April 1943). Just a year prior, Alexandria had been a site of violent race riots resulting in the mass arrests of black soldiers. See Fred Stanton, ed., *Fighting Racism in World War II* (New York: Pathfinder, 1980), 149.

9. See introduction, in R. G. Frey and Christopher Morris, eds., *Violence, Terrorism and Justice* (New York: Columbia University Press, 1991).

10. Victor Daly, *Not Only War: A Story of Two Great Conflicts* (New York: McGrath Publishing Company, 1969). Originally published in 1932 (Boston: Christopher Publishing House).

11. Chester Himes, *If He Hollers Let Him Go* (New York: Thunder's Mouth Press, 1945).

12. William Gardner Smith, *Last of the Conquerors* (New York: Lancer, 1965). Originally published in 1948 (New York: Farrar, Strauss and Cudahy).

13. Martha Hodes, "Wartime Dialogues on Illicit Sex," in *Divided Houses: Gender and the Civil War*, ed. Catherine Clinton and Nina Silber (New York: Oxford University Press, 1992), 237.

14. Hent De Vries and Samuel Weber, eds., *Violence, Identity, and Self-Determination* (Stanford, Calif.: Stanford University Press, 1997).

15. Ibid., 2.

16. Ibid.

17. For an analysis of the "Brownsville Incident," see Bernard Nalty, *Strength for the Fight: A History of Black Americans in the Military* (New York: Free Press, 1986), 90–97; for the Houston Riots, see ibid., 98–110; also see Arthur Barbeau and Florette Henri, *The Unknown Soldiers: African American Troops in WWI* (New York: DeCapo Press, 1996). 28–32.

18. In 1972, all were exonerated. Only one of the accused lived to see his named cleared.

19. For more on the Houston Riots, see Nalty, *Strength for the Fight*, 101–6; and Barbeau and Henri, *The Unknown Soldiers*, 21–32.

20. Barbeau and Henri, *The Unknown Soldiers*, xiv. This regiment, comprised of recruits from New York, earned the nickname "Harlem Hellfighters" and included the celebrated jazz musician James Reese Europe.

21. See ibid., 111–36.

22. W. E. B. Du Bois, "World War and the Color Line," in *The Emerging Thought of W. E. B. Du Bois: Essays and Editorials from the Crisis*, ed. Henry Lee Moon (New York: Simon and Schuster, 1972), 247. Originally published in the *Crisis* (November 1914).

23. Barbeau and Henri, *The Unknown Soldiers*, 114.

24. Bernard Nalty and Morris McGregor, *Blacks in the Military: Essential Documents* (Wilmington, Del.: Scholarly Resources, 1991), 88–89.

25. Ibid.

26. Barbeau and Henri, *The Unknown Soldiers*, 143.

27. Ibid.

28. J. Lee Greene, *Blacks in Eden: The African American Novel's First Century* (Charlottesville: University Press of Virginia, 1996), 140.

29. Ibid., 139.

30. René Girard, *Deceit, Desire and the Novel: Self and Other in Literary Structure* (Baltimore: Johns Hopkins University Press, 1965), 1.

31. Ibid., 4.

32. See Leslie Fiedler, *Love and Death in the American Novel* (New York: Stein and Day, 1966).

33. Ibid., 368.

34. Ibid.

35. See Robyn Weigman, "Fiedler and Sons," in *Race and the Subject of Masculinities*, ed. Harry Stecopoulos and Michael Uebel, 45–68 (Durham, N.C.: Duke University Press, 1997).

36. Eve Sedgwick, *Between Men: English Literature and Male Homosocial Desire* (New York: Columbia University Press, 1995), 16.

37. Quoted in Patricia Morton, *Disfigured Images: The Historical Assault on African American Women* (Westport, Conn.: Greenwood Press, 1991), 59. See W. E. B. Du Bois, *The Philadelphia Negro* (Philadelphia: University of Pennsylvania Press, 1889).

38. Review of *Not Only War: A Story of Two Great Conflicts*, by Victor Daly, *Crisis* 39 (April 1932): 138.

39. Greene also notes this as a character trait; see Greene, *Blacks in Eden*, 140.

40. Victor Daly, "Washington's Minority Problem," *Crisis* 40 (June 1939): 170.

41. W. E. B. Du Bois, "Our Special Grievances," in Moon, *Emerging Thought*, 256. Originally published in the *Crisis* (September 1918).

42. Lee Finkle, *Forum for Protest: The Black Press During WWII* (Rutherford, N.J.: Farleigh Dickinson University Press, 1975), 41.

43. W. E. B. Du Bois, "Close Ranks," in Moon, *Emerging Thought*, 256. Originally published in the *Crisis* (July 18, 1918).

44. W. E. B. Du Bois, "Returning Soldiers," in Moon, *Emerging Thought*, 261. Originally published in the *Crisis* (August 18, 1919).

45. W. E. B. Du Bois, *Dusk of Dawn* (New Brunswick, N.J.: Gregg Press, 1967), 264. Originally published in 1940 (New York: Harcourt, Brace and World).

46. Quoted in Michael Lee Lanning, *The African American Soldier from Crispus Attucks to Colin Powell* (Secaucus, N.J.: Birch Lane Press, 1997), 150. The senator was James K. Vardaman.

47. Walter White, *Rope and Faggot: A Biography of Judge Lynch* (New York: Alfred A. Knopf, 2001). Originally published in 1929 (New York: Alfred A. Knopf).

48. Walter White, *The Fire in the Flint* (Athens: University of Georgia Press, 1996). Originally published in 1924 (New York: Alfred A. Knopf).

49. Victor Daly, "Private Walker Goes Patrolling," *Crisis* 37 (June 1930): 199–201, 213.

50. Victor Daly, "Goats, Wildcats and Buffalo," *Crisis* 39 (March 1932): 91.

51. Finkle, *Forum for Protest*, 96–97.

52. Ibid., 112.

53. Ibid.

54. Many in the black left cited antifascism as a reason to resist a Soviet Union under Stalin's reign, and therefore as a reason to support the war. I thank James Smethurst for this insight.

55. "Why Communist Party Attacks 'Double V,'" in *Fighting Racism in World War II*, ed. Fred Stanton, 157–58 (New York: Pathfinder, 1980). The *Militant*'s disparaging comments about some in the black left was part of a strategy designed to suggest the ideological inferiority of American Stalinists. The editorial specifically attacks Eugene Gordon, a black journalist for the *Daily Worker*.

56. Nalty, *Strength for the Fight*, 164.

57. Grant Reynolds, "What the Negro Thinks About This War," in *A Documentary History of the Negro People in the United States, 1933–1945*, ed. Herbert Aptheker, 491 (New York: Citadel Press, 1974). Originally published in *Crisis* 51 (September, October, November 1944): 289–91, 299; 316–18, 328; 352–53, 357.

58. See Trudier Harris, *Exorcising Blackness: Historical and Literary Lynching and Burning Rituals* (Bloomington: Indiana University Press, 1984).

59. Chester Himes, "Democracy Is for the Unafraid," in *Primer for White Folks*, ed. Bucklin Moon, 479–83 (Garden City, N.Y.: Doubleday, 1946).

60. Ibid., 480.

61. For a history of this magazine, see Bill Mullen, "Popular Fronts: *Negro Story Magazine* and the African American Literary Response to WWII," *African American Review* 30, no. 1 (Spring 1996): 5–15.

62. Chester Himes, "A Night of New Roses," *Negro Story* 2, no. 2 (December–January 1945): 10.

63. Chester Himes, "A Penny for Your Thoughts," *Negro Story* 1, no. 5 (March–April 1945): 15.

64. Chester Himes, "One More Way to Die," *Negro Story* 2, no. 3 (April–May 1946): 15.

65. De Vries and Weber, *Violence*, 2.

66. These lectures have recently been collected and published. See Michel Foucault, *Society Must Be Defended* (New York: Picador, 2003).

67. Beatrice Hanssen, *Critique of Violence: Between Poststructuralism and Critical Theory* (New York: Routledge, 2000), 102–3.

68. Himes wrote an essay for the *Crisis*, "Zoot Riots Are Race Riots" (July 1943), 200–201, 222. The article's title probably refers to Eleanor Roosevelt's controversial characterization of the four-day disturbance prompted by U.S. sailors in Los Angeles, California, as "race riots." In this piece, Himes claims psychosexual causes for the clashes, arguing that white servicemen were guilty of improprieties toward Mexican American women that angered young Mexican American men. The article is accompanied by a picture of white sailors armed with clubs looking for both black and Mexican American "Zoot Suiters."

    Mexican American men and white sailors had repeatedly clashed during the spring of 1943. On May 31, several U.S. servicemen claimed that while downtown, they had been viciously attacked by Mexican American "pachucos," the argot for young Mexican American males believed to be associated with gangs. While the exact circumstances creating the confrontation on that date are a matter of debate, one sailor was severely hurt. On June 3, a band of sailors decided to retaliate, many saying that they had been subject to continued harassment by the "pachucos" for months prior. Over the course of several days, the group declaring war on young Mexican American men grew from the original group of fifty sailors to hundreds of serviceman, some traveling to Los Angles from other stations in California. The rioters began targeting all Zoot Suiters, including black American men. (As Robin D. G. Kelley notes, in the dominant culture's imagination, the suits, first worn by African Americans, had come to signify an "anti-American" counterculture). The attacks rapidly spread, moving from downtown into East L.A. At the height of the clashes, over 5,000 servicemen and civilians congregated downtown as a show of force against the youth. Advocates for the Mexican American men noted that sailors had gathered by the hundreds a month prior, attacking Latino youth who were leaving a social, claiming that a sailor had been knifed by someone in attendance. Only Mexican Americans were arrested, however. The Mexican American community also felt it had been under siege since a highly publicized murder case a year earlier. Labeled "The Sleepy Lagoon Murder," the case involved the alleged homicide of a young man of Mexican descent. While the autopsy revealed he had died of blunt force trauma to the head, many argued he had been hit by a car—not bludgeoned by the several other "pachucos" who were tried and convicted of murder. The sensationalist media coverage merely fueled anti-Latino sentiment in those hungry for "evidence" of Latino criminality.

    There is much literature on the riots; for more, see Edward J. Escobar, *Race, Police, and* the Making of a Political Identity: Mexican Americans and the Los Angeles Police Department, 1900–1945 (Berkeley: University of California Press, 1999). See also Mauricio Mazon, The Zoot-Suit Riots: The Psychology of Symbolic Annihilation (Austin: University of Texas Press, 1984). For more on African Americans and Zoot culture, see Robin D. Kelley, "The Riddle of the Zoot: Malcolm Little and the Cultural Politics During WWII," in Race and the Subject of Masculinities, ed. Harry Stecopoulos and Michael Uebel (Durham, N.C.: Duke University Press, 1997).

69. Chester Himes, "Negro Martyrs Are Needed," in Black on Black: Baby Sister and Other Writings (New York: Doubleday, 1973), 230–35.

70. Ibid., 231–32.

71. Ibid., 232, 233.

72. Cleaver made this statement in Eldridge Cleaver, Soul on Ice (New York: Dell, 1968).

73. Anne Cahill, Rethinking Rape (Ithaca: Cornell University Press, 2001), 18.

74. See Angela Davis, "The Myth of the Black Rapist," in Women, Race, and Class (New York: Vintage Books, 1983), 171–201.

75. Ibid.

76. Quoted in Davis, Women, 198.

77. Ibid.

78. Michel Fabre, "A Case of Rape," in The Critical Responses to Chester Himes, ed. Charles L. P. Silet (Westport, Conn.: Greenwood Press), 31.

79. Chester Himes, A Case of Rape (New York: Carroll and Graf Publishers, 1994).

80. Thurgood Marshall, "The Gestapo in Detroit," Crisis 55, no. 8 (August 1948): 232–84, 246–47.

81. See Ed Potter, The Liberators: Fighting on Two Fronts in WWII (New York: Harcourt, Brace, Jovanovich, 1992).

82. Ibid., 219.

83. "Negroes, Nazis, and Jews," in Aptheker, A Documentary History, 345. Originally published as an unsigned editorial in Crisis 45 (December 1938): 12.

84. William Patterson, "We Charge Genocide," in Aptheker, A Documentary History, 31–52.

85. Clarence Lusane, Hitler's Black Victims: The Historical Experiences of Afro-Germans, European Blacks, Africans, and African Americans in the Nazi Era (New York: Routledge, 2003), 165–72.

86. McKay, "Once More the Germans to Face Black Troops," Opportunity 17, no. 11 (1939): 324–28.

87. Paul Gilroy, Against Race (Cambridge: Belknap Press of Harvard University Press, 2000), 142. Also see Lusane, Hitler's Black Victims, 78–83.

88. Gilroy, Against Race, 142.

89. Lusane, Hitler's Black Victims, 95–101.

90. Because of the provocative name Smith gives this character, I wish to point out that he does not offer any homoerotic narrative involving Homo.

91. Michel Foucault, The History of Sexuality, An Introduction, vol. 1 (New York: Vintage Books), 149.

92. Sander Gilman, "Plague in Germany, 1939/1989: Cultural Images of Race, Space and Disease," in Nationalisms and Sexualities, ed. Andrew Parker, Mary Russo, Doris Sommer, and Patricia Yaeger (New York: Routledge, 1992), 182.

93. Ibid., 181.

94. Lusane, *Hitler's Black Victims*, 80.

95. Gilroy, *Against Race*, 7.

96. Ibid., 311.

97. For good discussions, see Perry Biddiscombe, "Dangerous Liaisons: The Anti-Fraternization Movement in the U.S. Occupation Zones of Germany and Austria, 1945–1948," *Journal of Social History* 34, no. 3 (2001): 611–47; and Petra Goedde, "From Villains to Victims: Fraternization and the Feminization of Germany, 1945–1947," *Diplomatic History* 23, no. 1 (Winter 1999): 1–20.

98. Susanne zur Nieden, "Erotic Fraternization: The Legend of German Women's Quick Surrender," in *Home/Front: The Military, War and Gender in Twentieth Century Germany*, ed. Karen Hagemann and Stefanie Schüler-Springorum (New York: Berg, 2002), 300.

99. Ibid., 302.

100. Ibid., 299.

101. Biddiscombe, "Dangerous Liaisons," 625.

102. See Biddiscombe, "Dangerous Liaisons"; also Goedde, "From Villains to Victims."

103. The Red Army in particular is accused of having committed mass rapes in the taking of Berlin and in the subsequent occupation of Berlin; see Biddiscombe, "Dangerous Liaisons."

104. Leroy S. Hodges, *Portrait of an Expatriate: William Gardner Smith, Writer* (Westport, Conn.: Greenwood Press, 1985), 12.

105. John Whiteclay Chambers II, ed., *The Oxford Companion to American Military History* (New York: Oxford University Press, 1999), 125.

106. I have yet to locate a copy of the original 1948 edition and therefore do know not whether it was published with a different image adorning the jacket.

107. For a discussion of the Gillem Plan, see Nalty, *Strength for the Fight*, 214–16.

108. See Hodges, *Portrait of an Expatriate*.

109. Frantz Fanon, *Black Skin, White Masks* (New York: Grove Weidenfield, 1967), 217.

110. Ibid., 218.

111. Ibid., 221.

112. Ibid., 222; original emphasis.

113. Edward Said, *Culture and Imperialism* (New York: Alfred A. Knopf, 1993), 5, 8.

CHAPTER SIX

1. Claude McKay, *Home to Harlem* (Boston: Northeastern University Press, 1987). Originally published in 1928 (New York: Harper and Brothers).

2. Wayne F. Cooper, *The Passion of Claude McKay: Selected Poetry and Prose, 1912–1948* (New York: Schocken Books, 1973), 9.

3. Ibid., 11–13.

4. Winston James, *Holding Aloft the Banner of Ethiopia: Caribbean Radicalism in the Early Twentieth Century* (London, U.K.: Verso, 1998), 168–69.

5. Claude McKay, *A Long Way from Home* (New York: Arno Press, 1969), 154. Originally published in 1937 (New York: Lee Furman).

6. Tyrone Tillery, *Claude McKay: A Black Poet's Struggle for Identity* (Amherst: University of Massachusetts Press, 1992), 64–69.

7. Vladimir I. Lenin, *Socialism and War* (Peking, China: Foreign Language Press, 1970), 8.

8. Claude McKay, "Report on the Negro Question," *International Press Correspondence* 3 (January 5, 1923): 16–17.

9. James, *Holding Aloft*, 169.

10. Tillery, *Claude McKay*, 61–62.

11. "Theses on the Negro Question," November 30, 1922, <http://www.workersaction.org.uk/McKay.htm>, 4–5 (September 6, 2006). Italicized words are my emphasis.

12. James, *Holding Aloft*, 180–82.

13. A. L. McLeod, ed., *Trial by Lynching: Stories about Negro Life in America*, translated by Robert Winter (Mysore, India: University of Mysore Press, 1977), iv.

14. Cooper, *The Passion of Claude McKay*, 237.

15. Ibid., 239, 238.

16. See, for instance, John Lowney, "Haiti and Black Transnationalism: Remapping the Migrant Geography of *Home to Harlem*," *African American Review* 34, no. 3 (2000): 413–29; Heather Hathaway, *Caribbean Waves: Relocating Claude McKay and Paule Marshall* (Bloomington: Indiana University Press, 1999); Michelle A. Stephens, "Black Transnationalism and the Politics of National Identity: West Indian Intellectuals in Harlem in the Age of War and Revolution," *American Quarterly* 50, no. 3 (1998): 592–608.

17. Wayne Cooper, *Claude McKay: Rebel Sojourner in the Harlem Renaissance* (New York: Schocken Books, 1990), 232.

18. McKay, *A Long Way*, 323.

19. McKay, *Home to Harlem*, 285.

20. Paul Gilroy, *The Black Atlantic: Modernity and Double Consciousness* (Cambridge: Harvard University Press, 1993), 7.

21. Cooper, *The Passion of Claude McKay*, 97.

22. Quoted in Tillery, *Claude McKay*, 45. Originally published as "The Capitalist Way: Lettow-Vorbeck," *Workers' Dreadnought* (February 7, 1920). Lettow-Vorbeck, Tillery writes, was a German commander who had commented on the superior performance of his black troops, which prompted this sharp rebuke from McKay.

23. McKay, *A Long Way*, 349.

24. Cooper, *The Passion of Claude McKay*, 49.

25. Victor Daly, *Not Only War: A Story of Two Great Conflicts* (McGrath Publishing Company, 1969). Originally published in 1932 (Boston: Christopher Publishing House).

26. See Melvin Small, "The United States and the German 'Threat' to the Hemisphere, 1905–14," *Americas: A Quarterly Review of Inter-American Cultural History* 28, no. 3 (January 1972): 252–70.

27. See James Weldon Johnson, "Self-Determining Haiti," in *The Conquest of Haiti: Articles and Documents reprinted from The Nation* (New York: Nation, 1920), 39–40. Originally published as a series in the *Nation* 111 (August 28–September 25, 1920). These articles were the products of an investigation by the NAACP. Also see W. E. B. Du Bois, "The African Roots of War," in *W. E. B. Du Bois: A Reader*, ed. David Levering Lewis, 642–51 (New York: Henry Holt, 1995). Originally published in the *Atlantic Monthly* 115 (May 1915): 707–14. For an excellent study on the U.S. cultural response to the occupation, see Mary A. Renda, *Taking Haiti: Military Occupation and the Culture of U.S. Imperialism* (Chapel Hill: University of North Carolina Press, 2001).

28. Quoted in Stephens, "Black Transnationalism," 599.

29. Claude McKay, "Once More the Germans to Face Black Troops," *Opportunity* 17, no. 11 (1939), 325.

30. Ibid.; see 326–27.

31. McKay, *A Long Way*, 74.

32. Ibid., 75.

33. McKay, "Once More," 327.

34. Ibid.; McKay, *A Long Way*, 75.

35. McKay, *A Long Way*, 279.

36. Ibid., 281.

37. Arthur E. Barbeau and Florette Henri, *The Unknown Soldiers: African American Troops in World War I* (New York: De Capo Press, 1996), 102.

38. Ibid.

39. Emmett J. Scott, *Scott's Official History of the American Negro in the World War* (New York: Arno Press, 1969), 327. Originally published by the author in 1919.

40. McKay, "Once More," 325.

41. Quoted in Wilson Jeremiah Moses, *The Golden Age of Black Nationalism, 1850–1925* (New York: Oxford University Press, 1978), 222.

42. McKay, *A Long Way*, 67.

43. McKay, "Once More," 324.

44. Melvin E. Page, ed., *Africa and The First World War* (London, U.K.: Macmillan Press, 1987), 9. See also Richard Rathbone, "World War I and Africa: Introduction," *Journal of African History* 19, no. 1 (1978): 1–9.

45. See Glenford Howe, "West Indian Blacks and the Struggle for Participation in the First World War," *Journal of Caribbean History* 28, no. 1 (1994): 27–62; also, Hans Schmidt, *The United States Occupation of Haiti, 1915–1934* (New Brunswick, N.J.: Rutgers University Press, 1971).

46. See Small, "The United States."

47. See Howe, "West Indian Blacks."

48. Frantz Fanon, *The Wretched of the Earth* (New York: Grove Press, 1963), 52, 53.

49. McKay, *A Long Way*, 354.

50. See Frantz Fanon, "The Negro and Recognition," in *Black Skin, White Masks* (New York: Grove Press, 1967), 210–22.

51. Randi Gray Kristensen, *Intertextuality: Maroonage as History and Metaphor across Genres and Centuries* (unpublished MS). Kristensen argues that the popular Montague Summers 1915 edition had made *Oroonoko* a more widely read text; see Montague Summers, ed., *The Works of Aphra Behn* (London, U.K.: Heinemann, 1915). Another edition was also available: Ernest A Baker, ed., *The Novels of Aphra Behn* (London, U.K.: George Routledge and Sons, 1913).

52. Cooper, *The Passion of Claude McKay*, 36; Aphra Behn, *Oroonoko; or, The Royal Slave*, in *Oroonoko and Other Writings*, ed. Paul Salzman (New York: Oxford University Press, 1994), 31.

53. Leon Trotsky, "A Letter to Comrade McKay," March 13, 1923. This version is from an English translation first published in *International Press Correspondence* on the above date and republished in Leon Trotsky, *The First Five Years of the Communist International*, 2 vols. (Lon-

don, U.K.: New Park, 1973), 2:354–56. Originally published in 1924 (Moscow: State Publishing House). In *A Long Way*, McKay writes that he is not certain whether the open letter was published in *Izvestia* or *Pravda*.

54. McKay, *A Long Way*, 182.

55. Ibid., 182.

56. McKay, "Report on the Negro Question," 17.

57. Gramsci, quoted in Manning Marable, *Blackwater: Historical Studies in Race, Class Consciousness and Revolution* (Dayton, Ohio: Black Praxis Press, 1981), 87.

58. McKay, "Report on the Negro Question," 17.

59. For one reading of McKay as a queer writer, see Marlon B. Ross, *Manning the Race: Reforming Black Men in the Jim Crow Era* (New York: New York University Press, 2004).

60. McKay, *A Long Way*, 69.

61. Claude McKay, *Banjo: A Story without a Plot* (New York: Harper and Brothers, 1929),

62. Tillery, *Claude McKay*, 128.

63. McKay, *A Long Way*, 249–52.

64. Claude McKay, *Banjo*, 325.

65. McKay, *A Long Way*, 69.

CHAPTER SEVEN

1. Gwendolyn Brooks, *Maud Martha* (Chicago: Third World Press, 1993), 177. Originally published in 1953 (New York: Harper and Row).

2. "Five Poems," *Harper's Weekly*, February 1945, 218–19.

3. Gwendolyn Brooks, *Blacks* (Chicago: Third World Press, 1987), 64. Brooks republished several of her other works in this compilation, including *A Street in Bronzeville* (New York: Harper and Brothers, 1949) and *Annie Allen* (New York: Harper and Brothers, 1949).

4. Gwendolyn Brooks, *Report From Part One* (Chicago: Broadside Press, 1972), 156.

5. Roderick A. Ferguson, *Aberrations in Black: Toward a Queer of Color Critique* (Minneapolis: University of Minnesota Press, 2004), 104.

6. bell hooks, *Ain't I a Woman: Black Women and Feminism* (Boston: South End Press, 1981), 33. hooks, like other scholars of the period, theorizes that women were "masculinized" as a justification for forcing black women to engage in "male" tasks such as field labor. Conversely, they were employed in distinctly "feminine" roles, as wet nurses, for instance. They were also ascribed "male" sexual appetites so that white men could claim that they were somehow victimized by a sexual force more powerful than they. This alleged sexual appetite was also an extension of existing narratives that positioned women as sinful creatures whose lack of restraint causes man's downfall, as in the biblical story of Eve. As a result of this cultural fantasy, black women were imagined as having both male and female characteristics; the black female body thus became an overdetermined cultural "grotesque," existing somewhere between the categories of "male" and "female."

7. Black women's genital excessiveness was "confirmed" by images such as those of the famous "Venus Hottentot," the name given Sartje Baartman, a South African woman whose clitoris and buttocks were allegedly oversized. Baartman was exhibited in American freak shows during the second decade of the nineteenth century.

8. Harry B. Shaw, "*Maud Martha*: The War with Beauty," in *A Life Distilled: Gwendolyn Brooks,*

Her Poetry and Fiction, ed. Maria K. Mootry and Gary Smith (Chicago: University of Illinois Press, 1987), 269.

9. Gwendolyn Brooks, "Why Negro Women Leave Home," *Negro Digest*, March 1951, 26–28.

10. Ibid., 28.

11. See Henri-Jacques Stiker, *A History of Disability* (Ann Arbor: University of Michigan Press, 1999), 125–39.

12. See ibid., 174–75.

13. I originally learned of this from a conversation with former Lt. Cdr. Aaron C. James, U.S. Navy (February 14, 1998). John Oliver Killens's novel also contains a scene in which a Filipino woman asks black soldiers to see their buttocks to confirm the truth of the rumor. See *And Then We Heard the Thunder* (Washington, D.C.: Howard University Press, 1983), 301.

14. See Philip McGuire, "Judge Hastie, World War II, and Army Racism," *Journal of Negro History* 62, no. 4 (October 1977): 356–57. It is also important to note here that Charles Drew, the black physician and blood plasma pioneer who headed the American Red Cross during part of the war, did not resign his position in protest over this issue, as popular lore maintains. The policy was only fully implemented after he had departed, though later he spoke publicly against it. See Spencie Love, *One Blood: The Death and Resurrection of Charles Drew* (Chapel Hill: University of North Carolina Press, 1996).

15. Elaine Scarry, *The Body in Pain: The Making and Unmaking of the World* (New York: Oxford University Press, 1985).

16. Ibid., 122.

17. See the opening paragraph of Chapter 5.

18. For instance, one 1942 memorandum describes Miller as "Husky and weighing more than 200 pounds at 19," mentioning he was a former high school fullback.

19. Sharon Patricia Holland, *Raising the Dead: Readings of Death and (Black) Subjectivity* (Durham, N.C.: Duke University Press, 2000), 28.

20. David Gerber, "Heroes and Misfits: The Troubled Social Reintegration of Disabled Veterans of WWII in *The Best Years of Our Lives*," in *Disabled Veterans in History*, ed. David Gerber (Ann Arbor: University of Michigan Press, 2000), 81.

21. See ibid., 74–75.

22. Ibid.

23. Philip McGuire, ed., *Taps for a Jim Crow Army: Letters from Black Soldiers in WWII* (Lexington: University Press of Kentucky, 1993), 205–8.

24. Ibid., 225.

25. Ibid., 217.

26. Ibid., 162.

27. Ibid.

28. See Robert F. Jefferson, " 'Enabled Courage': Race, Disability and Black World War II Veterans in Postwar America," *Historian* 65 (Fall 2003): 1104–5. Jefferson offers helpful statistics on black disability and psychological trauma: "114,000 were wounded . . . 24,526 underwent varying degrees of hospitalization . . . 29,000 black G.I.'s . . . had been hospitalized for neuropsychiatric disorders." See 1110. The refusal of disability compensation also occurred after World War I. See K. Walter Hickel, "Medicine, Bureaucracy, and Social Welfare: The Politics of Disability Compensation for American Veterans of WWI,"

in *The New Disability History*, ed. Paul K. Longmore and Lauri Umansky (New York: New York University Press, 2001), 237.

29. Jefferson, "Enabled Courage," 1116.

30. McGuire, *Taps*, 162.

31. Brian H. Chermol, "Wounds Without Scars: Treatment of Battle Fatigue in the U.S. Armed Forces in the Second World War," *Military Affairs* 49, no. 1 (January 1985): 9.

32. Ibid., 10.

33. Ibid., 11.

34. McGuire, *Taps*, 156.

35. Ibid., 159.

36. Jefferson, "Enabled Courage," 1106–8.

37. Rufus E. Clement, "Problems of Demobilization and Rehabilitation of the Negro Soldier After World Wars I and II," *Journal of Negro Education* 12, no. 3 (Summer 1943): 542.

38. The filmic incarnation of *Home of the Brave*, released by a major Hollywood studio, United Artists, altered the character's ethnic identity from Jewish to black. Foreman had worked for Frank Capra's film unit, responsible for the *The Negro Soldier*, the propaganda film released in 1944 and meant to inspire patriotism among black Americans. *Home* was produced by Stanley Kramer, whose sanitized vision of racial relations would culminate in his direction of the 1967 Sidney Poitier vehicle, *Guess Who's Coming to Dinner?* After writing this chapter, I found an interesting article treating *Home* that offers a different reading of the therapy scene: Michael Rogin, "Democracy and Burnt Cork: The End of Black Face, the Beginning of Civil Rights," in *Refiguring American Film Genres: History and Theory*, ed. Nick Browne, 171–207 (Berkley: University of California Press, 1998).

39. Quoted in Jefferson, "Enabled Courage," 1118.

40. Review of *Home of the Brave*, *Nation*, May 21, 1949, 590–91.

41. " 'Home of the Brave' is Brave Venture for Movie Makers," *Chicago Defender*, April 30, 1949, 16.

42. As such, it might have been capitulating to the propagandistic tendencies of much of the artistic output of that period. In much the same way that images of a white, hetero-patriarchal household were part of the nationalist/anticommunist campaign to showcase American wholesomeness, scholars have convincingly argued that the presentation of fabricated scenarios of racial harmony were intended to dispel perceptions of the United States abroad: that, for all of its protestations of democracy, it was a little more than a racially ill society whose history of segregation and antiblack violence betrayed its claim to moral superiority. This may be part of the reason Foreman made the character black rather than Jewish, though he suggested that he based the character on a black friend from his years in the military. See note 35. A recent book exploring the impact of the Cold War on integration argues that the United States's need to be viewed favorably played a significant part in desegregation efforts. See Mary Dudziak, *Cold War Civil Rights: Race and the Image of American Democracy* (Princeton: Princeton University Press, 2000). James Smethurst has suggested that the black-white interracialism can also be read as an "appeal to Popular Front sentiments" still prevalent within Left circles; in fact, as he points out, many involved in the film were blacklisted.

43. For a mention of this, see Jefferson, "Enabled Courage," 1120. The need for separate organizations arose, in part, from the exclusion of blacks from white veterans' groups.

44. Ibid., 1112.

45. Rosemarie Garland-Thomson, "Seeing the Disabled: Visual Rhetorics of Disability in Popular Photography," in *The New Disability History*, ed. Paul K. Longmore and Lauri Umansky (New York: New York University Press, 2001), 344.

46. Ibid.

47. Brooks, *Blacks*, 110.

48. From review printed on the back cover of *Maud Martha*.

49. Lennard Davis, *Enforcing Normalcy: Disability, Deafness and the Body* (London, U.K.: Verso, 1995).

50. Jacques Lacan, quoted in ibid., 134.

51. Jacques Lacan, *Ecrits: A Selection* (New York: W. W. Norton, 1977), 1.

52. Davis, *Enforcing Normalcy*, 132.

53. Lacan, *Ecrits*, 3.

54. Davis, *Enforcing Normalcy*, 134.

55. Lacan, *Ecrits*, 11, 3.

56. Davis argues that Freud's theory of the "uncanny" applies here, the term Freud gives the experience of registering something as strange yet inexplicably familiar. As Freud explains, "the uncanny is in reality nothing new or foreign, but something familiar and old-established in the mind that has been estranged only [in] the process of repression." See Davis, *Enforcing Normalcy*, 141. Equally appropriately, Lacan himself suggests that these imagos are figures of repressed aggression. See Lacan, *Ecrits*, 13–29.

57. My emphasis.

58. Margaret Sanger, *Woman and the New Race* (New York: Brentano's, 1920).

59. Ibid., 4.

60. Ibid., 229.

61. Margaret Sanger, *The Pivot of Civilization* (Amherst, N.Y.: Humanities Books, 2003), 8. The book was originally issued in 1922 (New York: Brentano's).

62. See Angela Y. Davis, *Women, Race and Class* (New York: Vintage, 1981), 202–21.

63. Although the Negro Project, developed in 1939 with the help of the Birth Control Federation of America, had black support (including that of W. E. B. Du Bois), the program was tainted by Sanger's eugenicism and became subject to accusations of racial genocide. See "Birth Control or Race Control? Sanger and the Negro Project," *Margaret Sanger Papers Newsletter* 28 (Fall 2001), 1–5.

64. Sanger, *The Pivot of Civilization*, 7.

65. Sanger, *Woman and the New Race*, 2.

CONCLUSION

1. Walter A. Luski, *A Rape of Justice: MacArthur and the New Guinea Hangings* (New York: Madison Books, 1991), 158. Barnwell's report, dated April 12, 1942, is reproduced in its entirety in Luski's work; see 157–59. For more information on the experiences of black troops in Australia, see Sean Brawley and Chris Dixon, "Jim Crow Downunder? African American Encounters with White Australia, 1942–1945," *Pacific Historical Review* 71, no. 4 (2002): 607–32; also see Kay Saunders and Helen Taylor, "The Reception of Black American Servicemen in Australia During WWII: The Resilience of 'White Australia,'" *Journal of Black Studies* 25, no. 3 (January 1995): 331–48. These essays note that although Australia had its

own white supremacist practices leveled against its indigenous population, black American servicemen were treated quite well. In part, this is why white American troops insisted on reinforcing the U.S. military's segregationist policies.

2. Ibid., 157, 158.

3. Ibid., 159.

4. For more on such disturbances, see Alan M. Osur, *Blacks in the Army Air Forces During World War II: The Problem of Race Relations* (Washington, D.C.: Office of Air Force History, c. 1975), 86–122.

5. See Robert L. Allen, *The Port Chicago Mutiny* (New York: Warner Books, 1989). In 1944 a deadly munitions accident at Port Chicago killed 320 men, 202 of whom were African Americans assigned to load munitions. As a result of many factors, including post-traumatic responses and anger that blacks were given the most dangerous tasks, these fifty men refused to return to service. They were court-martialed and defended by Thurgood Marshall. All were found guilty, but a combination of pressure from the NAACP and the end of the war eventually prompted the Navy to reduce their sentences.

6. John Oliver Killens, *And Then We Heard the Thunder* (Washington, D.C.: Howard University Press, 1983). Originally published in 1963 (New York: Knopf).

7. Killens, *Thunder*, 448, 491, 489, and 493, respectively. These reviews are reproduced as an appendage to the novel, 487–95.

8. Killens, *Thunder*, 493. As I have mentioned elsewhere, Poston was an official black press liaison for the Roosevelt administration.

9. Organization of Afro-American Unity, "Statement of the Basic Aims and Objectives of the Organization of Afro-American Unity," in *Black Nationalism in America*, ed. John H. Bracey, August Meier, and Elliot Rudwick (New York: Bobbs-Merrill, 1970), 423. The statement was originally issued on June 28, 1964.

10. Ibid., 534. Originally published by the Black Panther Party, "What We Want Now! What We Believe," *Black Panther*, March 16, 1968, 4.

11. John Oliver Killens, *The Black Man's Burden* (New York: Trident Press, 1965).

12. Keith Gilyard, *Liberation Memories: The Rhetoric and Poetics of John Oliver Killens* (Detroit: Wayne State University Press, 2003), 43–46. "God Bless America" originally appeared in the *California Quarterly* in 1952.

13. Quoted in Gilyard, *Liberation Memories*, 50.

14. For instance, the Killens entry in *The Oxford Companion to African American Literature* (New York: Oxford University Press, 1997), omits such information.

15. See Gilyard, *Liberation Memories*, 47–49.

16. Gwendolyn Brooks, *Maud Martha* (Chicago: Third World Press, 1993), 151.

17. Killens, *The Black Man's Burden*, 75.

18. Leonard Cassuto, *The Inhuman Race: The Racial Grotesque in American Literature and Culture* (New York: Columbia University Press), 128.

19. For instance, Lerone Bennett's influential and groundbreaking history, *Before the Mayflower: A History of Black America* (New York: Penguin, 1988), was first published in 1962.

20. "Slave personality" was a term used in Stanley Elkins's controversial work, *Slavery: A Problem in American Institutional and Intellectual Life* (Chicago: University of Chicago Press, 1959).

21. See Gilyard, *Liberation Memories*, 50–57.

22. William Wells Brown, *The Negro in the American Rebellion: His Heroism and His Fidelity* (Miami: Mnemosyne Publishing, 1969), 157. Originally published in 1867 (Boston: Lee and Shepard).

23. See Paul R. Lehman, *The Development of the Black Psyche in the Writings of John Oliver Killens (1916–87)* (Lewiston, N.Y.: Edwin Mellen Press, 2003), 74–76.

24. John Oliver Killens, *Great Gittin' Up in the Morning* (Garden City, N.Y.: Doubleday, 1972).

25. John Oliver Killens, *Slaves* (New York: Pyramid, 1969).

26. Frederick Douglass, *Narrative of the Life of Frederick Douglass, An American Slave, Written by Himself* (New York: W. W. Norton, 1997), 15. Originally published in 1845 (Boston: Anti-Slavery Office).

27. Ibid.

28. Ibid.

29. Ibid., 36.

30. Ibid., 45.

31. See Elaine Scarry, *The Body in Pain: The Making and Unmaking of the World* (New York: Oxford University Press, 1985), 44–51.

32. Ibid.

33. Elizabeth Alexander, *The Black Interior* (St. Paul, Minn.: Graywolf Press, 2004), 192.

34. See Douglass, *Narrative*, 42–49.

35. I read his inclusion as pointing to Jewish-black alliances in the civil rights movement. In *The Black Man's Burden*, Killens calls whites who participate in black struggle "winter soldiers."

36. Scarry, *The Body in Pain*, 7.

37. Excerpted from Martin Luther King, "Beyond Vietnam: A Time to Break Silence," speech delivered on April 4, 1967, at Riverside Church in New York City.

38. Killens, *The Black Man's Burden*, 112.

39. Ibid., 122.

40. Ibid.

41. Ibid., 109.

42. Ibid., 113.

43. Thomas Jefferson, *Notes on the State of Virginia*, in *Jefferson: Writings*, ed. Merrill D. Peterson (Library of America, 1984). See Query 14, 289.

44. Ibid., Query 17, 264.

45. W. E. B. Du Bois, *Dusk of Dawn: An Essay Toward an Autobiography of a Race Concept* (New York: Transaction Publishers, 2000), 255. Originally published in 1940 (New York: Harcourt, Brace and World).

INDEX

representation, 143; vulnerability of, 272. *See also* Black female body; Black male body; Mulatto bodies

Black citizenship rights: and Attucks, 2–3; deferring of, 3, 33, 98, 187; and Dred Scott decision, 3; and passport metaphor, 5, 6, 129; warfare language as metaphor for struggle, 6, 187; and black male body, 11–12, 144; as Civil War issue, 12, 15, 56, 61; and black participation in war, 26, 33, 34, 49–50, 100, 133, 138, 148, 172, 181, 182, 215, 278; and reconciliation narratives, 60–61, 62, 90; in Harper's *Iola Leroy*, 78; and black imperial mobility, 129; and Fifteenth Amendment, 134; and Double VV program, 187, 188; and black veterans, 244

Black Codes, 38

Black female body: and Harper, 11, 234; and William Wells Brown, 11, 36, 37, 43, 44–45; military compensating for limits of, 160; consequences of violation of, 176; black men's lack of patriarchal power over, 178; as cultural "grotesque," 234, 304 (n. 6)

Black imperial mobility, 129, 130–31, 135–36, 142, 145–46

Black Laws, 37–38

Black left, 188, 298 (nn. 54, 55)

Black male body: and black political discourse, 11–12; exemption from violence of war, 31; and William Wells Brown, 34, 36, 37, 38, 40–41, 47, 48, 49, 50, 54, 120; technologically determined black male body, 131–32, 144, 145–46, 149–50, 164–65; white imperial masculinity contrasted with, 137–38, 139, 149; Wheeler's interpretation of, 139; defeminization of, 142; punishment of, 172

Black male narrative of sexual innocence: and public antilynching discourse, 169, 170; embedded in black participation in warfare, 170, 171; and interconnectedness of war, violence, and racism, 198–99, 205, 209; U.S. claims to innocence

compared to, 209–10; unmaking of black body, 237

Black male soldier-citizen: and perfected body, 16; courage demonstrated by, 19–20; manliness of, 19, 102; triumph over racist practices, 29; extraordinary body, 31; in reconciliation narratives, 59, 91; in Harper's *Iola Leroy*, 78–80; in Dunbar's *Fanatics*, 102; in Susie King Taylor's *Reminiscences*, 114–15, 117, 119–20, 124; in Steward's *Colored Regulars*, 144–45

Black masculinity: war as confirmation of, 12–13, 221; black masculinist war novels, 19–21, 30; demasculinization of black men, 19; idealized representations of, 20, 31; imperial masculinity contrasted with domestic interpretive frameworks, 129; black military-industrial masculinity, 134, 149, 153, 165

Black military service: history of, 2; in American Revolution, 3, 6, 15, 113, 145, 174, 284 (n. 14); opposition to, 3, 19, 215; black writings on, 5–6; and Harper's *Iola Leroy*, 7, 9, 61, 78–84, 172, 178; as origins of new race, 20–21; women's role in, 21–22; recruitment practices, 22; in Civil War, 35, 38, 39, 61, 78–84, 85, 92, 99, 100–101, 102, 133, 138, 145, 148, 172; and William Wells Brown, 35, 80, 148, 186; Jackson's speech on, 42, 284 (n. 14); motivations for, 49, 237, 266; and Dunbar's *The Fanatics*, 61, 85, 92, 99, 100–101, 102, 133; northern celebration of, 99; in Spanish-Cuban-American Wars, 126, 133, 134, 137–39, 145–46, 148, 212; and Nell, 129; and social advancement, 133, 188, 266, 268; and westward expansionism, 135; images of, 138–39; and World War II mobilization, 187; and McKay, 212–13, 215, 221; voluntary service as participation in debasement, 215; and Killens's *And Then We Heard the Thunder*, 266–70

Black Nationalism, 211, 213, 214, 216, 226, 263, 264, 265

service, 61, 129; and memory of slavery, 63, 64, 66; and civilizationism, 69; preserving black race, 74; "Coloured Women in America," 77; "Enlightened Motherhood," 77; "An Appeal to the American People," 78; and North/South binary, 94, 122; and divided house trope, 97; on Lincoln, 121; and nation-building black woman, 179; and Nell's festival, 279 (n. 11)

Harper's Magazine, 96

Harris, Joel Chandler, 101

Harris, Trudier, 189

Harrison, Hubert H., 211–12

Hartman, Saidiya, 93

Hawthorne, Nathaniel, "Chiefly about War Matters," 73

Hayes, Rutherford B., 56

Hegel, Friedrich, 144, 154, 208

Hemingway, Ernest, 217, 230

Henri, Florette, 175

Heteronormativity, 234, 241, 253, 259

Heterosexism, 235

Higginson, Thomas Wentworth: on black subordinates, 12–13, 16, 20, 123, 282 (n. 69); and Susie King Taylor's *Reminiscences*, 105–6, 107, 118–20, 122, 123; *Army Life in a Black Regiment*, 123

Higonnet, Margaret R., 104

Himes, Chester: *If He Hollers Let Him Go*, 8, 9, 170, 171, 189–90, 191, 192, 193–96, 198, 199–200, 271; and rhetoric of military interventionism, 166; "A Night of New Roses," 189, 197–98; "A Penny for Your Thoughts," 189; "Democracy Is for the Unafraid," 189; "One More Way to Die," 189; "Negro Martyrs Are Needed," 193, 195; *A Case of Rape*, 198–99; and quest for manhood, 209; "Zoot Riots Are Race Riots," 299 (n. 68)

Hine, Darlene Clark, 104

Hinton, Richard, 171

Hitler, Adolf, 188, 198, 200, 201, 202–3, 209, 219

"Hitlerism at home," 27

Hodes, Martha, 171

Hodges, Leroy, 208

Holland, Sharon, 50, 240–41

Home of the Brave (film), 244–46, 306 (nn. 38, 42)

Homosocial fraternity, 88–90, 97, 176, 178, 186, 209

hooks, bell, 234, 304 (n. 6)

Hopkins, Pauline, 97, 122; *Of One Blood*, 56; *Contending Forces*, 98

Houston Riots, 173–74

Howell, William Dean, 285 (n. 1)

Huiswood, Otto, 212

Hunter, David, 106

Hunton, Addie, 17, 19, 21, 22, 24

Immunes, 141, 294 (n. 47)

Imperialism: and purposes of war, 10; and racial uplift, 69; destabilization of, 70; black anti-imperialism, 124, 125–28, 131, 163–64, 165; and Susie King Taylor, 124; and racism, 126–27, 192, 214, 222; and domesticity, 127, 128–29, 142, 154, 156, 158; technological feasibility of, 129, 130, 131, 134; and determinism, 130, 154; relationship to subjects of, 134; southern anti-imperialism, 136; Booker T. Washington on, 140; and "other," 150–51; and incest narrative, 151, 156–58, 162; and lynching, 164; violence of, 165–66; and black masculinity, 207; McKay on, 213–14, 215; black dispersal caused by, 226

Indianapolis Freeman, 135, 147

Indian wars, 135, 141, 145

Industrialism, 130–32, 137, 140–41, 142, 143, 144

International Press Correspondence, 212

Interracial fraternity, 134, 178, 186, 246, 306 (n. 42)

Interracial homosociality, 176, 196

Interracial sex: and World War I, 29–30, 174–79, 181, 184, 185, 186; and black male citizenship, 170; and black male narrative of sexual innocence, 171, 190; punishment for, 172, 185, 202, 203, 206;

as substitute for integration, 186; characterized as rape, 195–96; and William Gardner Smith's *Last of the Conquerors*, 203–7; and McKay's *Home to Harlem*, 220–21. *See also* Lynching

Iraq war, 25

Jackson, Andrew, 42, 284 (n. 14)
Jackson, Mattie J., 121
Jacobs, Harriet, 21, 105, 107, 110, 116; *Incidents in the Life of a Slave Girl*, 109, 277
James, Winston, 213
Japanese people, 151, 193, 295 (n. 68)
Jefferson, Robert F., 242, 305 (n. 28)
Jefferson, Thomas, 11, 277–78
Jewish Frontier, 215
Jews, compared to black Americans, 199–203
Jim Crow, 73, 125, 152, 181, 185, 187, 198, 262
Johnson, H. T. J., 128
Johnson, James Weldon, 218, 296 (n. 5)
Johnson, Kathryn M., 17, 19, 21, 22, 24
Journal of Negro Education, 244

Kaplan, Amy, 19, 58, 72, 127, 131, 137, 138, 145
Keckley, Elizabeth, 21, 121; *Behind the Scenes*, 120
Kelley, Robin D. G., 299 (n. 68)
Kennedy, John F., 263
Kennedy, John Pendleton, 101
Kennedy, Robert, 263
Killens, John Oliver: *And Then We Heard the Thunder*, 9, 19, 20, 31, 261–75, 276, 277, 278, 305 (n. 13); and neoslavery, 20, 266–71; and rhetoric of military interventionism, 166; *Black Man's Burden*, 264, 265, 268, 271, 277, 278, 309 (n. 35); "God Bless America," 264; and military service, 264; *Slaves*, 269; *William Styron's Nat Turner*, 269
King, Edward, 110
King, Martin Luther, Jr., 263, 276, 277
King, Richard H., 151

Koenigsberg, Richard, 16
Korean War, 246
Kramer, Stanley, 306 (n. 38)
Kristensen, Randi Gray, 227
Kuglemass, Jack, 102
Ku Klux Klan, 66, 70, 183, 189, 199

Lacan, Jacques, 156, 254, 255
Lanning, Michael, 281 (n. 60)
Laurent, Arthur, 244
Lee, Jarena, 111
Lenin, V., 212, 213, 226
Levine, Robert, 117
Liberator, 211, 212
Limon, John, 54
Lincoln, Abraham, 38, 39, 65, 81, 87–88, 95, 120–23, 227
Lincoln, Mary Todd, 21
Lively, Robert, 78, 89
Lost Cause ideology, 59
Louis, Joe, 28–29, 31, 33
Louisiana Native Guards, 34
Lynching: threat of, 19, 182–83, 214; as spectacle, 50; war injury compared to, 50–52; as unjust, 52; lynch laws, 73; and sexual trespass, 162; and imperialism, 164; and body of innocent black male, 169; Du Bois on, 182; as barometer of racial relations, 188, 193; of black servicemen, 188, 214; and Himes's *If He Hollers Let Him Go*, 189, 191, 192, 271; as form of extermination, 192; treatment of European Jews compared to, 199

Maceo, Antonio, 125, 148
Marshall, George, 168
Marshall, Thurgood, 199, 308 (n. 5)
Marx, Karl, 227, 228–29, 231
Marxism, 130, 214, 216, 228–29, 231
Maryland Industrial Exposition, 142
Masses, 211
Mayo, A. D., 96
McClintock, Anne, 127
McClure's, 59, 100
McKay, Claude: *Home to Harlem*, 8, 9, 211,

Slavery dynamics: in black war novels, 20, 33; master/slave dialectic, 93, 208–9, 267; and black masculinity, 138–40; and military neoslave narrative, 266–69, 272; Jefferson on, 277–78

Slaves (film), 269

Smethurst, James, 298 (n. 54), 306 (n. 42)

Smith, Felipe, 13, 168, 181, 296 (n. 5)

Smith, Sidonie, 117

Smith, William Gardner, 166; *Last of the Conquerors*, 9, 170, 171, 201–8, 209

Snow, Valaida, 200

Social Darwinism, 66

Sollors, Werner, 151, 156–57

Spanish-Cuban-American Wars: and Gilmore's *The Problem*, 9, 20; and imperialism, 124; black military service in, 126, 133, 134, 137–39, 145–46, 148, 212; and technology, 130–31, 134; and blacks' racial reorientation, 134, 135, 150

Stanford, Ann Folwell, 8

State: exclusion of blacks, 5, 6; obscuring or mythological language of, 31, 239; reliance on violence for development of, 58; as author of violence, 83–84

Stevens, Thaddeus, 87

Steward, Theophilus Gould: *The Colored Regulars in the United States Army*, 9, 128, 129, 134, 144–50, 165; and black imperial mobility, 130–31, 135–36, 142; and technologically determined black male body, 131–32, 144, 145–46, 149–50, 164–65; and American Negro Academy, 132, 134–35; and black masculinity, 133, 135, 149, 163, 165; on Theodore Roosevelt, 138; and Columbian Exhibition, 142–43, 144; *Genesis Re-Read*, 142; "Two Years in Luzon," 163; and imperial violence, 166; and inflicting and receiving injury, 247; background of, 292 (n. 10)

Stewart, Maria, 263

Stiker, Henri-Jacques, 51–52, 233, 235–36, 241, 245, 258

Still, William, 64, 65, 66, 71; *The Underground Railroad*, 65

Stowe, Harriet Beecher, 97, 116, 123; *Uncle Tom's Cabin*, 20

Stuckey, Sterling, 278

Styron, William, 269

Takaki, Ronald, 46–47

Tal, Kali, 81

Tanner, Benjamin, 57

Tate, Claudia, 77, 78

Taylor, Russell, 111

Taylor, Susie King: services to Union army, 103; and racial uplift, 105, 111; male performative of, 149

Technology, 129–32, 142–43, 144, 165

Tenth U.S. Cavalry, 19, 133, 137, 138

Terrorism, 66, 170, 194, 243

Third Communist International, Fourth Congress of, 212, 213, 227, 228–29

Thirteenth Amendment, 37

Thirty-third U.S. Colored Troops, 103, 110, 118

Thompson, James, 187

Thompson, Kathleen, 104

Thompson, L. S., 121

Till, Emmett, 272

Tillery, Tyrone, 217

Toussaint L'Ouverture, François, 39, 125, 148, 227

Transnationalism, 135, 217, 218, 225

Trotsky, Leon, 227–28

Trowbridge, C. T., 118, 119, 120, 122, 123

Truman, Harry, 28

Truth, Sojourner, 21, 105, 111

Tubman, Harriet, 21, 81, 106–7, 119, 265–66

Turner, Nat, 38, 40, 147, 148

Tuskegee Airmen, 28

Twenty-fifth Infantry, 133, 142, 162, 173

Twenty-fourth Infantry, 133, 173

Under Fire with the U.S. Calvary (Cashin and Alexander), 9, 134, 138, 140

Union army, 15, 16–17, 38, 39, 49, 79, 104

U.S. Army Nurse Corps, 21

USS *West Virginia*, 167–68